Paul on Marriage and Celibacy

Paul on Marriage and Celibacy

The Hellenistic Background of 1 Corinthians 7

Will Deming

WILLIAM B. EERDMANS PUBLISHING COMPANY
GRAND RAPIDS, MICHIGAN / CAMBRIDGE, U.K.

Wm. B. Eerdmans Publishing Co.

255 Jefferson Ave. S.E., Grand Rapids, Michigan 49503 /
P.O. Box 163, Cambridge CB3 9PU U.K.

Printed in the United States of America

08 07 06 05 04   7 6 5 4 3 2 1

Library of Congress Cataloging-in-Publication Data

Deming, Will, 1956-
    Paul on marriage and celibacy: the hellenistic background of 1 Corinthians 7 /
    Will Deming. — 2nd ed.
        p.   cm.
    Includes bibliographical references and indexes.
    ISBN 0-8028-3989-4 (pbk.: alk. paper)
    1. Bible. N.T. Corinthians, 1st, VII — Criticism, interpretation, etc. 2. Marriage —
    Biblical teaching. 3. Celibacy — Biblical teaching. 4. Cynics (Greek philosophy).
    5. Stoics.   I. Title.

    BS2675.6.M3D46   2004
    227'.206 — dc22

                                                                2004064206

www.eerdmans.com

For Maidee Elizabeth Coffman Deming and Andrew S. Deming

Contents

Foreword

In the waning decades of the twentieth century, New Testament scholarship for the first time began to consider seriously the fact that the text that Paul composed for the benefit of the Christians of Corinth during the early 50s C.E. was a real letter. The attention paid to the epistolary nature of 1 Corinthians has led scholars to reflect more than previously had been the case on who it was that received the letter and who it was that wrote it. First Corinthians, like any real letter, is an occasional piece of writing that must be understood in the light of the specific situation that existed when the letter was composed.

Will Deming's study of the Hellenistic background of 1 Corinthians 7 greatly clarifies the situation that prompted Paul to write about marriage and human sexuality in his letter. The analysis of Stoic and Cynic texts illustrates the popular ethos that prompted concerned Corinthians to write to Paul about the sexual relationship between a man and a woman.

Any sexual relationship is complex; relationships vary from case to case, from individual situation to individual situation. Aware of this double reality, Paul did not provide a "one size fits all" response to the Corinthians' question. Rather, he addressed individual cases and particular sets of circumstances, providing a nuanced yet simple response to a number of different situations.

Sorting out the varying witness of Stoic and Cynic sources, Deming has shown that the Corinthians' questions arose from a Stoic ethos coupled with an apocalyptic expectation that undoubtedly accompanied their acceptance of the Pauline gospel. Should their faith entail that they espouse such radical views on sexuality and marriage as are known to us from the writings of the Cynics? Essentially Paul's answer was "no." With regard to human sexuality, he was, if anything, a realist. For him radical sexual asceticism, as a goal for those who aspire to live the Christian life, was incompatible with the reality of human sexuality and the nature of marriage. With a deft analytical use of the pertinent texts of the philosophic moralists, Deming sheds considerable light on the complexity of Paul's response to the complex naivete summed up in the slogan, "It is well for a man not to touch a woman" (1 Cor. 7:1).

Paul did not write a treatise on marriage; neither did he compose an all-encompassing essay on human sexuality. What he wrote was a letter that responded in ad hoc fashion to the Corinthian concern. Illustrating as he does the reality of their situation, Deming carefully distinguishes among asceticism, sexual asceticism, and celibacy. He shows that the Corinthians' concern did not stem from Gnostic enthusiasm and that Paul should not be considered as the first witness to the later Christian ideal of sexual asceticism. The philosophical roots of the latter were far different from the popular philosophical views that abounded in mid-first-century Corinth.

With his study of 1 Corinthians 7 Deming has written an important chapter in the history of early Christian thought on human sexuality, marriage, and sexual asceticism. Perhaps Deming has most of all shown that in 1 Corinthians we have a real letter written by Paul to flesh-and-blood people whose views on and questions about human sexuality arose from the real world in which they processed their thoughts and lived their lives.

RAYMOND F. COLLINS

Acknowledgments

In origin this book was my doctoral dissertation, which was accepted by the University of Chicago Divinity School in August of 1991. For having reached this stage in my career as a teacher and scholar I am indebted to many people, but first of all to my parents, to whom this book is dedicated: to my mother, who taught me patience and curiosity, and to my father, who taught me to think logically and muster a good argument. Throughout the many years of my graduate education they generously supplied me with both financial support and encouragement, two of a scholar's most precious resources.

I am also indebted to my dissertation adviser Hans Dieter Betz for his exacting reading and rereading of this work, and to Elizabeth Asmis for her thoughtful criticisms of my Greek translations.

Beyond this I wish to express my gratitude to the many other teachers I have had at the University of Chicago and at Göttingen University in Germany. Among these are Wendy Doniger and Frank Reynolds, who initiated me into the study of symbolism and comparative religious ethics; the late David Wilmot, who imparted to me, and to all his students, a passion for reading Greek; and Hartmut Stegemann, Robert Hanhart, and Berndt Schaller, under whom I had the privilege of studying Hellenistic Judaism.

Finally, a special thanks is due to my wife, Lauren Wellford Deming, for reading through the manuscript as a nonspecialist, offering suggestions regarding style and clarity, and to my good friend the Reverend Owen Guy for providing me with a quiet place to work while I wrote the last two chapters.

THIS SECOND EDITION OF *Paul on Marriage and Celibacy* differs from the first in several ways. To begin with, I have made small changes throughout in an attempt to clarify and strengthen the argument. Here and there I have also added new evidence from the primary sources, shored up loose translations, and corrected faulty citations. Second, I have retranslated the pieces from Antipater and Ocellus[1] in appendices A and B, and supplied a Greek text for each. In this way I offer readers the benefit of several more years on my part of working with these authors, as well as convenient access to the Greek. Third, I have tried to give some account of the most recent scholarship on 1 Corinthians 7 and related topics. In this I have been very selective, however, adding to the secondary literature only when it enhanced the discussion. Where the literature was already adequate to define the issues under consideration, I saw no reason to multiply references.

Although much has changed in New Testament scholarship since this project was conceived, and a great deal has been written on marriage, asceticism, and sexuality in the ancient world, as well as the Greco-Roman aspects of Paul's ministry, I remain convinced of the fundamental soundness of this study and its conclusions. Thus the only new section I have added is an addendum to chapter 1, which summarizes several new publications; I have made no changes to the original thesis. Indeed, for whatever reason, only a few scholars to date have seriously engaged the arguments presented by this study, and there persists in New Testament and early patristic scholarship a confusion between "celibacy" and "asceticism," on the one hand, and asceti-

---

1. The work *On the Nature of the Universe* that bears his name is spurious.

cism and sexual asceticism, on the other.[2] I therefore reiterate, as something of a challenge, this important aspect of my thesis:

> Asceticism encompasses renunciation generally, while *sexual* asceticism pertains specifically to renouncing sexual activities. As a way of life or a primary task of religion, *sexual* asceticism is hardly mentioned in Greco-Roman or Jewish sources before the second century C.E.
>
> Celibacy is the single life — i.e., living without marriage or a spouse — and it is only from the end of the first century C.E. that we find clear evidence that *sexual* asceticism is a goal or principal consideration of celibacy.

In my view, until scholars appreciate fully the implications of these discrete practices — asceticism, sexual asceticism, and celibacy — it will be impossible to chart the development of sexual asceticism in the first hundred years of Christianity or fathom the beginnings of a distinctively Christian ethic of marriage, celibacy, and sexuality.

2. On the inability of New Testament scholars to define "asceticism," see Elizabeth A. Clark, *Reading Renunciation: Asceticism and Scripture in Early Christianity* (Princeton: Princeton University Press, 1999), 15; and Will Deming, review of *Asceticism,* ed. Vincent L. Wimbush and Richard Valantasis, *JR* 80 (2000): 668-69.

AB	Anchor Bible
AGJU	Arbeiten zur Geschichte des antiken Judentums und des Urchristentums
ALGHJ	Arbeiten zur Literatur und Geschichte des hellenistischen Judentums
ANRW	*Aufstieg und Niedergang der römischen Welt*
ARW	*Archiv für Religionswissenschaft*
ASNU	Acta seminarii neotestamentici upsaliensis
ATANT	Abhandlungen zur Theologie des Alten und Neuen Testaments
BBB	Bonner biblische Beiträge
BETL	Bibliotheca ephemeridum theologicarum lovaniensium
BFCT	Beiträge zur Förderung christlicher Theologie
BHT	Beiträge zur historischen Theologie
Bib	*Biblica*
BJS	Brown Judaic Studies
BU	Biblische Untersuchungen
BWANT	Beiträge zur Wissenschaft vom Alten und Neuen Testament
BZ	*Biblische Zeitschrift*
BZNW	Beihefte zur ZNW
CBQ	*Catholic Biblical Quarterly*
CP	*Classical Philology*
CQ	*Classical Quarterly*
CSCO	Corpus Scriptorum Christianorum Orientalium
CTM	*Concordia Theological Monthly*
EBib	Etudes bibliques
ERE	*Encyclopædia of Religion and Ethics*
ErFor	Erträge der Forschung

EvT	*Evangelische Theologie*
FB	Forschung zur Bibel
FRLANT	Forschungen zur Religion und Literatur des Alten und Neuen Testaments
GTA	Göttinger theologische Arbeiten
HKNT	Handkommentar zum Neuen Testament
HNT	Handbuch zum Neuen Testament
HNTC	Harper's New Testament Commentaries
HR	*History of Religions*
HTR	*Harvard Theological Review*
HTS	Harvard Theological Studies
ICC	International Critical Commentary
IDB	*Interpreter's Dictionary of the Bible*
IDBsup	Supplementary volume to *IDB*
Int	*Interpretation*
JAAR	*Journal of the American Academy of Religion*
JBL	*Journal of Biblical Literature*
JETS	*Journal of the Evangelical Theological Society*
JHS	*Journal of Hellenic Studies*
JR	*Journal of Religion*
JTC	*Journal for Theology and the Church*
LCC	Library of Christian Classics
LCL	Loeb Classical Library
MeyerK	H. A. W. Meyer, ed., Kritisch-exegetischer Kommentar über das Neue Testament
MTZ	*Münchener Theologische Zeitschrift*
NICNT	New International Commentary on the New Testament
NovT	*Novum Testamentum*
NovTSup	*Novum Testamentum*, Supplements
NRT	*La nouvelle revue théologique*
NTAbh	Neutestamentliche Abhandlungen
NTF	Neutestamentliche Forschungen
NTS	*New Testament Studies*
NTTS	New Testament Tools and Studies
OBO	Orbis biblicus et orientalis
PG	*Patrologia Graeca*, ed. J. Migne
PL	*Patrologia Latina*, ed. J. Migne
POxy	Oxyrhynchus Papyri
PW	*Paulys Real-Encyclopädie der klassischen Altertumswissenschaft*
QD	Quaestiones disputatae
RAC	*Reallexikon für Antike und Christentum*
RB	*Revue biblique*

RevScRel	*Revue des sciences religieuses*
RHE	*Revue d'histoire ecclésiastique*
Rh. Mus.	*Rheinisches Museum für Philologie*
RSR	*Recherches de science religieuse*
SBB	Stuttgarter biblische Beiträge
SBLDS	Society of Biblical Literature Dissertation Series
SBLGRS	Society of Biblical Literature Graeco-Roman Series
SBLMS	Society of Biblical Literature Monograph Series
SBLSBS	Society of Biblical Literature Sources for Biblical Study
SBLSPS	Society of Biblical Literature Seminar Papers Series
SBLTT	Society of Biblical Literature Texts and Translations
SBT	Studies in Biblical Theology
SCHNT	Studia ad corpus hellenisticum novi testamenti
SJLA	Studies in Judaism in Late Antiquity
SNT	Studien zum Neuen Testament
SNTSMS	Society for New Testament Studies Monograph Series
SPB	Studia postbiblica
SR	*Studies in Religion/Sciences religieuses*
SUNY	State University of New York
SVF	*Stoicorum Veterum Fragmenta*
SVTP	Studia in Veteris Testamenti pseudepigrapha
TDNT	*Theological Dictionary of the New Testament*
TLZ	*Theologische Literaturzeitung*
TQ	*Theologische Quartalschrift*
TRE	*Theologische Realenzyklopädie*
TRu	*Theologische Rundschau*
TU	Texte und Untersuchungen
TynBul	*Tyndale Bulletin*
VC	*Vigiliae Christianae*
WD	*Wort und Dienst*
WMANT	Wissenschaftliche Monographien zum Alten und Neuen Testament
WUNT	Wissenschaftliche Untersuchungen zum Neuen Testament
ZKG	*Zeitschrift für Kirchengeschichte*
ZNW	*Zeitschrift für die neutestamentliche Wissenschaft und die Kunde der älteren Kirche*
ZST	*Zeitschrift für systematische Theologie*
ZTK	*Zeitschrift für Theologie und Kirche*

THE SEVENTH CHAPTER OF Paul's first letter to the Corinthians is one of the most influential discussions of marriage and celibacy in the Christian tradition. Not only is it the most extensive treatment of these topics in the New Testament, but in the centuries following its appearance its importance grew to such an extent that one leading church historian has called it "the one chapter that was to determine all Christian thought on marriage and celibacy for well over a millennium."[1] In recent times there has been a resurgence of interest in this text. During the last century 1 Corinthians 7 has been the subject of innumerable articles on marriage, sexuality, gender issues, and feminism, as well as the focus of several book-length inquiries.[2]

One result of this recent scholarship is that most interpreters today support the view advanced by some of Paul's earliest interpreters, that Paul held a very low opinion of marriage and consequently encouraged his readers in the

1. Peter Brown, *The Body and Society: Men, Women, and Sexual Renunciation in Early Christianity*, Lectures in the History of Religions, n.s., 13 (New York: Columbia University Press, 1988), 54.

2. Namely, Darrell J. Doughty, "Heiligkeit und Freiheit: Eine exegetische Untersuchung der Anwendung des paulinischen Freiheitsgedankens in 1 Kor 7" (Ph.D. diss., Göttingen University, 1965); Werner Wolbert, *Ethische Argumentation und Paränese in 1 Kor 7*, Moraltheologische Studien, systematische Abteilung 8 (Düsseldorf: Patmos, 1981); Norbert Baumert, *Ehelosigkeit und Ehe im Herrn: Eine Neuinterpretation von 1 Kor 7*, FB 47 (Würzburg: Echter, 1984); O. Larry Yarbrough, *Not Like the Gentiles: Marriage Rules in the Letters of Paul*, SBLDS 80 (Atlanta: Scholars, 1985); Vincent L. Wimbush, *Paul, the Worldly Ascetic: Response to the World and Self-Understanding according to 1 Corinthians 7* (Macon, Ga.: Mercer University Press, 1987); and Brian S. Rosner, *Paul, Scripture, and Ethics: A Study of 1 Corinthians 5–7*, AGJU 22 (Leiden: Brill, 1994; reprint, Grand Rapids: Baker, 1999).

direction of sexual asceticism. Yet, as widely accepted as this picture of Paul is, it is open to question on the grounds that it simply leaves many important aspects of 1 Corinthians 7 unexplained or otherwise obscure. Especially telling is the fact that scholars have never reached a consensus regarding Paul's *reasons* for favoring asceticism over marriage.

Part of the difficulty, naturally, is that Paul did not write 1 Corinthians 7 as a theological treatise. It is his response to a particular situation that arose among certain Christians in first-century Corinth, and as such represents only one part of a dialogue between Paul and this elusive readership. But, with the possible exception of Romans, circumstances like these pertain to all of Paul's letters and therefore cannot be the whole problem with understanding the chapter. The main difficulty, in my opinion, is that interpreters have actually lost touch with much of the conceptual framework that undergirds Paul's discussion. Without the original context or worldview for his ideas, or those of the Corinthians with whom he is corresponding, it has been impossible to second-guess his meaning. Many scholars, to be sure, have come to this same conclusion and have suggested contexts for Paul's words based on their investigations of various Christian and non-Christian groups within the Greco-Roman world. As I have indicated above, however, and will show more thoroughly in the next chapter, these solutions do not do justice to the information in the text.

The goal of this study is to offer a new assessment of Paul's understanding of marriage and celibacy. I will base this assessment on a hypothesis that has, to date, gained only minimal acceptance among those working on 1 Corinthians 7. Beginning with the insight, often overlooked by scholars, that not all forms of celibacy stem from a theology of sexual asceticism, I will argue that in writing 1 Corinthians 7 Paul drew his basic concepts of marriage and its alternatives from a centuries-old debate on marriage that had been shaped by political and intellectual developments in the Hellenistic world. In Paul's day the line that separated the antagonists in this debate was drawn between a Stoic and a Cynic position, both of which presented married life as primarily a matter of duty and responsibility to a larger human community, not as the starting point of sexual activity in the life of an individual.

The Stoics and their supporters favored marriage, and for a reason which, to us, might seem rather curious: they saw it as the salvation of the city-states. Marriage, they reasoned, was the one institution that could halt the decline of local autonomy and traditional life in the Hellenistic world. If more people would take seriously the responsibilities of marriage, concerned citizens and stable households would result, insuring the future of the city-states. The Cynics, by contrast, renounced the institutions of the city-state, including marriage. By avoiding wedlock, they argued, a person secured the free time necessary to pursue philosophy and achieve virtue and well-being. To complicate matters, there was also a certain amount of crossover between the Stoic and Cynic camps. Some Stoics took a hybrid position, holding that while under normal conditions it was one's moral obligation to marry, special considerations in one's life, such as poverty or the advent of war, could force a person to forgo marriage and concentrate on the philosophical life.

In using this marriage debate as the backdrop for Paul's discussion in 1 Corinthians 7, I will show that the dynamics of the two are remarkably similar. Paul, like the Stoics and Cynics, defines marriage principally in terms of responsibility, not sexual activity; and he takes the position, much like the Stoic hybrid view, that under certain circumstances the duties of married life interfere with one's allegiance to a higher cause — which, in Paul's case, was allegiance to God through Christ. Beyond demonstrating that the dynamics of the Hellenistic debate and Paul's discussion are comparable, however, I will also show that 1 Corinthians 7 actually contains a number of Stoic and Cynic terms, phrases, and ideas. From this I will argue that Stoic and Cynic thought had a clear and decisive impact on how Paul and his readers conceived of marriage.

Central to this study, therefore, is the thesis that the understanding of 1 Corinthians 7 held by most scholars and church leaders today derives from an early Christian reinterpretation of Paul, and that this text has been essentially misunderstood almost since its composition. Briefly stated, the decisive moment appears to have been near the end of the first century c.e. As this century passed into the second, intellectuals of the age turned their attention away from the city-state to notions of earthly and cosmic *empires*. With much searching and introspection they weighed the benefits of a purely spiritual life against the vicissitudes and evils of mere physical existence. In this context marriage became more than a means of involving oneself in the local community: it symbolized an ominous bond with the material world. In line with these developments, the fathers of the church began to view 1 Corinthians 7 with a new eye. Some of what Paul said became mysterious or unintelligible to these interpreters, while other statements were cast in an ascetic mold never intended by the apostle. In the centuries that separate us from Paul, the worldview from within which he wrote was all but forgotten. This state of affairs has left modern interpreters with little to go on, and has encouraged them to follow the lead of their patristic and medieval counterparts. As a consequence, they have explained Paul's position on marriage in terms of a vision of the world that may not have existed in Paul's day, let alone informed his thought.

The implications of interpreting 1 Corinthians 7 from this perspective are far-reaching. No longer will it be possible to understand Paul as Christianity's first champion of sexual asceticism. Instead, we will find him to be a cautious and measured proponent of the single lifestyle, a form of celibacy aimed at freeing one from the responsibilities of marriage, and for which the absence of sexual fulfillment was simply a consequence and an inconvenience, not an end in itself.

1 The Motivation for Celibacy in 1 Corinthians 7: A Review of Scholarly Opinion

As a preliminary step in our reassessment of Paul's understanding of marriage and celibacy, this chapter will present a critical review of the work of other scholars. This will be an important aid in determining which options for interpretation are open to us and which are not, especially since it will reveal an extensive history of the misinterpretation of 1 Corinthians 7.

In all the research that has been done on 1 Corinthians 7, the aspect of this chapter that has fascinated and perplexed theologians and biblical scholars more than any other is its characterization of Christian marriage as the necessary alternative to certain forms of celibacy. In 7:2 Paul states, "Because of sexual immorality, let each man have his own wife, and let each woman have her own husband." In 7:9 he advises, "It is better to marry than to burn"; and in 7:36 he tells a single man that if he is "over the limit," he should marry without delay. Without much exaggeration one could even say that Paul's topic in 1 Corinthians 7 is not so much marriage but the benefits and limitations of celibacy. As one scholar lamented, "one looks in vain for a positive appreciation of love between the sexes or of the richness of human experience in marriage and family."[1]

Because celibacy looms so large in Paul's discussion, scholars have directed most of their efforts to determining the theological motivation for this celibacy — both for that which the Corinthians promote and which Paul, in

---

1. Günther Bornkamm, *Paul* (New York and Evanston, Ill.: Harper and Row, 1971), 208. Cf. Johannes Weiß, *The History of Primitive Christianity* (New York: Wilson-Erickson, 1937), 2:582; Kurt Niederwimmer, *Askese und Mysterium: Über Ehe, Ehescheidung und Eheverzicht in den Anfängen des christlichen Glaubens*, FRLANT 113 (Göttingen: Vandenhoeck & Ruprecht, 1975), 66, 67.

part, seeks to restrain, and for that which Paul himself promotes. A few have argued for the influence of Stoic and Cynic thought. This is the theory for which there is the most evidence, and the one that will guide the investigations in chapters 2, 3, and 4 of this study. As I will show here, however, the manner in which this theory has been presented until now needs to be rethought in light of a fuller understanding of the primary sources. The vast majority of scholars, by contrast, hold a very different view. They assume the importance of a theology of sexual asceticism in the thinking of Paul and the Corinthians, although there is little agreement as to its shape or source. Some point in the direction of Hellenistic Judaism while others see it as arising from ascetic tendencies thought to be sui generis products of first-century Christianity. Still others contend that Paul and his readers were motivated by considerations similar to those which inspired Christians of the second, third, and fourth centuries. In reviewing the work of these scholars I will argue that all such theories of an ascetic basis for the discussion in 1 Corinthians 7 rest on very little evidence indeed. I shall show, in fact, that most of what has been offered as evidence for these theories is both inconsistent with the information provided by 1 Corinthians 7 and a poor fit in the context of the mid–first century C.E. In concluding this chapter I will return to this matter of insufficient evidence and offer other methodological observations as well.

Paul in the Light of Stoic and Cynic Materials

Perhaps the first to connect Paul's statements on marriage and celibacy with Stoic and Cynic thought was Clement of Alexandria in the second century. As we will see in the next chapter, Clement identified Paul so closely with the Stoics on this matter that he had considerable difficulty distinguishing Paul's arguments from theirs. Almost a millennium and a half after Clement, the Dutch humanist and theologian Hugo Grotius picked up on this same thread. He began his treatment of 1 Corinthians 7 by pointing out that the question of marriage was frequently debated among the Greek philosophers, and he mentioned two Stoics by name, Musonius Rufus and Hierocles. He further speculated that the faithful in Corinth were "really philosophers under the name of Christians (although nonetheless Christians)."[2]

In recent times, especially since the publication of Johannes Weiß's com-

---

2. Hugo Grotius, *Annotationes in Novum Testamentum* (Paris: Pelé, 1646), 2:377-78.

mentary on 1 Corinthians, it has become commonplace for scholars to cite parallels between 1 Corinthians 7 and Stoic and Cynic authors, although the implications of these parallels are rarely explored.[3] An exception is the work of David Balch, Larry Yarbrough, and Vincent Wimbush. Despite the contribution these three scholars have made to our understanding of 1 Corinthians 7, however, their efforts to interpret this chapter with reference to Stoic and Cynic texts have left many matters unexplored. This is because none of them develops a clear picture of the central issues of Stoic and Cynic discourse on marriage. Balch's understanding of this discourse relies almost entirely on a topology he finds in an anthology of ancient literature compiled by Johannes Stobaeus around the fifth century. In this anthology Stobaeus collected excerpts on marriage from a wide range of authors, including not only Stoics and Cynics but also philosophers such as Thales, Socrates, and Plato, tragedians such as Euripides and Sophocles, comic poets such as Menander and Aristophanes, and orators such as Demosthenes and Lycurgus. These Stobaeus arranged under seven general headings: (1) marriage is best (or most beautiful), (2) it is not good to marry, (3) for some marriage is helpful but for others the life of those who marry will produce inconvenience, (4) courtship, (5) in marriages one should give thought to the ages of those marrying, (6) in marriages one should not give thought to social standing or wealth, (7) the censure of women.[4] Stobaeus then follows with sections on marriage precepts, children, parents, relatives, social status, and household management. Somewhat arbitrarily, Balch chooses Stobaeus's first three headings on marriage and uses them to define the parameters of what he calls the "Stoic debates about marriage." From the start, then, Balch's method for determining the issues is too oblique. In consequence he identifies Stoic elements only in verses 32-35 of 1 Corinthians 7, and he presents an abbreviated and somewhat confused picture of Stoic thinking.[5]

3. E.g., Johannes Weiß, *Der erste Korintherbrief*, MeyerK 5 (Göttingen: Vandenhoeck & Ruprecht, 1925), 169-210 (passim); Alfred Juncker, *Die Ethik des Apostels Paulus* (Halle an der Saale: Max Niemeyer, 1919), 2:188-90, 209-11; Hans Conzelmann, *1 Corinthians: A Commentary on the First Epistle to the Corinthians*, Hermeneia (Philadelphia: Fortress, 1975), 114-46 (passim); Werner Georg Kümmel, in Hans Lietzmann, *An die Korinther I·II*, 5th ed., HNT 9 (Tübingen: Mohr, 1969), 176.

4. Stobaeus 4.494-568, Wachsmuth and Hense.

5. David Balch, "1 Cor 7:32-35 and Stoic Debates about Marriage, Anxiety, and Distraction," *JBL* 102 (1983): 429-39. Aside from excluding consideration of the *Cynic Epistles* (439 n. 35), Balch mistakenly concludes that Musonius held what was considered a "Cynic" position on

Yarbrough also fails to define the concerns of Stoic and Cynic thinking on marriage, although with Yarbrough this is partly by design, for he makes clear that his interest lies with the sociological *function* of what Paul says on marriage, not its theological or philosophical basis.[6] From this methodological starting point he draws a comparison between 1 Corinthians 7 and Paul's statements in 1 Thessalonians 4:3-8. According to Yarbrough, the second passage consists of general moral admonitions, or parenesis, which serve to establish "boundaries" between Christians and non-Christians on the basis of sexual morality. This is its sociological function in the Christian community at Thessalonica. By contrast he sees 1 Corinthians 7 as Paul's adaptation of this parenesis to deal with actual problems at Corinth. While 1 Corinthians 7 may also function to define the distinctiveness of Christians over against "outsiders," Paul is concerned here mainly with the *internal* affairs of the community.[7]

From this Yarbrough concludes that the sociological function of 1 Corinthians 7 is similar to that of both rabbinic literature on sexual norms[8] and Greco-Roman discussions of marriage. His handling of the Greco-Roman material, however, moves thematically and somewhat freely between chronological periods and philosophical contexts.[9] Moreover, he sees no need to focus specifically on Stoic or Cynic authors, and does not venture much beyond a general comparison with their writings.[10] Due, then, to his interest in the sociological function of 1 Corinthians 7 and the corresponding goals he has set for his investigation, the connections Yarbrough draws between Paul and Stoic and Cynic texts are too tangential for our purposes.

Finally, Vincent Wimbush has made use of Stoic and Cynic materials in an attempt to explain Paul's understanding of celibacy in the context of a general trend toward ascetic behavior that he sees arising in the Hellenistic

---

marriage (433 and n. 17; cf. 434, 439), and fails to notice that Epictetus advocated both Stoic and Cynic positions (435 and n. 25, 436, 439 n. 35). See my treatment of these authors below, pp. 75-76, 80-84; cf. Roy Bowen Ward, "Musonius and Paul on Marriage," *NTS* 36 (1990): 281-89.

6. O. Larry Yarbrough, *Not Like the Gentiles: Marriage Rules in the Letters of Paul*, SBLDS 80 (Atlanta: Scholars, 1985), 3-5.

7. Yarbrough, 7-18, 77-88, 92, 96-97, 114, 117-22; see also 5, 8, 28, 69. Cf. Wayne A. Meeks, *The First Urban Christians: The Social World of the Apostle Paul* (New Haven and London: Yale University Press, 1983), 100, 105.

8. Yarbrough, 18-29.

9. Yarbrough, 31-63.

10. Yarbrough, 63; see also 32, 105, 109-10.

world.[11] Beginning with the assumption that 1 Corinthians 7 is largely Paul's attempt to clarify his position on sexual asceticism in the face of misunderstanding at Corinth,[12] Wimbush isolates two passages as the essence of Paul's views on celibacy, arguing that they constitute a digression in Paul's discussion for the purpose of clarification. These passages are 7:29-31, where Paul discusses eschatological detachment from the world, and 7:32-35, where Paul contrasts married life with single-minded devotion to the Lord. The first passage is important because it seems to "represent a direct expression of Paul's understanding of the appropriate mode of Christian existence in the world," while the second is a "reinterpretation and application" of the first.[13] Thus in 7:32-35, according to Wimbush, Paul relativizes the importance of Christ's imminent return and offers a new basis for Christian detachment from the world. This is the ideal of "indifference" or "lack of concern," which Wimbush sees expressed in the Greek words ἀμέριμνος and ἀπερισπάστως in verses 32 and 35, and which he identifies with the philosophical notion of ἀπάθεια, "freedom from 'passion,'" or as he translates it, "spiritual detachment."[14] Relying almost exclusively on Festugière's popular study, Wimbush traces the notion of detachment through Greek and Roman philosophical traditions, giving special attention to its use among the Stoics.[15] Then, following Balch, he points to the similarity between Stoic discussions on marriage and 7:32-35, and concludes that Paul's model of celibacy in 1 Corinthians 7 derives from a Panhellenistic spirit of detachment which both the Stoics and Paul had brought to bear on the question of marriage.[16]

The problem with Wimbush's conclusion, aside from whether one can accept his assumptions regarding the purpose of 1 Corinthians 7 or the centrality of 7:29-35, is that it depends on equating the notion of living a life free from distraction, which Paul invokes in 7:32-35 and some Stoics invoke in their dis-

---

11. Vincent L. Wimbush, *Paul, the Worldly Ascetic: Response to the World and Self-Understanding according to 1 Corinthians 7* (Macon, Ga.: Mercer University Press, 1987), 3; cf. 10. Note that Johannes Weiß, *Korintherbrief*, 171, considered and rejected a similar view.

12. Wimbush, 6-7, 9, 12-13; cf. 17 n. 14.

13. Wimbush, 7, 21, 44-47, 50; see also 10, 13, 73, 85, 95.

14. Wimbush, 50, 56, 69, 87.

15. Wimbush, 56-62, encompassing a grand sweep from Plato to Plotinus, with little concern for chronological issues (3 n. 9). See 59 n. 37 and cf. André-Jean Festugière, *Personal Religion among the Greeks*, Sather Classical Lectures 26 (Berkeley: University of California Press, 1954; reprint, Westport, Conn.: Greenwood, 1984), 37-65.

16. Wimbush, 62-69, 87.

cussions of marriage, with the Stoic ideal of ἀπάθεια. Yet these are not analogous concepts. The former has to do with the proper management of one's outward routine, the result of which is a measure of freedom from civic, social, and economic obligations, and access to leisure time. The latter, by contrast, concerns release from mental and emotional attachment to things and people, resulting in an inner freedom of the soul. For this reason, too, the notion of ἀπάθεια plays no part in the Stoics' discussions of marriage. Although some Stoics maintained that marital obligations could divert a philosopher's attention from his true purpose, none entertained the thought that marriage could endanger a philosopher's inner freedom.[17] Wimbush's attempt to understand 7:29-35 in terms of a Hellenistic trend toward ascetic detachment by virtue of its similarity to Stoic discussions on marriage is consequently without foundation. Moreover, since his understanding of Stoic and Cynic views on marriage depends entirely on Balch's interpretation of the texts, with Wimbush we advance little, if any, beyond Balch.[18]

Thus, while several scholars have examined 1 Corinthians 7 in light of Stoic and Cynic marriage discussions, there is still a need to articulate the main issues of these discussions. Without this articulation, one cannot show the full extent to which Stoic and Cynic principles have shaped Paul's statements on marriage and celibacy. This will be our task in the subsequent chapters of this study. At present, however, we continue with our critical review of scholarly theories.

Motivations for Celibacy from Hellenistic Judaism

Asceticism and Revelation

Let us now turn our attention to two scholars who suggest a Hellenistic Jewish context for the celibacy in 1 Corinthians 7. The first, curiously, is David Balch, who as we just saw also argues for a Stoic interpretation of some of the

17. According to Diogenes Laertius, Stoics held that the wise man was free from emotion (ἀπαθής), and married and had children (Diogenes Laertius 117, 121). See also Epictetus, *Discourses* 2.14.8-12; Seneca, *Epistle* 9.17-19; and Teles, frag. 2.18.183-97 O'Neil.

18. See, e.g., Wimbush, 64, 65. For a critical review of Wimbush's work from another perspective, see David R. Cartlidge, review of *Paul, the Worldly Ascetic,* by Vincent L. Wimbush, *JBL* 108 (1989): 355-57.

verses in this chapter (see also the addendum at the end of this chapter). In the latter half of an article devoted to 2 Corinthians 3, Balch proposes that the Corinthian church practiced celibacy out of a desire to receive revelations from God.[19] His point of departure is a passage from Philo's *Life of Moses* in which Moses, in his role as priest and prophet, prepares himself to receive such revelations. As part of this preparation, Philo tells us, Moses abstained from sexual intercourse.[20] Because Philo's description (which follows Exod. 34:29-35) also states that when Moses descended Mount Sinai his face shone with God's divine radiance, and because Paul emphasizes this same detail in his discussion of the new covenant in 2 Corinthians 3:4-18, Balch postulates a connection between the asceticism Philo attributes to Moses and the celibacy in evidence in 1 Corinthians 7. To strengthen his position he notes further that Philo presents Moses as a divine man, or "ascetic θεῖος ἀνήρ," which Balch interprets as a sort of model or ideal that was imitated by many Jews, "including Corinthian Jewish-Christians."[21]

This theory has several questionable aspects. To begin with, Balch misunderstands the notion of divine men in antiquity. They are not ideals intended as "an actual possibility for all men," but rather ideal types. That is, they are rare human beings possessed of divine powers quite unattainable by normal men and women.[22] If Balch were correct, we would expect to find many examples of divine men in Philo's writings, including Philo himself. But Balch has only the example of Moses, together with other glorified figures from Israel's past.[23] Be-

---

19. David L. Balch, "Backgrounds of I Cor. vii: Sayings of the Lord in Q; Moses as an Ascetic ΘΕΙΟΣ ΑΝΗΡ in II Cor. iii," *NTS* 18 (1971/72): 351-64. Supporters of this theory include S. Scott Bartchy, *ΜΑΛΛΟΝ ΧΡΗΣΑΙ: First-Century Slavery and the Interpretation of 1 Corinthians 7:21*, SBLDS 11 (Missoula: University of Montana Press, 1973), 145-48; and Benedetto Prete, *Matrimonio e continenza nel cristianesimo delle origini: Studio su 1 Cor. 7,1-40*, Studi Biblici 49 (Brescia: Paideia, 1979), 74-86.

20. Philo, *De vita Mosis* 2.66-70.

21. Balch, "Backgrounds," 358-61. On asceticism as characteristic of the divine man, see Ludwig Bieler, *ΘΕΙΟΣ ΑΝΗΡ: Das Bild des "göttlichen Menschen" in Spätantike und Frühchristentum* (Vienna: Oskar Höfels, 1935), 1:70-73. Cf. Balch, 356, where Balch discusses Noah as a divine man with ascetic tendencies.

22. See the catalogue of divine men in Greco-Roman antiquity collected in H. D. Betz, "Gottmensch II," in *RAC* 12 (1983), 235-88.

23. Balch, "Backgrounds," 356. On Moses as divine man in Philo, see Carl R. Holladay, *"Theios Aner" in Hellenistic Judaism: A Critique of the Use of This Category in NT Christology*, SBLDS 40 (Missoula, Mont.: Scholars, 1977), 103-98; and I. W. Scott, "Is Philo's Moses a Divine Man?" *Studia Philonica Annual* 14 (2002): 87-111.

yond this, although Philo presents Moses as a divine man, it is primarily in his role as priest and prophet that the latter abstains from sexual intercourse in *Life of Moses* 2.66-70. The idea of priestly consecration for the purpose of receiving a revelation does not occur, however, in Paul's discussion in 1 Corinthians 7.[24] Finally, we must question the appropriateness of Balch's attempt to connect ideas from Philo's *Life of Moses* with 1 Corinthians 7 via 2 Corinthians 3. First, Balch has not shown that any connection exists between *Life of Moses* and 2 Corinthians 3 other than the fact that both Philo and Paul have an Old Testament narrative in common and perhaps a similar haggadic tradition of interpretation. Regarding asceticism in particular, Paul makes no mention of ascetic practices in 2 Corinthians 3, nor may we safely posit any here on the basis of Balch's suggestion that *Life of Moses* 2.66-70 is representative of a larger haggadic tradition that reads an ascetic theology into Moses' actions at Mount Sinai.[25] And second, I do not think Balch has successfully demonstrated a connection between 2 Corinthians 3 and 1 Corinthians 7, for neither his claim that the interpretation of Exodus 34 was a "central part of the Corinthians' theology" nor his claim that this theology was "one source of the asceticism which appears in I Cor. vii" can be viewed as reliable.[26]

Asceticism as Marriage to Sophia

In contrast to Balch's theory that the Corinthians practiced asceticism in order to receive revelations, Richard Horsley proposes that they had renounced physical marriage in view of participating in a "spiritual marriage" between them-

24. More recently Balch, with Carolyn Osiek, has suggested that the asceticism of certain Egyptian priests described by Chaeremon of Alexandria may also have some bearing on the celibacy in 1 Cor. 7: Carolyn Osiek and David L. Balch, *Families in the New Testament World: Households and House Churches* (Louisville: Westminster/John Knox, 1997), 108-9. The connection between the Corinthians and the ritual asceticism of (married) Egyptian priests is not obvious, however; nor is it justified to speak of Chaeremon's report as "current Stoic opinion" (114).

25. For which he cites several late rabbinic sources, "Backgrounds," 360. His suggestion on p. 364 employs the same reasoning: "Moses' vision (Exod. xxxiii–xxxiv) as interpreted in Jewish exegesis [i.e., rabbinic sources] contained the notion that Moses was transformed to similarity with the divine 'image' seen by him. . . . Transformation into likeness with the divine Image might well have been supposed by the Corinthians to include the overcoming of sexual differentiation."

26. Cf. the criticism of Balch's theory in Niederwimmer, *Askese und Mysterium*, 81-82 n. 6.

selves and the personification of divine wisdom, Sophia. Horsley, who has elsewhere argued for the importance of Hellenistic Jewish wisdom traditions at
Corinth,[27] bases this theory primarily on material from the Wisdom of Solomon and from Philo, where he finds several passages that speak of a marriage
between Sophia (or her equivalent) and the wise man's mind or soul.[28] In one
particular text, moreover, Horsley sees an instance of actual asceticism stemming from this line of metaphorical thought. This is *On the Contemplative Life,*
in which Philo depicts a community of Jewish mystics called Therapeutae, who
live somewhere in the Egyptian countryside around Alexandria.[29]

As supporting evidence Horsley cites two other texts. One is Philo's description of Moses in *Life of Moses* 2.66-69, which, as we have seen, Balch also
uses. The second is Apuleius's *Golden Ass,* or *Metamorphoses,* chapter 11. Here
a devotee of Isis named Lucius speaks of practicing sexual abstinence as part
of his preparation to receive a vision from the goddess. Noting that there are
certain similarities between Sophia and Isis, Horsley argues for affinities with
the wise man's marriage to Sophia, calling Lucius's relation to his goddess a
"spiritual marriage with Isis."[30]

Following the analysis of these texts from Wisdom, Philo, and Apuleius,
Horsley turns to 1 Corinthians 7. He contends that the Corinthians' interest in
wisdom, especially apparent in 1 Corinthians 1–4, resulted in a similar form of
asceticism. Here he considers the evidence of the Therapeutae particularly
cogent. In his opinion "extensive parallels" exist between this ascetic community and the Corinthians, including an interest in the symbolic interpretation
of Scripture, "ecstatic experiences and revelation of wisdom," and a belief in
the "dualistic division between body and soul."[31]

---

27. Richard A. Horsley, "Pneumatikos vs. Psychikos: Distinctions of Spiritual Status among
the Corinthians," *HTR* 69 (1976): 269-88; Horsley, "Wisdom of Word and Words of Wisdom in
Corinth," *CBQ* 39 (1977): 224-39; Horsley, "'How Can Some of You Say That There Is No Resurrection of the Dead?': Spiritual Elitism in Corinth," *NovT* 20 (1978): 203-31; and Horsley, "Gnosis
in Corinth: I Corinthians 8.1-6," *NTS* 27 (1980/81): 32-51. For still other research on the influence
of wisdom traditions in 1 Corinthians, see Gerhard Sellin, "Hauptprobleme des Ersten
Korintherbriefes," in *ANRW* 2.25.4 (1987), 3021-22.

28. E.g., Wisd. of Sol. 8:2 and Philo, *Posterity and Exile of Cain* 78, where Philo speaks of
Understanding as the spouse of wise men (τὴν σοφῶν σύμβιον ἐπιστήμην), and lauds their be-
trothal to the logos. These and other passages are cited in Richard A. Horsley, "Spiritual Marriage with Sophia," *VC* 33 (1979): 32-37.

29. Horsley, "Spiritual Marriage with Sophia," 39-40.

30. Horsley, "Spiritual Marriage with Sophia," 43, 54.

31. Horsley, "Spiritual Marriage with Sophia," 49-51.

The difficulty with Horsley's theory is twofold. First, it is doubtful he has proven that a form of asceticism based on the wisdom tradition's notion of spiritual marriage with Sophia was very widespread; and second, it is equally doubtful he has identified this form of asceticism among the Corinthians. In reality Horsley has only one clear instance of asceticism understood as a spiritual marriage with Sophia, namely, among Philo's Therapeutae. Regarding his examples of the wise man's marriage to Sophia elsewhere in Philo and Wisdom, Horsley himself admits that this is no more than a metaphor, and carefully suggests that these texts are "tending toward a general asceticism," or "clearly a step in that direction."[32] He also proposes that we see an "ascetic inclination" in Philo's own religiosity, citing Philo's many prohibitions against illicit sexual practices and his insistence that sexual intercourse be engaged in only for procreation.[33] But this is far from sexual asceticism, and these same things are found elsewhere in texts that heartily endorse marriage — as does Philo.[34] As for Lucius's ascetic behavior in the *Metamorphoses,* this is described as preparation for a vision and modeled after the celibacy of the priests of Isis.[35] There is no evidence here of a spiritual marriage with the goddess, which even if it did exist, might have little in common with a spiritual marriage to Sophia given the significant differences between Jewish wisdom and Greek mysteries.[36]

Thus the Therapeutae, we again stress, are Horsley's only clear example of asceticism described as spiritual marriage. But even here his treatment of the evidence is open to criticism. We must first object to his readiness to accept Philo's account at face value. While the Therapeutae may have been "an actual mystical ascetic group" — a matter open to *some* question, at least — Horsley surely overlooks Philo's apologetic tendencies when he reports summarily that Philo speaks of them as "almost typical of the devout Jews who 'pursue wisdom.'"[37] In addition, Horsley generalizes Philo's account without

32. Horsley, "Spiritual Marriage with Sophia," 35, 39; cf. 38.

33. Horsley, "Spiritual Marriage with Sophia," 39.

34. E.g., *Testaments of the Twelve Patriarchs;* on Philo see below, pp. 87-93. Horsley, "Spiritual Marriage with Sophia," 36-37, also points to a Platonic estrangement from the body in Philo, from which he says Philo "draws ascetic conclusions." But these have to do with Philo's description of the soul's recovery of a symbolic "virginity," not actual asceticism.

35. Apuleius, *Metamorphoses* 11.6, 19. The same is true of Horsley's reference to the priestesses of Ceres ("Spiritual Marriage with Sophia," 46).

36. Despite the similarities Horsley sees between Sophia and Isis. Cf. Helmut Koester, review of *Weisheit und Torheit,* by Ulrich Wilckens, *Gnomon* 33 (1961): 594, who denies any close relation between the two.

37. Horsley, "Spiritual Marriage with Sophia," 40, 41.

sufficient cause: it is not, as he believes, *all* the Therapeutae who remain celibate for the sake of a spiritual marriage with Sophia, but only the women.[38] And finally, Horsley never considers the very real possibility that Philo has simply read his own wisdom tradition and metaphorical language onto the practices of the Therapeutae. Philo may have had little interest in reporting their actual motivation for celibacy. It is conceivable, in other words, that Horsley may not even have this one instance of spiritual marriage to point to.

Horsley's evaluation of the evidence from 1 Corinthians is likewise open to serious questioning. On the one hand, his "extensive parallels" between the Corinthians and the Therapeutae must all be taken with a grain of salt. The Therapeutae's fascination with symbolic and spiritual interpretation of Scripture as described by Philo really has no close counterpart at Corinth, and a passage such as 1 Corinthians 10:1-13, to which Horsley points to support this claim, is common enough in Paul's other letters, as well as elsewhere in the New Testament, that we need not account for it by postulating the influence of a certain brand of Jewish wisdom theology. As for the ecstatic forms of worship and the body-soul dualism that Horsley finds in both groups, these, too, are fairly common in the Mediterranean world in this period.[39] But by far the greatest difficulty Horsley has to overcome in extending his thesis of spiritual marriage to Corinth is the fact that a divine personification of wisdom is nowhere mentioned in either 1 or 2 Corinthians, and we find no mention of wisdom in any form in 1 Corinthians 7 — as Horsley himself admits.[40] To my mind this is no basis on which to claim that the "vortex" of a "whole Corinthian pattern of religious thinking is the divine figure Sophia."[41]

---

38. Horsley, "Spiritual Marriage with Sophia," 43; see Philo, *De vita contemplativa* 68. Nor can we simply assume the men were included: e.g., in some orders of the Roman Catholic tradition nuns are thought of as "brides of Christ," but to assume that priests are also symbolically married to Christ would be a mistake. Horsley's claim that some Therapeutae women "are ascetically separated from husbands" (50 and n. 48) is equally unsupported by the text.

39. E.g., on ecstatic speech see Johannes Behm, "γλῶσσα, ἑτερόγλωσσος," in *TDNT* 1 (1964), 719-27.

40. Horsley, "Spiritual Marriage with Sophia," 49. 1 Cor. 7:32-35 does contrast the marriage relationship with devotion to Christ, but this is not marriage to Christ, nor is Christ a personification of wisdom. On the latter point see Koester, 593-95.

41. So Horsley, "Spiritual Marriage with Sophia," 48.

Motivations for Celibacy from First-Century Christianity

A Sociological Approach

In his book on the body and sexuality in late antiquity, Peter Brown suggests a sociological explanation for the celibacy at Corinth. Rather than investigating influences or ideologies that outsiders may have imposed on the Corinthians, his analysis focuses on the dynamics within the church in Corinth, understood as a social group. He reasons that general disorder in the community, so evident in 1 Corinthians, has led directly to asceticism. Confusion at the Lord's Supper, class problems, differing views on meat offered to idols, and the refusal of women to wear veils prompted some Corinthians to do away with the social structures they perceived to be causing this disorder, one of these structures being marriage.[42] While Brown makes a creative departure from the lines of research employed by other scholars, I question whether his notions of cause and effect really hold. In my mind, to make a convincing case for his theory Brown would have to either demonstrate from 1 Corinthians that the Corinthians did in fact consider marriage a source of their many problems or offer other examples from this period showing how social disruption within a small group brings about renunciation of marriage. He does neither.

Fear and Confusion as the Cause of Celibacy

An option pursued by a number of other scholars posits an ascetic theology among the Corinthians that arose from their confusion over Paul's teachings on holiness and eschatology. As Johannes Weiß explains, these "earnest, fearful, unfree souls" were frightened by the apostle's condemnation of sexual sins, such as one finds in 1 Corinthians 6, and by the nearness of the end.[43]

---

42. Peter Brown, *The Body and Society: Men, Women, and Sexual Renunciation in Early Christianity*, Lectures in the History of Religions, n.s., 13 (New York: Columbia University Press, 1988), 52-53.

43. Johannes Weiß, *Korintherbrief*, 169. See also Yarbrough, 120-21; Herbert Preisker, *Christentum und Ehe in den ersten drei Jahrhunderten: Eine Studie zur Kulturgeschichte der alten Welt*, Neue Studien zur Geschichte der Theologie und der Kirche 23 (Berlin: Trowitzsch und Sohn, 1927; reprint, Aalen: Scientia, 1979), 129-30; and Heinrich August Wilhelm Meyer, *Critical and Exegetical Handbook to the Epistles to the Corinthians*, Critical and Exegetical Commentary

The most avid recent supporter of this view has been Kurt Niederwimmer. Adamant that the celibacy in 1 Corinthians 7 is to be derived from the basic, founding principles of the Corinthian church, he goes further than Weiß in identifying the puritanical, sexually negative parenesis to which he thinks the Corinthians were exposed. Whereas Weiß had pointed specifically to 6:12-20, which he claimed was a fragment of a letter that preceded 1 Corinthians 7,[44] Niederwimmer defines a much broader base, citing Hellenistic catalogues of vices and Hellenistic Jewish wisdom literature as the source of both 6:12-20 and Paul's baptismal teachings in general. Noting that a denunciation of illicit sex, or *porneia,* is prominent in all these traditions, he postulates a "thoroughly pessimistic character of the churches in Paul's time regarding sexuality."[45] At Corinth, therefore, it was a matter of course that marital relations should be viewed with suspicion, virginity seen "as an advantage," and believers gripped with the fear "that the hitherto 'pure' virgins could be profaned through marriage."[46]

The difficulty with this approach to 1 Corinthians 7 is clear. It confuses or requires that the Corinthians confused illicit sex with sex in general, and draws the conclusion, supposedly held by the Corinthians, that sexual abstinence equates to holiness. Yet this sort of confusion is highly unlikely on two counts. First, not one text from the extensive list cited by Niederwimmer gives any evidence of such a confusion between sex and *porneia,* let alone questions the propriety of marriage on this basis. A case in point is the *Testaments of the Twelve Patriarchs,* where we find abundant warnings against *porneia,* yet marriage is never challenged: all twelve patriarchs are married, and they encourage their sons in this endeavor.[47] Second, there is no indication in 1 Corinthians 7, or anywhere else in the letter, that such a confusion took place. To the contrary, 7:2 promotes marriage as a protection against *porneia,* which rules

on the New Testament 5 (Edinburgh: T. & T. Clark, 1892), 192-93, who cites earlier commentators.

44. Johannes Weiß, *Korintherbrief,* 169.

45. Niederwimmer, *Askese und Mysterium,* 67-74, 81-82.

46. Niederwimmer, *Askese und Mysterium,* 65, 80-81, 98 (where he states that the "fundamental question" facing couples at Corinth was "whether baptism abrogates marriage," and that behind 1 Cor. 7:10-11 stands the question "whether or not the new existence, into which they have come through baptism, demands divorce"), 108, 115; Niederwimmer, "Zur Analyse der asketischen Motivation in 1. Kor 7," *TLZ* 99 (1974): 242-43. Cf. Darrell J. Doughty, "Heiligkeit und Freiheit: Eine exegetische Untersuchung der Anwendung des paulinischen Freiheitsgedankens in 1 Kor 7" (Ph.D. diss., Göttingen University, 1965), 178, 189.

47. See, e.g., *T. Levi* 9:6–10:1.

out any identification between the two; and since Paul states his position here without further justification, we may assume that the Corinthians shared this basic (and common) understanding of marriage, sex, and *porneia*.[48]

Finally, a note on Gerhard Delling is in order here. In his oft-cited book *Paulus' Stellung zu Frau und Ehe,* Delling takes the position that the misunderstanding Weiß, Niederwimmer, and others attribute to the Corinthians is actually no misunderstanding at all. The Corinthians, he maintains, have understood Paul correctly. For Paul sex is an action against Christ that mixes Christ's members, which belong to the Spirit, with the flesh: in marriage a person is "ruled by a foreign power — as also in extra-marital relations — instead of letting oneself be ruled by Christ." By practicing celibacy, therefore, the Corinthians have done nothing more than take Paul's theology to its logical conclusion. It is Paul, says Delling, who has not followed through with his views; his promotion of marriage and his stance against celibacy in 7:1-24 are clear evidence of his inability to think consistently on this matter.[49]

Against Delling we may object simply that if it is difficult to comprehend the Corinthian position in terms of a misunderstanding of what Paul said, it is all the more difficult to see their position as a valid reading of his theology. Indeed, Delling's treatment of Paul must be viewed as something of a curiosity for another reason as well. In 1923, eight years before Delling wrote, a clearly stated "corrective" to much of what he said about Paul appeared in a book bearing a title very similar to his.[50]

---

48. See also 7:14, where Paul argues that marriage with an unbeliever makes the latter "holy"; and Wolfgang Schrage, "Zur Frontstellung der paulinischen Ehebewertung in 1 Kor 7 1-7," *ZNW* 67 (1976): 230 n. 65. In this context we may also note that Walter Schmithals proposed a similar theory of confusion, to which Conzelmann replied reasonably enough that such a position attributes to the Corinthians "a high degree of ignorance of language and morals — even to the point of stupidity" (Conzelmann, *1 Corinthians,* 115 n. 11, commenting on Walter Schmithals, *Gnosticism in Corinth: An Investigation of the Letters to the Corinthians* [Nashville and New York: Abingdon, 1971], 234-35, where the latter argues that the tendency toward celibacy in 7:1-16 was motivated by the Corinthians' misunderstanding of Paul's denunciation of intercourse with prostitutes. His halfhearted reply to Conzelmann is found in the addendum to his work, p. 386).

49. Gerhard Delling, *Paulus' Stellung zu Frau und Ehe,* BWANT, 4th ser., 5 (Stuttgart: W. Kohlhammer, 1931), 62-69, 80; cf. 78-79, 86. "Indeed, Paul says [in 7:5] that the Holy Spirit cannot be in people during sexual intercourse" (65).

50. P. Tischleder, *Wesen und Stellung der Frau nach der Lehre des heiligen Paulus: Eine ethisch-exegetische Untersuchung,* NTAbh 10/3-4 (Münster: Aschendorff, 1923), esp. 95-97. Cf.

Secondary Christological Motivations

Along with developing a theory explaining the Corinthians' motivation for celibacy from first-century Christian principles, Niederwimmer has made a similar proposal regarding Paul's own motivations. This theory defines three distinct sources for the apostle's celibate tendencies.[51] The first may be seen in 7:1b, where he finds "a general ascetic motivation about which nothing more detailed is said," but behind which stands "a radical sharpening of the sexual taboo." It is neither theologically grounded nor even Christian, according to Niederwimmer, but represents a "taboo asceticism" based on the "fear of ritual uncleanness" and hails from Paul's pre-Christian days.[52] Paul's second motivation for celibacy, for which Niederwimmer cites 7:26-31, is inspired by the nearness of the end. This, like the first, is not specifically Christian, and actually holds little interest for Niederwimmer since, as he says, it "is obviously a secondary rationalization" of the first.[53] The third source stems from a "Christological justification of sexual asceticism," and is found in 7:32-35.[54] Like the second, it is a rationalization of Paul's taboo asceticism;[55] but unlike the second, it is completely Christian in origin, coming "from the center of Paul's faith."[56] For this reason Niederwimmer ascribes particular importance to 7:32-35 as containing the "decisive motivation" of the chapter: "Taboo asceticism (sexuality is damaging to body and spirit) is here directly tied in with Christologically justified asceticism (Christ demands unconditional, undivided devotion)."[57]

---

the brief criticism of Delling in Yarbrough, 3-4. One source of Delling's misunderstanding of 1 Cor. 7 is his reliance on Tertullian's exegesis (*Paulus' Stellung*, 64 n. 61, 65 n. 64, 66 n. 67).

51. Niederwimmer, *Askese und Mysterium*, 122; "Zur Analyse," 243-44.

52. Niederwimmer, "Zur Analyse," 243-44; *Askese und Mysterium*, 122 and 84-85, where he also speaks of the "demonizing of the γυνή [woman] in 7.1" and reasons "that for Paul any manifestly sexual activity at all is inadvisable." Cf. Conzelmann, *1 Corinthians*, 115: "Paul's view has an ascetic stamp; he does not give reasons for it"; and Delling, *Paulus' Stellung*, 64: "deep in [Paul] lies the fear of pollution."

53. Niederwimmer, *Askese und Mysterium*, 122. See also 108 n. 138, 109 and n. 144; "Zur Analyse," 244. Here Niederwimmer may be following Johannes Weiß, *History of Primitive Christianity*, 2:582.

54. Niederwimmer, *Askese und Mysterium*, 113.

55. Niederwimmer, "Zur Analyse," 244; *Askese und Mysterium*, 84 n. 21 (where he is much less emphatic; cf. 83 n. 15).

56. Niederwimmer, *Askese und Mysterium*, 112-13 (cf. 122 where he states that 7:32b-35 is the only passage where "specifically Pauline elements play a role"); "Zur Analyse," 244.

57. Niederwimmer, "Zur Analyse," 244; *Askese und Mysterium*, 115; cf. 108: "Here, here first

In assessing the reasonableness of Niederwimmer's theory, we may ask, first of all, whether he is justified in seeing three separate and distinct motivations behind Paul's understanding of celibacy. It is far from "obvious," for example, that Paul's eschatological argument in 7:26-31 and his christological argument in 7:32-35 can be neatly categorized as independent rationalizations of taboo fear. It is even doubtful that such a sharp caesura should be placed between these two passages on any basis. While 7:26-31 and 7:32-35 may differ in emphasis, they are in fact juxtaposed and flow one into the other as part of the same discussion. Their differences, I would suggest, are better explained in terms of the development of Paul's argument than as contradictory motivations, for there is no reason why the "idea of radical and undivided devotion to the Kyrios" need necessarily exclude an eschatological withdrawal from worldly obligations.[58] The end result of Niederwimmer's method, moreover, is that it rules out, without any apparent warrant, the possibility of identifying a coherent theology of celibacy in 1 Corinthians 7. For this reason it also runs the risk of psychoanalyzing Paul on the basis of these forty verses. It leads Niederwimmer, for instance, to talk of an "overdetermination" in Paul's thought, brought on by "contradictory" and "overlapping" ascetic motivations which the apostle is unable to reconcile in the course of the chapter. Paul's advice, we are told, is borne along by tides of "unconscious constraint," "unconscious taboo fears," and "unconscious defense mechanisms."[59]

Aside from these considerations, Niederwimmer's contention that Paul's basic, driving motivation throughout chapter 7 is taboo asceticism, and that this can be seen in 7:1b, has two serious weaknesses. First, there is nothing in 7:1b that specifically points to taboo fears; and second, there is still no consensus among scholars that this half-verse even represents Paul's opinion. Indeed, many scholars see it as the Corinthians' viewpoint, with which Paul, for the sake of argument, tacitly agrees[60] — an interpretation I shall attempt to

---

and here only . . ." (emphasis Niederwimmer's); and 113, where he reasons, "the person who is married cannot completely belong to Christ (according to the clear wording of the text)."

58. See 7:26a, 28b, 32a. Cf. Niederwimmer's contention that vv. 29-31 are in tension with the overall argument because they do not speak of the advantage of being single but of inner distance from the world ("Zur Analyse," 248 n. 20).

59. Niederwimmer, "Zur Analyse," 244; *Askese und Mysterium,* 121-23. Cf. the psycho-phenomenological approach taken by Johannes Weiß, *Korintherbrief,* 170-71, where he derives Paul's celibacy, in part, from the apostle's personal constitution, which he describes as characteristic of "very great, very inward looking personalities."

60. For bibliography see John Coolidge Hurd, Jr., *The Origin of I Corinthians* (London:

substantiate below in chapter 3. Finally, we may ask whether this hypothesis really explains very much. Even if we grant that taboo asceticism is Paul's true (albeit unconscious) motivation for his stance in 1 Corinthians 7, Nieder-wimmer still does not clarify why this motivation should come to expression christologically — in terms of so radical a devotion to Christ — or why the christological side should so outweigh the eschatological considerations of 7:26-31. Ultimately, I suspect, Niederwimmer's real reason for adopting this circuitous route stems not from anything he finds in the text, but from his own theological (and somewhat polemical) agenda of identifying a purely Christian origin for the church's asceticism in the first century.[61]

Enthusiasm and Realized Eschatology

Yet another way scholars have argued for a first-century Christian origin for the celibacy in 1 Corinthians 7 is to trace it to the spiritual "enthusiasm" of the primitive church. The first to propose this theory was W. Lütgert in 1908. Challenging the widely held opinion of F. C. Baur that the various difficulties Paul faced at Corinth arose from the activities of a Jewish party, Lütgert sug-gested that Paul's opponents were "enthusiasts."[62] Under this rubric he envi-sioned a group of Christians who had put undue emphasis on Paul's claim that they possessed God's Spirit. This led them to believe they had access to knowledge, or "gnosis," which gave them a freedom of action even beyond what Paul taught or imagined.[63] It was this misinterpretation of Paul, accord-ing to Lütgert, that lay at the root of all the Corinthian problems: it caused the Corinthians to question the resurrection of the dead, it was the impetus behind their effort to emancipate women and slaves, it led to speaking in

---

SPCK, 1965; reprint, Macon, Ga.: Mercer University Press, 1983), 67-68, 163; and Yarbrough, 93-96.

61. See Niederwimmer, *Askese und Mysterium*, 10.

62. W. Lütgert, *Freiheitspredigt und Schwarmgeister in Korinth: Ein Beitrag zur Charakteristik der Christuspartei*, BFCT 12/3 (Gütersloh: C. Bertelsmann, 1908), 43-62. "Enthusi-asts" was popularized during the Reformation — see Gerhard Ebeling, "Der Grund christlicher Theologie: Zum Aufsatz Ernst Käsemanns über 'Die Anfänge christlicher Theologie,'" *ZTK* 58 (1961): 230-31. This may be where Lütgert gets the term, since he once says Paul stood in the same relation to his opponents as Luther did to his (86).

63. Lütgert, 58, 67, 76, 86, 119-20. "Pneumatics must at the same time be gnostics" (105).

tongues and abuses at the Lord's Supper, and it promoted, paradoxically, both licentiousness and asceticism.[64]

Regarding this last point, Lütgert explained how the same theology could spawn diametrically opposed attitudes toward sex in the following way. Licentiousness, or sexual "libertinism" as he called it, was an inevitable product of the enthusiasts' zeal for freedom and their exaggerated emphasis on the spirit, the corollary of which was a complete devaluation of the physical body.[65] Their celibacy, on the other hand, was partly a reaction against this libertinism, as well as their former pagan lifestyles, on which this libertinism was modeled. But more importantly, it was grounded in the selfsame overemphasis of the spirit and subsequent deprecation of the body that produced libertinism.[66]

In one form or another Lütgert's explanation has received wide support. Scholars have been particularly enamored with the ability of his theory to derive both asceticism and libertinism from the same theology, since these facets of the Corinthian situation appear curiously juxtaposed in 1 Corinthians 5–7.[67] But Lütgert's theory has also undergone a major development. In the 1960s, expanding on ideas that C. H. Dodd had presented earlier in the century, Ernst Käsemann presented his thesis that Christianity in its earliest form in Palestine was thoroughly apocalyptic. On Greek soil, he argued further, this apocalypticism evolved into a theology of enthusiastic freedom similar to what Lütgert had described but fueled by the belief that Christians had come into possession of the eschaton.[68] As a result of this proposal scholars began

---

64. Lütgert, 124-35.

65. "Everything belonging to nature," wrote Lütgert, "is, as such, free — that is, exempted from the moral canon 'good and evil.' . . . For the pneumatic, the entire area of sexuality as well lies, with all of nature, outside of the opposition of good and evil" (124; cf. 128-29).

66. Lütgert, 124-28, 135.

67. See, e.g., Bornkamm, 207.

68. Ernst Käsemann, "On the Subject of Primitive Christian Apocalyptic," in *New Testament Questions of Today* (Philadelphia: Fortress, 1969), 130-31. Cf. Käsemann, "Sentences of Holy Law in the New Testament," in *New Testament Questions of Today*, 72-73, 78-81. The idea of a realized eschatology in 1 Cor. 15 goes back as far as John Chrysostom — see Jack H. Wilson, "The Corinthians Who Say There Is No Resurrection of the Dead," *ZNW* 59 (1968): 95-97. On Käsemann's thesis generally, see Jürgen Becker, "Erwägungen zur apokalyptischen Tradition in der paulinischen Theologie," *EvT* 30 (1970): 593-609, esp. 596-97; and A. J. M. Wedderburn, *Baptism and Resurrection: Studies in Pauline Theology against Its Graeco-Roman Background*, WUNT 44 (Tübingen: Mohr, 1987). Cf. C. H. Dodd, *The Apostolic Preaching and Its Developments: Three Lectures* (Chicago and New York: Willett-Clark, 1937), 93-108, although Käsemann

to view the many problems at Corinth not only as the products of a theology of the spirit and freedom, but also as products of a "realized eschatology."[69] With regard specifically to 1 Corinthians 7, the notion of a realized eschatology opened up two new possibilities for more closely defining the Corinthians' practice of celibacy.

First, some scholars suggested that the Corinthians saw themselves as participating in a postresurrection existence in which people no longer married but lived "like angels," a concept found in Mark 12:25. Here Jesus states, "For when they rise from the dead they neither marry nor are they given in marriage, but are like angels in Heaven." Luke's version of this tradition, moreover, is suggestive of ascetic practices in the here and now, and was interpreted in this way by several patristic authors, beginning in the second century. It reads: "The sons of this age marry and are given in marriage, but those counted worthy to receive that age and the resurrection from the dead neither marry nor are given in marriage" (Luke 20:34-35).[70] Scholars have argued for a link between this notion of angelic existence and 1 Corinthians 7 in one of two ways. On the basis of Paul's mention of "tongues of angels" in 1 Corinthians 13:1, some scholars suggest that the Corinthian practice of "speaking in tongues" is evidence they are living a life of angels.[71] Other scholars note that

---

never cites Dodd. For further information on Dodd, see Clayton Sullivan, *Rethinking Realized Eschatology* (Macon, Ga.: Mercer University Press, 1988).

69. See, e.g., Anthony C. Thiselton, "Realized Eschatology at Corinth," *NTS* 24 (1977/78): 512: "distortions or imbalance in the area of eschatology stand in direct causal relationship to errors about the gifts and work of the Holy Spirit. . . . In specific terms, *an over-realized eschatology leads to an 'enthusiastic' view of the Spirit*" (emphasis Thiselton's); cf. 523. See also Niederwimmer, *Askese und Mysterium*, 76. Lütgert (118) himself seems to have entertained this view, but never explores it.

70. On the ascetic "life of angels" in the patristic period, see Peter Nagel, *Die Motivierung der Askese in der alten Kirche und der Ursprung des Mönchtums*, TU 95 (Berlin: Akademie, 1966), 34-48; and Jean-Paul Broudéhoux, *Mariage et famille chez Clément d'Alexandrie*, Théologie Historique 11 (Paris: Beauchesne et ses Fils, 1970), 105 n. 36. On Tatian, specifically, see G. Quispel, "The Syrian Thomas and the Syrian Macarius," *VC* 18 (1964): 228-29; D. Plooij, "Eine enkratitische Glosse im Diatessaron," *ZNW* 22 (1923): 13-16; and Arthur Vööbus, *History of Asceticism in the Syrian Orient*, CSCO 184 (Louvain: Secrétariat du CSCO, 1958), 42-43.

71. David R. Cartlidge, "1 Corinthians 7 as a Foundation for a Christian Sex Ethic," *JR* 55 (1975): 230; see also Balch, "Backgrounds," 354 n. 4; Bartchy, 149-51; and Meeks, *The First Urban Christians*, 121. Yarbrough, 120, says the mention of "gifts" in 1 Cor. 7:7 indicates a connection between speaking in tongues and the Corinthians' celibacy; and Adolf Hilgenfeld, *Die apostolischen Väter: Untersuchungen über Inhalt und Ursprung der unter ihrem Namen erhaltenen Schriften* (Halle: C. E. M. Pfeffer, 1853), 81 n. 9, suggested a connection between the

the rare causative γαμίζω occurs both in the Gospel passages (in the passive "are given in marriage") and in 1 Corinthians 7:38. From this they conclude that a version of Jesus' statement, perhaps the Lukan version, was known at Corinth and used there in an ascetic theology.[72]

The second possibility scholars have seen for defining the Corinthians' celibacy in terms of a realized eschatology comes from the suggestion that the Corinthians saw their heavenly existence beginning with baptism. While this was not Paul's understanding of baptism, it is argued that the enthusiasts interpreted Paul in this manner.[73] Pointing to Paul's claim in Galatians 3:26-28 that "in Christ" "there is no male and female," and noting that the baptismal formula in 3:28 is reflected (although without this particular clause)[74] in 1 Corinthians 12:13 and, significantly, 7:17-24, these scholars suggest that the Corinthians' realized eschatology included the denial of sexual distinctions, and hence celibacy.[75] Thus, on the basis of Mark 12:25 par. and Galatians 3:28,

---

Spirit-filled Christians of 1 Cor. 14 and the celibates of chap. 7 on the basis of 7:40, where Paul grounds his authority in his possession of the Spirit. Both these theories are highly speculative.

72. Balch, "Backgrounds," 357; cf. Cartlidge, "1 Corinthians 7," 227, 229-30. See also Wayne A. Meeks, "The Image of the Androgyne: Some Uses of a Symbol in Earliest Christianity," *HR* 13 (1973/74): 202; and Werner Wolbert, *Ethische Argumentation und Paränese in 1 Kor 7*, Moraltheologische Studien, systematische Abteilung 8 (Düsseldorf: Patmos, 1981), 117, who gives the unlikely view, "If the Corinthian enthusiasts knew a saying of the Lord in the manner of Luke 20.34-36 and appealed to it, it would also be understandable why Paul (v. 25) expressly emphasizes that he knows of no saying of the Lord regarding this topic." Confessions of ignorance in matters of law or moral argumentation are generally not a strong suit.

73. E.g., Cartlidge, "1 Corinthians 7," 228: "The Corinthians have taken a Pauline baptismal formulation, — for example, Romans 6.1-10 — and have turned the future tense of the apodosis into a present tense: having died with Christ in baptism, we are already raised into the heavenly life." See also James M. Robinson, "Kerygma and History in the New Testament," in *Trajectories through Early Christianity*, ed. James M. Robinson and Helmut Koester (Philadelphia: Fortress, 1971), 30-40; and Hans Conzelmann, "Zur Analyse der Bekenntnisformel I. Kor. 15,3-5," *EvT* 25 (1965): 10-11 n. 59. Cf. Käsemann, "Primitive Christian Apocalyptic," 125; and Hans von Soden, "Sakrament und Ethik bei Paulus: Zur Frage der literarischen und theologischen Einheitlichkeit von 1 Kor. 8-1," in *Urchristentum und Geschichte: Gesammelte Aufsätze und Vorträge*, vol. 1, *Grundsätzliches und Neutestamentliches*, ed. Hans von Campenhausen (Tübingen: Mohr, 1951), 259.

74. But see, e.g., Hans Dieter Betz, *Galatians: A Commentary on Paul's Letter to the Churches in Galatia*, Hermeneia (Philadelphia: Fortress, 1979), 200, who suggests that in 1 Corinthians Paul retracted his Galatians position on the equality of women.

75. E.g., Meeks, "Image of the Androgyne", 180-89, 202, 207; Bartchy, 131; and cf. Käsemann, "Primitive Christian Apocalyptic," 126, 131. For use of the tradition "no male and female" in later ascetic groups, see Niederwimmer, *Askese und Mysterium*, 177-79, 217; Gerhard Delling,

scholars have posited two ways a realized eschatology at Corinth could have promoted ascetic practices there. As a final step, many have considered these to be complementary and have combined them.[76]

Although the theory of realized eschatology and enthusiasm has gained the approval of a great number of scholars, it is nonetheless open to criticism from several angles. We may begin by considering the eschatological aspects that were added to Lütgert's original theory of enthusiasm. First, it seems to me that those scholars who posit a connection between 1 Corinthians 7 and *both* Mark 12:25 par. *and* Galatians 3:28 have all too quickly assumed that these latter passages are supportive of the same realized eschatology. Mark, however, speaks of an existence devoid of marriage, while Galatians speaks of one in which there is "no male and female," and these are not necessarily compatible concepts. Thus in Mark 12:18-23 par., the Sadducees evidently assume that there will be sexual distinctions in the new age, for it is on this basis that they object to the notion of a bodily resurrection. On logical grounds, they argue, a bodily resurrection presented an impossible situation in light of the practice of levirate marriage: In the new age, who would be paired with whom?[77] Although Jesus overrules their objection, he does not attack their assumption that sexual differentiation continued in the resurrection. Rather, as Luke explains, he faults them for overlooking the fact that marriage is not needed in the hereafter, due to immortality: those participating in the resurrection do not marry, "for they are no longer able to die"; they no longer take part in the human cycle of procreation but are "sons of God, being sons of the resurrection" (Luke 20:36). According to Luke's Jesus, therefore, it is not sexual distinction that is inconsistent with bodily resurrection but marriage and procreation, since resurrection implies immortality.[78]

"Geschlechter," in *RAC* 10 (1978), 790-93; Nagel, 50-55; and Ton H. C. van Eijk, "Marriage and Virginity, Death and Immortality," in *Epektasis: Mélanges patristiques offerts au Cardinal Jean Daniélou*, ed. Jacques Fontaine and Charles Kannengiesser (Paris: Beauchesne, 1972), 214-35.

76. E.g., Nils A. Dahl, "Paul and the Church at Corinth according to 1 Corinthians 1:10–4:21," in *Christian History and Interpretation: Studies Presented to John Knox*, ed. W. R. Farmer, C. F. D. Moule, and R. R. Niebuhr (Cambridge: Cambridge University Press, 1967), 333; Elaine H. Pagels, "Paul and Women: A Response to Recent Discussion," *JAAR* 42 (1974): 540. Cf. Käsemann, "Primitive Christian Apocalyptic," 130-31.

77. Josephus also knew of a tradition that imagined marriage in the hereafter: Josephus, *Antiquities* 15.69 (cf. *Jewish War* 1.441); and *Antiquities* 17.349-53 (cf. *Jewish War* 2.116).

78. See Lucien Legrand, *The Biblical Doctrine of Virginity* (London: Geoffrey Chapman, 1963), 46; cf. Luke 7:28, where the participants of the kingdom are contrasted with "those born of women."

If this is an accurate picture of the synoptic traditions,[79] there is no warrant for thinking of the angels in Mark 12:25 par. as "either asexual or bisexual,"[80] nor can these passages be closely tied to the notion in Galatians 3:28 of "no male and female." But perhaps this conclusion is not so surprising, for if we consider the relevance of Galatians 3:28 in its own right, apart from Mark 12:25 par., we find it has nothing to do with a *future* existence. Paul's claim here is that there is in the *here and now* "no male and female" for those baptized into Christ, just as there is neither "Jew nor Greek," "slave nor free," which are also claims for the present.[81] It remains to be seen, then, why the Corinthians would draw a connection between Paul's baptismal teaching in Galatians 3:28 and an eschatology, realized or not.

But, returning to the synoptics, neither can we acknowledge that all is well for the theory that links Mark 12:25 par. to the Corinthians' realized eschatology. As we saw above, the only connections scholars have been able to draw between the Corinthian situation and these passages are the mention of "tongues of angels" at 1 Corinthians 13:1 and the verb γαμίζω in 7:38. But 13:1 does not actually prove that the Corinthians saw angelic language as a sign of their new existence,[82] and furthermore, we have no reason to assume that angelic speech is part of the heavenly existence described in Mark 12:25 par., for these passages say nothing on the subject. In fact, the use of angelic language

---

79. Since Luke is the only Gospel to add this or any explanation to Jesus' statement about the resurrection and since his reasoning draws on ideas current in several ancient authors, I would argue, lacking any evidence to the contrary, that this same reasoning is also operative in Mark 12:25 and Matt. 22:30. See Cartlidge, "1 Corinthians 7," 230; Richard A. Baer, Jr., *Philo's Use of the Categories Male and Female*, ALGHJ 3 (Leiden: Brill, 1970), 78 n. 1; and the excellent study, Eijk, 209-35. Cf. the following texts: *1 Enoch* 15:3-7; *Sib. Or.* 2:327-29; Sir. 30:4; Clement of Alexandria, *Stromateis*, bk. 3, chap. 6.45.3 (2.217.5-10 Stählin) and parallels; bk. 3, chap. 6.49.3 (2.218.26-30 S.); bk. 3, chap. 9.63.2 (2.225.4-7 S.).

80. The phrase is John G. Gager's in *Kingdom and Community: The Social World of Early Christianity* (Englewood Cliffs, N.J.: Prentice-Hall, 1970), 34. In fact, one piece of evidence from this period strongly indicates otherwise. A very famous, or infamous, group of angels, known as the "Watchers," receives mention in a wide variety of texts precisely because they, unlike God's other angels, made use of their sexual potential. See, e.g., Jude 6; Philo, *Quaestiones et solutiones in Genesin* 1.92; *T. Reub.* 5:5-7; and generally, Johann Michl, "Engel II (jüdisch)," in *RAC* 5 (1962), 60-97. A much stronger case can be made for angels being only male: they bear masculine names such as Gabriel and Michael, and they appear on earth in the form of men (although see Zech. 5:9). Cf. L. William Countryman, *Dirt, Greed, and Sex: Sexual Ethics in the New Testament and Their Implications for Today* (Philadelphia: Fortress, 1988), 182-83.

81. These are all "accomplished facts" (Betz, *Galatians*, 189).

82. See the discussion in Conzelmann, *1 Corinthians*, 221 n. 27.

by human beings is a notion very poorly documented for this whole period. Our one and only clear instance is in the *Testament of Job,* where Job's daughters — three legendary figures from Israel's past — speak in various heavenly dialects by the power inherent in their father's phylacteries.[83] On the other hand, with regard to the presence of γαμίζω in both Mark 12:25 par. and 1 Corinthians 7:38, the following needs to be said. While it is true that this verb is extremely rare, it does occur in Matthew 24:38//Luke 17:27, which make no reference to either angelic existence or ascetic practices,[84] and in the second-century grammarian Apollonius Dyscolus, in a discussion of transitive and intransitive verbs.[85] Since Matthew 24:38 and Luke 17:27 are from the "Q" source of the synoptic traditions, whereas Mark 12:25 par. are not, and since Apollonius Dyscolus has no apparent relation to the Gospels at all, it is clear that the verb γαμίζω had a wide enough currency apart from the tradition in Mark 12:25 par. that, lacking other evidence, there is no necessary connection implied between it and 1 Corinthians 7:38 simply on the basis of this verb.

Beyond these two considerations, however, there is a final problem with drawing connections between Mark 12:25 par. and a realized eschatology at Corinth. For a long time scholars have had difficulty understanding how the Corinthians imagined themselves to be fully resurrected or fully part of a heavenly existence. Did this mean they considered themselves immortal? And if so, how did they explain sickness or death in their community (see 1 Cor. 11:30)? Julius Schniewind, for example, went so far as to propose that the Corinthians explained away death as being only a mirage or mistaken "appearance."[86] More recently, complaining that the case for realized eschatology is

---

83. *T. Job* 48–52. See the note in R. P. Spittler, "Testament of Job," in *The Old Testament Pseudepigrapha,* ed. James H. Charlesworth (Garden City, N.Y.: Doubleday, 1983), 1:866 n. 48f. *Testament of Job* is dated ca. first century B.C.E.–first century C.E., but the passage in question could be a Montanist gloss from the second century (Spittler, 833-34). If this is true, the case for speaking in angelic tongues in 1 Corinthians or the synoptic traditions becomes even weaker.

84. Balch's attempt ("Backgrounds," 355-56) to see an ascetic bent in these passages based on Philo's description of Noah and his sons abstaining from sexual relations in the ark (*Quaestiones et solutiones in Genesin* 2.49) rests on extremely circumstantial evidence. Schrage, "Zur Frontstellung," 227, and Niederwimmer, *Askese und Mysterium,* 81-82 n. 6, both express misgivings regarding his logic. See also the critique of Balch's argument in C. M. Tuckett, "1 Corinthians and Q," *JBL* 102 (1983): 613-16.

85. Apollonius Dyscolus, *De syntaxi* 3.153.

86. Julius Schniewind, "Die Leugner der Auferstehung in Korinth," in *Nachgelassene Reden und Aufsätze,* ed. Ernst Kähler, Theologische Bibliothek Töpelmann 1 (Berlin: Alfred Töpelmann, 1952), 117-18, alluding to Wisd. of Sol. 3–4 as his sole evidence.

"usually lost by sheer overstatement," Anthony Thiselton has contributed the following clarification: "The question was *not* whether the Corinthians believed that their resurrection was past, but whether they placed such weight on the experience of transformation in the past and present that when they thought about resurrection the centre of gravity of their thinking was no longer in the future. . . . Paul is speaking to those who made too little of the future in their Christian outlook."[87] Yet if Thiselton is correct — and his appears to be the most reasonable formulation to date — a connection between 1 Corinthians 7 and Mark 12:25 par. is again open to question. This is because the absence of marriage for those participating in the resurrection according to Mark 12:25 par. is predicated, as we just saw, on the very fact that these people *are* immortal, "no longer able to die." One could avoid this discrepancy by claiming that those in Corinth who remained unmarried did so out of anticipatory imitation of the celestial existence depicted in Mark 12:25 par.,[88] but we should at least be clear that this entails yet one more layer of speculation: it is an assumption as to how the Corinthians might have interpreted a tradition we are not even sure they knew.

Having now examined the central elements of the argument that a realized eschatology promoted asceticism at Corinth, we may question its validity from two additional perspectives. The first involves asking if this understanding of 1 Corinthians 7 is compatible with the notion, held almost universally by advocates of realized eschatology, that this same realized eschatology also promoted libertinism at Corinth, as seen in 1 Corinthians 5–6. Even if we grant, as Lütgert maintained, that the Corinthians' exaggerated emphasis on freedom and the spirit could produce the diametrically opposed attitudes of asceticism and libertinism, it is much less obvious that these initial attitudes could then play themselves out so fully in the life of a community that opposing *visions of salvation* — a marriageless angelic life and a life of complete dissipation — could result and coexist. It should come as no surprise that supporting this view has, for some scholars, resulted in projecting a dubious schizophrenia onto the Corinthians.[89]

---

87. Thiselton, 523, 524 (emphasis Thiselton's); cf. 510.

88. Cf. Herbert Preisker, "Ehe und Charisma bei Paulus," *ZST* 6 (1928/29): 94.

89. So Cartlidge, "1 Corinthians 7," 230, who writes, "The encratic practices of the Corinthians are a bold statement by these Christians that they have fully achieved the heavenly reality. We should perhaps see their sexual libertinism in the same light (6.12-20)" — having written six pages earlier, "It is even quite possible that it is the same people in Corinth who are celibate in marriage, or, within the Christian community, yet relieve their sexual drives with a πόρνη [pros-

The second additional perspective from which we may question whether a realized eschatology promoted sexual asceticism in Corinth concerns Paul's use of apocalyptic language in 1 Corinthians 7. It is often maintained, for the letter as a whole, that the presence of a realized eschatology at Corinth can be measured by Paul's reaction to it in the form of apocalyptic ideas, since these ideas emphasize that the eschaton still lies in the future.[90] Yet even if this theory can explain the apocalyptic elements in other parts of 1 Corinthians, it does not work for 1 Corinthians 7. This is because, as several scholars have noted, the apocalyptic traditions in the chapter make reference emphatically to the present: Paul says the frame of the world *is* passing away, the time *is* constricted, and he speaks of the *present* distress.[91] If the usual understanding of apocalyptic material in the rest of the letter carries any weight, then this is certainly not the tack one would expect from Paul if chapter 7 represents his efforts to fight an enthusiastic asceticism stemming from a realized eschatology. And this, moreover, is doubly apparent when we consider that Paul is using the apocalyptic material in 7:26-31 to *promote* celibacy, not refute it, a fact that has been almost completely overlooked in this context.[92]

---

titute] (6.15)" (224). Likewise Gordon D. Fee, *The First Epistle to the Corinthians*, NICNT (Grand Rapids: Eerdmans, 1987), 12, 276. Cf. Fee, "1 Corinthians 7.1 in the N.I.V.," *JETS* 23 (1980): 314. Hurd, 164, favors avoiding this problem by taking the position that 1 Cor. 6:12-20 does not reflect the existence of actual libertinism at Corinth, but represents only a theoretical discussion about freedom and its misuse (cf. 277-78). Similarly, Yarbrough, 96-97, also denies that there were libertines at Corinth, reasoning that the problems there were not caused by disputes between ascetics and libertines, but by ascetics who had arrogated themselves above married Christians (cf. 119-20, 124).

90. Käsemann, "Primitive Christian Apocalyptic," 125, 132, 133. Käsemann is followed, among others, by Wolfgang Schrage, "Die Stellung zur Welt bei Paulus, Epiktet und in der Apokalyptik: Ein Beitrag zu 1 Kor 7,29-31," *ZTK* 61 (1964): 150-51; Thiselton, 514-15, cf. 519, 520; and Wayne A. Meeks, "Social Functions of Apocalyptic Language in Pauline Christianity," in *Apocalypticism in the Mediterranean World and the Near East*, ed. David Hellholm (Tübingen: Mohr, 1983), 699.

91. 1 Cor. 7:26-31. See, e.g., Doughty, 209-11; Gottfried Hierzenberger, *Weltbewertung bei Paulus nach 1 Kor 7,29-31: Eine exegetisch-kerygmatische Studie*, Kommentare und Beiträge zum Alten und Neuen Testament (Düsseldorf: Patmos, 1967), 65-66, cf. 99; Norbert Baumert, *Ehelosigkeit und Ehe im Herrn: Eine Neuinterpretation von 1 Kor 7*, FB 47 (Würzburg: Echter, 1984), 192-255; Wimbush, 34-44; Fee, *The First Epistle*, 336; and see below, p. 182.

92. Schrage, "Die Stellung zur Welt," 151, suggests that Paul is not promoting celibacy in 7:26-31 but relativizing the "definitive character" of marriage. Yet this is a rather fine distinction, and the larger context (7:25-38) tells against it. It should be noted that a growing number of scholars question the notion of realized eschatology in 1 Corinthians altogether. See, e.g., Jack

Having now considered the eschatological elements that scholars have added to Lütgert's thesis of enthusiasm, let us return to his original formulation of this thesis. Lütgert, as I noted above, specified two ways he considered it possible for ascetic behavior to arise from an enthusiastic theology that emphasized freedom in the Spirit. First, he saw asceticism as a reaction to libertinism, and second, he proposed that asceticism was inspired by a narrow focus on the spirit and a consequent disregard for the body, the same narrow focus in fact that also inspired libertinism. Despite their popularity, neither suggestion fares well under close scrutiny.

As for the first, Lütgert never explains why it is reasonable to think that those who were appalled by the libertine activities of their fellow Christians would react, or overreact, with asceticism. There is nothing logically compelling about this argument, nor can we cite other instances of such a phenomenon from antiquity. To the contrary. Many Greek and Roman moralists were also outraged at the licentiousness of their compatriots, but they never resorted to asceticism to counteract it. The same can be said of Hellenistic Jews, who criticized the sexual promiscuity of the surrounding Gentile peoples at great length. In fact, it is just as logical, or illogical, to suppose the reverse — that the Corinthians' libertinism was a reaction to the asceticism of certain Christians there.[93] Apart from these considerations, however, it must also be said that the idea of asceticism as the opposite number of libertinism smacks of the old argument that asceticism at Corinth came about as a reaction to the dissipation for which that port city was famous. While this argument was popular in Lütgert's time and before, and still has some supporters even today, it is now generally rejected as completely unfounded.[94]

Wilson, 90-107; Wayne G. Rollins, "The New Testament and Apocalyptic," *NTS* 17 (1970/71): 454-76; Klaus Koch, *The Rediscovery of Apocalyptic: A Polemical Work on a Neglected Area of Biblical Studies and Its Damaging Effects on Theology and Philosophy*, SBT, 2nd ser., 22 (Naperville, Ill.: Alec R. Allenson, [1972]), 73-93; Horsley, "How Can Some," 203-4; Horsley, "Spiritual Marriage with Sophia," 47; and cf. J. Christiaan Beker, *Paul's Apocalyptic Gospel: The Coming Triumph of God* (Philadelphia: Fortress, 1982), 66-69. Even supporters of the theory now express some hesitancy: see Thiselton, 514-15; Yarbrough, 119.

93. Schrage, "Zur Frontstellung," 219, asks, if libertine and ascetic attitudes come from the same source, how can one be a reaction to the other?

94. See, e.g., Peter Brown, "The Notion of Virginity in the Early Church," in *Christian Spirituality: Origins to the Twelfth Century*, ed. Bernard McGinn and John Meyendorff, World Spirituality: An Encyclopedic History of the Religious Quest 16 (New York: Crossroad, 1985), 441, speaking of early Christian ascetic practices generally. For supporters of this discredited theory, past and present, see F. F. Bruce, *Paul: Apostle of the Heart Set Free* (Grand Rapids: Eerdmans,

With regard to Lütgert's second suggestion, that asceticism derives from the same spiritual freedom and enthusiastic devaluation of the body that produced libertinism, there is again the problem of finding comparative materials. Darrell Doughty, for example, cites several models of behavior from the Hellenistic world which he believes are equivalent to the Corinthian situation. These include practices associated with Greek and Roman religious observances, mystery religions, Jewish apocalyptic sects, and Cynic philosophy.[95] In none of these, however, do we have an instance of both asceticism and libertinism stemming from the same source.

Indeed, this dearth of comparative materials is no small problem for supporters of Lütgert's thesis, since his principal argument for associating the celibacy in chapter 7 with the other enthusiastic phenomena of the letter is precisely this proposed "dialectic" of asceticism and libertinism which he sees at work in the Corinthians' attempts to actualize their spiritual freedom. Realizing this, scholars have tended to press a comparison between the Corinthians and second-century gnostics, who, according to patristic writers, also derived ascetic and libertine practices from the same theology. Lütgert himself seems to have used these patristic reports in formulating his theory, since he often refers to the Corinthian enthusiasts as "gnostics" and sees Paul's struggles with them as a forerunner of the church's fight against gnosticism in the second and third centuries.[96] Yet this comparison is flawed by the facile manner in which it understands gnosticism as a unified entity. It is not one "gnosticism" that the church fathers describe as practicing both asceticism and libertinism, but individual gnostic groups that practiced either one or the other. Thus there is no evidence even in gnosticism that one religious community could derive opposing sexual practices from the same theological principles.[97]

This lack of supporting evidence for Lütgert's supposed dialectic of asceticism and libertinism at Corinth does not of course rule out his theory altogether. But it is worth stressing once again that the ability of his theory to

---

1977), 249; the authors cited in Schrage, "Zur Frontstellung," 219 n. 21; and the lucid description of Johann Lorenz von Mosheim, *Erklärung des Ersten Briefes des heiligen Apostles Pauli an die Gemeinde zu Corinthus*, ed. Christian Ernst von Windheim, 2nd ed. (Flensburg: Kortem, 1762), 275, who compares the hot and passionate temperate zones of Greece to the cooler, more rational climes of his native Germany.

95. Doughty, 132, 141-43.

96. Lütgert, 8, 79-80, 95-96, 105, 109, 111, 118, 126, 128, 134.

97. See the discussion of gnosticism later in this chapter.

establish an enthusiastic motivation behind the Corinthians' celibacy hangs essentially on this one point. Since Lütgert and his following contend that all the other problems Paul addresses in 1 Corinthians are explicable in terms of an enthusiastic *libertinism,* 1 Corinthians 7 stands out as an anomaly. His proposal of a libertine-ascetic dialectic has thus been defended by his followers as the key to setting chapter 7 in an enthusiastic context as well. Without this key the inclusion of chapter 7 makes little sense.[98]

The Use of Second-, Third-, and Fourth-Century Sources

General Considerations

Rather than looking solely to the primitive church for clues that would explain the celibacy in 1 Corinthians 7, several scholars have formulated theories based on ascetic practices from second-, third-, and fourth-century Christianity. Working backward through the evidence, they identify Paul and the Corinthians as precursors of these later forms of Christian asceticism.[99] Niederwimmer, for example, despite his interest in first-century ascetic motivations, maintains that the Corinthians practiced abstinence after baptism in observance of a usage that some church fathers associated with Marcion and Tatian in mid-second-century Rome, and which is otherwise documented in Syria in the third century.[100] Other scholars suggest that

---

98. It is telling that several scholars who propose an enthusiastic explanation for the issues addressed in 1 Corinthians "hesitate" noticeably when it comes to treating 1 Cor. 7. A good illustration of this is Bornkamm. In a preliminary sketch of the various problems caused by enthusiasts at Corinth, he discusses all but those found in chap. 7 (Bornkamm, 71-74). Ben Witherington III, *Women in the Earliest Churches,* SNTSMS 59 (Cambridge: Cambridge University Press, 1988), 39-40, suggests that an enthusiasm behind the celibacy in 1 Cor. 7 is apparent at 7:40, where Paul appeals to his own possession of the Spirit. He interprets this verse as an ironic criticism of the Corinthian "spiritualists." Yet this overlooks the fact that Paul's remark here *favors* celibacy. Cf. Adolf Hilgenfeld, *Die Glossolalie in der alten Kirche, in dem Zusammenhang der Geistesgaben und des Geisteslebens des alten Christenthums: Eine exegetisch-historische Untersuchung* (Leipzig: Breitkopf und Härtel, 1850), 135. Regarding the syntax of 7:40, see chap. 3, n. 418.

99. On this generally, see Johannes Weiß, *Korintherbrief,* 204, followed by E.-B. Allo, *Première épitre aux Corinthiens,* 2nd ed., EBib (Paris: Librairie Lecoffre, 1934; reprint, 1956), 183.

100. Niederwimmer, "Zur Analyse," 242-43, and *Askese und Mysterium,* 98, cf. 124. For Marcion see Vööbus, 53-54, and for Tatian see 36, 42-43. For the later history of the practice, see Niederwimmer, *Askese und Mysterium,* 176-86.

Paul's denial in 7:28 and 7:36 that marriage is a sin indicates that certain Corinthians had taken a solemn vow of virginity which, they felt, would be sinful to break — our first certain information on such vows coming from the second or third century.[101] Again, based on what appears to be Paul's begrudging preference for marital relations over fornication, still others maintain that Paul understood marriage as a "necessary evil" after the manner of Saint Jerome. According to these scholars, Paul defended the institution of marriage solely as a "lesser evil," to prevent "worse evils from breaking out in their midst."[102]

Aside from displaying a disregard for matters of chronology and geographic location, however, these theories involve a more serious methodological problem. This manner of using materials from the second century and beyond to clarify 1 Corinthians 7 completely overlooks the theological contexts of the ascetic practices involved. As several scholars have pointed out, even practices that outwardly appear to be identical may in reality have nothing in common with one another in motivation or theological justification.[103] Thus the practice of sexual abstinence following baptism finds its jus-

101. E.g., Johannes Weiß, *Korintherbrief,* 194; Helmut H. Rex, "Das ethische Problem in der eschatologischen Existenz bei Paulus" (diss., University of Tübingen, 1954), 85; and Wimbush, 20. On vows of virginity see Hugo Koch, *Virgines Christi: Die Gelübde der gottgeweihten Jungfrauen in den ersten drei Jahrhunderten,* TU 31/2 (Leipzig: J. C. Hinrichs, 1907), 63-64, 109-11; Broudéhoux, 103-4; Georg Kretschmar, "Ein Beitrag zur Frage nach dem Ursprung frühchristlicher Askese," *ZTK* 61 (1964): 29-30; Robert Schilling, "Vestales et vierges chrétiennes dans la Rome antique," *RevScRel* 35 (1961): 117-21; and Bernhard Lohse, *Mönchtum und Reformation* (Göttingen: Vandenhoeck & Ruprecht, 1963), 27-28.

102. E.g., Jerome, *Adversus Jovinianum* 1.7, 9. The phrases are from Ethelbert Stauffer, "γαμέω, γάμος," in *TDNT* 1 (1964), 648-57; and David L. Dungan, *The Sayings of Jesus in the Churches of Paul: The Use of the Synoptic Tradition in the Regulation of Early Church Life* (Philadelphia: Fortress, 1971), 86. Rudolf Bultmann, *Theology of the New Testament* (New York: Charles Scribner's Sons, 1951), 1:202, says that for Paul marriage is "an unavoidable evil." For other examples, see the authors cited in Doughty, 5 n. 3; and Wolfgang Schrage, *Die konkreten Einzelgebote in der paulinischen Paränese: Ein Beitrag zur neutestamentlichen Ethik* (Gütersloh: Gütersloh, 1961), 218.

103. David Ray Cartlidge made this insight a major emphasis of his Harvard dissertation: "Competing Theologies of Asceticism in the Early Church" (Th.D. diss., Harvard University, 1969), esp. 22. Karl Rahner observed that only in his day were scholars making the necessary distinctions between different types of asceticism: Marcel Viller and Karl Rahner, *Aszese und Mystik in der Väterzeit: Ein Abriß* (Freiburg: Herder, 1939), vi. See also the careful studies by Kretschmar, "Ein Beitrag zur Frage nach dem Ursprung frühchristlicher Askese"; and Eijk, "Marriage and Virginity, Death and Immortality."

tification in an encratitic understanding of the world,[104] while perpetual virginity, vows of chastity, and the claim that marriage is a necessary evil presuppose either a dualistic view of the world that understands physical existence as morally deficient,[105] the related notion that moral purity is achieved through sexual abstinence,[106] or the belief that Christian women can be joined to Christ in spiritual wedlock.[107] In 1 Corinthians 7, however, we find no evidence for any of these. In our search for the motivations that stand behind this chapter, therefore, these comparisons are of little value.[108]

Two further comparisons of this sort have been put forth, one involving gnostic ascetic practices, the other an institution known as *virgines sub-introductae*. Since both have been accorded considerable credence by the scholarly community, we shall examine them here in detail.

1 Corinthians 7 as a Case of Gnostic Asceticism

Several scholars have attempted to understand the Corinthians' celibacy as a reflection of gnostic thought, arguing that it was motivated by gnostic ideas of material dualism and devaluation of physical existence. In order to be convincing, however, this theory needs to overcome a series of difficulties. The central difficulty, of which the others are extensions, is that 1 Corinthians 7

---

104. See, e.g., Martin Elze, *Tatian und seine Theologie*, Forschungen zur Kirchen- und Dogmengeschichte 9 (Göttingen: Vandenhoeck & Ruprecht, 1960), 88-100, 108-18.

105. See, e.g., Bornkamm, 208; Tischleder, 4, 9, 23-24; Johannes Weiß, *Korintherbrief*, 581; Bultmann, 1:202; and cf. Schrage, *Die konkreten Einzelgebote*, 25.

106. See, e.g., Niederwimmer, *Askese und Mysterium*, 108, 115; Johannes Weiß, *Korintherbrief*, 194, 195.

107. Cf. Niederwimmer, *Askese und Mysterium*, 80. Tertullian is the first on record to use the phrase "brides of Christ" for Christian women; see Schilling, 116; and Niederwimmer, *Askese und Mysterium*, 186-98. On the "anticosmic" perspectives of the second-, third-, and fourth-century church fathers, see the insightful study by Rosemary Radford Ruether, "Misogynism and Virginal Feminism in the Fathers of the Church," in *Religion and Sexism: Images of Women in the Jewish and Christian Traditions* (New York: Simon and Schuster, 1974), 150-83.

108. This was seen as early as Martin Luther: *Commentaries on 1 Corinthians 7, 1 Corinthians 15, Lectures on 1 Timothy*, ed. Hilton C. Oswald, in *Luther's Works* 28, ed. Jaroslav Pelikan and Helmut Lehmann (Saint Louis: Concordia, 1973), 47-54. See also C. F. Georg Heinrici, *Das erste Sendschreiben des Apostel Paulus an die Korinthier* (Berlin: Wilhelm Hertz, 1880), 205, 209, 211-12, 216-17; Juncker, 2:183-91; Meyer, 226, 231, and 192 n. 3; and Doughty, 6, who objects to the "unqualified claim to a general self-explanatory nature" that usually accompanies this use of second-, third-, and fourth-century materials.

contains no evidence whatsoever that supports such an interpretation. One scholar who has been particularly outspoken on this point is Walter Schmithals, who rejects the whole notion of gnostic asceticism here. Indeed, the only connection with gnosticism that Schmithals has detected in 1 Corinthians 7 is in verse 40, which he understands as Paul's polemic against gnostics at Corinth who *oppose* ascetic practices.[109] This judgment, it seems to me, is especially noteworthy when we consider that no scholar in this century has done more than Schmithals to promote the idea of gnostic influence at Corinth.

Faced with this complete lack of direct evidence from within the chapter, those who support a gnostic explanation for the Corinthians' celibacy base their argument entirely on what we have termed the "dialectic" between ascetic and libertine attitudes that some scholars posit in second-century gnostic thought.[110] For this reason they assign great importance to the fact that chapter 7 immediately follows a passage in which many scholars, including Schmithals, have identified a form of gnostic libertinism. The chapter is thus seen as the logical "companion piece" to the gnostic libertinism of 6:12-20: it is the "ethical counter-pole" in a gnostic "bipolarity of libertinism and asceticism," a system which supports both these attitudes toward sexuality from the same "radical devaluation of everything bodily and worldly."[111] Of course, this sounds much like Lütgert's theory of enthusiasm, which is not surprising when we remember that Lütgert, too, seems to have relied on second-century gnostic models. As a consequence, this theory is open to some of the same criticisms as Lütgert's, as well as some new ones.

To begin with, it is now generally recognized that first-century gnosticism differed from the second-century phenomenon in many important ways.[112] Wolfgang Schrage and others have attempted to address this problem

---

109. Schmithals, *Gnosticism in Corinth*, 234, 236, 387.

110. On this ascetic-libertine dialectic in gnosticism, see the treatments in Henry A. Green, *The Economic and Social Origins of Gnosticism*, SBLDS 77 (Atlanta: Scholars, 1985), 216-38; Hans Jonas, *Gnosis und spätantiker Geist*, vol. 1, *Die mythologische Gnosis*, 3rd ed. (Göttingen: Vandenhoeck & Ruprecht, 1964), 233-38, 313-15; and cf. Niederwimmer, *Askese und Mysterium*, 200-219; Erhardt Güttgemanns, *Der leidende Apostel und sein Herr: Studien zur paulinischen Christologie*, FRLANT 90 (Göttingen: Vandenhoeck & Ruprecht, 1966), 226-40; and John Ernest Leonard Oulton and Henry Chadwick, *Alexandrian Christianity*, LCC 2 (London: SCM Press, 1954), 22-33.

111. Schrage, "Zur Frontstellung," 217-18; cf. 219-20.

112. E.g., Koester, 595; Hans-Friedrich Weiß, "Paulus und die Häretiker: Zum Paulusverständnis in der Gnosis," in *Christentum und Gnosis*, ed. Walther Eltester, BZNW 37

by speaking of a "nascent" gnosticism in Corinth, which implies a gradual and predictable development; and Schrage has pointed out that the later gnostic mythologies and metaphysical speculations are not prerequisite for the development of ascetic and libertine tendencies within the movement.[113] Luise Schottroff lends some credibility to this latter claim, inasmuch as her analysis of 1 Corinthians 1, 2, and 15 argues that while there is no evidence for a gnostic redeemer myth in 1 Corinthians, Paul's opponents do seem to have promoted a gnostic dualism.[114]

Yet this does not necessarily settle the matter, for once we entertain the possibility that the Corinthians' gnosticism was a gnosis in its initial stages, our ground for assuming parallels between it and later, fully developed gnostic systems becomes potentially very tenuous. As Jack Wilson reminds us, "It is methodologically incorrect to call one group at one time Gnostic, another at another time Gnostic, then assume that since both are Gnostic their attributes can be interchanged!"[115] The entire problem is further complicated by the fact that even those scholars who entertain a gnostic interpretation for parts or all of 1 Corinthians vary greatly in their conceptions of this gnosticism. Robert Grant, for example, speaks of a gnosticizing "tendency" at Corinth deriving (à la Käsemann) from the experience of the Spirit and a "fully-realized eschatology,"[116] while John Painter sees the influence of mys-

---

(Berlin: Alfred Töpelmann, 1969), 116-28; Carsten Colpe, "Vorschläge des Messina-Kongresses von 1966 zur Gnosisforschung," in *Christentum und Gnosis*, 129-32; and George W. MacRae, review of *Gnosticism in Corinth: An Investigation of the Letters to the Corinthians*, by Walter Schmithals, *Int* 26 (1972): 489-91.

113. Schrage, "Zur Frontstellung," 220 n. 26; cf. Conzelmann, *1 Corinthians*, 15 and 108.

114. Luise Schottroff, *Der Glaubende und die feindliche Welt: Beobachtungen zum gnostischen Dualismus und seiner Bedeutung für Paulus und das Johannesevangelium*, WMANT 37 (Neukirchen-Vluyn: Neukirchener, 1970), 115-227. Christian Maurer, "Ehe und Unzucht nach 1. Korinther 6,12–7,7," *WD*, n.s., 6 (1959): 166, suggests that the libertinism in 1 Cor. 6 was based on a gnostic anthropology and a docetic Christology. Specifically on 1 Cor. 7, however, Sellin, "Hauptprobleme," 3003, has pointed out that there is no evidence for an "anthropologic-dualistic" gnostic asceticism here.

115. Jack Wilson, 99. Cf. Dahl, 333. Even Schmithals has had to admit that there are difficulties in correlating the Corinthians' gnosticism with second-century examples. To explain the discrepancies he had argued for a "certain lack of correctness in Paul's train of thought," suggesting that Paul was not really aware that his opponents in Corinth were gnostics (*Gnosticism in Corinth*, 233). The potential pitfalls inherent in this sort of reasoning are obvious — see R. McL. Wilson, "How Gnostic Were the Corinthians?" *NTS* 19 (1972/73): 71.

116. R. M. Grant, *Gnosticism and Early Christianity*, 2nd ed. (New York and London: Columbia University Press, 1966), 157-58. Gerhard Sellin, "'Die Auferstehung ist schon geschehen':

tery religions.[117] Gerhard Sellin, in turn, detects the presence of a dualistic spiritualism which he also finds in Philo, and Horsley argues that the Corinthians' form of gnosis is close to Jewish wisdom literature.[118] Given, therefore, the potential for differences between first- and second-century forms of gnosticism, and the difficulty of defining gnosticism at Corinth, it is far from clear that the same dynamics responsible for producing the second-century "dialectic" of libertinism and asceticism are operative behind 1 Corinthians 6–7, especially since chapter 7 supplies no support at all for this theory.[119]

Finally, two further difficulties arise from this attempt to see 1 Corinthians 7 as reflecting one-half of a gnostic dialectic of sexuality. The first we have already addressed in the context of Lütgert's theory of enthusiasm, namely, that it is problematic to attribute both asceticism and libertinism to the Corinthians on the basis of second-century gnostic models since we know of no

---

Zur Spiritualisierung apokalyptischer Terminologie im Neuen Testament," *NovT* 25 (1983): 221, notes the indiscriminate use of "enthusiasm" among scholars for both gnosticism and realized eschatology; cf. Thiselton, 516-26, who attempts to distinguish between the two. Jörg Baumgarten, *Paulus und die Apokalyptik: Die Auslegung apokalyptischer Überlieferungen in den echten Paulusbriefen*, WMANT 44 (Neukirchen-Vluyn: Neukirchener, 1975), 199-200, questions the usefulness of the term "enthusiasm" altogether precisely because of its duplicity.

117. John Painter, "Paul and the Πνευματικοί at Corinth," in *Paul and Paulinism: Essays in Honour of C. K. Barrett*, ed. M. D. Hooker (London: SPCK, 1982), 237-50.

118. Gerhard Sellin, *Der Streit um die Auferstehung der Toten: Eine religionsgeschichtliche und exegetische Untersuchung von 1 Korinther 15*, FRLANT 138 (Göttingen: Vandenhoeck & Ruprecht, 1986), 54-63; Horsley, "Gnosis in Corinth," 33-34, referring to Bultmann, 1:692-96, 709-10.

119. Recent research on possible gnostic influence in 1 Corinthians has in fact tended sharply away from seeing close parallels to the second-century phenomenon. See Sellin, "Hauptprobleme," 3020-21; Edwin M. Yamauchi, *Pre-Christian Gnosticism: A Survey of the Proposed Evidences* (London: Tyndale, 1973), 39-43, 173-86; Sasagu Arai, "Die Gegner des Paulus im I. Korintherbrief und das Problem der Gnosis," *NTS* 19 (1972/73): 430-37, esp. 436-37; Bernhard Spörlein, *Die Leugnung der Auferstehung: Eine historisch-kritische Untersuchung zu I Kor 15*, BU 7, Münchener Universitäts-Schriften, Katholisch-Theologische Facultät (Regensburg: Friedrich Pustet, 1971), 174-81; R. McL. Wilson, "Gnosis at Corinth," in *Paul and Paulinism*, 102-44; R. McL. Wilson, "Gnosis/Gnostizismus II," in *TRE* 13 (1984), 535-50; Birger Albert Pearson, *The Pneumatikos-Psychikos Terminology in 1 Corinthians: A Study in the Theology of the Corinthian Opponents of Paul and Its Relation to Gnosticism*, SBLDS 12 (Missoula, Mont.: SBL, 1973); R. McL. Wilson, "Philo, Gnosis and the New Testament," in *The New Testament and Gnosis: Essays in Honour of Robert McL. Wilson*, ed. A. H. B. Logan and A. J. M. Wedderburn (Edinburgh: T. & T. Clark, 1983), 73-89; cf. Carsten Colpe, "Gnosis II (Gnostizismus)," in *RAC* 11 (1981), 602-7. For an alternative interpretation of 1 Cor. 5–6, see now Will Deming, "The Unity of 1 Corinthians 5–6," *JBL* 115 (1996): 291-315.

one gnostic group in that or following centuries that embraced both these extremes. What we have, rather, are reports of ascetic gnostics on the one hand and libertine gnostics on the other.[120] Reconciling himself to these facts, Schrage has attempted to show that the texts speak for a "double front" — a libertine front in chapter 6 and an ascetic front in chapter 7.[121] What his argument overlooks, however, is that the opposing forms of sexual conduct reported for gnosticism are not merely the result of different gnostic groups drawing conflicting conclusions from one basic gnostic doctrine — "simply different forms of degradation of the body that comes with dualism."[122] Rather, they reflect divergent views of the world. This is a point Brown has recently highlighted, stressing "the great diversity of the radical groups that had emerged in the course of the second century."[123] Thus Schrage's explanation of 1 Corinthians 6–7 in terms of gnostic libertinism and gnostic asceticism, respectively, implies the coexistence of two distinct systems of thought. This in itself seems unlikely, and nothing Paul says in these chapters speaks in its favor.

Second, a very serious difficulty with appealing to a gnostic dialectic to interpret 1 Corinthians 7 stems from the recent conclusion reached by a wide consensus of scholars that gnostic libertinism was never widespread.[124] Based on information from the newly edited Coptic texts discovered at Nag Hammadi, gnostic libertinism is now understood by scholars to be largely an

120. Schmithals has recognized the seriousness of this problem and comes to the following emphatic conclusion: "I deny that the same Pneumatics *at the same time* demand asceticism and libertinism, for reasons of logic as well as the lack of religio-historical parallels for such a procedure, and for the Corinthian situation moreover on the basis of the texts, which neither require nor suggest such an interpretation" (*Gnosticism in Corinth*, 387-88, emphasis Schmithals's); cf. Niederwimmer, "Zur Analyse," 242.

121. Schrage, *Die konkreten Einzelgebote*, 217 n. 141, in reply to Schmithals's declaration as cited in the previous note. Schmithals stands by his position, however: *Neues Testament und Gnosis*, ErFor 208 (Darmstadt: Wissenschaftliche Buchgesellschaft, 1984), 30, 32. On "two-front" hypotheses in the research on 1 Corinthians see Sellin, "Hauptprobleme," 3018-19.

122. Schrage, "Zur Frontstellung," 219, cf. 220.

123. Brown, *The Body and Society*, 86; cf. xiv, where he speaks of "the range of options faced by Christians in the remarkable fifty years that stretched from the generation of Marcion, Valentinus, and Tatian to that of Tertullian and Clement of Alexandria." Even attempts at grouping gnostic theologies of asceticism into one unified phenomenon using a broad psychological interpretation (e.g., Niederwimmer, *Askese und Mysterium*, 208-19, esp. 218-19) distort this diversity — see, e.g., Brown, 65-139.

124. See R. van den Broek, "The Present State of Gnostic Studies," *VC* 37 (1983): 49-50; Klaus Berger, "Gnosis/Gnostizismus I," in *TRE* 13 (1984), 522.

invention of the leaders of the orthodox church for the purpose of discrediting their opponents. As Grant observed, "Earlier the Christians, now the Gnostics, were being accused of actions harmful to marriage and the family."[125] What this means for our investigation is that the libertine-ascetic dialectic, which is the sole basis for a gnostic interpretation of 1 Corinthians 7, appears to have been an extremely rare phenomenon even *between* different groups of gnostics, let alone within one religious community. In short, the attempt to interpret 1 Corinthians 7 by an asceticism based on a gnostic theology draws its inspiration from a dated and rare model of gnosticism that poorly fits the information provided by 1 Corinthians.

Spiritual Marriages

In 1902 Hans Achelis, following the suggestion of two scholars at the end of the nineteenth century, offered his solution to the enigmatic 1 Corinthians 7:36-38. He attempted to prove that the relationship between a man and "his virgin" which Paul describes here was a "spiritual marriage," an arrangement in which a couple lived together, sharing all the responsibilities and benefits of a normal marriage, with the important exception of the sexual relationship. The man's virgin in 7:36-38, according to Achelis, was thus one of the *virgines subintroductae* spoken of by later church fathers.[126]

---

125. Robert M. Grant, "Early Christians and Gnostics in Graeco-Roman Society," in *The New Testament and Gnosis,* 180; the quote continues: "A glance at A. Berger's *Encyclopedic Dictionary of Roman Law* immediately shows how offenders would be subject not only to social condemnation but also to legal penalties: Adulterium, Incestus, Stuprum, not to mention Homicidium. Beyond that came the general social attitudes which supported marriage and the family, notably under the Antonine emperors. . . . We conclude that the charges against the Gnostics are intended to show that they were outcasts from Graeco-Roman society." The polemical nature of the patristic reports was seen with remarkable clarity by Gibbon: see Edward Gibbon, *The History of the Decline and Fall of the Roman Empire* (New York: A. L. Burnt, 1845), 1:595-97.

126. Hans Achelis, *Virgines Subintroductae: Ein Beitrag zum VII. Kapitel des I. Korintherbriefs* (Leipzig: J. C. Hinrichs, 1902); preceded by Carl Weizsäcker, "Die Anfänge christlicher Sitte," *Jahrbücher für Deutsche Theologie* 21 (1876): 33, cf. Weizsäcker, *Das apostolische Zeitalter der christlichen Kirche,* 1st ed. (Freiburg im Breisgau: Mohr, 1886), 675-76; and Eduard Grafe, "Geistliche Verlöbnisse bei Paulus," *Theologische Arbeiten aus dem rheinischen wissenschaftlichen Predigerverein,* n.s., 3 (1899): 57-69. Achelis was the first to research a full history of spiritual marriage; Grafe had only alluded to possible occurrences in *Hermas.*

Beginning with the "more certain" evidence and venturing backward in time to "questionable" cases of this institution, Achelis opens his analysis with the church father Cyprian, who around 249 writes with concern about several Christian men known to him (one being a deacon) who were cohabiting with virgins vowed to chastity.[127] His next instance is Eusebius's account of Paul of Samosata, a bishop of Antioch who was deposed in 268. Paul, it seems, along with his presbyters and deacons, lived in chastity with women the people of Antioch had nicknamed συνείσακτοι, the Greek equivalent of the later *subintroductae*.[128] Following this, Achelis cites Origen's stay with the virgin Juliana (235-37 C.E.),[129] and Tertullian's proposal (ca. 210) that those who wished to marry after the death of their first wife take a "spiritual wife," by which he meant an aged widow who could offer a man chaste companionship and housekeeping.[130]

Achelis then turns to five cases of spiritual marriage from the late to middle second century. The one on which he spends the most time is the *Shepherd of Hermas, Similitudes* 9.10.6–11.8, where the seer Hermas encounters twelve virgins with whom he spends the night, but "as a brother, and *not* as a husband."[131] Achelis's other cases involve: followers of Valentinus; the Montanist Alexander and a prophetess; Marcion's disciple Apelles, a woman called Philumene, and another woman who is not named; and several followers of Tatian.[132] Finally, Achelis arrives at 1 Corinthians 7:36-38. Challenging the church's traditional explanation of this passage, which envisioned a father agonizing over whether he should marry off his daughter, and discounting the idea that the virgin here is an orphan who was raised by a patron and is now being threatened by his sexual advances, Achelis proposes that we "as-

127. Achelis, *Virgines Subintroductae*, 7-8, citing Cyprian, *Epistle* 4, *To Pomponius*. Achelis (9) also cites *Epistle* 13.5 and 15.3, but these speak only of general promiscuity in the church.

128. Achelis, *Virgines Subintroductae*, 9-11, citing Eusebius, *Church History* 7.30.12. Our first evidence for the Latin *subintroductae* is from Atticus of Constantinople in 419, in his Latin translation of the proceedings of the Council of Nicea — cited by Pierre de Labriolle, "Le 'mariage spirituel' dans l'antiquité chrétienne," *Revue Historique* 137 (1921): 214 n. 4.

129. Achelis, *Virgines Subintroductae*, 12, citing Palladius, *Lausiac History* 147. Achelis is unsure whether this is really a spiritual marriage, however.

130. Achelis, *Virgines Subintroductae*, 12-14, citing Tertullian, *De exhortatione castitatis* 12, and *De monogamia* 16.

131. ὡς ἀδελφός, καὶ οὐχ ὡς ἀνήρ; Achelis, *Virgines Subintroductae*, 14-19.

132. Achelis, *Virgines Subintroductae*, 19-20, citing Irenaeus, *Against Heresies* 1.6.3; Eusebius, *Church History* 5.18.6; Tertullian, *De praescriptione haereticorum* 30; and Epiphanius, *Haereses* 47.3.1, respectively. He also surveys possibilities from later periods (34-59, 63, 69).

sume with Paul the institute of the *subintroductae* in its fully developed form."[133]

A major problem, though by no means the only problem, with this interpretation is in fact the passage itself, for nothing in these verses points distinctly to a spiritual marriage.[134] Indeed, Achelis openly conceded this much, and underscored the tenuous nature of his interpretation, as did Carl Weizsäcker and Eduard Grafe before him.[135] Beyond the absence of any clear evidence from 7:36-38, however, the most obvious difficulty with Achelis's work is chronological. Even if we accept his analysis of the materials from Cyprian to *Hermas*, his earliest case of *subintroductae* before we reach Paul is

---

133. Achelis, *Virgines Subintroductae*, 26. Achelis's theory, with some modification, has achieved a fairly wide acceptance among scholars. See the bibliography in Werner Georg Kümmel, "Verlobung und Heirat bei Paulus (I. Cor 7 36-38)," in *Neutestamentliche Studien für Rudolf Bultmann*, ed. Walther Eltester, BZNW 21 (1954), 275-76 n. 1 and 278 n. 11. See also Roland H. A. Seboldt, "Spiritual Marriage in the Early Church: A Suggested Interpretation of 1 Cor. 7:36-38," *CTM* 30 (1959): 113-19, 176-89; and Niederwimmer, *Askese und Mysterium*, 117-20. Some scholars have even argued for extending the notion of spiritual marriages over the entire section 7:25-38. This was actually the brainchild of Weizsäcker in 1876, when he first proposed a connection between 1 Cor. 7 and spiritual marriages (Weizsäcker, "Anfänge," 32-33), a fact overlooked in Albrecht Oepke's polemic, "Irrwege in der neueren Paulusforschung," *TLZ* 77 (1952): 450-51. Weizsäcker, in turn, was followed by Johannes Weiß in his influential commentary on 1 Corinthians (*Korintherbrief*, 194-96), and by Rudolf Steck, "Geistliche Ehen bei Paulus? (I. Kor. 7,36-38)," *Schweizerische Theologische Zeitschrift* 34 (1917): 185-89. Yet as Adolf Jülicher has shown, this proposal raises more problems than it solves ("Die Jungfrauen im ersten Korintherbrief," *Protestantische Monatshefte* 22 [1918]: 114-15; see also Juncker, 2:192-200). Other scholars have sought to reinstate the traditional father-daughter understanding of this passage, an interpretation that goes back at least to Clement of Alexandria (*Stromateis*, bk. 3, chap. 12.79.2 [2.231.21-23 S.]), but which is impossible on philological grounds. See Kümmel, "Verlobung," 279-86, and 276 nn. 2-3. Still other scholars have developed interpretations based on comparisons with late rabbinic sources, a methodology that is suspect for several reasons. For these theories see Kümmel, 289-95; Seboldt, 107-13; Niederwimmer, *Askese und Mysterium*, 116-17; J. Massingberd Ford, "St. Paul, the Philogamist (I Cor. vii in Early Patristic Exegesis)," *NTS* 11 (1964/65): 326-48; and J. Duncan M. Derrett, "The Disposal of Virgins," in *Studies in the New Testament* (Leiden: Brill, 1977), 1:184-92.

134. See Plooij, 4; Adolf von Schlatter, *Paulus der Bote Jesu: Eine Deutung seiner Briefe an die Korinther* (Stuttgart: Calwer, 1934; reprint, 1956), 246; and Franz Fahnenbruch's apt characterization of the elusiveness of the passage in his "Zu 1 Kor 7,36-38," *BZ* (Freiburg i. B.) 12 (1914): 392 — which parrots Achelis's own (*Virgines Subintroductae*, 22).

135. A fact most present-day supporters of the *subintroductae* theory choose to overlook. See Achelis, *Virgines Subintroductae*, 26 n. 1; Achelis, "AGAPĒTÆ," *ERE* 1 (1926): 179; Weizsäcker, *Das apostolische Zeitalter*, 675-76; Grafe, 57.

in the middle of the second century, almost one hundred years after the apostle writes.[136] The anachronism of Achelis's theory is further indicated by the fact that no Greek or Latin church father *ever* interprets 7:36-38 as referring to spiritual marriage, although many discuss it. Even in the church's many debates on the propriety of *subintroductae,* this passage is never used as a proof text, even though these debates lasted from the third to the seventh century and employed many biblical proof texts.[137]

Well aware of these shortcomings to his argument, Achelis attempted to explain the silence of the Fathers in light of two developments within the church: beginning in the third century, spiritual marriage fell into disrepute; and already in the second century, the marriage of a virgin vowed to a life of

---

136. See Richard Kugelmann, "1 Cor 7:36-38," *CBQ* 10 (1948): 66; Kümmel, "Verlobung," 289; P. Ladeuze, review of *Virgines Subintroductae,* by Hans Achelis, *RHE* 6 (1905): 61; and Roger Gryson, *Les origines du célibat ecclésiastique: Du premier au septième siècle,* Recherches et synthèses, section d'Histoire 2 (Gembloux: J. Duculot, 1970), 36-38. Cf. Conzelmann, *1 Corinthians,* 135 n. 45; and Hugo Koch, 59-112. Even supporters of Achelis are obliged to concede that "the historical gap is great" (Seboldt, 189). Some scholars have sought to close this gap by proposing that *Didache* 11.11, a text which may come from the late first or early second century, also speaks of spiritual marriages — e.g., Preisker, *Christentum und Ehe,* 158-60. But there is really nothing in this passage that points to spiritual marriages. It speaks of strange practices of itinerant prophets, which, the text says, are not to be imitated by the congregation as a whole. These could be almost anything. Further, the text never mentions prophetesses or female companions to these prophets, nor does it refer to their associating with women of the local congregations. Indeed, the only thing that even *remotely* connects *Didache* 11.11 with spiritual marriages is an exegesis of this passage developed by certain fathers in the Syrian church. On this see Alfred Adam, "Erwägungen zur Herkunft der Didache," *ZKG* 68 (1957): 20-37; Conzelmann, *1 Corinthians,* 136 n. 45; Kümmel, "Verlobung," 278 n. 9; and Niederwimmer, *Askese und Mysterium,* 191-92. Achelis, we should note, never mentions the passage. He was, however, prepared to consider Philo's Therapeutae in the historical trajectory of spiritual marriage, and even compares the dancing of Hermas's virgins with the religious activities of the female Therapeutae ("AGAPÉTÆ," 179; *Virgines Subintroductae,* 71; 29, 32). Cf. Kirsopp Lake, *The Earlier Epistles of St. Paul: Their Motive and Origin,* 2nd ed. (London: Rivingtons, 1914), 188-89.

137. See Joseph Sickenberger, "Syneisaktentum im ersten Korintherbriefe?" *BZ* 3 (1905): 49-57; Kugelmann, 67. Cf. Kümmel, "Verlobung," 276 n. 2, 289. On the nature of the church's debates, see Achelis, *Virgines Subintroductae,* 34-35, 42-43. Achelis (23 n. 2) attempted to argue that John Chrysostom's use of ἀσχημοσύνη and ἀσχημονεῖν in his two treatises on *subintroductae* had reference to 1 Cor. 7:36, but this is not at all compelling; cf. Sickenberger, 58 n. 1. It is only in the Syrian church, in Saint Ephraem's commentary on Paul from the mid–fourth century (extant in Armenian), that 1 Cor. 7:36-38 is interpreted in light of spiritual marriages — see Kugelmann, 67-68; Franz Herklotz, "Zu 1 Kor 7, 36ff.," *BZ* (Freiburg i. B.) 14 (1916/17): 344-45. On spiritual marriage in the Syrian church, see Vööbus, 78-83.

continence was regarded a serious sin. According to Achelis, the church fathers found it impossible to interpret Paul in a manner that would have given either of these practices an air of legitimacy. While Henry Chadwick and others have seconded Achelis's suggestion, it is unclear how much this argument from silence can explain. If we grant that the Greek and Latin Fathers rejected a *subintroductae* interpretation for 7:36-38, does it then follow that not one of them would have ventured to refute such an interpretation by showing how it was in error?[138]

Thus far we have assumed that Achelis accurately construed his patristic sources, but this, too, is problematic. Let us consider his evidence for the second century. Regarding the followers of Valentinus, Achelis's source, Irenaeus, tells us only that these gnostics proposed ascetic cohabitation with women as a ruse, in order to lure them away from their husbands.[139] As for the Montanist Alexander, Eusebius's informant Apollonius states that the former had a relationship with a prophetess but leaves the actual nature of this relationship poorly defined. He says only in passing that the woman lived or "cavorted" with Alexander, for Eusebius's real concern was with discrediting this Montanist as a thief.[140] With Tatian's followers the matter is different. Here we learn from Epiphanius that they were found among women, that they led the women astray, traveled with them, lived with them as companions, and let themselves be served by them.[141] But whether this corresponds to spiritual marriage or simply an ascetic community, Epiphanius does not say. Concerning Marcion's disciple Apelles, by contrast, Tertullian states specifically that his first relation with a woman involved *leaving* the ascetic regiment of his teacher *(desertor continentiae Marcionensis)*, while his second relationship began when he "forced himself" *(impegit)* on the virgin Philumene, who thereafter became a prostitute.[142]

---

138. See Achelis, *Virgines Subintroductae*, 28 n. 3; H. Chadwick, "'All Things to All Men' (I Cor. ix.22)," *NTS* 1 (1954/55): 267, and Seboldt, 105-6, who offers the unlikely theory that some manuscripts of 1 Cor. 7:38 read ἐκγαμίζων in place of γαμίζων to prevent someone from interpreting the latter as the equivalent of γαμῶν, and thus as referring to spiritual marriages.

139. Irenaeus, *Against Heresies* 1.6.3.

140. The expression Eusebius uses is συνεστιάω τινί, *Church History* 5.18.6.

141. Epiphanius, *Haereses* 47.3.1.

142. Tertullian, *De praescriptione haereticorum* 30.5-6. One could argue, of course, that in their zeal against the heretics the church fathers distorted some of these reports for polemic reasons. But even if this were the case, it would be precarious to speculate further on this basis that the heretics practiced spiritual marriages.

Of Achelis's five examples of spiritual marriage from the second century, this leaves us with only *Hermas, Similitudes* 9.10.6–11.8.[143] Here Hermas is left by his spiritual guide, the Shepherd, to spend the night with twelve virgins who are watching over a tower (πύργος). Initially Hermas is reluctant, but after some persuasion gives in. Further on in the narrative we learn that these virgins are holy spirits and powers of God (δυνάμεις). The Shepherd instructs Hermas that he must clothe himself with these spirits and receive their power in order to please God, and he contrasts them with ten women dressed in black, who lead people astray. We also learn the names of the twelve virgins: Faith, Temperance, Power, Patience, Simplicity, Innocence, Holiness, Joyfulness, Truth, Understanding, Concord, and Love.

Achelis, of course, realized that this passage reported a vision. Even so, he argued, the author relates the incident of staying overnight in such a matter-of-fact manner that we must presuppose familiarity with spiritual marriages in *Hermas*. Robert Schilling has supported this view, adding that the scene with the virgins could hardly be an invention of Hermas's imagination.[144] Other scholars, however, object. Pierre Labriolle, for example, finds it difficult to compare Hermas's one-night mystical experience with the practice of spiritual marriage; and noting the simple logistics of Hermas's lodging arrangements, J. Massingberd Ford remarks, rather wryly one hopes, that "polygamous *subintroductae* relationships would hardly be possible."[145]

143. Achelis also cites *Hermas, Visions* 1.1.1, in his *ERE* article ("AGAPĒTÆ," 179), to which we may add *Visions* 2.2.3, which Plooij (4-6) cites. In these passages Hermas enters into a new relationship with two women: with Rhoda, whose servant Hermas once was, and with his wife. In *Visions* 1.1.1, however, Hermas says only that after many years he reacquainted himself with his former mistress and began to love her as a sister (ἠρξάμην αὐτὴν ἀγαπᾶν ὡς ἀδελφήν). He does not say that he took up residence with Rhoda and thus initiated a spiritual marriage (cf. Kugelmann, 66-67). *Visions* 2.2.3, on the other hand, depicts Hermas receiving instructions that he should continue to live with his wife but cease sexual relations with her. Yet here we must ask whether this represents the beginning of a spiritual marriage or simply the application of Hermas's rigorism to an already existing marriage. In any case, Hermas's wife is not a *virgo subintroducta*.

144. Achelis, "AGAPĒTÆ," 179; Schilling, 115. See also Lietzmann, 36. Cf. Niederwimmer, *Askese und Mysterium*, 196; and Bultmann, 1:103.

145. Labriolle, 210; J. Massingberd Ford, *A Trilogy on Wisdom and Celibacy,* Cardinal O'Hara Series: Studies and Research in Christian Theology at Notre Dame 4 (London and Notre Dame, Ind.: University of Notre Dame Press, 1967), 135 n. 39. See also Kümmel, "Verlobung," 278 n. 9; and cf. Kugelmann, 66-67. As early as 1905 scholars had raised doubts about the inclusion of the *Hermas* passage in Achelis's survey — see G. Ficker, review of *Virgines Subintroductae*, by Hans Achelis, *TRu* 8 (1905): 117-18.

But quite apart from these considerations is the fact that *Similitudes* 9.10.6–11.8 appears to be fashioned after the erotic scenes one finds in ancient novels. Novelistic elements that occur here include Hermas's overnight stay with the virgins as well as the suggestive exchange that takes place just before this, regarding the propriety of these arrangements.[146] Achelis had taken note of this, but denied any risqué intent on Hermas's part, explaining that the naïveté and innocence of the mid–second century toward sex — whatever that means — ruled out giving this scene so bawdy a reading.[147] Yet in another piece of literature from this period, which also displays novelistic influence, we find many important similarities. This is the story *Joseph and Aseneth*, dated somewhere between the first century B.C.E. and the early second century C.E.[148] Here Joseph and Aseneth, like Hermas and his virgins, address each other as "brother" and "sister" on the basis of their chaste behavior toward one another; they engage in suggestive banter; and Aseneth is accompanied by seven virgins who live with her in a tower (πύργος), just as those in *Hermas* are associated with a tower.[149] This last similarity is particularly intriguing when we consider that Hermas knows of yet another group of women who are stationed by a tower, this time seven in number. These women, moreover, are a variation on the twelve with whom he spends the night: they have "powers" (δυνάμεις); those who serve them will be counted among God's saints; and their names are Faith, Continence, Simplicity, Innocence, Knowledge, Reverence, and Love.[150]

---

146. *Hermas, Similitudes* 9.11.3-6. As part of this scene the virgins kiss and embrace Hermas and begin to play with him, dancing, gavotting, and singing. Cf. Martin Dibelius, *Der Hirt des Hermas,* HNT Ergänzungsband: Die Apostolischen Väter 4 (Tübingen: Mohr, 1923), 618-19; and Peter Lampe, *From Paul to Valentinus: Christians at Rome in the First Two Centuries,* trans. Michael Steinhouser, ed. Marshall D. Johnson (Minneapolis, Minn.: Fortress, 2003), 218-20, 227-31.

147. Achelis, *Virgines Subintroductae,* 15-19. Steck (185) proposed that the scene reflected a testing of Hermas's continence *(Keuschheitsprobe),* since "Christians felt themselves so secure in their blameless purity that they found it a pleasure to be tested through intimate fellowship between persons of the opposite sex" — even though Achelis (66-67) had denied that any such test was involved.

148. See C. Burchard, "Joseph and Aseneth," in *The Old Testament Pseudepigrapha,* 2:186-217; Richard I. Pervo, "Joseph and Asenath and the Greek Novel," *SBL 1976 Seminar Papers: 112th Annual Meeting,* SBLSPS 10 (Missoula, Mont.: Scholars, 1976), 171-81.

149. *Joseph and Aseneth* 2.1 [2.1-2]; 7.1–8.7; 14.5; 19.10–21.1 [19.3; 19.11–20.10] (brackets indicate alternate versification).

150. *Hermas, Visions* 3.8.1-8. While it is true that these seven are not virgins, this is only because they are daughters of one another, symbolizing the fact that faith, continence, etc., give birth to one another. On this aspect of the women cf., e.g., the tradition in Rom. 5:1-5.

Given these parallels between *Hermas* and *Joseph and Aseneth,* it is an open question as to how much of *Similitudes* 9.10.6–11.8 we may reasonably attribute to actual practices in Hermas's church in Rome, and how much to the influence of novelistic topoi. In all, it is clear that we cannot take Achelis's assessment of the patristic materials at face value, for neither he nor those who accept his theory have succeeded in producing a clear instance of spiritual marriage before the third century.

Finally, Achelis's hypothesis must be criticized from the perspective of theological context. We may ask, namely, whether it is meaningful to call an asceticism based on the Montanists' apocalyptic expectations, one inspired by Tatian's encratitic theology, a third inspired by Hermas's rigorism, and still others motivated by Marcion's or Valentinus's dualism all forms of the same practice.[151] Has Achelis, in other words, given sufficient consideration to the vast theological differences that separate his various cases of spiritual marriage? Although he was in part aware of this problem, the answer must be no. According to Achelis, spiritual marriage was the "natural product of two opposing tendencies in ancient Christianity," intimate brotherly love and a "strong aversion, based on religious feelings, to sexual intercourse."[152] But even if Achelis were to establish this as the motivation behind the relationship in 1 Corinthians 7:36-38, which he cannot, the simplistic notion of an asceticism based on "religious feelings" is so vague and all-encompassing that it provides no real explanation for any ascetic practice, let alone spiritual marriage.

This same confusion about motivation, moreover, is also found among the proponents of Achelis's theory. Thus Jean Héring suggests "eschatological enthusiasm" as a motivating force, while Käsemann and John Hurd maintain that spiritual marriages developed out of a desire to live like angels. Schmithals and Roland Seboldt contend that anticipation of apocalyptic times of distress played a part, and Chadwick suggests that Paul may have accidentally created spiritual marriage by advising the Corinthians not to form new marriages, while at the same time insisting that they honor the relationships established by their wedding engagements.[153] As with Achelis, none of

151. So also Adolf Jülicher, "Die geistlichen Ehen in der alten Kirche," *ARW* 7 (1904): 378-80.

152. Achelis, "AGAPĒTÆ," 178; cf. *Virgines Subintroductae,* 61.

153. Jean Héring, *The First Epistle of Saint Paul to the Corinthians* (London: Epworth, 1962), 64 (cf. Weizsäcker, "Anfänge," 33: "Frucht einer krankhaften Schwärmerei"); Käsemann, "Primitive Christian Apocalyptic," 130-31; Hurd, 276-78; Schmithals, *Gnosticism in Corinth,* 235, 387; Seboldt, 187-88; Chadwick, 268 n. 1 (cf. Schmithals, 235 n. 159).

these scholars argues for a motivation that convincingly links this passage to any other putative case of spiritual marriage. And consequently, the motivations responsible for these other cases shed no light on 7:36-38.

Conclusion

With the analysis of Achelis our review of the secondary literature comes to a close. It began with an examination of several authors who argue for Stoic or Cynic influence on 1 Corinthians 7. Their work, as we saw, is both imprecise, in that it poorly represents Stoic and Cynic discussions on marriage, and incomplete, in that it deals with only small sections of Paul's discussion. The remainder of this chapter was then devoted to reviewing the many and diverse theories that interpret 1 Corinthians 7 in light of a theology of sexual asceticism. These theories argue for influences from Hellenistic Judaism or first-century Christianity, or from attitudes toward sexuality similar to what we find in the later church. In all, none of them stands out as particularly convincing, the reason for this being twofold. First, none of the authors we have examined offers any decisive comparative material. Texts from Philo, Wisdom, or Apuleius; Hellenistic catalogues of vices; reports of gnostic groups; and possible second-century examples of *subintroductae* all fall short of providing close parallels to the celibacy attested in 1 Corinthians 7. Second, and rather surprisingly, no author deals extensively with the text of 1 Corinthians 7 itself. Apart from Niederwimmer's psychological approach to 1b, 26-31, and 32-35 — passages he examines in isolation from one another — *all these theories stand or fall on the interpretation of only a few of the chapter's forty verses.*

Approaching this from another direction, I would suggest that the common, fundamental fault of these latter theories is their assumption, stated or otherwise, that 1 Corinthians 7 is best comprehended within a "trajectory" of Judeo-Christian thinking on sexuality that leads directly into the asceticism of the later church. This text is seen either as the starting point of such a trajectory or as part of some vaguely defined continuum that began earlier with ascetic practices in Hellenistic Judaism or primitive Christianity. But as our survey has made abundantly clear, construing the data in this way does justice neither to 1 Corinthians 7 nor to the comparative materials.

In the pages that follow I will pursue the hypothesis that Paul's discussion of marriage and celibacy is best understood against the backdrop of Stoic and Cynic discourse on these topics. I will first examine the entire range of Stoic and Cynic positions on the marriage question, and then demonstrate, point for point, how this material relates to specific statements in 1 Corinthians 7, and how Stoic and Cynic traditions have shaped the thinking of both Paul and the Corinthians. In the end I will have made clear that Paul's discussion cannot be fitted into any presumed trajectory of ascetic thought. Rather, his words draw on a reservoir of ideas about marriage and celibacy that is neither ascetic, nor Judeo-Christian in origin, nor confluent with much of the later church's thinking, but one fed by many of the enduring concerns of Greek culture in the Hellenistic age.

Addendum

The purpose of this addendum is to address the work of several authors not treated in the first edition. In what follows I will briefly summarize and reflect on each work from the perspective of this study.

1. In their book *Families in the New Testament World,* Carolyn Osiek and David Balch propose that a theology of celibacy at Corinth can be understood, in part, by reference to first-century medical theory. Citing from Cornelius Celsus and Soranus of Ephesus, they show that sexual abstinence and virginity were recommended by some ancient physicians to maintain good health.[154] Citing from Galen of Pergamum (fl. mid–second century C.E.), they also note that the release of "sperm" by both men and women during intercourse was believed to deplete a person's "vital spirit" and hence physical strength. Since the Corinthians may have styled themselves spiritual people (see 1 Cor. 2:14–3:1), Osiek and Balch reason that they may have promoted sexual asceticism out of a desire for the spiritual gifts Paul discusses in 1 Corinthians 12 and 14.

Yet nothing in 1 Corinthians indicates that Paul or the Corinthians would have understood the spirit (or Spirit) primarily as the source of one's physical strength, and therefore connected with one's "sperm."[155] Furthermore, there is little to suggest that Greco-Roman moralists or theologians in the first century used these medical opinions to justify a life of sexual asceticism. Indeed, a fairly wide consensus existed among them that sexual renunciation was an

---

154. Osiek and Balch, 104-6.

155. Osiek and Balch, 106-7. Nor is this a satisfactory explanation for the celibacy of Philo's Therapeutae, as Osiek and Balch suggest (107-8).

extreme that should be avoided.[156] Even in the medical community, to the extent that these opinions played a practical rather than a purely theoretical role, they were used to justify the training regimes of athletes and to argue for moderation in sexual activity, not to promote complete sexual renunciation.[157]

2. In an article entitled "Paul without Passion," Dale Martin proposes that Paul's understanding of sexuality has been determined by his aversion to "desire" (ἐπιθυμία).[158] Martin argues from 1 Corinthians 7:9 that Paul viewed marriage as a cure for sexual desire because repressed sexuality was the cause of desire, and marriage provided a sanctioned outlet for sexuality. Yet because of his emphasis on avoiding desire, what Paul envisioned, according to Martin, were marital relations devoid of passion, romance, and love — that is, all that was related to "desire."[159]

If this striking conclusion were true, it would give us invaluable insight into Paul's conceptualization of marriage, sexual asceticism, and celibacy. The problem is that it confuses an ancient understanding of "desire" with a modern one. Among Greek philosophers and Greco-Roman moralists, ἐπιθυμία almost always denoted *excessive* longing or compulsiveness, and in a sexual context it meant "lust." It did not refer to "natural" or "proper" sexual desires, which were seen as God-given impulses toward correct moral conduct.[160] Thus when Martin states that both Stoics and Paul saw the goal of the virtuous person as "to have sex without desire," he is wrong to assert that this excludes love, passion, or romance from marital relations.[161] What it excludes is lust and sexual excess. Stoics (and others) did not object to a man "loving his wife too much," as Martin claims,[162] but to loving her as a paramour or a prostitute, without regard for her dignity and status as a wife.[163] As we shall

156. E.g., Philo, *De Decalogo* 107-10; Seneca, *Epistle* 5.2-6; *De ira* 2.12.3-5; Plutarch, *Moralia* 125B-126D; 654C; on the Cynic tradition, see the next chapter.

157. See the more balanced discussion in Brown, *The Body and Society*, 17-23; cf. Dale B. Martin, "Paul without Passion: On Paul's Rejection of Desire in Sex and Marriage," in *Constructing Early Christian Families: Family as Social Reality and Metaphor*, ed. Halvor Moxnes (London and New York: Routledge, 1997), 204-5.

158. Martin, "Paul without Passion," 201-15; see also Martin, *The Corinthian Body* (New Haven and London: Yale University Press, 1995), 198-228.

159. Martin, "Paul without Passion," 201-2, 205-6, 213.

160. See below, p. 69 n. 70 and p. 128 nn. 85-86.

161. Martin, "Paul without Passion," 206.

162. Martin, "Paul without Passion," 206.

163. E.g., Seneca, *De constantia sapientis* 7.4; cf. Plutarch, *Moralia* 145A. Martin's confusion

see in the next chapter, Stoics promoted the idea of marriage as a "partnership" in which spouses shared their bodies with one another — an idea, as I shall argue in chapter 3, that is also reflected in 1 Corinthians 7:3-4.[164]

3. Finally, Brian Rosner, in his *Paul, Scripture, and Ethics,* and Calvin Roetzel, in his *Paul: The Man and the Myth,* argue that much of what Paul says about celibacy can be clarified through an examination of biblical, Qumranic, and rabbinic practices of sexual asceticism.[165] The difficulty here is that sexual asceticism is seldom encountered in these materials outside of ritual renunciation or priestly activities, and as I noted above, ritual and priestly motivations have no apparent bearing on the celibacy described in 1 Corinthians 7.[166] Beyond this: Rosner and Roetzel confuse asceticism with sexual asceticism, and sexual asceticism with celibacy;[167] Rosner's characterization of rabbinic sources as "contemporary Jewish interpretation of Torah" vis-à-vis Paul is far too generous;[168] and Roetzel mistakenly attributes sexual asceticism to the Old Testament Nazarite tradition, and assumes a sexual interpretation of 1 Corinthians 7:32-34 that is unsupported by the text.[169]

---

stems from his reliance on Martha C. Nussbaum, *The Therapy of Desire: Theory and Practice in Hellenistic Ethics* (Princeton: Princeton University Press, 1994), whose description of the "passions" as "emotions" is misleading (see, e.g., pp. 190, 319n.4, and 358). More recently she has attempted to clarify her position in "*Erōs* and Ethical Norms: Philosophers Respond to a Cultural Dilemma," in Martha C. Nussbaum and Juha Sihvola, eds., *The Sleep of Reason: Erotic Experience and Sexual Ethics in Ancient Greece and Rome* (Chicago: University of Chicago Press, 2002), 76-86.

164. See below, pp. 117-20. In Stoic ethics, sexual pleasure was classified as a "preferred indifferent" (see Seneca, *Epistle* 74.17; Diogenes Laertius 7.102; Philo, *Quaestiones et solutiones in Genesin* 4.147; cf. Seneca, *Epistle* 116.1-3; and Diogenes Laertius 7.149).

165. Brian S. Rosner, *Paul, Scripture, and Ethics: A Study of 1 Corinthians 5–7,* AGJU 22 (Leiden: Brill, 1994; reprint, Grand Rapids: Baker, 1999), 147-61; Calvin Roetzel, *Paul: The Man and the Myth* (Minneapolis: Fortress, 1999), 135-45.

166. See above, pp. 7-8.

167. Rosner, 153-58; Roetzel, 138-40.

168. Rosner, 176.

169. Roetzel, 138, 146.

2 The Stoic–Cynic Marriage Debate

IN THE HELLENISTIC WORLD there existed several conceptions of marriage and celibacy quite different from the ones advanced by the fathers of the church. In this chapter we will explore those commonly held by Stoics and Cynics, our goal being to establish an appropriate context for interpreting 1 Corinthians 7.

One reason scholars have not satisfactorily pursued a comparison between Stoic and Cynic discussions on marriage and Paul is the fragmentary state in which the former have come down to us. Indeed, these discussions seem to have been mostly an oral affair. It is telling, for example, that two of our most important witnesses, the lectures of Musonius Rufus and Epictetus, survive only as the class notes of devoted students.[1] What Stoics, Cynics, and their followers did manage to write down, moreover, received rough treatment at the hands of the church fathers. Willing conduits for the works of Aristotle, Plato, Philo, and Josephus, the Fathers balked when it came to Stoic and Cynic writings on marriage. Preferring their own, Christian treatments of the subject, they tended to adopt Stoic and Cynic ideas as their own or ignore them completely. They saw no reason to pass the works of these pagan moralists on to future generations. In consequence, it fell to a relatively obscure anthologist, Johannes Stobaeus, to preserve some of our most valuable sources. Stobaeus, however, offers only excerpts or "fragments," not complete texts, and hence much has been lost.

---

1. See Cora E. Lutz, "Musonius Rufus 'The Roman Socrates,'" in *Yale Classical Studies* 10, ed. Alfred R. Bellinger (New Haven: Yale University Press, 1947), 5-8; and Arrian's dedication to Lucius Gellius, which prefaces his publication of Epictetus's *Discourses*.

The course of Stoic and Cynic thinking on marriage must therefore be reconstructed. We will begin this task with an overview of their respective positions — as I have pieced these together from the extant materials — for the purpose of identifying the central issues and tensions in their considerations of marriage. The bulk of this chapter will then be given over to an examination of the extant materials themselves. Here I will chart the development of Stoic and Cynic arguments for and against marriage, starting with antecedents in early Greek philosophy and ending several centuries later in the patristic period. This chronological survey will not only demonstrate the longstanding popularity and extensive influence that Stoic and Cynic ideas on marriage had in the ancient world, but it will also provide a considerable amount of comparative material with which to interpret Paul. This interpretive venture will take place in chapters 3 and 4.

Issues and Dynamics in the Stoic-Cynic Marriage Debate

Stoic and Cynic discussions on marriage are available to us from the second century B.C.E. to the second century C.E.[2] While none individually can be

2. The classic survey of the Stoic discussions, often referred to as the περὶ γάμου topos, is Karl Praechter, *Hierokles der Stoiker* (Leipzig: Dieterich, 1901), 121-50, as well as 4-6, 66-90. See also Ernestus Bickel, *Diatribe in Senecae philosophi fragmenta*, vol. 1, *Fragmenta de matrimonio* (Leipzig: B. G. Teubner, 1915); O. Larry Yarbrough, *Not Like the Gentiles: Marriage Rules in the Letters of Paul*, SBLDS 80 (Atlanta: Scholars, 1985), 33-46; Lise Henrion, "La conception de la Nature et du rôle de la Femme chez les philosophes cyniques et stoïciens" (Ph.D. diss., Université de Liège, 1942/43), 36-62, 125-81; Claude Vatin, *Recherches sur le mariage et la condition de la femme mariée à l'époque hellénistique*, Bibliothèque des Écoles Françaises d'Athènes et de Rome 216 (Paris: E. de Boccard, 1970), 17-40; O. Hense, "Zu Antipatros von Tarsos," *Rh. Mus.*, n.s., 73 (1920-24): 300-302; Susan Treggiari, *Roman Marriage: "Iust Congiuges" from the Time of Cicero to the Time of Ulpian* (Oxford: Clarendon Press, 1991), 183-319; and Albrecht Oepke, "Ehe I," in *RAC* 4 (1959), 651-55. For general discussions of precursors to the περὶ γάμου material in the classical and archaic periods, see Marylin B. Arthur, "Early Greece: The Origins of the Western Attitude toward Women," in *Women in the Ancient World: The "Arethusa" Papers*, ed. John Peradotto and J. P. Sullivan, SUNY Series in Classical Studies (Albany: SUNY Press, 1984), 7-58; Sarah B. Pomeroy, *Goddesses, Whores, Wives, and Slaves: Women in Classical Antiquity* (New York: Schocken Books, 1975), 18-23, 33-38, 48-49; Yarbrough, 32-33; Walter Erdmann, *Die Ehe im alten Griechenland*, Münchener Beiträge zur Papyrusforschung und antiken Rechtsgeschichte 20 (Munich: C. H. Beck, 1934), 139-47, 155-61; and W. K. Lacey, *The Family in Classical Greece*, Aspects of Greek and Roman Life (London: Thames and Hudson, 1968), 9, 176. See also Stobaeus 4.532-49 Wachsmuth and Hense.

Scholars are correct in pointing to a relationship between the περὶ γάμου and the περὶ ἔρωτος thought of as a "debate" in the strict sense of the word, two considerations allow us to treat them collectively as the products of a larger, unified debate rather than simply as the writings of two schools of thought quite isolated from one another. First, the arguments used by Stoics and Cynics, respectively, correspond sufficiently to warrant the conclusion that these two camps stood consciously in dialogue with one another on the subject of marriage. And second, arguments identified specifically as "Cynic" were adopted by certain Stoics. This resulted in an *inner*-Stoic debate on marriage based on the opposition between "Stoic" and "Cynic" positions, a phenomenon we can document as early as Cicero, and which comes into full bloom in the *Discourses* of Epictetus.[3]

The starting point for this "Stoic-Cynic marriage debate," as we shall refer to it, was the recognition of a basic datum of free Greek society: marriage involved a man in weighty responsibilities. Marriage joined a man socially and financially to another human being, his wife. To a greater or lesser extent her cares and concerns now became his as well. But marriage also meant accepting the responsibilities of a father, a householder, and a citizen.[4] This is because marriage in the ancient world almost always resulted in the birth of children. In marrying, a man thus obligated himself to providing for a family. He would need to raise and educate children; he would need to establish a household (οἶκος, οἰκία), a financial endeavor that was the ancient world's ideal of a small business; and he would need to become active in the social, political, and economic life of his hometown, since a household could not survive without the political protection and economic environment provided

---

literature: see Praechter, 148-50; Friedrich Wilhelm, "Zu Achilles Tatius," *Rh. Mus.*, n.s., 57 (1902): 55-75; Daniel Babut, *Plutarque et le Stoïcisme* (Paris: Presses Universitaires de France, 1969), 108-15. But this is taken to an extreme in Lisette Goessler, "Plutarchs Gedanken über die Ehe" (Ph.D. diss., University of Basel, 1962), e.g., 31-32. Michel Foucault, *The Care of the Self*, History of Sexuality 3 (New York: Pantheon Books, 1986), 191-277, is right to discuss Plutarch, *Amatorius;* Achilles Tatius, *Leucippe and Clitophon* 2.35-38; and [Lucian], *Amores*, as a category of literature in its own right. See also Hubert Martin, Jr., "Amatorius (Moralia 748E-771E)," in *Plutarch's Ethical Writings and Early Christian Literature*, ed. Hans Dieter Betz, SCHNT 4 (Leiden: Brill, 1978), 443-49.

Vettius Valens's περὶ γάμου κ.τ.λ. and ἄλλως περὶ γάμου μετὰ ὑποδείγματος (second century c.e.), in which the author speaks of his subject as ὁ περὶ γάμου τόπος (bk. 2, chap. 37; 114.22, 24 Kroll), has nothing to do with the literature under consideration here; the same applies to the fifth chapter of Maximus Astrologus's περὶ καταρχῶν (second century c.e. or later), also entitled περὶ γάμου.

3. See the remarks in Praechter, 69, and the discussion below.

4. Cf. Michel Foucault, *The Use of Pleasure*, History of Sexuality 2 (New York: Pantheon Books, 1985), 150-51.

by the Greek city-state (πόλις). The effect was cumulative: through marriage a man left the freedom of his bachelor days behind and began the settled life of a responsible citizen with all its cares and concerns.

There were, to be sure, various means by which a married man in antiquity could avoid children and thereby alleviate some of the responsibilities of married life. These included abortion and exposure, and several forms of contraception.[5] But aside from the fact that abortion and exposure were dangerous or otherwise unattractive, and contraceptives unreliable, Stoics and Cynics alike ruled out the option of family planning because it was "contrary to nature."[6] Thus Antipater of Tarsus, Ocellus Lucanus, Musonius Rufus, and Hierocles the Stoic implicitly condemn all these methods with their insistence that the goal of sexual intercourse was the producing of children; and Musonius condemns abortion and exposure outright. Hierocles, moreover, speaks of a wife being "worn out by pregnancies"; Dio Chrysostom maintains in a treatise on household management that "the begetting of children is a work of necessity"; and in the *Cynic Epistles* the birth of a child is referred to as "what had to come."[7] The inevitability of having and raising children is emphasized among these authors, finally, by the set phrase "marrying and

5. In general, see Emiel Eyben, "Family Planning in Graeco-Roman Antiquity," *Ancient Society* 11/12 (1980-81): 5-82; David Michael Feldman, *Birth Control in Jewish Law* (New York: New York University Press; London: University of London, 1968). On contraception see also John T. Noonan, Jr., *Contraception: A History of Its Treatment by the Catholic Theologians and Canonists*, rev. ed. (Cambridge: Harvard University Press, 1965); M. K. Hopkins, "Contraception in the Roman Empire," *Comparative Studies in Society and History* 8 (1965): 124-51; Norman Edwin Himes, *Medical History of Contraception* (London: Geo. Allen and Unwin; Baltimore: Williams and Wilkins, 1936; reprint, New York: Gamut, 1963). On abortion see also R. Crahay, "Les moralistes anciens et l'avortement," *L'Antiquité Classique* 10 (1941): 9-23; P. A. Brunt, *Italian Manpower: 225 B.C.–A.D. 14* (Oxford: Clarendon, 1971), 147-48; and J. H. Waszink, "Abtreibung," in *RAC* 1 (1950), 55-60. On exposure see also John Boswell, *The Kindness of Strangers: The Abandonment of Children in Western Europe from Late Antiquity to the Renaissance* (New York: Pantheon Books, 1988), 53-179; Averil Cameron, "The Exposure of Children and Greek Ethics," *Classical Review* 46 (1932): 105-14; and W. W. Tarn and G. T. Griffith, *Hellenistic Civilization*, 3rd ed. (London: Edward Arnold, 1959), 100-104 (inscriptional evidence).

6. See, e.g., Paul Veyne, "La famille et l'amour sous le Haut-Empire romain," *Annales: Économies, Sociétés, Civilisations* 33 (1978): 48-49.

7. Hierocles 63.26 von Arnim (in Stobaeus 5.699.9-10 W.-H.), τετρυμένη κυοφορίαις — cf. Aline Rousselle, *Porneia: On Desire and the Body in Antiquity* (New York: Basil Blackwell, 1988), 34-35, 39; Dio Chrysostom, frag. 9 Cohoon and Crosby (vol. 5), τὸ μὲν γὰρ τίκτειν ἀνάγκης ἐστὶν ἔργον; *Cynic Epistle of Crates* 33 (82.20 Malherbe), ὅπερ ἐχρῆν ἥκειν; on Musonius, see below, pp. 75-76, 79.

having children," which recurs throughout their discussions,[8] often as a synonym for "marrying."[9]

Marriage and all that it implied thus spelled responsibility in the eyes of both Stoics and Cynics, and it is around this realization that their discussions on marriage turn. The basic question they asked was: Should the intelligent, informed, morally upright person take on such responsibility? They often framed this question in terms of what the wise man would do, since the *sophos,* acting on the basis of a perfectly moral disposition, was seen as the model for human behavior. The Stoics based their answer on the belief that the universe was governed by a divine principle, and that it was not only in a man's best interests, practically speaking, to conduct his life in harmony with this principle, but he was morally obligated to do so. From this they argued in favor of marriage by pointing out that various gods patronized marriage, or that the Creator, or nature, seen as a divine entity, had decreed that men and women should come together in marriage for the purpose of populating and repopulating the earth. The real backbone of the Stoic discussions, however, was provided by two more complex lines of argumentation. Although often used in conjunction with one another, they were nonetheless distinct and, at times, even in conflict with each other.

The first focused on the presumed structure of the universe, or *kosmos,* and the place of marriage within it, this structure reflecting the divine will, variously, of nature, reason, the Creator, God, or "the gods." The *kosmos,* the Stoics contended, consisted of a plurality of city-states, for men were designed by nature to be political beings and their existence — that is, their meaningful, civilized, natural existence — required that they organize themselves into city-states. These city-states, in turn, consisted of citizens organized into a plurality of households; and households, finally, had their beginnings in the union of men and women in marriage. From this understanding of the structure of the *kosmos,* the Stoics argued that marriage was indispensable. Not only did it hold a key position in the divine plan, but more than any other element it insured the future of the whole. It was only through marriage that succeeding generations of householders could arise, guaranteeing a con-

---

8. Praechter, 67, notes that these terms are "readily joined"; see, e.g., Hierocles 55.22 v. A. (Stobaeus 4.603.9 W.-H.); Epictetus, *Discourses* 3.22.67, 68; Diogenes Laertius 6.16; 7.121; cf. 10.119.

9. E.g., Musonius, frag. 14.96.3-6 Lutz (76.11-14 Hense). Theon, *Progymnasmata* 120.30 Spengel, even uses "having children" as an abbreviation for marrying and having children.

tinuous supply of responsible citizens, and thus insuring the future of the
city-states and of the *kosmos*.[10]

In origin this line of argumentation draws on Aristotelian thought, a fact
made clear by the first book of Aristotle's *Politics*. Here Aristotle also assumes
a progression from marriages to households to city-states, insisting that this
is the work of nature.[11] In advancing this schema he even parts company with
his teacher Plato, who had characterized the household as a kind of miniature
city-state. The household, Aristotle stresses, is an entity in its own right; it is
the step in the natural progression that allows one to see the dependence of
the city-state on the institution of marriage.[12] In adopting Aristotle's vision
of human existence, the Stoics made an important change. Whereas Aristotle
had understood nature as that which prompted a thing to realize its full, inherent potential, the Stoics identified nature as a divine principle. As A. A.
Long explains:

> Aristotle does not conceive nature as a rational agent; nature for him is that
> factor within each individual organism which accounts for its efforts to per-
> fect itself. Though Aristotle sometimes speaks of nature as "divine" he can-
> not in his mature system identify God and nature, since God is not "in the
> world." . . . The Stoics, by setting Nature/God within the world, have united
> under a single principle functions which Aristotle kept apart. Stoic Nature

10. See Hense, "Zu Antipatros," 299, and the discussion below.

11. Aristotle, *Politics* 1.1252a 17-1253a 39; cf. *Nicomachean Ethics* 8.1162a 16-19; and Arius
Didymus in Stobaeus 2.147.26–150.13 W.-H., translated in David Balch, "Household Codes," in
Greco-Roman Literature and the New Testament: Selected Forms and Genres, ed. David E.
Aune, SBLSBS 21 (Atlanta: Scholars, 1988), 41-44. See also R. G. Mulgan, *Aristotle's Political
Theory: An Introduction for Students of Political Theory* (Oxford: Clarendon, 1977), 18-25, 30-
38, 140-41; Manfred Riedel, *Metaphysik und Metapolitik: Studien zu Aristoteles und zur
politischen Sprache der neuzeitlichen Philosophie* (Frankfurt: Suhrkamp, 1975), 73-80; and Elisabeth Schüssler Fiorenza, *Bread Not Stone: The Challenge of Feminist Biblical Interpretation*
(Boston: Beacon Press, 1984), 73: "Aristotle, in contrast to the Sophists, stressed that the patri-
archal relationships in household and city . . . are based not on social convention but on 'nature.' He therefore insisted that the discussion of political ethics and household management
begin with marriage."

12. Aristotle, *Politics* 1.1252a 7-16; 2.1260b 36-1261a 29. See Günther Bien, *Die Grundlegung
der politischen Philosophie bei Aristoteles*, 3rd ed. (Freiburg and Munich: Karl Alber, 1985), 303-13;
Erwin R. Goodenough, *The Politics of Philo Judaeus: Practice and Theory* (New Haven: Yale University Press, 1938), 49 n. 28; and Mulgan, 21: "[Aristotle] gives especial emphasis to the naturalness of the household as if this were the most solid part of the argument."

resembles the Aristotelian Prime Mover in being a rational agent which is the ultimate cause of all things.[13]

The upshot of this Stoic innovation was that it put a moral edge on Aristotle's schema. The Stoics could now set the city-state in a divine *kosmos* and argue that marriages, households, and city-states not only came about naturally, but in fact *ought* to come about.[14] As for marriage in particular, they maintained that any man who respected the divine will would count it as his moral duty to marry and have children.

The second major line of argumentation used by the Stoics was more indigenous to their own school of philosophy, deriving from their work in systematic ethics. For this reason it was also more cosmopolitan, for instead of envisioning the *kosmos* primarily as a collection of individual city-states, it stressed that the *kosmos* itself was a grand city-state or "cosmopolis."[15] This difference in emphasis meant that the actions of an individual were assigned ethical value first in terms of their impact directly on the whole rather than through the intermediary of the city-state. The starting point for this second line of argumentation was the Stoics' assumption that virtue (ἀρετή) was the sole requisite for happiness and well-being (εὐδαιμονία), and that a person progressed toward virtue through the continual practice of actions that were "in accordance with nature," which they termed "fitting" (καθῆκον) actions. These, they reasoned, brought one's disposition into harmony with virtue and also provided natural advantages in the quest for virtue. Actions that

13. A. A. Long, *Hellenistic Philosophy: Stoics, Epicureans, Sceptics*, 2nd ed. (Berkeley: University of California Press, 1986), 151-52. See also F. H. Sandbach, *Aristotle and the Stoics*, Cambridge Philological Society, suppl. 10 (Cambridge: Cambridge Philological Society, 1985), 38-40; and Maximilian Forschner, *Die stoische Ethik: Über den Zusammenhang von Natur-, Sprach- und Moralphilosophie im altstoischen System* (Stuttgart: Klett-Cotta, 1981), 17-24.

14. Regarding the absence of this moral edge in Aristotle himself, see D. W. Hamlyn, *A History of Western Philosophy* (Harmondsworth: Penguin Books, 1987), 74: "On certain conceptions of morality there is little about morality in what Aristotle has to say. He is simply clear that there is such a thing as the good life in some sense of those words and that a man is thought εὐδαίμων, happy, to the extent that he attains it."

15. On the Stoic idea *oikeiosis*, which denoted the natural affinity between human beings in this world community, see S. G. Pembroke, "Oikeiōsis," in *Problems in Stoicism*, ed. A. A. Long (London: University of London Press, Athlone Press, 1971), 114-49; Margherita Isnardi Parente, "Ierocle Stoico: Oikeiosis e doveri sociali," in *ANRW* 2.36.3 (1989), 2201-26; and Troels Engberg-Pedersen, *The Stoic Theory of Oikeiosis: Moral Development and Social Interaction in Early Stoic Philosophy*, Studies in Hellenistic Civilization 2 (Aarhus: Aarhus University Press, 1991).

were contrary to nature, on the other hand, were either directly in opposition to virtue or resulted in natural disadvantages, and so were to be avoided. Beyond this basic dichotomy the Stoics also reasoned that many actions classified as fitting could be *dis*advantageous if performed under adverse circumstances. These, which in themselves were morally neither good nor bad, they further classified as "intermediate" (μέσον) actions.[16] It is into this subcategory, ultimately, that marrying falls, with the consequence that Stoics could argue that marriage, being in accordance with nature, was incumbent upon a man unless special circumstances stood in his way.

These, then, were the two basic lines of argumentation employed by the Stoics in their discussions of marriage. What they make clear is that Stoics evaluated marriage as an important component in a larger system of morality. The act of marrying was a sign of allegiance to a higher metaphysical order; it was the equivalent of acquiescing to the divine will. We may gain some insight into why they took such a stalwart position if we now inquire into the historical impetus that gave rise to their discussions, for in fact the Stoic marriage discussions reflect one of the great issues that faced intellectuals in the Hellenistic period, namely, whether the Greek city-state could continue as the social, economic, and political center of a person's life.

From the time of Alexander the Great's conquests near the end of the fourth century, the Greek city-state lost ground as an important political unit. It was obliged to accept an ever diminishing role in the minds of its citizens due to the attention now focused on the successive empires of Alexander, his generals, and finally Rome. The gradual disappearance of local autonomous rule from the political map of Greece, and the tendency toward cosmopolitan thinking, whereby a man considered himself a citizen of the world rather than of any one city-state, were both the cause and the end of this development. As a consequence, many intellectuals of the time feared that citizens would find participation in local politics and the responsibility associated with establishing a household and raising future generations of citizens increasingly unattractive, abandoning their loyalty to the city-states altogether.[17] Several even maintained that the new cosmopolitan spirit proved

16. On these aspects of Stoic ethics see Long, 179, 187, 189-205, 213-16; and I. G. Kidd, "Stoic Intermediates and the End for Man," in *Problems in Stoicism*, 150-72.

17. See Pomeroy, 120; Otto Kiefer, *Sexual Life in Ancient Rome* (London: George Routledge and Sons, 1938), 35; Paul Veyne, "The Roman Empire," in *A History of Private Life*, vol. 1, *From Pagan Rome to Byzantium*, ed. Paul Veyne (Cambridge: Harvard University Press, Belknap Press, 1987), 38; Gustave Glotz, *The Greek City and Its Institutions* (New York: Knopf, 1951; reprint, Ann

the underlying cause of the depopulation of the Greek city-states.[18] As proof they pointed to the fact that authorities in some areas had found it necessary to pass measures requiring citizens to marry and have children under penalty of law.[19]

It is in this traditionalist reaction to the changing social and political cli-

---

Arbor: University Microfilms, 1965), 295-96 (cited by Richard J. Devine, "Holy Virginity: A Study of the New Testament Teaching on Virginity and Celibacy" [Ph.D. diss., University of Fribourg, 1964], 70); Yarbrough, 36-37, 41-46, 60; Max Pohlenz, *Freedom in Greek Life and Thought: The History of an Ideal* (Dordrecht: D. Reidel; New York: Humanities, 1966), 116-19; Eduard Zeller, *Die Philosophie der Griechen in ihrer geschichtlichen Entwicklung*, 5th ed. (Leipzig: Fues [O. R. Reisland], 1922/23), 3.1.1-22, 283-92; Long, 3-4; Émile Bréhier, *Chrysippe* (Paris: Félix Alcan, 1910), 262-70; Tomas Hägg, *The Novel in Antiquity* (Berkeley: University of California Press, 1983), 88-90, who traces this development through epic, tragedy, and the novel; Pál Csillag, *The Augustan Laws on Family Relations* (Budapest: Akadémiai Kiadó, 1976), 39-40; and Wayne A. Meeks, *The Moral World of the First Christians*, Library of Early Christianity (Philadelphia: Westminster, 1986), 26-31.

18. Even though there is little evidence that such depopulation was ever widespread. The most famous example is perhaps Polybius 36.17. On this passage see Praechter, 84-86. See also L. P. Wilkinson, *Classical Attitudes to Modern Issues: Population and Family Planning, Women's Liberation, Nudism in Deed and Word, Homosexuality* (London: William Kimber, 1978), 22; Martin P. Nilsson, *Geschichte der griechischen Religion*, 2nd ed., Handbuch der Altertumswissenschaft 5/2 (Munich: C. H. Beck, 1961), 2:310-11; Pierre Salmon, *Population et dépopulation dans l'Empire romain*, Collection Latomus 137 (Brussels: Latomus, 1974); Vatin, 228-40; Tarn and Griffith, 100-104; Brunt, esp. 131-55; and Cameron, 113.

19. On the marriage laws enacted by Augustus Caesar, the *Lex Iulia de adulteriis* and the *Lex Iulia de maritandis ordinibus* (18 B.C.E.), and the *Lex Papia Poppaea* (9 C.E.), see Csillag, 24-25; Brunt, 558-66; James A. Field, Jr., "The Purpose of the *Lex Iulia et Papia Poppaea*," *Classical Journal* 40 (1944/45): 398-416; Michel Humbert, *Le remariage à Rome: Étude d'histoire juridique et sociale*, Università di Roma: Pubblicazioni dell' Istituto di diritto Romano e dei diritti dell' oriente mediterraneo 44 (Milan: A. Giuffrè, 1972), 138-80; Leo Ferrero Raditsa, "Augustus' Legislation concerning Marriage, Procreation, Love Affairs and Adultery," in *ANRW* 2.13 (1980), 278-339; Richard I. Frank, "Augustus' Legislation on Marriage and Children," *California Studies in Classical Antiquity* 8 (1975): 41-52; Max Kaser, *Das römische Privatrecht*, vol. 1, *Das altrömische, das vorklassische und klassische Recht*, 2nd ed., Handbuch der Altertumswissenschaft, Rechtsgeschichte des Altertums 10.3.3.1 (Munich: C. H. Beck, 1971), 318-21, cf. 328-29; Diana E. E. Kleiner, "The Great Friezes of the Ara Pacis Augustae: Greek Sources, Roman Derivatives, and Augustan Social Policy," *Mélanges de l'École Française de Rome: Antiquité* 90 (1978): 772-76, 778-81; and J. P. V. D. Balsdon, *Life and Leisure in Ancient Rome* (New York: McGraw-Hill, 1969), 82-90. On the precursors of Augustus's marriage laws, see Field, 404-5; Cicero, *Laws* 3.3.7 (cf. *Pro Marcello* 23, and *Pro Caelio* 18.42); Dionysius of Halicarnassus, *Roman Antiquities* 2.15 and 9.22.2; Plutarch, *Vitae* 129D-E *(Camillus)*; 451B-C *(Lysander)*; Gellius, *Attic Nights* 1.6.1-2; Suetonius, *Augustus* 89; and Dio Cassius, *Roman History* 56.6.4.

mate of the Hellenistic world that the Stoic marriage discussions have their place.[20] Given the various social responsibilities that marriage implied in the ancient world, the Stoics' support of marriage was the equivalent of promoting active involvement in the life of the city-state. This is evident particularly in their insistence that marriage was linked via the household to the city-state, and that the *kosmos,* that entity for which all actions are ultimately performed, was no less than the sum total of all city-states.[21] What was really at stake in their "marriage discussions," in other words, was not marriage per se, but the promotion of a traditional view of human society.[22] In posing the

20. Similarly, Adolf Bonhöffer, *Die Ethik des Stoikers Epictet* (Stuttgart: Ferdinand Enke, 1894; reprint, Stuttgart–Bad Connstatt: Friedrich Frommann, 1968), 87, describes the high value the Stoics placed on marriage as part of their "conservative perspective" on the communal nature of human beings. See also Brent D. Shaw, "The Divine Economy: Stoicism as Ideology," *Latomus* 44 (1985): 16-54; Long, 3; and the older treatment in André Baudrillart, *Moeurs païennes, moeurs crétiennes,* vol. 1, *La famille dans l'antiquité païenne et aux premiers siècles du christianisme* (Paris: Bloud et Gay, 1929), 63-70.

21. Cf. Meeks, *Moral World,* 61: "It seems to us in retrospect that the fundamental issue of the [Hellenistic] times must have been how the humane values achieved in the classical polis and the Roman Republic could be made effective in the vastly enlarged and transformed political and social world of the empire"; and Lacey, 9. On the importance of the city-state in Stoic ethical theory, see Max Pohlenz, *Die Stoa: Geschichte einer geistigen Bewegung,* 2nd ed. (Göttingen: Vandenhoeck & Ruprecht, 1959), 1:139-40, 165-66; Zeller, 3.1.300-302; Arnold Ehrhardt, *Politische Metaphysik von Solon bis Augustin,* vol. 1, *Die Gottesstadt der Griechen und Römer* (Tübingen: Mohr, 1959), 180-85; and Eleuterio Elorduy, *Die Sozialphilosophie der Stoa,* Philologus, suppl. 28/3 (Leipzig: Dieterich, 1936), 135-39. Cf. Arthur W. H. Adkins, *Merit and Responsibility: A Study in Greek Values* (Oxford: Oxford University Press, 1960), 197, 226-32, 348-51.

22. These discussions are thus correctly understood as "propaganda" for a larger apologetic — see Emiel Eyben, "De latere Stoa over het huwelijk," *Hermeneus: Tijdschrift voor antieke Cultuur* 50 (1978): 21; cf. Johannes Stelzenberger, *Die Beziehungen der frühchristlichen Sittenlehre zur Ethik der Stoa* (Munich: Max Hueber, 1933), 440-41 and n. 7; and Holger Thesleff, *An Introduction to the Pythagorean Writings of the Hellenistic Period,* Acta Academiae Aboensis, Humaniora 24/3 (Åbo, Finland: Åbo Akademi, 1961), 72. The larger apologetic is aptly brought out by Hans Jonas's description of Stoic popular philosophy in the time of the empire: "'To play one's part' — that figure of speech on which Stoic ethics dwells so much — unwittingly reveals the fictitious element in the construction. . . . In the phrase of playing one's part there is a bravado that hides a deeper, if proud, resignation. . . . To be sure, the strained fervor by which man's integration in the whole was maintained, through his alleged affinity to it, was the means of reserving the dignity of man and thereby of saving a sanction for a positive morality. This fervor, succeeding that which had formerly been inspired by the ideal of civic virtue, represented a heroic attempt on the part of intellectuals to carry over the life-sustaining force of that ideal into fundamentally changed conditions. But the new atomized masses of the Empire, who had never shared in that noble tradition of *areté,* might react very differently to a situation in which they

question of whether a man should take on the responsibilities of marriage, the Stoics were actually asking a much more profound question: Should a man affirm the traditional Greek understanding of human society and consequently become involved in the life of his city-state, beginning with marriage, procreation, and the establishment of a household?[23]

Turning now to the Cynic side of the marriage debate, we observe that while the Stoics met this question with an affirmative response, the Cynics answered with an abusive no. Theirs, too, was a position fostered by the social and political developments of the Hellenistic age, but in contrast to the traditionalism of the Stoics, the Cynics denied the importance of the Greek city-states, promoting instead a radical cosmopolitanism. They held that the social structures of marriage, household, and city-state had their origin in mere human convention, not divine purpose, and in their place they demanded individualism and self-sufficiency.[24]

At the center of their philosophy was the idea of freedom, both freedom for something and freedom from something. It was freedom *for* the pursuit of philosophy, since they believed it was only through living a life guided by philosophy that an individual could achieve the goal of happiness and well-being. Indeed, many Cynics considered philosophy a full-time profession and insisted on devoting all their "free time" (σχολή) to it — that is, all the time not taken up with providing for the necessities of life. This meant that the Cynic idea of freedom necessarily also included freedom *from* the responsibilities of conventional existence: "from all care about food, clothing, house, home, marriage, children, etc.; freedom from all ties which morality, law, state, and community life in general may put upon the individual."[25] For this reason they resolutely excluded marriage from their sphere of moral concern. Marriage and all that it implied — the duties of husband, father, householder,

---

found themselves passively involved: a situation in which the part was insignificant to the whole, and the whole alien to the parts" (*The Gnostic Religion*, 2nd ed. [Boston: Beacon Press, 1963], 249).

23. Veyne, "La famille," 39, says of the Stoics in the first century c.e., "one no longer forms wise men, one confirms and conforms men in their role as good citizens." Cf. Yarbrough, 41-46.

24. I. G. Kidd, "Cynics," in *Encyclopedia of Philosophy*, ed. Paul Edwards, vol. 2 (1967), 284-85; cf. Zeller, 2.1.324-26; 3.1.306-7.

25. Ragnar Höistad, "Cynic Hero and Cynic King: Studies in the Cynic Conception of Man" (inaugural diss., University of Uppsala, 1948), 15. See also Rudolf Helm, "Kynismus," in *PW* 12.1 [half-vol. 23] (1924), 10-12, although he does not adequately distinguish between Epictetus and the Cynics.

and citizen — represented for the Cynics a burden of responsibility that involved them in a vision of the world for which they had no sympathy, and reduced the time available to them for the practice of their true profession, the philosophical life.

In sum, the Stoic-Cynic marriage debate was essentially a forum for defining an individual's allegiances to a higher cause. It pitted Stoic dedication to traditional Greek life in the city-state against the Cynic calling to the philosophical life. One could even say that marriage became the central issue in this debate unwittingly, due to the claims it made on an individual regarding one of these two causes, for no participant in the debate ever evaluates marriage solely on its own merits.[26]

Having now defined the basic issues of the Stoic-Cynic marriage debate, let us proceed to a chronological examination of the evidence from antiquity. The first period we will treat stretches from the mid–fifth century to the beginning of the third century B.C.E. This will bring us up to the start of the marriage debate, affording us glimpses of several antecedents.

The Fifth to the Third Century B.C.E.

Anaxagoras, Antiphon, Democritus

The first examples we have of the conflict that lies at the heart of the Stoic-Cynic marriage debate come from the middle of the fifth century B.C.E. If we can believe the later accounts, it is at this time that the philosopher Anaxagoras (ca. 500–ca. 428) gave up his patrimony — and with it presumably his marriage — and abandoned all concern for his city-state in order to devote his energies to the study of physical theory.[27] As Plutarch describes it, he chose the life of a theoretical philosopher over that of a man active in the

---

26. Musonius's eulogy of marriage in frag. 13A, *What Is the Chief Aspect of Marriage?* is often misunderstood in this respect. Its proper context, as frag. 13B and the similar discussions in Antipater and Hierocles indicate, is the Stoic understanding of marriage as a natural advantage for the wise man in his effort to live in accord with nature. Kurt Deißner, *Das Idealbild des stoischen Weisen: Rede anläßlich der Reichsgründungsfeier der Universität Greifswald am 18. Januar 1930*, Greifswalder Universitätsreden 24 (Greifswald: L. Bamberg, 1930), 10-11, is quite correct in seeing this "deepest and most noble appraisal of marriage" as stemming from the Stoics' sense of duty toward the *kosmos*.

27. Diogenes Laertius 2.7.

affairs of his city-state.[28] Similarly two other philosophers in this early period criticize the constraints of married life. Antiphon of Athens, an early fifth-century sophist, complains of the manifold burdens brought on by a wife and children in his treatise *On Harmony,* and the atomist Democritus (b. ca. 470) advises against having children due to the trouble of providing for them.[29] Later reports have it that Democritus, like Anaxagoras, abandoned both private and public responsibilities in order to pursue philosophy.[30]

Xenophon

Anaxagoras, Antiphon, and Democritus are examples of an attitude that Cynic authors would later espouse. A very different viewpoint is presented in the first half of the fourth century by the philosopher and statesman Xenophon (ca. 430–ca. 354). In his treatise *Household Management,* in a dialogue between Socrates and the successful, if somewhat childlike, householder Ischomachus, Xenophon outlines the purpose of marriage, the instruction of one's wife, and the proper division of labor within the household.[31] Far from being a burdensome and time-consuming responsibility, marriage is depicted here as that which affords Ischomachus his life of leisure. Because he has a wife adept at household management, he is able to "en-

28. Plutarch, *Vitae* 162B-D *(Pericles),* θεωρητικοῦ φιλοσόφου βίος versus πολιτικοῦ. For a popular treatment of the idea of philosophical retirement among the Greeks, see André-Jean Festugière, *Personal Religion among the Greeks,* Sather Classical Lectures 26 (Berkeley: University of California Press, 1954; reprint, Westport, Conn.: Greenwood, 1984), 53-67.

29. Antiphon, frag. 49 (87 B49 Diels and Kranz); Democritus, frags. 275-76 (68 B275-6 D.-K.) and 170 (68 A170 D.-K.). On these authors see W. K. C. Guthrie, *A History of Greek Philosophy,* vol. 3, *The Fifth-Century Enlightenment* (Cambridge: Cambridge University Press, 1969), 287-89.

30. Cicero, *Tusculan Disputations* 5.39.115; Horace, *Epistle* 1.12.12; Philo, *De vita contemplativa* 14. See also the story of the philosopher Epaminondas (late fifth century–362 B.C.E.), who forgoes marriage for philosophy and the single life due to poverty: Plutarch, *Vitae* 279E-F *(Pelopidas);* cf. Epictetus, *Discourses* 3.22.78. Stobaeus preserves a tradition in which Epaminondas is questioned on the advantage of not marrying and having children. He responds, "Not hesitating to die for the fatherland" (4.520.19-22 W.-H.). Foucault, *Care of the Self,* 156, speaks of the "incompatibility between the goal of philosophy (the care of one's own soul, the mastery of one's passion, the search for peace of mind) and what was traditionally described as the agitation and troubles of married life," as being a perennial problem in Greek philosophy.

31. Xenophon, *Oeconomicus* 7.4–9.19. See the discussion in Foucault, *The Use of Pleasure,* 152-65.

joy free time" (σχολάζειν),[32] which he spends in the pursuit of activities out-side the home, such as civic affairs and philosophy. It is this attitude toward a wife and household that most Stoics would promote, evincing a similar inter-est in the details of establishing and managing households.[33]

Early Cynics

About the time of Xenophon's *Household Management,* we find evidence for the first Cynic positions on marriage, although in this early period there is no consensus. The reputed founder of the movement, Antisthenes (ca. 445–ca. 360), argued in favor of marriage, citing the need for men to procreate.[34] This is similar to one of the arguments used in the later Stoic discussions, and it may be that the contents of Antisthenes' treatise *On Procreation, or on Mar-riage,* of which only the title survives, resembled these. In support of this con-jecture, his treatise on household management, also lost, seems to indicate his concern for the efficient operation of the business end of marriage.[35]

A position close to that taken by the later Cynics was championed by

32. Xenophon, *Oeconomicus* 7.1.

33. Some Stoics even show familiarity with Xenophon's dialogue, directly or otherwise — see Antipater (app. A), lines 44-58; Praechter, 122 n. 2 (regarding Hierocles and Musonius). In the first century B.C.E. Xenophon's *Oeconomicus* was translated into Latin by Cicero (*De officiis* 2.24.87). On the relation between the περὶ γάμου literature and the οἰκονομικός literature, see Albrecht Dihle, "Ethik," in *RAC* 6 (1966), 657; Peter Fiedler, "Haustafel," in *RAC* 13 (1986), 1067; Friedrich Wilhelm, "Die Oeconomica der Neopythagoreer Bryson, Kallikratidas, Periktione, Phintys," *Rh. Mus.* 70 (1915): 162-64, cf. 182, 222; and Klaus Thraede, "Ärger mit der Freiheit," in *"Freunde in Christus werden . . . ,"* ed. Gerta Scharffenort and Klaus Thraede (Gelnhausen: Burckhardthaus, 1977), 67, cf. 63. The best survey and discussion of the οἰκονομικός literature is now Ernst Dassmann and Georg Schöllgen, "Haus II (Hausgemeinschaft)," in *RAC* 13 (1986), 801-906. Although the authors intend to be comprehensive (816), they overlook certain texts. The most obvious omission is [Aristotle] *Oeconomica* 3; for others, see the discussion below. On the history of the topos περὶ οἰκονομίας, see also David L. Balch, *Let Wives Be Submissive: The Domestic Code in I Peter,* SBLMS 26 (Chico, Calif.: Scholars, 1981), 23-62.

34. Diogenes Laertius 6.11. See the discussion in J. M. Rist, *Stoic Philosophy* (Cambridge: Cambridge University Press, 1969), 56-57.

35. Diogenes Laertius 6.16, περὶ παιδοποιίας ἢ περὶ γάμου, and περὶ νίκης οἰκονομικός. The latter, rather odd name is evidently not to be separated into περὶ νίκης (*On Victory*) and οἰκονομικός (*Household Management*) — see Fernanda Decleva Caizzi, ed., *Antisthenis Fragmenta,* Testi e Documenti per lo Studio dell' Antichitá 13 (Milan: Istituto Editoriale Cisalpino, 1966), 81.

Antisthenes' contemporary and the movement's most colorful figure, Diogenes of Sinope (ca. 400–ca. 325). Diogenes rejected the duties of a citizen and took a stand against conventional marriage, offering two alternatives. He suggested that men take joint responsibility over several women and their children, and define marriage simply as intercourse between the "man who persuades" and the "woman who is persuaded";[36] he also appears to have advocated the practice of masturbation in place of all forms of sexuality that demanded a partner,[37] being accredited with the remark that sexual love is "an activity of those who have time to waste" (τὸν ἔρωτα σχολαζόντων ἀσχολίαν).[38] Finally, a third Cynic of this period, Diogenes' disciple Crates (ca. 365–ca. 285), may have stood somewhere between Antisthenes and Diogenes on the marriage issue, at least in his personal life. While he married, it was no marriage in the conventional sense, for though he raised a daughter, he seems to have neither founded a household nor carried out the duties of a citizen, from which, as a foreigner, he was excluded in any case.[39]

The Academy, the Peripatetics, and Epicurus

Neither Plato (ca. 429-347) nor his student Aristotle (384-322) seems to have given much credence to the notion of an inevitable conflict between the duties of a married man and the call of a philosopher, although Plato does demand that the philosopher-guardians of his ideal state hold their wives in common, as Diogenes would also suggest.[40] Both do, however, recognize the necessity of marriage for the prosperity of the city-state.[41] Further, Aristotle

36. Diogenes Laertius 6.72.

37. See Zeller, 2.1.322-23.

38. Diogenes Laertius 6.51. See also Rist, 59-61; cf. Diogenes Laertius 6.54. It may be noted here that no Cynic or Stoic author advocating celibacy explicitly demanded abstinence from sexual activity.

39. See Rist, 61-62.

40. E.g., Plato, *Republic* 5.449A-65C. See Mulgan, 38; Susan Moller Okin, *Women in Western Political Thought* (Princeton: Princeton University Press, 1979), 31-45; and cf. *Phaedo* 66B; *Theaetetus* 172C-76A. On Aristotle see Adkins, 347; on Plato's teacher Socrates, see Zeller, 2.1.166-71.

41. On Plato see, e.g., *Republic* 5.460A, 461A-C; W. K. C. Guthrie, *A History of Greek Philosophy*, vol. 5, *The Later Plato and the Academy* (Cambridge: Cambridge University Press, 1978), 354-56. On Aristotle see, e.g., *Politica* 7.1334b 29-1336a 2; see also Arius in Stobaeus 2.152.18-22 W.-H.

and another of Plato's students, Xenocrates, who headed the Academy from 339 to 314, wrote on household management,[42] and Aristotle seems to have addressed several related topics in other tractates as well.[43]

The situation changes significantly with two of Aristotle's students, Theophrastus (ca. 370-285) and his contemporary Dicaearchus, who championed the "theoretical" and the "practical" life, respectively.[44] In these authors we are already able to make out the basic polarities that characterized the later Stoic-Cynic debate.[45] Similar to the later Cynic position, Theophrastus held that married life and philosophy were incompatible due to the cares and responsibilities imposed on a married man by his wife. He also criticized the notions that a wife was the best of all helpers and companions, and that marriage was necessitated by the need to raise children.[46] In sharp contrast to this, and anticipating later

42. Aristotle, *Politica* 2.1253b 1-1260b 24; Diogenes Laertius 4.12. [Aristotle] *Oeconomica* 1, the anonymous work of an early Peripatetic, is also devoted to household management; on its date, authorship, and relationship to Xenophon, *Oeconomicus*, see Dassmann and Schöllgen, 818. These authors (816-17) maintain that philosophical reflection on household management begins with Plato's teacher Socrates (citing Xenophon, *Memorabilia* 1.2.48, 64; 4.1.2); yet Hesiod should also be seen as a candidate (see *Works and Days* 373-78, 397-413, 695-705). The creation of a technical vocabulary may begin with Aristotle (*Politica* 1.1253b 8-11).

43. I.e., in his περὶ συμβιώσεως ἀνδρὸς καὶ γυναικός, his νόμοι ἀνδρὸς καὶ γαμετῆς, and his ὑπὲρ τοῦ μὴ γεννᾶν. On these see Fritz Wehrli, ed., *Die Schule des Aristoteles: Texte und Kommentar*, vol. 4, *Demetrios von Phaleron*, 2nd ed. (Basel and Stuttgart: Schwabe, 1968), 60. Cf. the discussion in Praechter, 121-31. Saint Jerome held that Aristotle also wrote a book entitled *On Marriage* (*Adversus Jovinianum* 1.49, "scripserunt Aristoteles et Plutarchus et noster Seneca de matrimonio libros"). Bickel, 106-28, thinks Jerome refers to Aristotle's περὶ συμβιώσεως ἀνδρὸς καὶ γυναικός, known to him from a Neoplatonic collection of Aristotle's writings by Porphyrus, but this is speculation.

44. See Cicero, *Ad Atticum* 2.16.3; *De finibus* 5.4.11; Zeller, 2.2.858-59, 862-64, 891-93; and Alberto Grilli, *Il problema della vita contemplativa nel mondo greco-romano*, Filologia e Letterature Classiche 1 (Milan and Rome: Fratelli Bocca, 1953), 125-33.

45. Praechter, 129-31, and Konrad Graf Preysing, "Ehezweck und zweite Ehe bei Athenagoras," *TQ* 110 (1929): 93-94, think Theophrastus may have been writing against Zeno or another early Stoic, but this is conjecture.

46. Our source for this information is his work *On Marrying*, from which Saint Jerome preserves an excerpt: *Adversus Jovinianum* 1.47 (*PL* 23:289-90); Jerome's knowledge of this tractate may go back to a translation or partial translation made by Seneca; see Marion Lausberg, *Untersuchungen zu Senecas Fragmenten*, Untersuchungen zur antiken Literatur und Geschichte 7 (Berlin: Walter de Gruyter, 1970), 1 n. 2; Winfried Trillitzsch, "Hieronymus und Seneca," *Mittellateinisches Jahrbuch* 2 (1965): 43-44; and H. B. Gottschalk, "Aristotelian Philosophy in the Roman World from the Time of Cicero to the End of the Second Century A.D.," in *ANRW* 2.36.2 (1987), 1140-41 n. 297. Bickel questions whether the original name was *De nuptiis*. He suggests,

Stoic discussions, Dicaearchus is reported to have argued that marriage was properly understood as one of the philosopher's true tasks in life.[47]

Whether Demetrius of Phaleron, a Peripatetic philosopher, statesman, and close associate of Theophrastus, supported the latter's views about marriage in his treatise *On Marriage* is not known, as only its title survives.[48] Concerning yet another contemporary, however, we are better informed. According to two late sources, the philosopher Epicurus (341-270) held a posi-

---

rather, that Jerome's excerpt was part of a book entitled περὶ βίων *(On Lifestyles)*, for three reasons: the list of Theophrastus's works in Diogenes Laertius 5.42-50 does not contain a περὶ γάμου, but it does contain three volumes entitled περὶ βίων (5.42); Philon of Larissa (160/159–ca. 80) demonstrates that εἰ γαμητέον τῷ σοφῷ is a topic handled by tractates entitled περὶ βίων (Stobaeus 2.41.7-11 W.-H.); and the Academic Eudoros of Alexandria (fl. ca. 25 B.C.E.) names ὁ περὶ γάμου [λόγος] as part of ὁ περὶ βίων λόγος (Stobaeus 2.44.26–45.1, 6 W.-H.). See Bickel, 214-15; Robert Philippson, "Hierokles der Stoiker," *Rh. Mus.*, n.s., 82 (1933): 110, who sees influence of the Middle Stoa on Eudoros. On the Theophrastus excerpt in Jerome generally, see Bickel, 129-220; Zeller, 2.2.858-59, 862-64; Stelzenberger, 432-33 n. 122; and Ralph Hanna and Traugott Lawler, eds., *Jankyn's Book of Wikked Wyves*, vol. 1, *The Primary Texts* (Athens: University of Georgia Press, 1997), 8-16.

47. Dicaearchus, frag. 31 Wehrli: "Nor does it seem to Dicaearchus that these things behove wise men, for [he contends] neither did the ancients philosophize with mere discourse. Rather, back then wisdom was in fact devotion to good works, but in time it became an art of popular discourses. Thus at present, the one who engages persuasively in dialectic is thought to be a great philosopher, whereas in ancient times the good man alone was a philosopher, even if he could not craft celebrated and crowd pleasing sayings. For these men did not investigate whether in fact one should practice politics or how, rather they practiced politics well — nor if one had to marry, rather, having married in the manner that one should marry, they shared a common life with their wives. These things, he says, are works of men and pursuits of wise men, but these clever sayings are a tiresome matter." This is *Codex Vaticanus* 435, which is attributed to "the *Roman Sayings* of Plutarch or Caecilius [first century B.C.E.]"; see Hans von Arnim, "Ineditum Vaticanum," *Hermes* 27 (1892), 120, lines 13-14. Cf. Plutarch, *Moralia* 797D *(An seni respublica gerenda sit)*, and Epictetus, *Discourses* 3.21.4-6. My suspicion is that it is a Stoic presentation of Dicaearchus.

48. Diogenes Laertius 5.81. Menander, the acclaimed poet of New Comedy, student of Theophrastus and friend of Demetrius, may also have been influenced by Theophrastus's dark view of marriage. See T. B. L. Webster, *Studies in Menander*, 2nd ed., Publications of the University of Manchester 309, Classical Series 7 (Manchester: Manchester University Press, 1960), 214-17; Webster, *An Introduction to Menander* (Manchester: University of Manchester Press; New York: Barnes and Noble, 1974), 46-48. Stobaeus preserves two sayings from Menander that point in this direction: "To have a wife and to be a father of children, Parmenon, entails many cares in life" (4.517.12-14 W.-H.; frag. 575 Körte); "To marry, if one would examine the truth, is an evil, but a necessary evil" (4.527.5-7 W.-H.; frag. 578 K.). Cf. Menander, *Sententiae* 141 Jaekel, "For a wife is bane and salvation to a household." On the theme of marriage in New Comedy generally, see Ph. E. Legrand, *Daos: Tableau de la comédie grecque* (Lyon: A. Rey, 1910), 148-84.

tion very similar to that of Theophrastus. Diogenes Laertius, for example, has this report: "Nor, again, will the wise man marry and rear a family: so Epicurus says in the *Problems* and in *De natura*. Occasionally he may marry owing to special circumstances (περίστασιν) in his life. Some too will turn aside from their purpose [by marrying]."[49]

Early Stoics

What we know of the early Stoics makes it clear that marriage was discussed from the inception of this school, and in terms not unlike what we find in the

---

49. Diogenes Laertius 10.119, text and trans. R. D. Hicks, *Diogenes Laertius: Lives of Eminent Philosophers*, LCL (London: Wm. Heinemann; Cambridge: Harvard University Press, 1925), 2:644-45; "[by marrying]" is my addition. The manuscript reads μὴν καὶ γαμήσειν instead of μηδὲ καὶ γαμήσειν, i.e., "the wise man *will indeed* marry . . . ," but given the next sentence, this would not change the sense significantly. For a discussion of this text, see Tad Brennan, "Epicurus on Sex, Marriage, and Children," *CP* 91 (1996): 346-52. The other source is Seneca, *De matrimonio*, in Jerome, *Adversus Jovinianum* 1.48: "Epicurus, the patron of pleasure . . . says that a wise man can seldom marry, because marriage has many drawbacks. And as riches, honors, bodily health, and other things which we call indifferent, are neither good nor bad, but stand as it were midway, and become good and bad according to the use and issue, so wives stand on the border line of good and ill. It is, moreover, a serious matter for a wise man to be in doubt whether he is going to marry a good or a bad woman" (trans. W. H. Fremantle, in A Select Library of Nicene and Post-Nicene Fathers of the Christian Church, 2nd ser., vol. 6, *St. Jerome: Letters and Select Works*, ed. Philip Schaff and Henry Wace [New York: Christian Literature Co., 1893; reprint, Grand Rapids: Eerdmans, n.d.], 385). Regarding Epicurus's views on marriage, see Vatin, 32 and n. 1; Wayne A. Meeks, "The Image of the Androgyne: Some Uses of a Symbol in Earliest Christianity," *HR* 13 (1973/74): 173-74; Grilli, 59-84; C. W. Chilton, "Did Epicurus Approve of Marriage?" *Phronesis* 5 (1960): 71-74; and Carlo Natali, "*Oikonomia* in Hellenistic Political Thought," in *Justice and Generosity: Studies in Hellenistic Social and Political Philosophy*, edited by André Laks and Malcolm Schofield, Proceedings of the Sixth Symposium Hellenisticum (Cambridge: Cambridge University Press, 1995), 109-14. See also *Vatican Sayings* 41 and 58. After Epicurus, the Epicureans voice little opinion on marriage. In his critique of non-Epicurean theories of household management, Philodemus of Gadara (ca. 110–ca. 40) questions simply whether it is necessary to have a wife (*On Household Management* col. 2-3, 9). Cf. Diogenes of Oenoanda 22S Long and Sedley. On Lucretius's views on marriage, see Martha C. Nussbaum, *The Therapy of Desire: Theory and Practice in Hellenistic Ethics* (Princeton: Princeton University Press, 1994), 185-91. Epictetus may have encountered some Epicureans who revived their founder's teachings on marriage; see below, p. 80. On Epicurean communities in this late period, see Wayne A. Meeks, *The First Urban Christians: The Social World of the Apostle Paul* (New Haven and London: Yale University Press, 1983), 83-84 (lit.).

later Stoic-Cynic debate. Diogenes Laertius tells us that Zeno (335-263), the school's founder, held that the wise man will marry and have children. Significantly he cites Zeno's *Politics* as his source, which suggests that the relationship between marriage and the well-being of the city-state posited by later Stoics was part of Zeno's understanding of marriage as well.[50] After Zeno, his student Persaeus and Chrysippus (ca. 280-207), third in line as head of the Stoa, wrote about marriage. Whereas only the title of Persaeus's treatise *On Marriage* survives,[51] our information on Chrysippus is somewhat better. According to Plutarch, Chrysippus always discussed the topics of marriage and raising children under the assumption that these activities formed part of a larger cosmic order under the sway of a divine principle, which Chrysippus described variously as "Good Fortune," "Zeus," "Destiny," "Providence," or "the Common Nature."[52] Plutarch's report, moreover, receives support from Seneca's remark that "Chrysippus ridiculously maintains that a wise man should marry, that he may not outrage Jupiter Gamelius and Genethlius."[53]

But to this picture of early Stoic views on marriage we must add one more consideration. Citing from Chrysippus's *On Politics* and again from Zeno's *Politics*, Diogenes Laertius reports that both these philosophers also advocated the idea of holding wives in common, as had Plato and Diogenes of Sinope.[54] This seeming disparity in their teachings on marriage may reflect a distinction that Zeno and Chrysippus drew between utopian vision and practical reality.[55] It may also point to Cynic influence on their thinking, however, for as Diogenes Laertius says elsewhere, Zeno, a onetime follower of Crates, wrote his *Politics* while still a Cynic.[56]

---

50. Diogenes Laertius 7.121.

51. Diogenes Laertius 7.36.

52. Plutarch, *Moralia* 1035B-C *(De Stoicorum repugnantiis)*.

53. That is, Zeus in his role as divine patron and guardian of marriage and the human race; Seneca, *De matrimonio*, in Jerome, *Adversus Jovinianum* 1.48, trans. Fremantle, in Schaff and Wace, 385.

54. Diogenes Laertius 7.33, 131.

55. So Pohlenz, *Die Stoa*, 1:137-39. On the utopian concept of "community of wives" in the ethnographic writers, see John Ferguson, *Utopias of the Classical World* (London: Thomas and Hudson, 1975), 19-21.

56. Diogenes Laertius 7.4. Cf. A. A. Long and D. N. Sedley, *The Hellenistic Philosophers*, vol. 1, *Translations of the Principal Sources with Philosophical Commentary* (Cambridge: Cambridge University Press, 1987), 435. On Zeno's view of marriage see also Rist, 65-67; H. C. Baldry, "Zeno's Ideal State," *JHS* 79 (1959): 9-10; and Praechter, 128-29, who suggests that the *Cynic Epistle of Diogenes* 47 (to Zeno) might reflect Zeno's position. In this connection we should also note

The Second to the First Century B.C.E.

Antipater of Tarsus and Ocellus Lucanus

The Stoic-Cynic marriage debate as described in the introduction to this survey appears to begin in the second century B.C.E. At least it is not until this period that we have texts complete enough to define clearly the respective Stoic and Cynic positions on marriage. One of these is the treatise *On Marriage* by the Stoic philosopher Antipater of Tarsus (fl. mid–second century).[57] In this text Antipater begins his discussion with the conviction that men are political beings destined by nature and the gods to play a part in a cosmic order composed of households and city-states. The institution of marriage, he maintains, serves as the foundation of this order, being the source of households and thus city-states. From this he concludes that all morally upright youths, in an effort to fulfill their obligations to the gods and express their allegiance to the divine plan, will consider marriage "among the primary and most necessary actions that are fitting (τῶν ἀναγκαιοτάτων καὶ πρώτων καθηκόντων)."[58]

Having thus identified marriage as a highly valued "fitting action," Antipater eulogizes its natural benefits. It is superior to all other "friendly affections of life," for in marriage the partners express their dedication to one another by sharing not only possessions and children, and their souls, but also their bodies. From this praise Antipater proceeds to criticize those who see a wife as a burden, saying this misconception arises from the inability of some men to select an appropriate mate — a matter to which he devotes another treatise[59] — and to instruct her in the art of managing a household and

---

that Zeno's student Ariston is said to have held that both πατρίς and οἶκος were products of civilization, not nature (Plutarch, *Moralia* 600E [*De exilio*]). On Ariston see Rist, 74-77. For Chrysippus see Rist, 79; Zeller, 3.1.302-3 n. 6; Diogenes Laertius 7.121; and Plutarch, *Moralia* 1033D (*De Stoic. repug.*). On the early Stoics generally, see also Grilli, 89-99.

57. *SVF* 3.254-57 (Stobaeus 4.507-12 W.-H.); a complete translation with Greek text is provided in app. A below. For a summary and discussion of this text, see Hermann Cohn, "Antipater von Tarsos: Ein Beitrag zur Geschichte der Stoa" (Ph.D. diss., University of Giessen, 1905), 15-18, 80-83; and André-Jean Voelke, *Les rapports avec autrui dans la philosophie grecque: D'Aristote à Panétius*, Bibliothèque d'histoire de la philosophie (Paris: J. Vrin, 1961), 149-52.

58. Antipater (app. A), line 14.

59. Antipater's περὶ γυναικὸς συμβιώσεως in *SVF* 3.254.3-22 (Stobaeus 4.539.5–540.6 W.-H.). Hense has argued that this fragment is actually part of Antipater's περὶ γάμου (Hense, "Zu Antipatros," 300-302), a theory made plausible by Nicostratus's περὶ γάμου, which contains similar material (Stobaeus 4.536-39, 593-99 W.-H.).

living piously. A wife who is properly chosen and instructed, he asserts, offers advantages essential to anyone who "loves the good." She becomes a help to her husband, like a second pair of hands, affording him "leisure time" (σχολή)[60] to pursue philosophy or politics. It is through her diligence in household matters that he can give his full attention to these pursuits, remaining "undistracted" (ἀπερίσπαστος)[61] by concerns for the necessities of life.

A text similar to this is *On the Nature of the Universe* 43b–51, mistakenly ascribed to the Pythagorean Ocellus Lucanus. According to Karl Praechter, its provenance is Stoic and it stems from perhaps around 150, making its author a contemporary of Antipater.[62] Here we find a view of the *kosmos* identical to Antipater's, being a system that reflects the divine will and consists of households and city-states, the foundation of which is marriage.[63] Unlike Antipater, however, its author does not argue the case for marrying per se, but, assuming marriage, proceeds to show that the married man must carry out the divine plan of the *kosmos* through the proper procreation of children. In his words, if a man wishes to protect his ancestral hearth, the altar of his city-state, and the altar of God, he is "obligated" (ὀφείλει) to replace each person death takes from his household and city-state.[64]

In a manner similar to Antipater, the author then criticizes those who have chosen wives badly, either for wealth or status, or wives too old to bear children. Stressing again the importance of marriage as a part of the larger system, he complains that the disharmony which results from these marriages is detrimental to the whole. Households are but the constituent parts, he states, and thus "whatever sort of things the parts happen to be, the Whole and the Entirety that are composed of such parts are also like this."[65]

Cynic Epistles

The next documents we need to consider come from a collection known as the *Cynic Epistles*. These are pseudepigraphic writings attributed to Greek

---

60. Antipater (app. A), line 74; cf. lines 79, 83.
61. Antipater (app. A), line 77.
62. Praechter, 138-41. A translation and text is provided in app. B below.
63. See Praechter, 140 n. 1, 141. Cf. [Ocellus Lucanus] *De legibus*.
64. [Ocellus] (app. B) *De universi natura* 45; cf. 47.
65. [Ocellus] (app. B) *De universi natura* 50-51.

philosophers of the classical and early Hellenistic periods, but which scholars have assigned to Cynic authors of the late Hellenistic period, situating them in the neo-Cynic revival that began in the second or first century B.C.E.[66] The particular letters in which we are interested, the *Cynic Epistles of Diogenes* 21, 35, 42, 44, 47 and the *Cynic Epistle of Heraclitus* 9, have been dated variously by scholars between the first century B.C.E. and the second century C.E., without the benefit of any true consensus.[67] Thus, while the dates of composition of some may extend beyond the first century B.C.E., it will be convenient for us to consider them all here rather than divide them up on some basis and treat some later. These letters contribute greatly to our understanding of the Stoic-Cynic marriage debate since they present a fairly uniform position against many of the Stoic teachings. In other words, they give us a glimpse of the other side of the debate.

In the *Cynic Epistle of Diogenes* 47 the author opens his discussion by flatly denying the position emphasized so strongly by Antipater, that a man should marry because a wife's partnership serves to make her husband's life easier. In his opinion a wife and children are a burden that the philosopher should avoid by living self-sufficiently and free from "passion," a term denoting disturbance of the soul. The author then challenges the Stoic position that marriage is necessary because it guarantees the future of the human race. To his mind the majority of people in the world are largely "uninformed as to the true nature of things" and therefore no more worth worrying about than the races of various insects.[68] In a similar vein, two other letters take issue with Stoic views on the purpose of sexual intercourse and the necessity of procreation. Letter 21 tacitly denies the Stoic claim that sexual intercourse must be performed solely for the sake of procreation, and the author of the *Cynic Epistle of Heraclitus* 9 suggests

66. On this revival see Margarethe Billerbeck, *Der Kyniker Demetrius: Ein Beitrag zur Geschichte der frühkaiserzeitlichen Popularphilosophie,* Philosophia Antiqua 36 (Leiden: Brill, 1979), esp. 1-11; Marie-Odile Goulet-Cazé, "Le cynisme à l'époque impériale," in *ANRW* 2.36.4 (1990), 2720-2833.

67. These texts have been edited and translated in Abraham J. Malherbe, ed., *The Cynic Epistles,* SBLSBS 12 (Missoula, Mont.: Scholars, 1977). For a summary of the various theories on dating the *Cynic Epistles of Diogenes,* see Malherbe, 14-17; on the *Cynic Epistles of Heraclitus* see Harold W. Attridge, *First-Century Cynicism in the Epistles of Heraclitus,* HTS 29 (Missoula, Mont.: Scholars, 1976), 12.

68. On this disdain for "nonphilosophical" persons among the Cynics, see Zeller, 2.1.314-16; Abraham J. Malherbe, *Paul and the Thessalonians: The Philosophic Tradition of Pastoral Care* (Philadelphia: Fortress, 1987), 21 and n. 59.

that the feared depopulation of the city-states could be halted by simply defining citizens on the basis of virtue rather than birth.[69]

Still another perspective on marriage is afforded by the *Cynic Epistle of
Diogenes* 44. Starting with the assumption, also held by the Stoics, that sexual
desires are natural and the satisfaction of these desires both natural and necessary,[70] its author argues that sexual relations in general, let alone marriage,
are too time-consuming for the philosopher in his pursuit of happiness and
well-being. To solve this dilemma he promotes the practice of masturbation,
which both conserves a Cynic's precious free time (σχολή) and helps him put
his life in order as a teacher of moderation and endurance.[71] From two other
letters, the *Cynic Epistles of Diogenes* 35 and 42, we learn that Cynics considered masturbation fully in accord with nature, the latter employing a comparison between satisfying one's sexual appetite and satisfying one's hunger.[72]

If we combine the information of these letters and place it against the
backdrop of what we know about the Cynics of this period more generally,[73]
the following picture of their position on marriage emerges. First, the Cynics
rejected the Stoic claim that a man is morally obligated to marry, have children, and establish a household, thereby providing a constant supply of citizens for the city-states. This rejection is consistent with the Cynic concept of
radical cosmopolitanism, and it is grounded in their more basic rejection of
the notion that "civilized life," or the life most worth living, is dependent on
the prosperity of the city-state.[74] Second, in place of the Stoic concept of allegiance to this cosmic order, the Cynics proposed a different ideal with a different set of allegiances. They maintained that the true nature of a man was
best served by a life devoted exclusively to a philosophy that promoted self-
sufficiency and inner freedom. This, in turn, excluded marriage inasmuch as

69. Cf. Dio Chrysostom, *Oration* 34.21-23.

70. Cf. Zeller, 2.1.321-22; Arthur O. Lovejoy and George Boas, *Primitivism and Related Ideas
in Antiquity* (Baltimore: Johns Hopkins University Press, 1935; reprint, New York: Octagon
Books, 1973), 121.

71. Cf. Dio Chrysostom, *Oration* 6.16-20; Galen, *De locis affectis* 6.5 (8.419 Kühn); and
Agathias Scholasticus, *Greek Anthology* 302 (sixth century C.E.). On the Cynic concern for
σχολή, see also *Cynic Epistle of Anacharsis* 5, and *Cynic Epistle of Heraclitus* 1.

72. Similarly, Plutarch, *Moralia* 1044B *(De Stoic. repug.)*; Diogenes Laertius 6.46, 69.

73. On this see Meeks, *Moral World,* 52-56; and the description of "austere Cynicism" in
Abraham J. Malherbe, "Self-Definition among Epicureans and Cynics," in *Jewish and Christian
Self Definition,* vol. 3, *Self-Definition in the Greco-Roman World,* ed. Ben F. Meyer and E. P.
Sanders (London: SCM Press, 1982), 50-59, 195 n. 30.

74. Cf. *Cynic Epistle of Crates* 5.

marriage introduced responsibilities that encroached on a wise man's self-sufficiency and made demands on his free time. The importance of marrying for the Stoic is thus mirrored by the importance of rejecting marriage for the Cynic. Indeed, according to the *Cynic Epistle of Diogenes* 44, shunning sexual relations with women (although not sexuality per se) was one of the things that distinguished a man from the nonphilosophical people of the world, earning him the title "Cynic."[75]

Arius and Cicero

From the end of the first century B.C.E. comes an epitome of Stoic ethics compiled by Arius Didymus, friend and teacher of Augustus Caesar.[76] Its importance lies in the fact that it details efforts within Stoicism to apply a systematic theory of ethics to the marriage debate. We have already seen some evidence of this in Antipater, both in his statement that marriage is the most necessary of those actions which are "fitting" and in his discussion of the natural advantages of married life. Arius's treatment, however, allows us to see the fuller implications of these efforts.

Arius tells us that Stoics classified marriage as an "indifferent thing" (ἀδιάφορον), which is what made marrying a "fitting action" under normal circumstances.[77] He says further that the wise or "good" man (σπουδαῖος) would correctly administer a household, and that the Stoics saw participation in the affairs of one's city-state as a "preferred thing" (προηγούμενον).[78] This much dovetails nicely with the assertions of Antipater and Ocellus that the *kosmos* is a hierarchy of marriages, households, and city-states. But Arius tells us one more thing — that the Stoics saw all these activities, including marriage, as ethically

---

75. *Cynic Epistle of Diogenes* 44 (174.11-15 M.). On the meaning "nonphilosophical" for ἰδιώτης here, see Musonius, frag. 3.40.35 Lutz (11.13 H.), and Epictetus, *Discourses* 3.16, passim.

76. For a summary and discussion of Arius's epitome, see Charles H. Kahn, "Arius as a Doxographer," in *On Stoic and Peripatetic Ethics: The Work of Arius Didymus*, ed. William W. Fortenbaugh, Rutgers University Studies in Classical Humanities 1 (New Brunswick, N.J.: Transaction Books, 1983), 3-13. For text and translation, see Arthur J. Pomeroy, ed., *Arius Didymus: Epitome of Stoic Ethics* SBLTT 44/SBLGRS 14 (Atlanta: Society of Biblical Literature, 1999).

77. Arius in Stobaeus 2.86.12-16 W.-H. Cf. Eudoros of Alexandria (fl. ca. 25 B.C.E.), who associates ὁ περὶ γάμου [sc. λόγος] with "fitting actions" (καθήκοντες, cited by Arius in Stobaeus 2.44.24 W.-H.). Cf. also Cicero, *De finibus* 3.17.58-19.64; 3.20.68-21.69; Diogenes Laertius 7.107-21.

78. Arius in Stobaeus 2.95.9-23 and 2.109.10-18 W.-H. See also 2.100.5 and 2.103.9-23 W.-H.

"missing the mark," or "sin" (ἁμάρτημα), when performed in a manner detrimental to one's well-being.[79] With this he raises the possibility, not considered by Antipater or Ocellus, that the morally upright man will not marry if the circumstances of his life prove marriage to be impractical or disadvantageous.

Approaching this matter from another perspective, we may isolate an even more profound difference between Arius, on the one hand, and Antipater and Ocellus on the other. All three emphasize an individual's allegiance to "nature," and hence to the *kosmos,* the embodiment of nature's will. In Antipater and Ocellus, however, this *kosmos* is pictured as the sum total of all city-states. Thus a man's place in the *kosmos* is defined in terms of his identity as a citizen of one of these city-states, leading to the conclusion that the part nature has destined a man to play is identical to his roles as husband, householder, and citizen. By contrast, the Stoic position that Arius describes pictures the *kosmos* as a single world community. In consequence, a man's obligation to marry and establish a household is less evident. It no longer derives primarily from his allegiance to a city-state, but from his identity as a citizen of the world who is first and foremost concerned for a community whose affairs sometimes take precedence over those of the city-state.

Thus, somewhat ironically perhaps, the ethical system described by Arius, which Stoics pressed into service in support of marriage, breathes the same cosmopolitan spirit that the Stoics' promotion of marriage originally sought to quell. The moral obligation to take on the responsibilities of married life has now been relativized in light of an allegiance higher than one's allegiance to the city-state. Not surprisingly, this ethical system becomes the means by which some Stoics were able to incorporate Cynic views into their thinking on marriage, leading to what I have termed an "inner-Stoic" marriage debate. Our first substantial evidence for this development is in Cicero's *De finibus,* written not long before Arius composed his epitome. Here Cicero tells us that the Stoics believed "the Wise Man should desire to engage in politics and government, and also to live in accordance with nature by taking to himself a wife and desiring to have children by her," adding, "As for the principles and habits of the Cynics, some say that these befit the Wise Man, if circumstances should happen to indicate this course of action; but other Stoics reject the Cynic rule unconditionally."[80] With this the door swings wide for

---

79. Arius in Stobaeus 2.86.11 W.-H. See also 2.99.8 and 2.109.16-18 W.-H.

80. Cicero, *De finibus* 3.20.68: ". . . Cynicorum autem rationem atque vitam alii cadere in sapientem dicunt, si qui eiusmodi forte casus inciderit ut id faciendum sit, alii nullo modo";

those Stoics who would shun the marital duties of a citizen in pursuit of the higher calling of philosophy.

As an additional note to Cicero, we should mention that our information concerning his own interest in the Stoic-Cynic marriage debate is intriguing, but mixed. We know he held that a proper youth entered into mature life by taking on the responsibilities of domestic and civic affairs,[81] that he was familiar with Stoic views on the structure of the *kosmos*,[82] and that he translated Xenophon's *Oeconomicus* into Latin, which suggests he had more than a passing interest in the theory of household management.[83] On the other hand, he was familiar with certain philosophers who distanced themselves from civic affairs in order to have sufficient time for study,[84] and at certain points in his career chose the contemplative life over the active.[85]

H. Rackham, ed. and trans., *Cicero: De finibus bonorum et malorum*, LCL (London: William Heinemann; New York: Macmillan, 1914), 289. Cf. Diogenes Laertius 7.121, where immediately after citing Zeno's position in favor of marriage, he cites Apollodorus on Stoics acting like Cynics. Depending on how we read back into the arrangement of Diogenes' source material, this idea of a Stoic taking a Cynic position on marriage could possibly be dated as early as Apollodorus, a contemporary of Antipater. On the idea that some Cynics of this period are "radical Stoics," see Donald B. Dudley, *A History of Cynicism* (London: Methuen, 1937; reprint, Hildesheim: Georg Olms, 1967), 96-103, 117-24, 137, and esp. 189-99; Miriam T. Griffin, *Seneca: A Philosopher in Politics* (Oxford: Clarendon, 1976), 297-314; Abraham J. Malherbe, "Cynics," in *IDBsup* (1962), 202; Cicero, *De officiis* 1.35.128; Arius in Stobaeus 2.114.22-25 W.-H.; Seneca, *De brevitate vitae* 14.2; *De beneficiis* 7.1.3; 8.2; and Epictetus, *Discourses* 3.22. Cf. Juvenal, *Satires* 13.122, and Ramsay MacMullen, *Enemies of the Roman Order* (Cambridge: Harvard University Press, 1966), 305 n. 2.

81. *Rei domesticae . . . reique publicae*, Cicero, *Pro Caelio* 42.

82. See Cicero, *Laws* 3.1.2-3; *De officiis* 1.17.54; *De finibus* 3.19.62-64; *De natura deorum* 2.51.128; and Pohlenz, *Die Stoa*, 1:269-70. On his knowledge of the Stoic concept of *oikeiosis*, see Pembroke, 121-22.

83. Cicero, *De officiis* 2.24.87. It is also about this time that the Epicurean Philodemus writes his περὶ οἰκονομίας, a critical discussion of Xenophon, *Oeconomicus*, [Aristotle] *Oeconomica* 1343a-1345b, and various Cynic views on household management; see Dassmann and Schöllgen, 819.

84. Cicero, *De officiis* 1.9.28; 1.20.69–21.70.

85. See Cicero, *De finibus* 5.4.11, and *Epitulae ad Atticum* 2.16.3; cf. *Topica* 82; *De oratore* 3.29.112; *De officiis* 1.20.69–21.73; and Plutarch, *Vitae* 862A *(Cicero)*. See also Neal Wood, *Cicero's Social and Political Thought* (Berkeley: University of California Press, 1988), 122-23; Grilli, 192-200. According to an anecdote passed on by Seneca, Cicero chose not to remarry after his divorce from Terentia so as to devote himself to philosophical studies (Seneca, *De matrimonio*, in Jerome, *Adversus Jovinianum* 1.48, cited below, p. 73). Yet this divorce took place in 47 B.C.E., and by the next year Cicero had married Publilia (although that union lasted only until 45).

The First to the Middle of the Second Century C.E.

Seneca

By the beginning of the first century C.E. the basic parameters of the Stoic-Cynic marriage debate had been established. Over the next century and a half the focus would sharpen on one particular issue already familiar to us from Antipater and the *Cynic Epistles of Diogenes,* namely, whether the responsibilities of married life are compatible with the pursuit of philosophy. This period is also noteworthy in that it supplies us with our richest cache of materials. The marriage debate enjoys great popularity, attracting the attention of a variety of authors, many of whom were contemporaries of the apostle Paul.

Some of our first information on the marriage debate in the first century comes from the Stoic philosopher and statesman Seneca (ca. 5 B.C.E.–65 C.E.). Here, as with Cicero, we encounter something of a mixed picture. On the one side Seneca is the author of a treatise devoted entirely to marriage. This is his *On Marriage,* parts of which are preserved by Saint Jerome in his polemical tractate *Against Jovinian.* While Jerome does not cite enough of Seneca's work for us to determine its full intent, it clearly dealt with whether marriage and philosophy were compatible, and two of the anecdotes it contains offer the sharply negative assessments of Epicurus and Cicero.[86] Regarding Cicero, for example, Seneca claims, "when Cicero after divorcing Terentia was requested by Hirtius to marry his sister, he set the matter altogether on one side, and said that he could not possibly devote himself to a wife and to philosophy."[87]

This negative attitude toward marriage seems inherent in several of Seneca's other writings as well. In two of his letters he portrays the wise man as favoring a cosmopolitan approach to public life that excludes participation in the affairs of any one community or city-state, and he comments on the philosopher's need for free time, maintaining that other aspects of life should be

---

86. Jerome, *Adversus Jovinianum* 1.41-49. The fragments of Seneca's *De matrimonio* have been edited by Bickel, 382-94, and by Winfried Trillitzsch, *Seneca im literarischen Urteil der Antike: Darstellung und Sammlung der Zeugnisse,* 2 vols. (Amsterdam: Adolf M. Hakkert, 1971), 2:370-75. For critical problems associated with this text, see Bickel, 288-372; Trillitzsch, 1:145-51; Trillitzsch, "Hieronymus und Seneca," *Mittellateinisches Jahrbuch* 2 (1965): 42-54; and Lausberg, 1 n. 2. (The discussion in Henrion, 146-53, is uninformed by Bickel.) Zeller, 3.1.750, believes this treatise, nonetheless, gave a positive evaluation of marriage.

87. Seneca, *De matrimonio,* in Jerome, *Adversus Jovinianum* 1.48, trans. Fremantle, in Schaff and Wace, 384; cf. Seneca, *De otio* 3.2. On Epicurus see above, n. 49.

allotted to whatever time is left over from the pursuit of philosophy, not the other way around.[88] In one of his dialogues he even complains of how much of a man's life is wasted in dealing with a mistress and arguing with a wife, stating that this time should be dedicated to philosophy.[89] But Seneca can also take a clear stand against the Cynic notion that philosophy and marriage are mutually exclusive. In his ninth epistle, arguing on the basis of the advantages that accrue from marriage, he maintains that the self-sufficiency required to give a man the time and the peace of mind to pursue philosophy is fully compatible with the responsibilities involved with marriage and raising children, relationships to which the philosopher is drawn by natural impulse.[90] Consistent with this, in his ninety-fourth epistle he demonstrates a knowledge of the theory of household management, which he assigns to an important category of philosophical precepts.[91]

In the final analysis, what we see reflected here is an ambiguity in Seneca's thought to which scholars have drawn attention especially in regard to his political theory.[92] In our terminology, Seneca's ambivalence displays the dynamics of the inner-Stoic debate on marriage. He is being drawn in two directions, one "Stoic" and one "Cynic" — options made possible by the very dissonance in Stoicism itself. On the one hand Seneca is mindful of his civic responsibilities, including marriage; on the other he lists to the higher calling of the philosophical life, a life which identifies him as a citizen of the world, responsible only to the world community.[93]

---

88. Seneca, *Epistles* 72.3-4; 53.9; cf. 64.6.

89. Seneca, *De brev. vit.* 3.2; 7.2; 14.2.

90. Seneca, *Epistles* 9.17-19.

91. Seneca, *Epistles* 94.1, 3, 15; on this see Balch, *Let Wives Be Submissive*, 51. Another Latin work from this period that shows knowledge of the literature on household management is Columella, *On Agriculture* 1.4.8–9.9 (ca. 60-65 C.E.).

92. E.g., Griffin, 315-66; Pohlenz, *Die Stoa*, 1:313-15; Pohlenz, *Freedom*, 147-49; and Grilli, 217-78. While the dialogues are earlier than the letters, there does not seem to be a consistent development in Seneca's thought on participation in either politics or marriage; see Griffin, 316-17, 334, 339.

93. Seneca's anecdote involving Epicurus (cited above, n. 49) suggests that he was aware of the classification of marriage as an "indifferent." See also Seneca, *De otio* 6.4-6; 8.1-4; *Epistle* 68.2; *De brev. vit.* 13.8–14.5.

Musonius Rufus

The ambiguities apparent in Seneca are completely absent from his contemporary and fellow Stoic philosopher Musonius Rufus (fl. middle to late first century C.E.). This is because, unlike Seneca, Musonius is untouched by cosmopolitan ideals in his thinking on marriage. As with Antipater and Ocellus before him, Musonius defines a man's allegiances and loyalties against the backdrop of a *kosmos* that is a collectivity of city-states. Man's nature, he maintains — his divinely sanctioned place in the *kosmos* — is that of a citizen, morally obligated to look after the affairs of his city-state. He must live with a wife, raise children, and establish a household. And for Musonius this rule would seem to have no exceptions.[94]

In line with these beliefs he devotes an entire treatise to refuting the (Cynic) claim that the philosopher cannot marry. His thesis is that a philosopher is no more and no less than a teacher and example of what is in accordance with nature's divine will; and if anything is in accordance with nature, and thus the business of the philosopher, it is marriage.[95] As an example, Musonius cites the early Cynic philosopher Crates, who despite hardships fulfilled this philosopher's duty. He also presents several arguments for the "naturalness" of marriage. He maintains that the Creator formed men and women with the intention that they join together in marriage; he claims that men's gregarious nature urges them to live together in city-states and act as responsible citizens, insuring stability and growth through stable households and procreation; and he points out that major gods of the Greek pantheon patronize the institution of marriage.[96] Beyond this, Musonius makes use of the ethical categories outlined in Arius. He refers several times to marriage as "appropriate" and "fitting,"[97] and he praises a wife's love for her husband as one of life's natural advantages.[98] In another treatise he develops the kindred notion, seen already in Antipater, that marriage is a beautiful relationship, characterized by the uncommon closeness of its partners.[99]

---

94. Musonius, frag. 14.92.33-8; 94.33–96.4; frag. 15.96.12-26 L. (73.8-15; 76.1-11; 77.6–78.6 H.).

95. Musonius, frag. 14, *Is Marriage an Impediment to the Pursuit of Philosophy?* see 14.92.6-9; 94.32–96.8 L. (71.7-11; 75.20–76.17 H.); cf. frag. 11.82.34-7 L. (60.19–61.2 H.).

96. Musonius, frag. 14.90.26–92.4 L. (70.14–71.5 H.); frag. 14.92.9–94.32 L. (71.11–75.20 H.).

97. προσήκειν, Musonius, frag. 14.92.17; 94.32, 33; 96.3, 4, 7 L. (72.4; 75.20, 21; 76.10, 12, 15 H.); προσῆκον, frag. 14.92.8 L. (71.10 H.); πρέπει, frag. 14.96.6 L. (76.15 H.).

98. Musonius, frag. 14.94.2-19 L. (73.17–75.5 H.).

99. Musonius, frag. 13A; see the discussion in Foucault, *Care of the Self,* 151-53.

Finally, Musonius's conviction that a man is morally obligated to marry, whether he is a layman or philosopher, is reflected in several writings devoted to the topics of choosing a capable wife,[100] family planning, and household management. As for family planning, Musonius maintains that sexual intercourse should be practiced only within marriage and only for the purpose of procreation, arguing further that all children who are born should be raised.[101] According to him, children are natural advantages to the wise man,[102] while abortion and the exposure of infants are an affront to the divine plan.[103] As for household management, in his treatise *That Women, Too, Should Pursue Philosophy* he again argues that there is no contradiction between marriage and philosophy, saying that household management is a "virtue" (ἀρετή) and that women who study philosophy can only become better guardians of the home.[104]

Quintilian, Theon, and Dio Chrysostom

Contemporary with Musonius are three orators who give us a sense of the considerable popularity the Stoic-Cynic marriage debate had achieved by the end of the first century c.e.[105] Their works witness to the fact that both Greek and Roman rhetorical schools had taken account of the debate in their discussions of the various strategies of argumentation common to philosophers

100. Musonius, frag. 13B.

101. Musonius, frag. 15 L. (15A-B H.).

102. Musonius, frag. 15.98.1-17; 100.2-16 L. (78.14–79.13; 80.11–81.13 H.).

103. Musonius, frag. 15.96.12–98.1 L. (77.4–78.14 H.). See the suggestion in Keith Hopkins, "A Textual Emendation in a Fragment of Musonius Rufus: A Note on Contraception," *CQ*, n.s., 15 (1965): 72-74, that Musonius's denunciation of childlessness (ἀτοκία) at frag. 15.96.20 L. (15A.77.13 H.) should be read as a condemnation of "contraceptives" (ἀτόκια).

104. Musonius, frag. 3.40.8–42.29 L. (9.17–13.3 H.). Concerning division of labor in the household, see frag. 4.44.13-14; 46.13-31 L. (14.9-11; 16.15–17.17 H.). Cf. Philodemus's report that wives, under the effects of Cynic philosophy, desert their husbands and go off with whom they choose (Philodemos, Περὶ Στωϊκῶν, *P. Herculaneum* 339, col. IX, lines 5-12 Crönert [p. 64]). Similarly, Lucian, *Fugitivi* 18, satirizes philosophers who seduce wives of others under the pretense of making them philosophers.

105. Plutarch is a fourth writer from this period who seems to know something about the debate, especially on the issue of the compatibility of philosophy and marriage. See Plutarch, *Moralia* 750C; 751E; 770A (*Amatorius*); 138B-C (*Coniugalia praecepta*); 493C, E (*De amore prolis*); 1035B-C (*De Stoic. repug.*); and Dicaearchus, frag. 29 W. (*Codex Vaticanus* 435), attributed to "the *Roman Sayings* of Plutarch or Caecilius" (cited above, n. 47). See also above, n. 2.

and statesmen.[106] Thus the standard rhetorical manuals of Quintilian (ca. 35–ca. 95) and Theon of Alexandria (fl. middle to late first century?) make frequent use of the question "Should one marry?" in their treatments of theses, and they discuss civic responsibility, procreation, and marriage in terms reminiscent of Stoic and Cynic authors.[107] The third orator, Dio Chrysostom (ca. 40–ca. 120), gives much the same picture in his now fragmentary discourse *On Peace and War.* Introducing marriage, the establishment of a household, and participation in local politics under the Stoic heading of "fitting actions,"[108] he reviews the way philosophers, as opposed to rhetoricians, handle these matters, describing strategies identical to what we find in Theon.[109] Dio

---

106. On this development see Praechter, 141-48.

107. On this development see Pohlenz, *Die Stoa*, 1:246. See, e.g., Theon, *Progymnasmata* 123.6-10; 125.9-20 S.: "For the sake of a model, let us take some beginning *thesis* from the category of practical *theses*, such as whether a wise man engages in politics. Now the person preparing to argue that it is necessary to engage in politics should say first that it is possible for the wise man to engage in politics; second, that it is in accordance with nature. . . . It is possible to bring to bear on the proposed *thesis* arguments based on examples of these things which are prior to the matter at hand, and which are contemporaneous with the very matter, and which come after the matter; but they will be clearer when brought to bear on other *theses*, such as whether one should have children. For taking marriage and generally everything that must exist prior to having children, we will commend them, showing them to be good (καλά), and beneficial (συμφέροντα), and pleasant, and whether, next, they go hand in hand with having children; then, after these, the positive consequences of having children, such as care and attention in one's old age, and the benefits and pleasures of children, and the like. For the refutation of this *thesis* we have at our disposal the opposites of these points." See also 120.12–121.17 and 128.3-21 S.; and Quintilian 2.4.24-5; 3.5.8, 12, 13, 16. On the *progymnasmata* literature and Theon, see Roland F. Hock and Edward N. O'Neil, eds., *The Chreia in Ancient Rhetoric*, vol. 1, *The "Progymnasmata,"* SBLTT 27/SBLGRS 9 (Atlanta: Scholars, 1986), 10-22, 63-66. Willy Stegemann, "Theon, 5," in *PW*, 2nd ser., 5/2 [half-vol. 10] (1934), 2047, wrongly maintains that the theses εἰ γαμητέον and εἰ παιδοποιητέον are out of place in the *progymnasmata* literature. For a correct assessment see H. I. Marrou, *A History of Education in Antiquity*, Wisconsin Studies in Classics (Madison: University of Wisconsin Press, 1982), 201; John Barns, "A New Gnomologium: With Some Remarks on Gnomic Anthologies," *CQ*, n.s., 1 [mistakenly 45] (1951): 13. Concerning the question of the compatibility of philosophy and marriage in Quintilian, see 12.1.5, 8; 11.1.35; 12.2.7; 1.6.36. A translation of Theon is available in James R. Butts, "The Progymnasmata of Theon: A New Text with Translation and Commentary" (Ph.D. diss., Claremont Graduate School, 1986); and George A. Kennedy, trans., *Progymnasmata: Greek Textbooks of Prose Composition and Rhetoric*, Writings from the Greco-Roman World, 10 (Atlanta: Society of Biblical Literature, 2003), 1-72.

108. Dio Chrysostom, *Oration* 22.1-3, περὶ τοῦ προσήκοντος; cf. 26.8.

109. Dio Chrysostom, *Oration* 22.3-4.

also shows knowledge of several arguments in favor of marriage used by Stoics,[110] and he is the author of a treatise titled *Household Management.*[111]

Hierocles the Stoic and Epictetus

Around the end of the first and the beginning of the second century, two further authors supply us with substantial materials from the Stoic-Cynic marriage debate. These are Hierocles the Stoic and Epictetus, the latter a student of Musonius Rufus. For the most part Hierocles (fl. early second century) stands squarely in the tradition of Antipater, Ocellus, and Musonius. He holds the conviction that a man has a moral obligation to a higher order, and that this obligation is defined by the fact that a man is a citizen of a city-state. There is no one, he claims in his *Elements of Ethics,* who is not part of a city-state.[112] As for marriage, it is the beginning of the city-state, being the "first and most elementary" partnership, for marriages produce households and households constitute city-states.[113] A man's moral duty is thus clear: he must marry, establish a household, and thereby ensure the future of his city-state.[114] This is nature's will,[115] and consequently what is "fitting"[116] for a man. Quite in accord with this perspective, a large portion of Hierocles' treatise *On Marriage* is devoted to reviewing the natural advantages of marriage — a wife, children, and the marriage relation itself. A wife and children, he states, lighten a man's burdens and

---

110. Dio Chrysostom, *Oration* 7.135; cf. 7.34, 50 (on the depopulation of the city-states).

111. Dio Chrysostom, frags. 4-9, assembled from Stobaeus in J. W. Cohoon and H. Lamar Crosby, eds. and trans., *Dio Chrysostom,* LCL (London: William Heinemann; Cambridge: Harvard University Press, 1951), 5:348-51. Cf. Dio Chrysostom, *Oration* 69.2. On the possibility that Dio was a student of Musonius, see Pohlenz, *Die Stoa,* 2:146.

112. οὐδεὶς γὰρ ἄνθρωπος ὃς οὐχὶ πόλεώς ἐστι μέρος, Hierocles, ἠθικὴ στοιχείωσις, col. 11, lines 15-16 (p. 43) von Arnim. On the contrasting notion of *oikeiosis* in Hierocles, see Pembroke, 125-27; and Parente, "Ierocle Stoico."

113. Hierocles 52.15-21 v. A. (Stobaeus 4.502.1-7 W.-H.). This is from his treatise *On Marriage,* the fragments of which have been assembled from Stobaeus by Hans von Arnim, *Hierokles ethische Elementarlehre,* Berliner Klassikertexte 4 (Berlin: Weidmann, 1906), 52-56. An English translation is available in Abraham J. Malherbe, *Moral Exhortation: A Greco-Roman Sourcebook,* Library of Early Christianity (Philadelphia: Westminster, 1986), 100-104.

114. Hierocles 56.21-32 v. A. (Stobaeus 4.604.27–605.16 W.-H.).

115. Hierocles 52.28–53.12; cf. 54.20-21 v. A. (Stobaeus 4.502.15–503.10; 4.505.12-14 W.-H.).

116. Hierocles 52.26-27; 53.3, 11 v. A. (Stobaeus 4.502.13-14; 4.502.22, 503.9 W.-H.).

make his life safer and more pleasant.[117] Like Antipater and Musonius, Hierocles also praises the extraordinary partnership by which husband and wife agree to hold all things in common, even each other's body and soul.[118] Again like Antipater, he marvels at those who consider a wife or married life burdensome. They only seem so to those who marry for the wrong reasons and find themselves unprepared for the responsibilities of being a hus-band,[119] a situation he seeks to rectify in a treatise on household manage-ment.[120]

Thus far there is little new in Hierocles. But Hierocles deviates from his predecessors in two respects. First, unlike Musonius, he does not insist that every child that is born must be raised. Rather, he says simply that it is in ac-cord with nature to raise "all *or at least most*" of one's offspring.[121] Second, he attends to an aspect of Stoic systematic ethics passed over by Antipater and Musonius. As we have seen, this ethical program describes marriage as a "fit-ting" action for human beings, but which, depending on circumstances, en-genders either advantages or disadvantages in one's life. Antipater and Musonius, however, spoke only of the advantages arising from married life, giving no indication that there might be circumstances in which it would be disadvantageous to marry. In fact, Musonius may have excluded this possibil-ity altogether, for he insists that even extreme poverty is not a circumstance which impedes marrying.[122] By contrast, Hierocles discusses such adverse circumstances with respect to both the layman and the philosopher. In a trea-tise entitled *On Households,* he states that marriage is to be preferred by the wise man "except in special circumstances (κατὰ περίστασιν)"; and, he con-

---

117. Hierocles 53.20–54.14; 55.16-20, 27-28 v. A. (Stobaeus 4.503.20–505.4; 4.506.26–507.5; 4.603.15-18 W.-H.).

118. Hierocles 54.14-27 v. A. (Stobaeus 4.505.5-22 W.-H.).

119. Hierocles 54.27–55.20 v. A. (Stobaeus 4.505.22–507.5 W.-H.).

120. Hierocles 62.21–63.30 v. A.; cf. 52.23 (Stobaeus 4.696.21–699.15; 4.502.9 W.-H.). English translation in Malherbe, *Moral Exhortation,* 98-99. On this treatise see Praechter, 64-66; on its original title see Philippson, 101, 103; and for a comparison between Hierocles and Seneca, *Epis-tle 94,* see 107-9.

121. Hierocles 55.22-24 v. A. (Stobaeus 4.603.9-12 W.-H.).

122. Musonius, frag. 15.98.17-27 L. (79.13 H. — only the very beginning of this passage ap-pears in the Hense ed.); cf. 14.92.1-4 L. (71.1-5 H.). For a comparison between Musonius and Hierocles, see Praechter, 5-6. On poverty and marriage, see also the two maxims attributed to Menander: "O thrice ill-fated, whoever being poor marries and has children!" (Stobaeus 4.514.11-12 W.-H.; frag. 335 Körte); "Whoever, being poor, wants to live pleasurably, let him keep away from marriage while others marry" (Stobaeus 4.519.7-9 W.-H.; frag. 576 K.).

tinues, "since we should imitate the man of intellect in those things we can, and marriage is preferred by him, it is evident that it would also be fitting for us except some circumstance prevent us."[123] Similarly, the Suidas lexicon reports that in book 2 of his *Philosophical Topics,* Hierocles "says with regard to the philosophers: 'Which of them did not marry, raise children, and manage property *when there was no obstacle?*'"[124]

In Hierocles, then, the moral duty of a man to marry and raise children has been relativized in comparison with the positions taken by Antipater and Musonius. Here, once again, we sense the dynamics of the inner-Stoic debate on marriage, for as Cicero explained, it was precisely on this matter of "circumstances" that some Stoics made the decision to follow Cynics in the rejection of marriage. Just how far a Stoic could relativize the importance of marriage on this basis will be made clear by our examination of Epictetus.

With the Stoic philosopher Epictetus (ca. 50–ca. 135) we reach a new level of sophistication in the Stoic-Cynic marriage debate. Like others in this debate, he addresses whether a man should take on the responsibilities of married life in the context of his moral obligations to a higher, divine order. Unlike them, however, he chooses to argue both for and against marriage, depending on whether he understands a man's primary allegiance as being to the individual city-state or to the *kosmos* as a whole. In this way his writings develop both sides of the inner-Stoic marriage debate, integrating Stoic and Cynic positions on marriage into one philosophical system.

The Stoic vision of a *kosmos* consisting of city-states, households, and marriages is very much in evidence in Epictetus's thinking, and as a consequence he, like Stoics before him, concludes that human existence as ordained by nature derives its meaning from men identifying themselves as citizens of city-states. Accordingly, he counts marriage and having children as part of the "purpose" or "business at hand" in a man's life, since these contribute to the fundamental well-being of the city-state.[125] This comes out, for example, in his caricature of the Epicurean vision of the city-state, in which marrying

---

123. Hierocles 52.23-27 v. A. (Stobaeus 4.502.9-14 W.-H.), trans. Malherbe, *Moral Exhortation,* 100. See the discussion in David L. Balch, "1 Cor 7:32-35 and Stoic Debates about Marriage, Anxiety, and Distraction," *JBL* 102 (1983): 434.

124. μηδενὸς ἐμποδὼν ὄντος, Suidas, s.v. "ἐμποδών (1)" (emphasis mine). This text is available in Praechter, 318, and in von Arnim, *Elementarlehre,* 64. On the *Philosophical Topics,* see Philippson, 107-12, 113; and Praechter, 10.

125. ἡ πρόθεσις and τὸ προκείμενον, respectively; Epictetus, *Discourses* 2.23.37-38. See also 3.21.5-6.

and raising of children are absent. "Where are the citizens [for this city-state] to come from?" he chides, maintaining that these two tasks are among the "preferred things" of life.[126] Epictetus seems to have been relatively well known for holding this position, moreover, for he is thus depicted in an anecdote that circulated not long after his death. As the satirist Lucian recounts, Epictetus once confronted the Cynic Demonax with the admonition to marry and raise children, saying, "this also is fitting for a man who pursues philosophy, namely, to leave behind for nature another in his place."[127]

But scratch Epictetus and you will not find his teacher Musonius. Like Hierocles, he recognized that certain conditions made it impossible for a man to marry and at the same time meet his moral obligations to nature and the gods.[128] He names two instances of this in passing in his *On the Cynic Life,* one of his longest discourses. They involve situations in which a man's energies are taken up by scholarship or the fulfillment of military duty.[129] A third instance, to which he devotes nearly a sixth of this discourse, involves a figure he calls the Cynic, whom he envisions as something of a philosopher's philosopher, called for a special mission by God.[130]

In this discussion of the Cynic's position on marriage, the initial question Epictetus seeks to answer is, Should the Cynic, like other men, choose marriage as a "preferred" indifferent?[131] Here, as earlier, we see clear reference to the categories of Stoic ethics. But as Epictetus proceeds, using further catego-

---

126. Epictetus, *Discourses* 3.7.19-28, τὰ προηγούμενα. At 3.7.20 he says Epicurean beliefs are "disruptive of the city-state, destructive of households" (ἀνατρεπτικὰ πόλεως, λυμαντικὰ οἴκων). See also 1.23.3-7; 2.20.20; and Heinrich Greeven, *Das Hauptproblem der Sozialethik in der neueren Stoa und im Urchristentum,* NTF, 3rd ser., 4 (Gütersloh: C. Bertelsmann, 1935), 121.

127. Lucian, *Demonax* 55, πρέπειν γὰρ καὶ τοῦτο φιλοσόφῳ ἀνδρὶ ἕτερον ἀντ' αὐτοῦ καταλιπεῖν τῇ φύσει.

128. E.g., Epictetus, *Discourses* 4.5.6. On this passage see Bonhöffer, 86. See also Long, 199; and Michel Spanneut, "Epiktet," in *RAC* 5.606-10.

129. Epictetus, *Discourses* 3.22.79.

130. Epictetus, *Discourses* 3.22.67-82. Too often the position on marriage Epictetus attributes to his Cynic is taken to be normative for Epictetus, e.g.: William Klassen, "Musonius Rufus, Jesus, and Paul: Three First-Century Feminists," in *From Jesus to Paul: Studies in Honour of Francis Wright Beare,* ed. Peter Richardson and John Coolidge Hurd (Waterloo, Ontario: Wilfrid Laurier University Press, 1984), 196, cf. 190-91; Balch, "Stoic Debates," 430-31; cf. Greeven, 123; and Bernhard Lohse, *Askese und Mönchtum in der Antike und in der alten Kirche,* Religion und Kultur der alten Mittelmeerwelt in Parallelforschungen 1 (Munich and Vienna: R. Oldenbourg, 1969), 66.

131. Epictetus, *Discourses* 3.22.67: γάμος δ' ἔφη, καὶ παῖδες προηγουμέμως παραληφθήσονται ὑπὸ τοῦ κυνικοῦ; cf. 3.22.76 and 3.14.7.

ries from this system, it is not without violence to these categories. In order to prove that a Cynic cannot marry, he essentially flips everything on its head. What holds true for the common man is wrong for the Cynic, and vice versa. Thus, Epictetus claims, the Cynic can marry *only* under "special circumstances."[132] In an ideal city-state, in which all are wise men and women, marriage is possible,[133] or when a Cynic falls passionately in love with a woman who is herself a Cynic. This was the case with Crates, Epictetus admits,[134] but Crates was a rare exception, not the rule, as Musonius had supposed.[135] Under "usual circumstances" the Cynic cannot view marriage as a "preferred" indifferent.[136]

The key to Epictetus's curious logic is his perception of society in his day. To his mind society stood "arrayed as for battle," a state of affairs in which common people were in need of moral guidance.[137] For this purpose God calls forth the Cynic, whose task it is to oversee society, showing people which things are good and which are bad.[138] This includes monitoring the doings of the dutiful householder, checking up on "those who have married, those who have had children."[139] For this same reason, however, the Cynic himself cannot marry. The adverse conditions that make his calling necessary require him to forgo the responsibilities of a husband, father, and householder. "In

132. Epictetus, *Discourses* 3.22.76. In this Epictetus comes very close to the positions held by Theophrastus and, especially, Epicurus.

133. Epictetus, *Discourses* 3.22.67-68. Early Stoics, as we saw, envisioned a community of wives in the ideal state. By the second century C.E., however, this notion, popularized through Plato's *Republic,* had come under strong criticism from many quarters: Epictetus, *Discourses* 2.4.8-10; frag. 15 Oldfather; Lucian, *Vitarum auctio* 17; *Fugitivi* 18; *Verae historiae* 2.19 (on this last see Ferguson, 174-76); Sextus Empiricus, *Outlines of Pyrrhonism* 3.205; Clement of Alexandria, *Stromateis,* bk. 3, chap. 2.10.2 (2.200.16-20 Stählin); bk. 3, chap. 2.5.1 (2.197.16-18 S.). This last has reference to a gnostic treatise *On Righteousness* by Epiphanes (fl. early second century). On Clement see Paul Wendland, *Quaestiones Musonianae: De Musonio Stoico Clementis Alexandrini Aliorumque Auctore* (Berlin: Mayer und Mueller, 1886), 14-15.

134. Epictetus, *Discourses* 3.22.76. Cf. the *Cynic Epistle of Crates* 1 and 28-33; *Greek Anthology* 7.413 (attributed to Antipater of Sidon, fl. 120 B.C.E.).

135. Praechter, 5 n. 1, calls Epictetus's use of Crates "almost like a polemic against his teacher." But cf. *Discourses* 4.1.159, where Epictetus is very close to Musonius.

136. Epictetus, *Discourses* 3.22.76, τῶν κοινῶν γάμων καὶ ἀπεριστάτων.

137. Epictetus, *Discourses* 3.22.69, ὡς ἐν παρατάξει. Cf. Philo's description of a "peacetime war" (κατ' εἰρήνην πόλεμος) in *Quod omnis probus liber sit* 34.

138. Epictetus, *Discourses* 3.22.72, 77. On the Cynic's divine appointment see Epictetus 3.22.2, 23, 53, 69; 4.8.31; *Encheiridion* 7.

139. Epictetus, *Discourses* 3.22.72, τοὺς γεγαμηκότας, τοὺς πεπαιδοποιημένους.

these present circumstances," Epictetus explains, marriage presents the Cynic with too many disadvantages — obligations to his in-laws and to his wife,[140] and the endless responsibilities involved in raising children, which Epictetus recounts at length: "he must get a kettle to heat water for the baby, for washing it in a bath-tub; wool for his wife when she has had a child; oil, a cot, a cup (the vessels get more and more numerous); not to speak of the rest of his business, and his distraction (τὴν ἄλλην ἀσχολίαν, τὸν περισπασμόν)." "Where, I beseech you," he despairs, "is left now . . . the man who had leisure for the public interest (ὁ τοῖς κοινοῖς προσευκαιρῶν)?"[141]

In better times a wife and in-laws would also have the Cynic's wisdom, children would be raised accordingly,[142] and there might not even be a need for the Cynic's profession.[143] But "given such conditions as prevail," Epictetus argues, the Cynic must keep himself "free from distraction" (ἀπερίσπαστος) and "wholly devoted to the service of God."[144] Can there be any free time (σχολή), he asks, for the man tied down to his own wife, children, and household affairs? While these things are "fitting" for the common man, they are nonetheless private duties,[145] and the Cynic's task involves grander issues.[146] He must show the common man where to look for true happiness and serenity precisely by *not* being married.[147] For this reason, and in contrast to Musonius's ideal of a philosopher, Epictetus's Cynic has much more of a "do as I say, not as I do" attitude: "'Look at me,' he says, 'I am without a home, without a city, without property. . . . I have neither wife nor children. . . . Yet what do I lack? . . . am I not free?'"[148] In this way the Cynic's calling takes precedence over the responsibilities of married life. Rather than concerning himself with raising a few "ugly-snouted" children of his own, he must look

140. Epictetus, *Discourses* 3.22.70, 76.

141. The tirade continues, peppered with belittling diminutives: "Come, doesn't he have to get little cloaks for the children? Doesn't he have to send them off to a school-teacher with their little tablets and writing implements, and little notebooks; and, besides, get the little cot ready for them?"; Epictetus, *Discourses* 3.22.70-72, 74, trans. W. A. Oldfather, *Epictetus: The Discourses as Reported by Arrian, the Manual, and Fragments,* LCL (Cambridge: Harvard University Press; London: William Heinemann, 1959), 2:155, 157.

142. Cf. *Cynic Epistle of Crates* 33.

143. Epictetus, *Discourses* 3.22.67-68; cf. Long, 205.

144. Epictetus, *Discourses* 3.22.69; cf. *Encheiridion* 15.

145. Epictetus, *Discourses* 3.22.74, καθήκουσιν ἰδιωτικοῖς.

146. Cf. Seneca, *De otio* 4.1-2; 6.4-5.

147. τὴν εὐδαιμονίαν καὶ ἀταραξίαν, Epictetus, *Discourses* 4.8.30-31.

148. Epictetus, *Discourses* 3.22.47-48, trans. Oldfather, 2:147.

upon all of society as his household — they are his children and he is their father.[149] And that is responsibility enough.[150]

Epictetus's presentation of his ideal philosopher includes much that we
have identified as belonging to the Cynic attitude toward marriage. It speaks
of marriage as impeding the work of the philosopher (the philosopher par excellence), and advocates his need for "free time"; it expresses something of
the Cynic disdain for the nonphilosophical population of the world in its remarks that belittle the rearing of children; and above all, it employs the name
"Cynic" for this extraordinary philosopher. It is not Cynic, however, but a
Stoicized Cynic. In the final analysis we must regard it as a compromise between Stoic and Cynic positions on marriage, between allegiance to the traditional values of the Greek city-state and the wholesale rejection of these values in favor of philosophy.[151] While Epictetus has succeeded in alleviating his
ideal philosopher — and himself, evidently[152] — of the responsibilities of
marriage, he has not made this into a general principle. Unlike the Cynics, he
does not espouse a radical cosmopolitanism that promotes complete freedom
from all social institutions.[153] Rather, he continues to affirm the Stoic belief
that the civilized world reflects a divine plan and that every man is morally
obligated to lend his support to the divine plan through marriage and raising
children. The one exception to this rule is the "Cynic," although this figure
also pledges his allegiance to this plan, being appointed by "special dispensa-
tion" as God's servant to oversee the workings of the whole.[154]

The Middle of the Second Century and Beyond

The teachings of Epictetus may in fact mark the culmination of the Stoic-
Cynic marriage debate. While the debate continues beyond the middle of the

149. Epictetus can also speak of God as the father and householder (οἰκοδεσπότης) of human society, and the Cynic as his representative, e.g., *Discourses* 3.22.1-8.

150. Epictetus, *Discourses* 3.22.77-82; see also 3.22.54, 96.

151. See Deißner, *Das Idealbild des stoischen Weisen.*

152. Lucian, *Demonax* 55.

153. Cf. the description of "mild Cynicism" in Malherbe, "Self-Definition," 56-57.

154. The phrase comes from R. D. Hicks, *Stoic and Epicurean,* Epochs of Philosophy (New
York: Charles Scribner's Sons, 1920), 138. On the Stoic aspects of Epictetus's Cynic, see Karl Suso
Frank, *Grundzüge der Geschichte des christlichen Mönchtums,* Grundzüge 25 (Darmstadt:
Wissenschaftliche Buchgesellschaft, 1979), 5-6; Malherbe, "Self-Definition," 50, 194 n. 27; and
Margarethe Billerbeck, *Epiktet: Vom Kynismus,* Philosophia Antiqua 34 (Leiden: Brill, 1978), 132.

second century, our sources become increasingly scarce and there is little to suggest that later authors took up the debate with the same fervor as the earlier ones. A possible exception is Aelius Herodianus, an Alexandrian-born grammarian who served under the Stoic emperor Marcus Aurelius, and to whom the *Etymologicum Magnum* attributes the treatise *On Marriage and Life Together.* Unfortunately, the only remnant of this work is an etymology for the word "male."[155] Another possible exception is the philosopher Aurelianus Nicostratus (fl. mid–second century?), a portion of whose treatise *On Marriage* is preserved by Stobaeus. All that survives, however, is a passage instructing how to choose a wife and how to exercise prudence and self-control within marriage. To what degree it addressed other issues raised by the Stoic-Cynic debate is unclear.[156]

Aside from Herodianus and Nicostratus, we may point to three other authors from the middle to the late second century who provide information on the marriage debate. These are the rhetorician Hermogenes (fl. mid–second century), the satirist Lucian of Samosata (ca. 120-85), and the sophist Maximus of Tyre (ca. 125–ca. 185).[157] From Hermogenes we learn that the thesis "Should one marry?" (εἰ γαμητέον) continues to be used as an exercise in the rhetorical schools.[158] Lucian, in turn, makes brief allusion to Stoic and Cynic views on marriage in his anecdote on the exchange between Demonax and Epictetus, and in his parodies of Diogenes the Cynic.[159] And Maximus makes a similar allusion in reporting the philosophical heroism of Diogenes. According to Maximus, after Diogenes "stripped off all the encumbering cir-

---

155. περὶ γάμου καὶ συμβιώσεως, *Etymologicum Magnum*, s.v. "ἄρσην" (cited below, p. 201).

156. Stobaeus 4.536-39, 593-99 W.-H.

157. On the influence of the marriage debate and the literature on household management on the neo-Pythagorean literature, probably also to be dated to this period, see Zeller, 3.2.158; Wilhelm, "Die Oeconomica," esp. 182-83; Alfons Städele, *Die Briefe des Pythagoras und der Pythagoreer,* Beiträge zur klassischen Philologie 115 (Meisenheim am Glan: Anton Hain, 1980), 166-69, 253-55, 267-68, 280, 321; Holger Thesleff, ed., *The Pythagorean Texts of the Hellenistic Period,* Acta Academiae Aboensis, Humaniora 30/1 (Åbo, Finland: Åbo Akademi, 1965), 151-54; Armand Delatte, *Essai sur la politique pythagoricienne* (Liège and Paris, 1922; reprint, Geneva: Slatkine, 1979), 163-68; and David L. Balch, "Neopythagorean Moralists and the New Testament Household Codes," in *ANRW* 2.26.1 (1992), 380-411. On the dating of these documents, see Dassmann and Schöllgen, 819-20, and the notes in Städele. Also see the Christianized Pythagorean collection, the *Sentences of Sextus* (second century, Egypt?) 230b, 232, 235, 237.

158. Hermogenes, *Progymnasmata* 11.

159. Lucian, *Demonax* 55; *Vitarum auctio* 8-9; *Verae historiae* 2.18.

cumstances (τὰς περιστάσεις πάσας) and liberated himself from fetters," he ranged the world as free as a bird, "not expending free time (ἀσχολούμενος) on the concerns of the city-state, not being strangled by the raising of children, not shut in by marriage."[160]

In the early third century, in his account of Augustus's speech to the married and unmarried men of Rome in 9 C.E., the Roman historian Dio Cassius mentions several issues that are now familiar to us from the marriage discussions.[161] Again, at the end of that century or the beginning of the next, the author of *Ars rhetorica* informs us that the thesis "Should one marry?" was still one of the most commonly assigned rhetorical exercises in the *progymnasmata* curriculum.[162] We may see this firsthand, moreover, in the writings of Libanius (fourth century) and Aphthonius (late fourth to early fifth century), although by the time we reach the *Progymnasmata* of the latter, only the first few lines of his thesis εἰ γαμητέον really bear any resemblance to the earlier discussions.[163] Finally, again in the fourth century, the emperor Julian shows some awareness of certain elements of the marriage debate, as does the author of the *Amores* earlier in the century.[164]

First-Century Judaism and Early Christianity

Thus far we have traced the Stoic-Cynic marriage debate through pagan philosophical traditions. In this section we turn to Jewish and Christian sources, with the exclusion of 1 Corinthians. Our goal here is to demonstrate the extent to which this debate found a hearing in intellectual and cultural circles similar to those associated with Paul's ministry. While most, if not all, of the Christian sources we will examine were written after Paul's day, the earlier ones nonetheless provide examples of how readily Stoic and Cynic views on marriage could be integrated into early Christian belief systems, while the later ones document the church's eventual disaffection with Stoic views on marriage, a development that explains the later ascetic interpretation of 1 Corinthians 7. Regarding the

---

160. Maximus, *Philosophumena* 36.5 Hobein. See also 32.9 H.

161. Dio Cassius, *Roman History* 56.1-10.

162. [Dionysius of Halicarnassus] *Ars rhetorica* 2.1-2.

163. Libanius, *Progymnasmata* 13.1 (*Opera* 8.550-61 Foerster); Aphthonius, *Progymnasmata* 13, trans. Ray Nadeau, "The Progymnasmata of Aphthonius," *Speech Monographs* 19 (1952): 264-85; and Kennedy, 120-24. On Libanius see Praechter, 143-47. On still other rhetoricians, see 143, 147-48.

164. Julian, *Oration* 6.185c-d; [Lucian] *Amores* 19. For still other texts, see Praechter, 150.

Jewish sources, we will confine ourselves to three Hellenistic Jewish authors from the first century C.E., Philo, Pseudo-Phocylides, and Josephus.[165]

Philo of Alexandria

The Jewish philosopher Philo of Alexandria (fl. early first century) was an eclectic thinker who drew on several Greek philosophical traditions in the expression of his religious heritage. In his ethical theory, and particularly his political theory, Philo borrowed a considerable number of ideas from Stoicism.[166] His conception of the *kosmos* is similar to that which the Stoic marriage discussions presume. He envisions it as consisting of city-states made up of households, the basis for which is marriage. The "economics" or "management" (οἰκονομία) of both household and city-state, Philo insists, begins with marriage, for without a wife a man is imperfect and homeless, but with a wife he has time for the affairs of his city-state while she attends to the management of the household.[167]

The influence of the Stoic marriage discussions on Philo's thinking may further be seen in his concern that the household provide the city-state with future generations of city dwellers. He claims that the violation of Mosaic regulations concerning legal, productive marriages undermines the affairs of households and cities alike, and he condemns pederasty and the exposure of newborns as practices that lead to the destruction of the cities.[168] "All true servants of God," he explains, "will fulfill the law of nature regarding the procreation of children,"[169] while persons involved in unfruitful marriages are

165. For Jewish sources before and after the first century C.E., see below, n. 188, and chap. 3, n. 58.

166. Emil Schürer, *The History of the Jewish People in the Age of Jesus Christ (175 B.C.–A.D. 135),* vol. 3, pt. 2, rev. Geza Vermes, Fergus Millar, and Martin Goodman (Edinburgh: T. & T. Clark, 1987), 887-88; Ray Barraclough, "Philo's Politics: Roman Rule and Hellenistic Judaism," in *ANRW* 2.21.1 (1984), 493-97, 533-42; Max Pohlenz, "Philon von Alexandreia," in *Nachrichten der Akademie der Wissenschaften zu Göttingen, philologisch-historische Klasse* 4 (1942), 461-78; Michel Spanneut, *Permanence du stoïcisme: De Zénon à Malraux* (Gembloux: J. Duculot, 1973), 119-23; Paul Wendland, "Philo und die kynisch-stoische Diatribe," in *Beiträge zur Geschichte der griechischen Philosophie und Religion,* ed. Paul Wendland and Otto Kern (Berlin: Georg Reimer, 1895), 3-75.

167. Philo, *De Josepho* 29, 38-39 (on the latter see Goodenough, 43-44, 48-50); *Quaestiones et solutiones in Genesin* 1.26; 4.165.

168. Philo, *De specialibus legibus* 3.31; *De Abrahamo* 135-41; *De vita contemplativa* 62; *De virtutibus* 131-32.

169. Philo, *De praemiis et poenis* 108, νόμον φύσεως τὸν ἐπὶ παιδοποιίᾳ; cf. *De Decalogo* 119.

"enemies of nature," overturning her statues.[170] A recurring theme in his writings, moreover, is his insistence that the goal of marriage is the procreation of legitimate children, not sexual pleasure.[171]

One also sees the influence of the Stoic marriage discussions in Philo's conception of the wise man. Philo tells us that the wise man is by definition well suited to civic affairs as well as household management.[172] The dissemination of philosophical virtue results in better households and city-states because it produces men capable of managing these.[173] Indeed, Philo views the very practice of the duties of householder and citizen as "virtues."[174] Finally, in several of his writings Philo employs the Stoic categories of the "good man" and the "bad man." In interpreting Deuteronomy 28:6, "You shall be blessed in your coming in and you shall be blessed in your going out," Philo sees a reference to the good man (ὁ σπουδαῖος) being blessed as he fulfills his duties as statesman and householder. By contrast, in his treatise *On the Giants,* Philo speaks of the bad man (ὁ φαῦλος) as one who is without a home or city-state, and an exile.[175]

The Stoic conception of marriage as a primary responsibility for the man seeking to act in accord with the divine will has thus made significant impact on Philo's thought. But Philo, like Epictetus and certain other Stoics, also accommodates a number of Cynic ideas on marriage within his ethical theory. We observe this in his writings in two ways, in his personal code of ethics and in his description of two groups of Jewish philosophers. Just as Epictetus attributed several Cynic views on marriage to an exemplary philosophical type, the Cynic, Philo too attributes these views to those he considers model philosophers, the Essenes and the Therapeutae. Whether these philosophers actually existed in the manner Philo supposes is a difficult question to an-

---

170. Philo, *De specialibus legibus* 3.36, ἐχθροὶ τῆς φύσεως.

171. E.g., Philo, *De virtutibus* 207; *Quod deterius* 102, 171; *Quaestiones et solutiones in Genesin* 4.68, 154; *De Abrahamo* 248-49, 253; *De Josepho* 43; *De vita Mosis* 1.28.

172. Philo, *Quaestiones et solutiones in Genesin* 3.33; *De ebrietate* 91-92.

173. Philo, *De mutatione nominum* 149. See also *Hypothetica* 7.3, 14, and *De specialibus legibus* 3.169-75, which reflect knowledge of the literature on household management. Wolfgang Schrage, "Zur Ethik der neutestamentlichen Haustafeln," *NTS* 21 (1974): 8, also sees the influence of this literature in *De Decalogo* 165-67, but there is nothing in this passage that cannot be accounted for in terms of Philo's Jewish heritage. The same applies to Schrage's assessment of 4 Macc. 2:10-12 (Schrage, 8).

174. ἀρετῶν, Philo, *De fuga et inventione* 36; cf. Musonius, frag. 3.42.28 L. (13.1 H.), cited above.

175. Philo, *De praemiis et poenis* 113; *De gigantibus* 67; cf. *Quaestiones et solutiones in Genesin* 4.165; *De specialibus legibus* 3.1-3.

swer.[176] It is enough for us, however, to know that Philo's description of them reflects knowledge of the Stoic-Cynic marriage debate, and that this knowledge had currency among his readership.

Philo describes the Essenes in two tractates, the *Hypothetica* and *Every Good Man Is Free*, in which the Essenes are brought in as an example, this latter being a philosophical treatise very much in the Stoic and Cynic tradition.[177] According to Philo, the Essenes are philosophers[178] who pursue a communal lifestyle that is the "clearest proof of a perfected and abundantly happy life."[179] What makes this life possible is freedom from the passions and from sensual desire, which Philo calls "the only true and real freedom."[180] Regarding marriage, a subject to which he devotes more than a fifth of the *Hypothetica*, Philo tells us that the Essenes "astutely perceive marriage as that which alone or for the most part is likely to undo their communal life."[181] This is because marriage forces a man to do things hostile to communal living by awakening in him the passions from which the Essenes seek to escape. A wife, Philo explains, is a selfish, jealous, and seductive creature, and when children arrive, a man is forced by the constraints of nature to care for them, too.[182] In the minds of the Essenes, marriage subjects a man to obligations that destroy his chances of attaining the true and only real freedom, consigning him to slavery.[183]

176. See, e.g., Emil Schürer, *The History of the Jewish People in the Age of Jesus Christ (175 B.C.–A.D. 135)*, vol. 2, rev. Geza Vermes, Fergus Millar, and Matthew Black (Edinburgh: T. & T. Clark, 1979), 579-80, 593-97; John J. Collins, "Marriage, Divorce, and Family in Second Temple Judaism," in *Families in Ancient Israel*, ed. Leo Perdue et al. (Louisville: Westminster/John Knox, 1997), 130-35; and Lawrence H. Schiffman, *Reclaiming the Dead Sea Scrolls* (New York: Doubleday, 1995), 51-53, 127-43.

177. Philo, *Quod omnis probus liber sit* 62-63, 75-91; cf. 121-26, where "Diogenes the Cynic philosopher" is used as an example of the perfectly free man. On Stoic and Cynic influence in this text see Madeleine Petit, ed., *"Quod omnis probus liber sit": Introduction, texte, traduction et notes*, Les œuvres de Philon d'Alexandrie 28 (Paris: Éditions du Cerf, 1974), 39-42, 48-57, 68-78, 83-86, 110-14. See also Otto Hense, "Bio bei Philo," *Rh. Mus.*, n.s., 47 (1892): 219-40; Schürer, *History*, 3.2:856; and Stanley Kent Stowers, *The Diatribe and Paul's Letter to the Romans*, SBLDS 57 (Chico, Calif.: Scholars, 1981), 69: "*Quod omnis probus liber sit* comes closer to being a typical diatribe than any of Philo's other works. Aside from a handful of allusions to the Pentateuch it could have been written by a Stoic."

178. Philo, *Quod omnis probus liber sit* 80-83, 88.

179. Philo, *Quod omnis probus liber sit* 91; cf. 84, and *Hypothetica* 11.1.

180. Philo, *Hypothetica* 11.3-4; *Quod omnis probus liber sit* 76-79, 88, 91.

181. Philo, *Hypothetica* 11.14.

182. Philo, *Hypothetica* 11.14, 16.

183. Philo, *Hypothetica* 11.17.

To be sure, this description of the Essenes' stance on marriage owes much to Jewish wisdom literature's negative assessment of women.[184] But Philo's reference to the responsibilities of married life, especially in the context of a discussion about philosophical freedom, points in the direction of Cynic ideas from the Stoic-Cynic marriage debate. This complex of ideas is given fuller expression in Philo's description of yet another group of Jewish philosophers, the Therapeutae.[185]

Like the Essenes, the Therapeutae are philosophers who live the communal life in pursuit of perfect happiness.[186] They are "theoretically" oriented, Philo tells us, meaning that they consider the contemplative part of philosophy to be the "best and most godlike." As a consequence they devote their entire day to philosophical studies.[187] To accommodate this lifestyle they abandon all responsibilities related to marriage and the household, believing that concern for the necessities of life and managing property are at odds with philosophy since, among other things, these consume time, and conserving time is essential for the philosopher.[188] Beyond this, they also free themselves of their responsibilities to their city-states. Eschewing city life altogether, they live in a loose philosophical community in the countryside as "citizens of heaven and the world."[189]

---

184. See John Strugnell, "Flavius Josephus and the Essenes: *Antiquities* XVIII.18-22," *JBL* 77 (1958): 110; and, e.g., Eccles. 7:26-28; Sir. 47:14-19; *T. Reub.* 5:3; 6:1, 3.

185. Cf. Paul Wendland, "Die Therapeuten und die philonische Schrift vom beschaulichen Leben," in *Jahrbücher für classische Philologie*, suppl. 22 (1896), 703-4: "[Philo] sees the Stoic ideal of the simple life in accord with nature actualized in the life-style of the Therapeutae. . . . With this, his thoughts are moving completely in the sphere of the Stoic-Cynic diatribe." See also 705; and Wendland, "Philo und die kynisch-stoische Diatribe," 66-67.

186. Philo, *De vita contemplativa* 2.11; 3.24; 11.90. As with the Essenes, Philo states several times that the Therapeutae are philosophers; e.g., 3.21, 22, 26, 28, 30.

187. Philo, *De vita contemplativa* 8.67; 4.34.

188. Philo, *De vita contemplativa* 2.13-18 (here χρόνος). As Wendland, "Die Therapeuten," 748-50, correctly points out, the need for "free time" for philosophy or academic study is also a theme elsewhere in Jewish literature. See Sir. 38:24, "the wisdom of the scribe comes about in opportunity for leisure" (σοφία γραμματέως ἐν εὐκαιρίᾳ σχολῆς); *m. Ketubot* 5.6; *m. Eduyot* 4.10; *t. Bekorot* 6.10-11; *b. Megillah* 27a; *b. Ketubot* 62; *b. Bar. Kidd.* 29b; and especially the rabbinic material on Rabbi Simeon ben Azzai, *t. Yebamot* 8.7; *b. Yebamot* 63b; *b. Sota* 4b. On the possibility of Stoic or Cynic influence on these texts, see Henry A. Fischel, *Rabbinic Literature and Greco-Roman Philosophy*, SPB 21 (Leiden: Brill, 1973), esp. 4-9, 90-97; Fischel, "Studies in Cynicism and the Ancient Near East: The Transformation of a Chreia," in *Religions in Antiquity: Essays in Memory of Erwin Ramsdell Goodenough*, ed. Jacob Neusner, Numen Supplements 14 (Leiden: Brill, 1968), 372-411. Cf. chap. 3, n. 58.

189. Philo, *De vita contemplativa* 2.19; 3.22; 11.90.

In comparing these two basically Cynic positions on marriage, it is instructive to note that Philo presents the Therapeutae as the "contemplative" counterparts to the Essenes, who by contrast live the "active life."[190] Thus, while the exclusive devotion to philosophy and extreme cosmopolitanism of the Therapeutae bring them very close to the position on marriage we saw in the *Cynic Epistles of Diogenes,* the "active" philosophy of the Essenes places them close to those Stoics known to Cicero who adopted a Cynic stance on marriage. As Philo explains, their philosophy encourages them in the practical matters of household management and politics (οἰκονομία, πολιτεία), and — although Philo is inconsistent on this point — the Essenes seem to live in city-states.[191] Inasmuch as the Essenes manage their households without the benefit of a wife (a view also held by Josephus), they may even represent a position criticized by Antipater and Hierocles, since the latter speak against such households as being "incomplete."[192]

From our examination of Philo's writings thus far, it is evident that this author, like Epictetus, is able to accommodate several views on marriage from the Stoic-Cynic debate within his philosophical system. For this reason, however, like Seneca, he also verges on inconsistency. Despite pronounced Stoic leanings, some of Philo's own beliefs pertaining to an individual's responsibilities to the city-state "tend to underline and enlarge upon the key ideas in 'De Vita Contemplativa'"[193] — i.e., his description of the Therapeutae.

With regard to cosmopolitan beliefs, Philo is largely Stoic.[194] But inherent in his cosmopolitanism is a sense of alienation that also reflects Cynic, Jewish mystical, and Platonic attitudes toward the *kosmos,* leading him ultimately to favor the contemplative life over the active one.[195] In the area of political and ethical theory, Erwin Goodenough points to a "warfare between

190. Philo, *De vita contemplativa* 1.1, τῶν θεωρίαν ἀσπασαμένων versus τὸν πρακτικὸν βίον.

191. Philo, *Quod omnis probus liber sit* 72, 82-83; *Hypothetica* 11.1. Josephus, *Jewish War* 2.124, 125, also says they live in city-states.

192. Antipater (app. A), line 3; Hierocles 52.20; 53.15 v. A. (Stobaeus 4.502.5-6; 4.503.12 W.-H.). On Josephus see next section. With regard to the Therapeutae, Philo says the young men among them behave toward the older men and women "like genuine sons toward fathers and mothers" (*De vita contemplativa* 9.72).

193. Barraclough, 544; cf. Wendland, "Die Therapeuten," 747-48. See also Goodenough, 66-75.

194. See, e.g., Barraclough, 539.

195. Barraclough, 539-40; Wendland, "Die Therapeuten," 734; Ehrhardt, 204-5. At one point Philo even boasts that the Jewish people are the "contemplative race" (*Quaestiones et solutiones in Exodum* 2.42).

statesman and philosopher in Philo's own life,"[196] for while Philo promotes marriage, household management, and political activities, "he alternates bewilderingly between this attitude toward the state and another one, the ascetic and individualistic attitude, which seems to have originated with the Cynics and to have run through much of Stoic and Sceptic teaching."[197]

Thus Philo's positive stance toward marriage is qualified by the fact that his philosophical and religious allegiances are divided between a Stoic attitude which recognizes certain civic responsibilities to the *kosmos* and an attitude which envisions an even higher calling to a contemplative, spiritual life.[198] It is this latter attitude that comes to expression in the famous opening lines to book 3 of his *Special Laws,* bringing to mind the Cynic position in the Stoic-Cynic debate. Here in a sonorous, doleful lament, Philo speaks nostalgically of a period in his life when he had "leisure time for philosophy" (φιλοσοφίᾳ σχολάζων) and contemplation of the *kosmos,* before he found himself violently plunged into "a great ocean of civil cares."[199]

To some extent Philo attempts to account for these inconsistencies — this division of allegiance — by means of a temporal solution. The practical life of the householder and statesman, he says in his treatise *On Flight and*

196. Goodenough, 83.

197. Goodenough, 69. As Goodenough further remarks: "The interesting thing is that Philo strongly upholds both solutions of this problem, insisting that the philosopher's concern with the true state, the world, cut him off from obligation or concern with society, and then insisting just as heartily that this contact with the world-state puts the philosopher under special obligation to serve the human organization" (69; see also 70-75).

198. Cf. Barraclough, 550: "Philo is concerned for a life of contemplation for the individual, stability for society and the *status quo* for the Jews in the Roman Empire. The contemplative life surpasses but does not contradict the political life" — perhaps, but they are in the very least mutually exclusive. See Goodenough, 72 and n. 40, and the following discussion.

199. Philo, *De specialibus legibus* 3.1-3. Cf. Philo's description of Moses commanding those in his charge to dedicate themselves to leisure "for the sole purpose of pursuing philosophy": σχολάζοντας . . . μόνῳ τῷ φιλοσοφεῖν (*De vita Mosis* 2.211); ἑνὶ μόνῳ σχολάζοντας τῷ φιλοσοφεῖν (*De opificio mundi* 128) — both passages cited by Johann Jakob Wettstein, *Novum Testamentum Graecum* (Amsterdam: Dommerian, 1752; reprint, Graz, Austria: Akademische Druck- und Verlagsanstalt, 1962), 2:126. Similarly, Philo, *De praemiis et poenis* 122, speaks of the wise man devoting leisure time to discourses on wisdom and thereby achieving the blessed and happy life (ἐνσχολάσει τοῖς σοφίας θεωρήμασι, μακαρίας καὶ εὐδαίμονος ζωῆς ἐπιλαχών). Occasionally Philo, like his Therapeutae, even expresses an aversion toward the city-states: *De specialibus legibus* 2.42-47; cf. *De Decalogo* 2-13; *De ebrietate* 99-103 (one also finds this in Musonius, frag. 11.84.10-11 L. [61.15-16 H.]: . . . τῶν ἀστικῶν κακῶν, ἅπερ ἐμπόδιον τῷ φιλοσοφεῖν). On the political realities of Philo's day see Barraclough, 417-86; Schürer, *History,* 3.2:842-44.

Finding, must come before the contemplative one, as a preparation and prelude to it. There is no justification, he says a few lines earlier in this treatise, for those — perhaps Cynics known to him in Alexandria — who go around filthy and destitute, having chosen a solitary life from the first.[200] By this measure he also castigates the early Greek philosophers Anaxagoras and Democritus for showing so little concern for their household affairs as they rushed off in pursuit of philosophy. The Therapeutae, by contrast, dispose of their goods thoughtfully, exercising good household management to the last.[201] Finally, Philo indicates that the Essenes and Therapeutae have fulfilled their civic responsibilities before taking up philosophical pursuits, for not only do the Therapeutae have households to dispose of, but members of both groups leave behind children from former marriages.[202] Even so, Philo's temporal solution does not solve all the problems. Not all Essenes have fulfilled the duty of procreation, and among the Therapeutae there are young unmarried men and women.[203] In fact, as we have seen, Philo himself admits to engaging in politics *after* pursuing the contemplative life, albeit against his will. The divisions in Philo's allegiances thus remain, and as Goodenough remarks, "his very inconsistency is a reflection of the spirit of the age."[204]

Pseudo-Phocylides and Josephus

A contemporary of Philo and perhaps also from Alexandria,[205] the author known as Pseudo-Phocylides also gives us some indication of the influence the Stoic-Cynic marriage debates had on certain groups of Jews in the first century. In a collection of aphorisms he arranged in the form of a poem, this author includes a section that deals successively with three relationships: between husband and wife, between parents and children, and between a master and his slaves.[206] Not only does this reflect the general schema of the literature on

---

200. Philo, *De fuga et inventione* 36, 33.

201. Philo, *De vita contemplativa* 13-17. Cf. Philodemus's criticism of similar actions on the part of Cynics in his day, *On Household Management* col. 12-13.

202. Philo, *De vita contemplativa* 13, 18; *Hypothetica* 11.13; cf. 11.3.

203. Philo, *Hypothetica* 11.13; *De vita contemplativa* 8.67-68.

204. Goodenough, 73.

205. P. W. van der Horst, *The Sentences of Pseudo-Phocylides,* SVTP 4 (Leiden: Brill, 1978), 81-83.

206. Pseudo-Phocylides, *Sentences* 175-227.

household management, but as several scholars have noted, many of the aphorisms in the first group have close parallels in Stoic discussions on marriage.[207]

Finally, late in the first century the Jewish historian Josephus shows some knowledge of the marriage debate. In his description of Jewish marriage laws he attributes to Moses the Stoic dogma that procreation of legitimate children contributes to the welfare of the household and the city-state.[208] Similarly, in two other passages he upholds the Stoic position that the purpose of sexual relations is procreation, not pleasure.[209] Beyond this, Josephus offers a picture of the Essenes which, consistent with Philo's, depicts them as supporting a modified Cynic position on marriage. According to Josephus, they are philosophers who have found marriage incompatible with their way of life and have established the sort of quasi households that Antipater and Hierocles would have labeled "incomplete." In a passage that seems to parody the literature on household management, he explains that they live unmarried and provide each other with services, thereby eliminating the need for wives or slaves. As for children, the third subject treated by works on household management, Josephus tells us that they adopt the children of others and treat them as family, "thereby not abrogating the institution of marriage and the offspring that results from it."[210] In this last remark we see an Essene response to the Stoic concern for procreation. But not all Essenes, Josephus adds, were satisfied with this response, for some married, siding with the (Stoic) view that without marriage the race would die out. These, moreover, required their wives to undergo tests of fertility, and they never engaged in intercourse while their wives were pregnant — proof that they married for procreation, not lust.[211]

The New Testament

In comparison to the Jewish materials just examined, the influence exerted by the Stoic-Cynic marriage debate on Christian literature of the first and early

---

207. E.g., van der Horst, 225-44.

208. Josephus, *Antiquities* 3.274.

209. Josephus, *Jewish War* 2.161; *Against Apion* 2.199. On Josephus's awareness of the literature on household management, see *Against Apion* 2.201 and the discussions of this passage in Meeks, "Image of the Androgyne," 177 n. 67; and Wendland, "Die Therapeuten," 712.

210. Josephus, *Antiquities* 18.21; *Jewish War* 2.120-21.

211. Josephus, *Jewish War* 2.160-61.

second centuries appears to have been relatively meager. Even so, excluding for the moment 1 Corinthians 7, which we will examine in the next chapter, we can point to at least two texts from the New Testament that may demonstrate some awareness of this debate. The first is Matthew 19:10-12. Here the disciples of Jesus respond to his prohibition of divorce (19:3-9) with the surprising conclusion that it is "not beneficial to marry" (οὐ συμφέρει γαμῆσαι). What stands behind this conclusion may be their refusal to become permanently involved in the responsibilities of a husband and householder in light of what they perceive to be a higher calling, the kingdom of heaven.[212] If this is accurate, then their position can be understood as a variation of the Cynic position that marriage was an impediment to the higher calling of philosophy. Carrying this interpretation a step further, we may also speculate on Matthew's purpose in juxtaposing this passage, which is from his special material ("M"), to Jesus' prohibition of divorce, which he received from Mark. It is possible that Matthew sought to bring a particularly Christian understanding of marriage — that it is permanent — to bear on the marriage debate, thereby condemning the sort of solution adopted by Philo's Essenes and Therapeutae, who simply abandoned their wives, families, and domestic responsibilities for the philosophical life. From Luke, moreover, we have evidence that such a solution may have had its advocates in early Christian circles, too.[213]

A second passage from the New Testament that merits our attention is Luke 10:38-42. Here Jesus is invited to the house of a woman named Martha. While Martha is distracted (περιεσπᾶτο) by her duties as hostess, her sister Mary sits attentively at Jesus' feet listening to his discourse. When Martha complains that Mary should also be helping, Jesus tells her that while she is concerned (μεριμνάω) about many things, Mary has chosen "the good portion" (τὴν ἀγαθὴν μερίδα). In all, I do not think it is unreasonable to see in this passage a reflection of the question so central to the marriage debate, whether involvement in domestic affairs distracted one from pursuing philosophy.[214]

212. On the possible Stoic flavor of the term συμφέρει, see chap. 3, n. 373. The disciples' response is similarly construed by the followers of Basilides, an early second-century gnostic group. They claimed that Jesus' disciples took this position "on account of the circumstances arising from marriage (διὰ τὰ ἐκ τοῦ γάμου συμβαίνοντα)," "fearing the demands on their leisure time (ἀσχολία) associated with providing for the necessities of life" (Clement of Alexandria, *Stromateis*, bk. 3, chap. 1.1.4 [2.195.14-17 S.]).

213. See Luke 18:28-30.

214. Several scholars have compared the Lukan passage to Epictetus's discussion of marital responsibilities and the Cynic (*Discourses* 3.22.67-82). See, e.g., Archibald Robertson and Alfred

Although this question was usually posed about men, Musonius Rufus, as we have noted, poses it with regard to women in his tractate *That Women, Too, Should Pursue Philosophy.*[215] Such an interpretation of this passage is also suggested by Luke's use of the verbs "to be distracted" (περισπάομαι) and "to be concerned" (μεριμνάω), which parallel Stoic usage in the marriage debate.[216]

Besides these two passages, influence of the Stoic-Cynic marriage debate may be indicated by the presence in several early Christian writings of a form of moral exhortation known as the *Haustafel,* or household code.[217] Recent scholarship has concluded that these household codes, the aim of which was to order Christian lifestyles on the model of a well-ordered household, derive their basic structure from the Hellenistic literature on household management.[218] Given the interest many Stoics took in this literature, indirect avenues of influence between Christian discussions of the well-ordered house-

Plummer, *A Critical and Exegetical Commentary on the First Epistle of St. Paul to the Corinthians,* 2nd ed., ICC (Edinburgh: T. & T. Clark, 1914), 158; Werner Wolbert, *Ethische Argumentation und Paränese in 1 Kor 7,* Moraltheologische Studien, systematische Abteilung 8 (Düsseldorf: Patmos, 1981), 130-31; cf. Kurt Niederwimmer, *Askese und Mysterium: Über Ehe, Ehescheidung und Eheverzicht in den Anfängen des christlichen Glaubens,* FRLANT 113 (Göttingen: Vandenhoeck & Ruprecht, 1975), 113 n. 162. See also Epictetus, *Discourses* 1.29.59.

215. Musonius, frag. 3.40.8–42.29 L. (9.17–13.3 H.). See also the *Cynic Epistle of Crates* 30, 32, 33; and Diogenes Laertius 6.98 (regarding Crates' wife Hipparchia). Cf. 1 Tim. 2:11-15.

216. See below, pp. 195-200. See also the discussion of this passage in Gerd Theissen, *Sociology of Early Palestinian Christianity* (Philadelphia: Fortress, 1977), 10-17; cf. 88, and Theissen, *The Social Setting of Pauline Christianity: Essays on Corinth,* edited and introduction by John H. Schütz (Philadelphia: Fortress, 1982), 39, 44-49. It is worth noting that starting with Origen the church fathers saw Martha and Mary as examples of the "active life" and the "contemplative life," respectively. On this see Ignace de la Potterie, "Le titre ΚΥΡΙΟΣ appliqué à Jésus dans l'Évangile de Luc," in *Mélanges bibliques: En hommage au R. P. Béda Rigaux,* ed. Albert Descamps and André de Halleux (Gembloux: J. Duculot, 1970), 129 n. 2 (lit.).

217. Aside from the texts usually named in this connection (Col. 3:18–4:1; Eph. 5:21–6:9; 1 Tim. 2:8–6:2; Titus 1:5-9; 2:2-10; 1 Pet. 2:18–3:7; *1 Clement* 1.3; 21.6-8; *Didache* 4.9-11; *Epistle of Barnabas* 19.5-7; Ignatius, *Polycarp* 4.1–6.2; and Polycarp, *Philippians* 4.2–6.1), the following should also be considered: Matt. 13:52 (cf. Seneca, *Epistle* 64.7); Heb. 3:2-6; 1 John 2:12-14; and *perhaps* Rom. 13:1, 5.

218. See Balch, *Let Wives Be Submissive,* 23-121; Balch, "Household Codes," 25-50; Klaus Thraede, "Zum historischen Hintergrund der 'Haustafel' des NT," in *Jahrbuch für Antike und Christentum,* suppl. 8: *Pietas: Festschrift für Bernhard Kötting,* ed. Ernst Dassmann and K. Suso Frank (Münster: Aschendorff, 1980), 359-68; and the overviews in Ben Witherington III, *Women in the Earliest Churches,* SNTSMS 59 (Cambridge: Cambridge University Press, 1988), 42-47; Fiorenza, 72-74; Fiedler, esp. 1070-71; and David C. Verner, *The Household of God: The Social World of the Pastoral Epistles,* SBLDS 71 (Chico, Calif.: Scholars, 1983), 16-23, 84-91, cf. 91-111.

hold and Stoic and Cynic discussions on marriage should not be ruled out. This is especially true for the extended household code in 1 Timothy 2:8–6:2, which stresses the importance of marriage and procreation and denounces certain persons who object to marriage,[219] perhaps a type of gnostic.[220]

Second- and Third-Century Christian Apologists[221]

After the period of the New Testament, as Christianity came more and more in contact with mainstream Greco-Roman culture, Stoic and Cynic arguments for and against marriage became increasingly appealing to leaders of the church. As several scholars have noted, four apologetic writings from the middle of the second to the early third century present a point of view that is prominent in many Stoic marriage discussions.[222] The passages in question, *Epistle to Diognetus* 5.4-6;[223] Athenagoras, *Legatio* 33.1-2; Minucius Felix, *Octavius* 31.5; and Justin Martyr, *Apology* 1.27.1-3 and 29.1, all maintain that the sole purpose of marriage is the procreation of children. In addition, Justin, who admits familiarity with both Stoic and Cynic authors, and specifically with Musonius,[224] incorporates this viewpoint into his theology in a manner reminiscent of Matthew 19:10-12, claiming that Christians "would not marry in the first place except to raise children, or forgoing marriage we would live perfectly continent," for which he provides examples.[225] Regarding

219. 1 Tim. 5:14, βούλομαι οὖν νεωτέρας γαμεῖν, τεκνογονεῖν, οἰκοδεσποτεῖν, cf. 2:15; and 4:3, κωλυόντων γαμεῖν — cf. Epictetus, *Discourses* 3.22.68, οὐδὲν κωλύσει καὶ γῆμαι αὐτὸν καὶ παιδοποιήσασθαι, regarding the Cynic in a city of wise men.

220. See Martin Dibelius and Hans Conzelmann, *The Pastoral Epistles*, Hermeneia (Philadelphia: Fortress, 1972), 65-67. On the possibility that early gnostics were influenced by the Cynic marriage discussions, see below, nn. 243-44; cf. Jonas, 145, commenting on Clement's report on Marcion in *Stromateis*, bk. 3, chap. 4.25 (2.207.6-25 S.): "Here the pollution by the flesh and its lust, so widespread a theme in this age, is not even mentioned . . . it is the aspect of *reproduction* which disqualifies sexuality" (emphasis Jonas's).

221. For this and the following sections, see Noonan, 76-85.

222. See Preysing, 85-110; Stelzenberger, 417-19; and Herbert Preisker, *Christentum und Ehe in den ersten drei Jahrhunderten: Eine Studie zur Kulturgeschichte der alten Welt*, Neue Studien zur Geschichte der Theologie und der Kirche 23 (Berlin: Trowitzsch und Sohn, 1927; reprint, Aalen: Scientia, 1979), 179-80.

223. The *Epistle to Diognetus* may be as late as the third century.

224. Justin, *Apology* 2.3, 7-8; *Dialogue with Tryphon* 2.

225. Justin, *Apology* 1.29.1 and 1.15.4-6.

Athenagoras, Preysing has argued that this author's use of the terms παιδοποιΐα (childbearing) and παιδοποιεῖσθαι (to bear children), as well as the metaphor of a farmer sowing seed, indicate the proximity of this text to Stoic discussions.[226] And in the *Epistle to Diognetus* we sense the issue of cosmopolitanism, so prominent in the marriage debate: "[Christians] dwell in their own fatherlands, but as if sojourners in them; they share all things as citizens, and suffer all things as strangers. Every foreign country is their fatherland, and every fatherland is a foreign country. They marry as all men, they bear children, but they do not expose their offspring."[227]

Clement of Alexandria

With Clement of Alexandria, at the end of the second century, we are in the presence of a church father who exhibits broad learning in Greek philosophical traditions. His ethical thought especially is influenced by Stoic ideas, in particular through the teachings of Philo and Musonius, and therefore it is not surprising that he also demonstrates currency with the marriage debate.[228] In book 2, chapter 23 of his *Stromateis* ("Miscellanies"), for example, he gives a short synopsis of various Greek positions, including those of Plato, Democritus, Epicurus, the Stoics, and the Peripatetics.[229] Here he also identi-

---

226. Preysing, 97-100.

227. *Letter to Diognetus* 5.5-6, trans. Kirsopp Lake, *The Apostolic Fathers*, vol. 2, *The Shepherd of Hermas, the Martyrdom of Polycarp, the Epistle to Diognetus*, LCL (Cambridge: Harvard University Press; London: William Heinemann, 1913), 359, 361.

228. Regarding Stoic influence on Clement's view of marriage, see Max Pohlenz, "Klemens von Alexandreia und sein hellenisches Christentum," in *Nachrichten der Akademie der Wissenschaften zu Göttingen, philologisch-historische Klasse* 5.3 (1943), 144; Jean-Paul Broudéhoux, *Mariage et famille chez Clément d'Alexandrie*, Théologie Historique 11 (Paris: Beauchesne et ses Fils, 1970), 115-37. See also Michel Spanneut, *Le stoïcisme des Pères de l'Eglise de Clément de Rome à Clément d'Alexandrie*, Patristica Sorbonensia 1 (Paris: Éditions de Seuil, 1957), 259-60; and Preisker, 200-211. Eusebius, *Church History* 5.10.1–11.2, says Clement's predecessor and teacher at the Christian catechetical school in Alexandria, Pantaeus, was a former Stoic. Concerning the influence of Philo on Clement's ethics of marriage, see Stelzenberger, 419-21. On Clement's knowledge of Musonius, see Wendland, *Quaestiones Musonianae*, 31-38, which he qualifies in Wendland, review of *C. Musonii Rufi reliquiae*, ed. O. Hense, *Berliner philologische Wochenschrift* 26 (1906): 197-202; and Charles Pomeroy Parker, "Musonius in Clement," *Harvard Studies in Classical Philology* 12 (1901): 191-200.

229. Clement of Alexandria, *Stromateis*, bk. 2, chap. 23.138.2-5 (2.189.12-20 S.).

fies the basic question of the debate, "should one marry" (εἰ γαμητέον), and states that it was discussed with respect to the various circumstances of a man's life. Marriage itself he defines as "the legal union of a man and a woman for the procreation of legitimate children."[230] Beyond this Clement knows of the Stoic classification of marriage as an "indifferent" (ἀδιάφορον),[231] as well as their arguments that nature designed the human body for sexual union; that a household without a wife is "incomplete"; and that one must marry for the sake of one's homeland, the succession of children, and the wholeness of the *kosmos*.[232] Regarding this last idea, he attributes to Plato the Stoic position that men who forgo marriage bring about a dearth of children and thereby destroy "both the cities and the *kosmos*, which is constituted by them."[233]

Clement not only knows of these various positions on marriage, he also adopts many of the Stoic arguments as his own. To some extent he regarded them as a welcome antidote to the dualistic ascetic groups of his day, such as the gnostics.[234] In the second book of his *Paedagogus*, for instance, he introduces chapter 10 with a clear statement of the Stoic position that marital relations are to be undertaken entirely for the purpose of procreation.[235] This dogma, in turn, runs like a leitmotiv through book 3 of his *Stromateis*.[236] He even reads it into Paul's statements in 1 Corinthians 7:3-5, interpreting

230. Clement of Alexandria, *Stromateis*, bk. 2, chap. 23.137.1, 3-4 (2.188.25-27; 189.1-8 S.). On Stoic influence here see Broudéhoux, 74, and the notes to the Greek text in the Stählin edition, 2.188-90.

231. Clement of Alexandria, *Stromateis*, bk. 2, chap. 23.138.5 (2.189.18-19 S.). On this see John R. Donahue, "Stoic Indifferents and Christian Indifference in Clement of Alexandria," *Traditio* 19 (1963): 438-46; Broudéhoux, 34 n. 94. Cf. *Stromateis*, bk. 3, chap. 5.40.2; 41.4; 42.5 (2.214.11-13, 30-31; 215.20-21 S.).

232. Clement of Alexandria, *Stromateis*, bk. 2, chap. 23.139.3; 140.1 (2.190.2-5, 15-18 S.).

233. Clement of Alexandria, *Stromateis*, bk. 2, chap. 23.141.5 (2.191.10-15 S.), τάς τε πόλεις καὶ τὸν κόσμον τὸν ἐκ τούτων.

234. See, e.g., Roger Gryson, *Les origines du célibat ecclésiastique: Du premier au septième siècle*, Recherches et synthèses, Histoire 2 (Gembloux: J. Duculot, 1970), 7-13; John Ernest Leonard Oulton and Henry Chadwick, *Alexandrian Christianity*, LCC 2 (London: SCM Press, 1954), 22-39. For a time it was believed that Clement, in the tradition of the Stoics, wrote a tractate of his own on marriage; see Broudéhoux, 8-10.

235. Clement of Alexandria, *Paedagogus*, bk. 2, chap. 10.83.1 (1.208.2-6 S.). On this see Broudéhoux, 77-79.

236. Clement of Alexandria, *Stromateis*, bk. 3, chap. 3.24.1; chap. 7.58.1-2; chap. 11.71.4; chap. 12.79.3; 81.4; 82.3; 89.2 (2.206.20-22; 222.27–223.1; 228.16-22; 231.23-25; 233.2-5, 21-25; 237.13-17 S.); cf. chap. 9.67.1 (2.226.19-25 S.). On this see Noonan, 76-77. In *Stromateis*, bk. 2, chap. 18.93.1 (2.163.8-12 S.), Clement states that the man who does not want children ought not marry.

the duty owed one's spouse in verse 3 as procreation, and concluding that this is also the object of the verb "to withhold or defraud" in verse 5.[237]

Another instance is book 7 of the *Stromateis*, where Clement defines the *true* gnostic as one who necessarily takes on the responsibilities of marriage, having been trained in marriage, procreation, and the oversight of a household.[238] This, too, Clement is able to read back into his own Christian tradition, maintaining not only that *all* of Paul's letters contain *innumerable* rules "on marriages and on begetting children and on management of the household," but also that Jesus taught monogamy "for the sake of begetting children and oversight of the household."[239] Clement, however, stops short of basing his understanding of morality on the Stoic conception of the *kosmos*. While willing to admit that procreation assures the permanence of the world,[240] in an exegesis of Luke 14:26 he uses the connection Stoics saw between marriage, households, cities, and the *kosmos* to warn Christians *against* involvement with "the world" through marriage and procreation.[241] Here we detect a Christian form of the alienation from the cities and the *kosmos* that we saw in Philo's writings. In fact, it is in accord with this sense of alienation that Clement, like Philo, can also lend his support to several Cynic arguments against marriage, as we see in this exegesis of 1 Corinthians 7:8: "But if someone wants to be unencumbered (εὔζωνος), choosing not to raise children because of the time involved in raising children (διὰ τὴν ἐν παιδοποιΐᾳ ἀσχολίαν), 'he should remain unmarried just as I do,' says the Apostle."[242]

---

237. Clement of Alexandria, *Stromateis*, bk. 3, chap. 18.107.5 (2.246.5-9 S.); and chap. 15.96.2; 97.1 (2.240.14-18, 21-24 S.).

238. Clement of Alexandria, *Stromateis*, bk. 7, chap. 12.70.6-7 (3.51.1-10 S.), οὐ προηγουμένως ἀλλὰ ἀναγκαίως.

239. Clement of Alexandria, *Stromateis*, bk. 3, chap. 12.86.1 (2.253.20-23 S.); bk. 3, chap. 12.82.3 (2.233.21-25 S.). On the degree to which Clement was influenced by the literature on household management, see Broudéhoux, 139-69, 182-83.

240. Clement of Alexandria, *Paedagogus*, bk. 2, chap. 10.83.1-2 (1.208.2-11 S.), τῆς τοῦ παντὸς διαμονῆς. See also bk. 2, chap. 10.96.1; 98.3 (1.215.1-5; 216.5-7 S.).

241. Clement of Alexandria, *Stromateis*, bk. 3, chap. 15.97.2-3 (2.240.24–241.2 S.): "But what [Christ] means is this: Do not let yourself be led astray by irrational impulses and have nothing to do with city customs (τοῖς πολιτικοῖς ἔθεσι). For a household consists of a family, and cities of households, as Paul also says of those who are absorbed in marriage that they aim to 'please the world' (κόσμῳ ἀρέσκειν [cf. 1 Cor. 7:33-34])," (trans. Chadwick in Oulton and Chadwick, 86). On the idea of raising children for the city-state in Clement, see Broudéhoux, 80.

242. Clement of Alexandria, *Stromateis*, bk. 3, chap. 10.68.2 (2.226.34–227.2 S.). Cf. Walther

Finally, we should point out that Cynic arguments are present in the views held by one of the heretical groups Clement describes. As noted above, the followers of Basilides understood the "eunuchs" in Matthew 19:12 to be those who, in Cynic fashion, rejected marriage on account of its time-consuming responsibilities (ἀσχολία).[243] Another of their considerations appears to have been that a man might be too poor to take on the responsibilities of raising children, an argument Musonius rejected in his treatise *Whether All Children Born Should Be Raised.*[244]

Tertullian

In Clement's North African contemporary Tertullian we again find detailed knowledge of the marriage debate.[245] In contrast to Clement, however, this church father finds only the Cynic position useful. In his *Exhortation to Chastity,* Tertullian employs Cynic arguments to justify his own stance on "second marriages," or marriages contracted upon the death of a spouse. Marriage takes up all one's time, he claims, but without a wife a man can give himself wholeheartedly to prayer, the study of Scripture, song, and the rebuking of demons, and put his full effort into such areas of Christian endeavor as martyrdom, persecution, and chastity.[246]

In Cynic fashion Tertullian also points to the burden of having children, which he considers the inevitable consequence of marriage. What wise man *(sapiens)*, he asks, would voluntarily take on such responsibilities?[247] In addition, Tertullian criticizes the Stoic arguments that one should marry in order to secure help in managing a household and governing a family, and to lighten domestic worries *(curas domesticas)*. These he writes off as mere excuses used

Völker, *Der wahre Gnostiker nach Clemens Alexandrinus,* TU 57 (Berlin: Akademie; Leipzig: J. C. Hinrichs, 1952), 199-204.

243. Clement of Alexandria, *Stromateis,* bk. 3, chap. 1.1.4 (2.195.14-17 S.); see above, n. 212.

244. Clement of Alexandria, *Stromateis,* bk. 3, chap. 1.2.4 (2.196.5-6 S.); Musonius, frag. 15.98.17-27 L. (79.13 H. — only the very beginning of this passage appears in the Hense ed.). The gnostic practice of masturbation may also be a sign of Cynic influence; see the discussion of Cynicism above, and Robert M. Grant, *Early Christianity and Society: Seven Studies* (San Francisco: Harper and Row, 1977), 172 n. 9.

245. See the discussion in Stelzenberger, 423-26.

246. Tertullian, *De exhortatione castitatis* 10, 12.

247. Tertullian, *De exhortatione castitatis* 12. Cf. *Acts of Thomas* 1.12 (early third century).

by insincere or unstable Christians who wish to contract second marriages. If a man takes his Christian faith seriously, says Tertullian, he will take a "spiritual wife" for these tasks — an aged, pious widow.[248] Finally, Tertullian makes a mockery of the arguments that marriage ensures that the temples will not be forsaken (used by Antipater) and is necessary for the survival of the city-states, saying that a Christian's citizenship is a heavenly one.[249]

Jerome and Beyond

After Clement and Tertullian, the impact made by the Stoic-Cynic marriage debate on the writings of the church fathers is rather slight. The one exception is Jerome, at the end of the fourth century.[250] As we noted earlier, in his polemic against the heretical monk Jovinian he cites from writings on marriage by Theophrastus and Seneca, and by way of the latter is familiar with a couple of anecdotes about Epicurus and Cicero.[251] Aside from this, Jerome also knows several Cynic commonplaces on the disadvantages of marriage, such as the trials posed by a wife's pregnancy, the annoyance of crying babies, and the cares of household management.[252] The presentation of these in his tractate *Against Helvidius* even bears a tacit resemblance to Epictetus's enumeration in his discourse on Cynicism.[253] Not surprisingly, Jerome, like Tertullian, sides with the Cynics over the Stoics.

248. *Uxorem spiritalem;* Tertullian, *De exhortatione castitatis* 12; *De monogamia* 16.

249. Tertullian, *De exhortatione castitatis* 12.

250. See Stelzenberger, 422-23, 426-38; Günther Christian Hansen, "Molestiae nuptiarum," *Wissenschaftliche Zeitschrift der Universität Rostock: Gesellschafts- und sprachwissenschaftliche Reihe* 2, no. 12 (1963): 215-19; and Marrou, 201 (on the use of the rhetorical thesis εἰ γαμητέον by the Fathers). On John Chrysostom see Peter Brown, *The Body and Society: Men, Women, and Sexual Renunciation in Early Christianity*, Lectures in the History of Religions, n.s., 13 (New York: Columbia University Press, 1988), 306-21. On Gregory Nazianzus, whom Jerome claimed as his teacher (*Adversus Jovinianum* 1.13), and Gregory of Nyssa, see the remarks in Rosemary Radford Ruether, "Misogynism and Virginal Feminism in the Fathers of the Church," in *Religion and Sexism: Images of Women in the Jewish and Christian Traditions* (New York: Simon and Schuster, 1974), 176-78.

251. On Jerome's dispute with Jovinian see Brown, *The Body and Society*, 359-61.

252. Jerome, *Letter* 22.2 *(To Eustochius).* In *Adversus Jovinianum* 1.13, commenting on 1 Cor. 7:32-34, Jerome concedes, "This is not the place to describe the difficulties of marriage and to revel in rhetorical commonplaces *(in communibus locis rhetorico).*"

253. Jerome, *Contra Helvidium: De perpetua virginitate beatae Mariae* 20. Compare also Jerome's treatment of procreation in *Adversus Jovinianum* 1.36 to the Cynics' disdain for raising citizens.

The general disinterest in the marriage debate among church fathers after the beginning of the third century, as well as their increasing dissatisfaction with the Stoic position in particular, may be accounted for in part by the interest the church took in the new ideals of virginity, continence, and sexual asceticism. These worked to de-emphasize the importance of marriage and cast a shadow of suspicion on arguments favoring the institution. Indeed, Ambrose, in his tractate *On Widows*, written around 337, is moved to declare that the real goal of the Augustan marriage legislation was not to increase the population but to thwart chastity.[254] Some forty years later Epiphanius would condemn the Elkesaites for the heresy of encouraging single people to marry;[255] and at that end of the century, Jerome would accuse his opponent Jovinian of praising marriage in order to denigrate virginity.[256] As Henri Crouzel so elegantly framed the matter: "The insistence of the sages of the Portico on the need to people the earthly city met with less enthusiasm from the Fathers. The society which counted most for them was the Church, and her growth was facilitated more by the spiritual fecundity of virginity than by marriage."[257]

254. Ambrose, *De viduis* 14.84.

255. Epiphanius, *Haereses* 19.1.7. See the discussion of this passage in Gerard P. Luttikhuizen, *The Revelation of Elchasai: Investigations into the Evidence for a Mesopotamian Jewish Apocalypse of the Second Century and Its Reception by Judeo-Christian Propagandists*, Texte und Studien zum Antiken Judentum 8 (Tübingen: Mohr, 1985), 119, 126, 202, 208.

256. Jerome, *Adversus Jovinianum* 1.3.

257. Henri Crouzel, "Marriage and Virginity: Has Christianity Devalued Marriage?" *The Way*, suppl. 10 (1970): 18. Cf. Noonan, 84-85: "The evaluation of virginity cut across the valuation of procreation. Procreative purpose was valued as a rational control of marital intercourse. . . . The connection between procreation and an increase of population was not explored." See also Brown, *The Body and Society*, 120-21, 138-39, 369; Brown, "The Notion of Virginity in the Early Church," in *Christian Spirituality: Origins to the Twelfth Century*, edited by Bernard McGinn and John Meyendorff, World Spirituality: An Encyclopedic History of the Religious Quest 16 (New York: Crossroad, 1985), 427-43; Ton H. C. van Eijk, "Marriage and Virginity, Death and Immortality," in *Epektasis: Mélanges patristiques offerts au Cardinal Jean Daniélou*, edited by Jacques Fontaine and Charles Kannengiesser (Paris: Beauchesne, 1972), 209-35; the rambling but well-documented account in Robin Lane Fox, *Pagans and Christians* (New York: Knopf, 1987), 351-74; and Ford, *A Trilogy on Wisdom and Celibacy*, The Cardinal O'Hara Series: Studies and Research in Christian Theology at Notre Dame 4 (Notre Dame, Ind., and London: University of Notre Dame Press, 1967), 230-33, who gives a table indicating the increased interest in virginity in the period from *1 Clement* to Jerome.

Conclusion

In this chapter I have outlined the central aspects of a debate on marriage that began in the Hellenistic period in Stoic and Cynic circles. I have also surveyed the extant texts that witness to this debate, a large number of which come from the first century c.e. and include both Jewish and Christian authors. The longevity of this debate, its wide dissemination, and its consistency through the centuries are an impressive indication that it addressed problems both basic and common to a wide range of people in the Greco-Roman period.

By presenting these materials, however, I do not wish to suggest that the Stoic-Cynic marriage debate was the only forum for discussing marriage, or that Stoic and Cynic conceptualizations of marriage dominated intellectual thought in Paul's day. Rather I have selected these particular texts for analysis in the belief that they are representative of a discrete worldview that also informs Paul's discussion of marriage in 1 Corinthians 7. For this reason as well I have resisted the temptation to focus solely on elements in the debate that point to a material connection with Paul. While I have highlighted Greek words and phrases from each author that are "parallels" in this sense, and while I will use these parallels liberally in the next chapter to show Stoic and Cynic influence on Paul, my primary concern has been to delineate the philosophical and theological framework of each author's position so as to clarify his premises and worldview.

What has emerged from this method of analysis is a uniform picture of marriage held by these authors that envisioned marriage as a set of responsibilities — responsibilities toward one's spouse, household, and community. Whether or not a person accepted these responsibilities, moreover, depended on his or her allegiance to a higher order or calling. Sometimes this was nature or reason, sometimes the will of Zeus, sometimes the will of the Judeo-Christian God. It is on this basis that one decided whether marriage was morally incumbent, as well as desirable and beneficial, or whether, in light of obligations that took precedence over marriage, celibacy was preferable. *Considerations such as a negative evaluation of human sexuality or sexual abstinence as a goal of celibacy played no part at all.* How these insights into the issues of the Stoic-Cynic marriage debate, as well as the worldview that underlies it, help us better understand Paul's views on marriage and celibacy is a matter I will explore in the next two chapters.

3 Stoic and Cynic Elements
in 1 Corinthians 7

A KNOWLEDGE OF STOIC AND CYNIC discussions of marriage is essential for understanding Paul's statements on marriage and celibacy in 1 Corinthians 7 — this thesis, which we will shortly put to the test, is neither new, as indicated in chapter 1, nor unreasonable. The Stoic-Cynic marriage debate, as we saw in chapter 2, flourished among Paul's philosophical contemporaries, and Corinth was a center of philosophical thought in the Hellenistic world, situated, so to speak, at a crossroad of other philosophical centers. With Rome to the northwest, Alexandria to the southeast, and Athens some fifty miles away on its eastern flank, this cosmopolitan port city regularly caught the intellectual breezes that circulated in the Roman Empire.[1] The prospect of Paul finding an audience at Corinth attuned to Stoic and Cynic arguments about marriage was therefore quite good. As for the apostle himself, a growing number of investigations have demonstrated the similarity between Paul's theology and ministry and that of Stoic and Cynic moralists of his day,[2] and several schol-

---

1. According to Acts, several early leaders in the church at Corinth hailed from Rome and Alexandria (18:2, 24; 19:1; cf. 1 Cor. 1:12; 3:4, 5, 6, 22; 4:6; 16:12), and Paul came to Corinth via Athens, where he encountered Stoics and Epicureans (Acts 17:18; 18:1).

2. Especially important in this respect is Abraham J. Malherbe, *Paul and the Popular Philosophers* (Minneapolis: Fortress, 1989), and Malherbe, *Paul and the Thessalonians: The Philosophic Tradition of Pastoral Care* (Philadelphia: Fortress, 1987). See also D. A. DeSilva, "Paul and the Stoa: A Comparision," *JETS* 38 (1994): 549-64; Troels Engberg-Pedersen, *Paul and the Stoics* (Louisville: Westminster/John Knox, 2000); J. Paul Sampley, ed., *Paul in the Greco-Roman World: A Handbook* (Harrisburg, Penn.: Trinity Press International, 2003); Gerd Theissen, *The Social Setting of Pauline Christianity: Essays on Corinth*, edited and introduction by John H. Schütz (Philadelphia: Fortress, 1982), 39-47; Robert M. Grant, *Early Christianity and Society: Seven Studies* (San

ars have argued that passages throughout 1 Corinthians betray an awareness of Stoic-Cynic thought.[3]

Given the plausibility of Stoic and Cynic influence in 1 Corinthians 7, if not its likelihood, the present chapter will attempt to reassess Paul's views on marriage and celibacy in the context of Stoic and Cynic ideas. My approach will be to locate in 1 Corinthians 7 patterns of thought, argumentative structures, terminology, and phrasing that draw directly or indirectly on Stoic and Cynic traditions, and explain how they function in Paul's discussion with the Corinthians. While this will not constitute a sustained verse-by-verse commentary on the chapter, which is beyond the scope of this book, the intricacies of many passages will nonetheless be dealt with in full.

What my analysis will demonstrate is that Paul utilized a number of Stoic and Cynic principles in addressing the various marital issues at Corinth — issues that included whether a Christian could forgo sexual relations with his or her spouse, whether a Christian should divorce a non-Christian "outsider," and whether Christians should marry in times of severe economic or social uncertainty. My analysis will also make clear, however, that Paul did not employ these principles in a purely Stoic or Cynic form. An important component of the investigation, consequently, will be an exploration of the way Paul reconciles Stoic and Cynic tenets with his own distinctive theological agenda,

---

Francisco: Harper and Row, 1977), 68-75; Howard Clark Kee, "Pauline Eschatology: Relationships with Apocalyptic and Stoic Thought," in *Glaube und Eschatologie: Festschrift für Werner Georg Kümmel zum 80. Geburtstag,* ed. Erich Gräßer and Otto Merk (Tübingen: Mohr, 1985), 147-58; Johannes Weiß, *Der erste Korintherbrief,* MeyerK 5 (Göttingen: Vandenhoeck & Ruprecht, 1925), passim; Kurt Deißner, "Das Sendungsbewußtsein der Urchristenheit," *ZST* 7 (1929/30): 782-87; and cf. Karl Heinrich Rengstorf, "ἀποστέλλω," in *TDNT* 1 (1964), 409-13. Paul's familiarity with Greek philosophical and rhetorical traditions more generally is demonstrated in Hans Dieter Betz, *Der Apostel Paulus und die sokratische Tradition: Eine exegetische Untersuchung zu seiner "Apologie" 2 Korinther 10–13,* BHT 45 (Tübingen: Mohr, 1972); Betz, *Galatians: A Commentary on Paul's Letter to the Churches in Galatia,* Hermeneia (Philadelphia: Fortress, 1979); Margaret M. Mitchell, *Paul and the Rhetoric of Reconciliation: An Exegetical Investigation of the Language and Composition of 1 Corinthians* (Louisville: Westminster/John Knox, 1991); and Paul A. Holloway, *Consolation in Philippians: Philosophical Sources and Rhetorical Strategy,* SNTMS 112 (Cambridge: Cambridge University Press, 2001).

3. E.g., 1 Cor. 3:22-23; 9:1-5; 11:14-15; 12:4-31. See Conzelmann, 80 n. 17, 152, 190, 211, 214; and Abraham J. Malherbe, "Determinism and Free Will in Paul: The Argument of 1 Corinthians 8 and 9," in *Paul in His Hellenistic Context,* ed. Troels Engberg-Pedersen (Minneapolis: Fortress, 1995), 231-55. Max Pohlenz, "Paulus und die Stoa," *ZNW* 42 (1949): 69-104, by contrast, questions the presence of direct Stoic influence in Paul; cf. Hans Conzelmann, *1 Corinthians: A Commentary on the First Epistle to the Corinthians,* Hermeneia (Philadelphia: Fortress, 1975), 10.

melding them with Judeo-Christian traditions from sapiential and apocalyptic worldviews.

Because of the complexity of both 1 Corinthians 7 and our manner of approaching it, a summary of these findings as well as a consideration of how they contribute to our understanding of Paul's view of marriage and celibacy will be reserved for chapter 4. In this way chapter 4 will provide a summation and conclusion to both the present chapter and the book as a whole.

A "Cynic" Position for Married Christians: 7:1-7

Our first indication that Stoic and Cynic ideas on marriage have had an impact on 1 Corinthians 7 appears in the opening words of the chapter. Scholars have long debated whether the words in 7:1b, "it is good for a man not to touch a woman," are Paul's own or, on the basis of 7:1a, "Now concerning what you wrote . . . ," a quotation from a letter he received from Corinth. John Hurd has argued persuasively for the latter option, pointing out that the statement in 7:1b contradicts what Paul says in favor of marital relations in 7:2-5, and that unless 7:1b is a quotation, Paul must be seen as having begun his discussion in 1 Corinthians 7 without any precise indication of his topic. Furthermore, Hurd and others have noted that Paul also appears to begin his discussion in 1 Corinthians 8 with a quotation, namely, the words "all have knowledge" (8:1).[4]

Against this line of reasoning, several scholars maintain that 7:1b represents Paul's own words since the expression καλόν, "it is good," appears again in 7:8 and 7:26 (twice), and is thus "Pauline style" or "typically Pauline."[5] But this view is mistaken, for the expression in 7:1b is not the simple

4. John Coolidge Hurd, Jr., *The Origin of I Corinthians* (London: SPCK, 1965; reprint, Macon, Ga.: Mercer University Press, 1983), 120-23, 163; cf. 67. See also Helmut Merklein, "'Es ist gut für den Menschen, eine Frau nicht anzufassen': Paulus und die Sexualität nach 1 Kor 7," in *Die Frau im Urchristentum*, ed. Gerhard Dautzenberg et al., QD 95 (Freiburg, Basel, and Vienna: Herder, 1983), 230-31; Werner Wolbert, *Ethische Argumentation und Paränese in 1 Kor 7*, Moraltheologische Studien, systematische Abteilung 8 (Düsseldorf: Patmos, 1981), 78; O. Larry Yarbrough, *Not Like the Gentiles: Marriage Rules in the Letters of Paul*, SBLDS 80 (Atlanta: Scholars, 1985), 93-96; and Wolfgang Schrage, "Zur Frontstellung der paulinischen Ehebewertung in 1 Kor 7 1-7," *ZNW* 67 (1976): 215-16.

5. So Conzelmann, 115 n. 10; Kurt Niederwimmer, *Askese und Mysterium: Über Ehe, Ehescheidung und Eheverzicht in den Anfängen des christlichen Glaubens*, FRLANT 113 (Göttingen: Vandenhoeck & Ruprecht, 1975), 81 n. 3. Gerhard Sellin, "Hauptprobleme des Ersten Korintherbriefes," in *ANRW* 2.25.4 (1987), 3002 n. 321, contends that if 7:1b were a quota-

καλόν, "it is good," but καλὸν ἀνθρώπῳ, "it is good for a man," which occurs only here and in 7:26b. This second instance, moreover, provides additional evidence that 7:1b is a quotation of some sort. The Greek of 7:26 reads, νομίζω οὖν τοῦτο καλὸν ὑπάρχειν διὰ τὴν ἐνεστῶσαν ἀνάγκην, ὅτι καλὸν ἀνθρώπῳ τὸ οὕτως εἶναι, which is usually understood to translate something like, "I think that this is good because of the present necessity, that it is good for a man to be thus." Accepting this manner of translation, several scholars have looked askance at Paul's wording of this verse because of the abruptness by which the second half is introduced, and because of the apparent redundancy of the repeated καλόν, "this is good . . . it is good." Weiß, for example, disparages the text as "not pretty," and reckons with the possibility that the second half of the verse is an interpolation. Neuhäusler proposes that the second καλόν should be read as the comparative "better," on the basis of Semitic syntax, which has no formal comparative; and Allo describes the second half of the verse as a "pleonastic" explanation of the first.[6] Still other scholars see this awkward sentence as an example of Paul's clumsiness. Meyer calls it a "manifest confusion of expression" stemming from repetition by Paul during the process of dictation, and Bachmann queries, "Does Paul hesitate to say what there is to say?"[7] The two strangest explanations be-

---

tion, Paul would have written ὅτι after 7:1a (as in 12:1; 16:1, 12), and there would be no δέ at the beginning of 7:2; but this is simply speculation. Regarding his argument that 7:1b agrees with what Paul says in 7:7, see our analysis of this verse below.

6. Weiß, *Korintherbrief*, 193; cf. Archibald Robertson and Alfred Plummer, *A Critical and Exegetical Commentary on the First Epistle of St. Paul to the Corinthians*, 2nd ed., ICC (Edinburgh: T. & T. Clark, 1914), 152; E. Neuhäusler, "Ruf Gottes und Stand des Christen: Bemerkungen zu 1 Kor 7," *BZ*, n.s., 3 (1959): 57 n. 40; E.-B. Allo, *Première épitre aux Corinthiens*, 2nd ed., EBib (Paris: Librairie Lecoffre, 1934; reprint, 1956), 177, cf. Thomas Charles Edwards, *A Commentary on the First Epistle to the Corinthians*, 2nd ed. (New York: A. C. Armstrong and Son, 1886), 190, and C. F. Georg Heinrici, *Der erste Brief an die Korinther*, MeyerK 5, 8th ed. (Göttingen: Vandenhoeck & Ruprecht, 1896), 237-39. In 1762 Mosheim, *Erklärung des Ersten Briefes des heiligen Apostles Pauli an die Gemeinde zu Corinthus*, ed. Christian Ernst von Windheim, 2nd ed. (Flensburg: Kortem, 1762), 311, also remarked that his contemporaries had difficulty with the syntax here.

7. Heinrich August Wilhelm Meyer, *Critical and Exegetical Handbook to the Epistles to the Corinthians*, vol. 1, *First Epistle, Ch. I.–XIII*, rev. William P. Dickson, Critical and Exegetical Commentary on the New Testament 5 (Edinburgh: T. & T. Clark, 1892), 220; cf. Paul Wilhelm Schmiedel, *Die Briefe an die Thessalonicher und an die Korinther*, HKNT 2/1 (Freiburg: Mohr, 1891), 104; and L. J. Rückert, *Der erste Brief Pauli an die Korinther*, Die Briefe Pauli an die Korinther 1 (Leipzig: K. F. Köhler, 1836), 200. Philipp Bachmann, *Der erste Brief des Paulus an die Korinther*, 4th ed., Kommentar zum Neuen Testament 7 (Leipzig: A. Deichert, 1936), 280.

long to Grosheide and Héring. Grosheide maintains that the τοῦτο (this) in
7:26a refers to "the virgin state" (see 7:25), while Héring reasons that it refers
back to 7:20, where Paul speaks of each Christian remaining in his or her
calling.[8]

The awkwardness that these scholars attribute to 7:26 vanishes, however,
if we punctuate the verse to account for a quotation: "I think that this is good
because of the present necessity, that 'it is good for a man' to be thus."[9] In this
interpretation the first καλόν may indeed be "Pauline style,"[10] while the second belongs to the expression καλὸν ἀνθρώπῳ, which Paul quotes as a catchword or "slogan." Since the sentence now reads in a logical manner, I would
maintain that this is the most plausible interpretation of 7:26, and consequently we have every reason to believe that the expression in 7:1b, "it is good
for a man not to touch a woman," also represents a quotation — especially
given Hurd's attractive explanation of 7:1 and the mistaken nature of arguments to the contrary. Indeed, this approach clarifies two other aspects of 7:1b
and 7:26b: it explains why in 7:1b Paul writes "it is good for a man not to . . ."
as opposed to the more natural "it is not good for a man to . . ."; and it makes
intelligible why Paul begins his discussion of virgins in 7:25 by stating what is
good for a *man* (7:26b) — it is because in both cases the expression is a catchword.[11]

If we assume that 7:1b is a quotation, it is possible, as Hurd and others have
suggested on the basis of 7:1a, that it derives from a letter Paul received from
the Corinthians, although there is no way to prove this. Even so, we may be
able to speak about its provenance in a more revealing way, for the aversion to
sexual intercourse expressed in 7:1b finds an analogy in the Cynic traditions we
examined in chapter 2 of this study. As we saw there, some Cynics argued

8. F. W. Grosheide, *Commentary on the First Epistle to the Corinthians*, NICNT (Grand
Rapids: Eerdmans, 1955), 175 n. 6; Jean Héring, *The First Epistle of Saint Paul to the Corinthians*
(London: Epworth, 1962), 57.

9. Or: ". . . present necessity: 'it is good for a man' to be thus." Cf. Hurd, 178-79, who also argues that 7:26 contained a quotation — because of the ὅτι, the repeated καλόν, and because
καλόν appears in 7:1b, which he held to be a quotation. Joachim Jeremias, "Zur Gedankenführung in den paulinischen Briefen," in *Abba: Studien zur neutestamentlichen Theologie und
Zeitgeschichte* (Göttingen: Vandenhoeck & Ruprecht, 1966), 273, wanted to put both of the
καλόν expressions in 7:26 in quotation marks.

10. Aside from 7:8, see 9:15, Gal. 4:18, and Rom. 14:21. But see below, pp. 203-6, for evidence
that Paul's use of καλῶς and κρεῖσσον in 1 Cor. 7:37-38 is Stoic.

11. In both verses, of course, ἄνθρωπος is generic ("man/human being"), as distinct from
ἀνήρ ("man/husband/male human being").

against both marriage and sexual relations generally, on the grounds that sexual relations take up leisure time, or σχολή, which otherwise could be devoted to philosophical studies and progress toward virtue.[12] Paul employs a similar line of reasoning in 7:5 when he maintains that spouses may refuse one another by mutual consent in order to "have leisure" for prayer. The term Paul chooses is σχολάζω, which he uses only here, although we see it and the noun σχολή frequently in documents relating to the Stoic-Cynic marriage debate.[13]

In addition to these clues, the words "it is good for a man" (καλὸν ἀνθρώπῳ) may also have philosophical roots.[14] While I have been unable to

---

12. See, e.g., *Cynic Epistle of Diogenes* 44 (174.7-14 Malherbe): "But incessant liaisons with women — leave these alone altogether, as they require a lot of spare time (σχολή). For there is no spare time (σχολή). . . . While intercourse with women brings enjoyment for many unphilosophical men, . . . you will learn to work the trick from those who learned from Pan."

13. E.g., Antipater (app. A), line 74 (cf. lines 79, 83); *Cynic Epistle of Diogenes* 44 (see previous note); Epictetus, *Discourses* 3.22.74; and Philo, *De specialibus legibus* 3.1-3. Johann Jakob Wettstein, *Novum Testamentum Graecum,* vol. 2 (Amsterdam: Dommerian, 1752; reprint, Graz, Austria: Akademische Druck- und Verlagsanstalt, 1962), 2:126, illustrates 1 Cor. 7:5 with Philo, *De vita Mosis* 2.211, and *De opificio mundi* 128 (cited chap. 2, n. 199). Similarly, Lodewijk Kasper Valckenaer, *Selecta e scholis Lud. Casp. Valckenarii in libros quosdam Novi Testamenti,* ed. Everwijn Wassenbergh (Amsterdam: Petri den Hengst et filii, 1817), 2:204-5, illustrates this passage with σχολάζειν τῇ φιλοσοφίᾳ ("to have leisure for philosophy"), *totum se tradere Philosophiae* ("to devote oneself completely to philosophy"), and *omnibus aliis relictis uni Philosophiae severa lege invigilare* ("all other things abandoned, to give strict attention to philosophy alone"), concluding that the extent to which 7:5 "belongs to precisely those types of sayings will also be easily perceived from Greek and Latin authors." As editor of one of the editions of Stobaeus, Valckenaer would have been familiar with Stoic discussions on marriage.

14. We should note in passing that several French scholars have argued for a connection between the expression καλὸν ἀνθρώπῳ and Gen. 2:18 in the Septuagint version, where God observes, "It is not good that the man be alone" (οὐ καλὸν εἶναι τὸν ἄνθρωπον μόνον). Yet there is a vast difference syntactically between Gen. 2:18 and 1 Cor. 7:1b, and the respective viewpoints of these passages are diametrically opposed: 1 Cor. 7:1b is a statement against sexual relations while Gen. 2:18 provides the rationale for marriage. To overcome these difficulties, these authors resort to theological constructs that go well beyond Paul's discussion in 1 Cor. 7. See Héring, 49; Xavier Léon-Dufour, "Mariage et virginité selon saint Paul," *Christus* 11 (1964): 186-94; Léon-Dufour, "Mariage et continence selon S. Paul," in *A la rencontre de Dieu: Mémorial Albert Gelin,* ed. A. Barucq et al., Bibliothèque de la Faculté Catholique Théologie de Lyon 8 (Le Puy: Xavier Mappus, 1961), 319, 323-27; Thaddée Matura, "Le célibat dans le NT d'après l'exégèse recente," *NRT* 97 (1975): 602; Jean Jacques von Allmen, *Pauline Teaching on Marriage,* Studies in Christian Faith and Practice 6 (London: Faith, 1963), 15-16; and Lucien Legrand, *The Biblical Doctrine of Virginity* (London: Geoffrey Chapman, 1963), 34, 35.

find the exact expression outside of 1 Corinthians 7,[15] a close parallel is ἀγαθὸν ἀνθρώπῳ, from Musonius Rufus. Not only did Stoics identify the concepts καλόν and ἀγαθόν in their famous maxim, "the morally beautiful (τὸ καλόν) alone is good (ἀγαθόν),"[16] but Musonius's use of ἀγαθὸν ἀνθρώπῳ shows that the activity of determining what is "good for a man" is not a chance idea but fundamental to his understanding of the philosophical enterprise. Advising a Syrian king, Musonius states: "Do you imagine . . . that it is more appropriate for anyone to study philosophy than for you, nor for any other reason than because you are a king? For the first duty of a king is to be able to protect and benefit men (ἄνθρωποι), and a protector and benefactor must know what is good for a man (τί μὲν ἀγαθὸν ἀνθρώπῳ) and what is bad."[17]

Similar expressions also play an important role in the philosophies of other Stoics. Epictetus says the task of his model philosopher, the Cynic, is to search out "what is friendly to men (τοῖς ἀνθρώποις φίλα) and what is hostile,"[18] and Dio tells us that during his exile people came to him asking about "good or evil" (ἀγαθὸν ἢ κακόν), and so he found it necessary to advise them "on what was fitting for men" (περὶ τῶν προσηκόντων τοῖς ἀνθρώποις).[19] This last expression also appears in Musonius's tractate on marriage, where he uses it three times in an attempt to prove the Stoic position that one must marry. His argument is that the philosopher is a "teacher and guide to men of all things fitting for a man" (ἀνθρώπῳ προσηκόντων), including marriage (τὸ γαμεῖν).[20] A denial of this position, whether by Cynics or by Stoics who took a

15. My assumption is that 1 *Clement* 51.3 knows this phrase from 1 Cor. 7 (cf. below, n. 81).

16. See, e.g., *SVF* 3.9.23–11.24. Philo, *De posteritate Caini* 133, knows this as "the Stoic dogma" (τὸ στωικὸν . . . δόγμα), and Diogenes Laertius 7.100-101 links it with the Stoic tenet that only the wise man is "good and morally beautiful" (ἀγαθὸς καὶ καλός). Niederwimmer, 84, notes that 7:1b speaks of what is good for a *human being,* not simply a Christian, and therefore contains nothing specifically Christian.

17. Musonius, frag. 8.60.6-11 Lutz (32.7-13 Hense), trans. Lutz, "Musonius Rufus 'The Roman Socrates,'" in *Yale Classical Studies* 10, ed. Alfred R. Bellinger (New Haven: Yale University Press, 1947), 61, slightly modified.

18. Epictetus, *Discourses* 3.22.24. In 3.22.23 he says the Cynic is sent by Zeus "to men, showing them concerning good things and bad" (πρὸς τοὺς ἀνθρώπους περὶ ἀγαθῶν καὶ κακῶν ὑποδείξων αὐτοῖς).

19. Dio Chrysostom, *Oration* 13.12-13.

20. Musonius, frag. 14.92.6-9 L. (71.8-11 H.); and see 14.94.32 L. (75.20-21 H.), προσήκειν ἀνθρώπῳ (twice). See also frag. 4.46.8 L. (16.9-10 H.), τὴν ἀνθρώπῳ προσήκουσαν ἀρετήν, "the virtue appropriate for a man"; and Seneca, *Epistle* 76.4, where Seneca explains that philosophical schools seek to ascertain "by what means a man is good" *(in quo vir bonus).*

Cynic stance against marriage, might have sounded much like what Paul writes in 7:1b.[21]

The passage from Dio, finally, may be significant in another respect, for it depicts the philosopher holding forth on "what was fitting for men" in response to inquiries from his public. This coincides with the circumstances of Paul's discussion, as indicated by his opening phrase, "Now concerning what you wrote . . ." (7:1a). Indeed, discussions on marriage occasioned by such inquiries may have been common among Paul's philosophical contemporaries. In Plutarch's *Amatorius,* for example, we learn of one that ostensibly took place when Plutarch and his friends were asked if it would be appropriate for a promising young gymnasium student to marry an influential widow in her thirties.[22] Similarly, Lucius begins Musonius's diatribe on marriage by having a young man ask the philosopher if marriage and life with a wife were impediments to the philosopher; and Arrian, in recording Epictetus's description of the ideal Cynic, has an interlocutor ask Epictetus if the Cynic will undertake marriage.[23] Regarding Musonius and Epictetus, I am aware, of course, that stock figures who ask leading questions are a literary convention in diatribe-style writing. Even so, this consideration does not exclude the possibility that these inquisitive straight men actually reflect the real world of the Greco-Roman moralist — a world, I am suggesting, that also peers through in 7:1.[24]

---

21. Note that Theon, *Progymnasmata* 125.15-20 Spengel (cited above, chap. 2, n. 107), explains that in making a case for having children one will maintain that marriage is "good" (καλός), while in refuting this thesis one will draw on the *opposite* arguments (ἐκ τῶν ἐναντίων).

22. Plutarch, *Moralia* 748E-771E, esp. 750A. While Hubert Martin, Jr., "Amatorius (Moralia 748E-771E)," in *Plutarch's Ethical Writings and Early Christian Literature,* ed. Hans Dieter Betz, SCHNT 4 (Leiden: Brill, 1978), 443, reminds us that the *Amatorius* "is a dramatic essay, not a historical document," he adds, "To say this is not to deny that its setting and circumstances may include factual elements and that it reflects the conversation and behavior of Plutarch and his circles."

23. Musonius, frag. 14.90.24-26 L. (70.11-13 H.), and see also 14.96.4-6, 7-8 L. (76.11-14, 16-17 H.); Epictetus 3.22.67, 77. See also Diogenes Laertius 6.3, where Antisthenes is asked by someone what sort of wife he should marry (told also of Bion, 4.48), and Theon, *Progymnasmata* 12.121.6-17 S.; cf. Juvenal, *Satire* 6. "O" 17 (between 6.365 and 6.366).

24. On this see Rudolf Bultmann, *Der Stil der paulinischen Predigt und die kynisch-stoische Diatribe,* FRLANT 13 (Göttingen: Vandenhoeck & Ruprecht, 1910), 10-19, 64-74; Stanley K. Stowers, *The Diatribe and Paul's Letter to the Romans,* SBLDS 57 (Chico, Calif.: Scholars, 1981), 53-58, 61. Stowers ventures that many of Epictetus's diatribes were "occasional responses addressed to specific problems, situations or individuals" (54). This tradition of requesting advice on marriage from moral leaders may have been institutionalized by the church near the end of the first century: Ignatius of Antioch, *To Polycarp* 5.2, maintains that it is proper (πρέπει) for

If, for these several reasons, we can understand 7:1b as representing a "Cynic" position, then 7:5 seems to represent a modification of that position, designed to meet the needs of married Christians. As we just saw, Paul allows for abstinence here *within marriage* so that Christians might spend time in prayer. It is only temporary abstinence that he authorizes, however, not a complete renunciation of marital intercourse, which would be the full Cynic position. For such abstinence to occur within marriage, moreover, Paul requires the mutual consent of husband and wife (σύμφωνος, 7:5), a provision he justifies using Stoic as well as Judeo-Christian moral reasoning.

The Judeo-Christian component of his argument appears most prominently in 7:2. Here Paul holds that marital relations are necessary because permanent abstinence exposes a spouse to the danger of fornication (αἱ πορνεῖαι).[25] This theme is then repeated at the end of 7:5, where Paul states that a couple practicing abstinence must ultimately resume marital relations "so that Satan might not tempt you through your lack of control," and in 7:6, where he states that his counsel is based on "concession" (συγγνώμη) rather than command, meaning, evidently, concession to Satan and to human weakness.[26]

Paul's argument in 7:3-4 and the beginning of 7:5, on the other hand, appears to draw on Stoic traditions. To begin with, I suspect that the rather heavy-handed conjunction ὁμοίως δὲ καί, "and likewise also," which Paul uses twice in 7:3-4 to stress the equality of roles between spouses, reflects a Stoic manner of comparison. In Arius's epitome of Stoic ethics, for example, this conjunction occurs fourteen times,[27] whereas in his account of Aristote-

---

those contemplating marriage to seek out the "advice" of the bishop (γνώμη — cf. 1 Cor. 7:25) to ensure that the resulting union is in accordance with the Lord rather than passionate desire (κατ᾽ ἐπιθυμίαν). Cf. 1 Tim. 5:14; Epictetus 3.22.72; Pseudo-Clement, *Letter of Clement to James* 7.1; and *Homily* 3, chap. 68.1.

25. On *porneia* as a concern for early Jews and Christians, see, e.g., 1 Cor. 5:1; 6:13; Gal. 5:18; Niederwimmer, 67-68, 73; and Friedrich Hauck and Siegfried Schulz, "πόρνη," in *TDNT* 6 (1968), 587-89. On marriage for the sake of avoiding *porneia*, see *T. Levi* 9:9-10 (cited in Yarbrough, 69). We should also not overlook that certain Stoics denounced extramarital relations as well: see [Ocellus] (app. B), *De univ. nat.* 44-45; Musonius, frag. 12, *On Sexual Relations;* Epictetus, *Discourses* 3.7.21; *Encheiridion* 33.8.

26. Cf. 7:7. Peter Brown, *The Body and Society: Men, Women, and Sexual Renunciation in Early Christianity,* Lectures in the History of Religions, n.s., 13 (New York: Columbia University Press, 1988), 55, paraphrases διὰ τὰς πορνείας in 7:2 as "'because of the temptation of immorality' that abstinence might bring."

27. Arius in Stobaeus 2.67.19; 70.3, 4; 71.6; 78.4, 13; 82.18; 84.19; 86.8; 100.10; 103.12; 108.14; 109.12; 112.13 Wachsmuth and Hense.

lian ethics it appears only once.[28] A similar pattern is found in Diogenes Laertius.[29] Moreover, in Musonius's treatise *That Women, Too, Should Pursue Philosophy,* the phrase occurs, as in Paul, in two consecutive sentences, again stressing equality between men and women.[30] Beyond this, the almost identical phrase, ὁμοίως τε καί, appears in Romans 1:27,[31] a passage which owes a considerable debt to Stoic thought, the context again being gender issues.[32] Finally, the simpler ὁμοίως, "likewise," appears often in Musonius's discussion of whether boys and girls should receive the same education.[33] In 1 Corinthians 7 it occurs in verse 22, where Stoic influence is once again evident.[34] Other than the passages just cited, the word is not found in Paul's writings.

A further connection between 7:3-4 and Stoicism is the topic of these verses, namely, marital responsibilities, which as we saw in chapter 2 was at the very heart of the Stoic-Cynic marriage debate. In verse 3 Paul states that spouses must "render" (ἀποδίδωμι) to one another "that which is owed" (τὴν ὀφειλήν). This, quite plainly, is the language of obligation, as can also be seen from other New Testament texts and from the papyri.[35] But more specifically,

---

28. Arius in Stobaeus 2.138.17 W.-H. — even though the expression occurs frequently in Aristotle's own writings in discussions of gender. Here we must distinguish between early usage (Aristotle) and later popularization (Stoicism). See next note.

29. In the accounts of Plato and Aristotle (Diogenes Laertius 3.1-109; 5.1-35), the term never occurs; in his account of Zeno (Diogenes Laertius 7.1-160) it appears eight times: 7.43, 87, 97, 107 (ὁμοίως δ' ἔχει καί), 122, 126 (ὁμοίως τε καί), 147, 148.

30. Musonius, frag. 3.38.30, 31 L. (9.5, 7 H.).

31. As the second part of a τε . . . τε construction; otherwise we might have had ὁμοίως δὲ καί here as well.

32. Rom. 1:26-28: "For this reason, God gave them over to dishonorable passions (πάθη), for their females exchanged natural sexual usage (τὴν φυσικὴν χρῆσιν) for that which is contrary to nature (τὴν παρὰ φύσιν), and likewise also (ὁμοίως τε καί) the males, leaving natural sexual usage (τὴν φυσικὴν χρῆσιν) of females, were inflamed by their desire for one another, males committing unseemliness (τὴν ἀσχημοσύνην) with males. . . . God gave them over to a base mind, to do those things which are not fitting (τὰ μὴ καθήκοντα)." This is followed in vv. 29-31 by a catalogue of vices, a literary form also used by Stoics.

33. Musonius, frag. 4.44.8, 16-17 (δ' ὁμοίως καί); 46.9, 10, 15 L. (14.2, 13; 16.10, 13, 18 H.). It also serves to introduce the roles of husbands and wives in the household code in 1 Pet. 3:1, 7 (cf. 5.5), and those of the "sisters" and "brothers" in the household code in Ignatius, *Polycarp* 5.1.

34. See below.

35. E.g., in Paul at Rom. 13:7; in the Gospels at Matt. 18:30, 34. In the papyri see, e.g., POxy II 278.17-19 (no. 286; 82 C.E.): ". . . so that they may secure us without liability or difficulty with regard to the aforementioned debt (ὀφειλήν), and repay it (ἀποδώσειν)." James Hope Moulton

it is the language of marital obligations, a fact made clear by marriage and divorce contracts from this period.[36]

With verse 4 Paul's consideration of marital responsibilities becomes more focused. Here he concentrates on the sexual obligations that spouses have to one another, stating that neither the husband nor the wife has final say over his or her own body. Several scholars have attempted to understand this statement in light of Genesis 2:24, where marriage is described as an act by which husband and wife become "one flesh." Niederwimmer, for example, speaks of a deeper "mythological" understanding of marriage deriving from the Genesis passage, and points out that Paul uses Genesis 2:24 in 1 Corinthians 6:16 in his discussion of prostitutes.[37] Against this, however, Bruns has argued that no advocate of this theory can explain the precise logic that connects Genesis 2:24 to 1 Corinthians 7:4. To the contrary, "If one wanted to derive justification for *potestas corporis* from Gen 2.24, the result would be either that both spouses have authority over the one body . . . , or that both spouses have authority over their own bodies as well as that of the partner."[38] Although, as we shall see shortly, Bruns overstates his case — for 7:4 probably does describe the mutual, not the exclusive, authority that spouses exercise over each other's body — the overall force of his objection is still valid, for Paul's reasoning carries no obvious allusion to the "one flesh" idea of Genesis 2:24.[39]

---

and George Milligan, *The Vocabulary of the Greek Testament: Illustrated from the Papyri and Other Non-Literary Sources*, pts. 1-8 (London: Hodder and Stoughton, 1915-29; reprint, Grand Rapids: Eerdmans, 1980), 61, comment that the verb ἀποδίδωμι "is the appropriate one everywhere for the 'paying' of a debt, or 'restoring' of a due of any kind."

36. Günter Häge, *Ehegüterrechtliche Verhältnisse in den griechischen Papyri Ägyptens bis Diokletian*, Graezistische Abhandlungen 3 (Cologne and Graz: Böhlau, 1968), 58, 76-77 n. 8, 78 n. 12, 115 and n. 49, 239 and n. 3, 240, 248-49, 278-80. See also Epictetus's claim that a husband must "render" (ἀποδιδόναι) various services to his wife and her relatives (*Discourses* 3.22.70). John Chrysostom evidently felt this language of obligation was too strong for his theological purposes, for he substitutes "the honor being due" (ὀφειλομένην τιμήν) (*PG* 61:152). Likewise, both he, the New Testament manuscripts K and L, and most minuscules read "the kindness being due" (ὀφειλομένην εὔνοιαν, *PG* 51:216).

37. Niederwimmer, 91-92; cf. Eph. 5:28-33. See also Darrell J. Doughty, "Heiligkeit und Freiheit: Eine exegetische Untersuchung der Anwendung des paulinischen Freiheitsgedankens in 1 Kor 7" (Ph.D. diss., Göttingen University, 1965), 174, and the studies by Greeven, Merk, and Maurer discussed in Bernhard Bruns, "'Die Frau hat über ihren Leib nicht die Verfügungsgewalt, sondern der Mann . . .': Zur Herkunft und Bedeutung der Formulierung in 1 Kor 7,4," *MTZ* 33 (1982): 179-80.

38. Bruns, 180.

39. Cf. P. Richardson, "'I Say, Not the Lord': Personal Opinion, Apostolic Authority and

Other scholars have suggested a rabbinic origin for the idea expressed in 7:4,[40] and still others that it derives from Hellenistic wedding vows;[41] but there is insufficient evidence to sustain either of these suggestions.[42] Bruns himself has argued that 7:4 represents a deep expression of Christian love, as seen in 13:5 and Philippians 2:3-4.[43] He maintains that the specific formulation of this love in terms of the marriage relation was occasioned by gnostics in Corinth who promoted the idea that individuals had complete power or freedom over their own bodies. According to Bruns, 1 Corinthians 7:4 must be seen as a polemical statement, an antithesis to a gnostic thesis that circulated in Corinth.[44] Bruns's theory, however, is based on two doubtful premises. First, he believes 6:12-20 and 1 Corinthians 7 represent libertine and ascetic manifestations of gnosticism, respectively — a notion we rejected in chapter 1; and second, he believes the verb ἐξουσιάζω ("to have power over something") in 7:4 is "typical gnostic usage," on the basis of his conviction that Paul uses the related ἔξεστιν ("it is lawful") in a gnostic manner in 6:12.[45] Yet, while ἐξουσιάζω and ἔξεστιν are etymologically akin to one another, and while 6:12b contains a wordplay based on this kinship, we have no indication that gnostics saw any significant connection between these two terms. In fact,

---

the Development of Early Christian Halakah," *TynBul* 31 (1980): 79: "For some reason Paul does not rely at all upon, nor even allude to the Hebrew Scriptures in chapter 7. Even such an obvious reference as 'the two shall become one flesh' does not appear. Thus, one of the fundamental authorities he frequently uses is absent" (cf. 85).

40. E.g., Rudolf Schnackenburg, "Die Ehe nach dem Neuen Testament," in *Theologie der Ehe: Veröffentlichung des Ökumenischen Arbeitskreises evangelischer und katholischer Theologen*, ed. Gerhard Krems and Reinhard Mumm (Regensburg: Friedrich Pustet; Göttingen: Vandenhoeck & Ruprecht, 1969), 22; Ford, *A Trilogy on Wisdom and Celibacy*, Cardinal O'Hara Series: Studies and Research in Christian Theology at Notre Dame 4 (Notre Dame, Ind., and London: University of Notre Dame Press, 1967), 65-66. Cf. Hermann L. Strack and Paul Billerbeck, *Kommentar zum Neuen Testament aus Talmud und Midrash* (Munich: C. H. Beck, 1956), 3:368-71. Against this see, e.g., Doughty, "Heiligkeit und Freiheit," 169.

41. Mosheim, 278-79; Wolbert, 82, 93.

42. Regarding the latter, Hans Julius Wolff, *Written and Unwritten Marriages in Hellenistic and Postclassical Roman Law*, Philological Monographs 9 (Haverford, Pa.: American Philological Association, 1939), 52, notes that the common rulership clause (κοινῇ κυριεύειν) is absent in marriage law from the imperial period and later.

43. Bruns, 190, cf. 181, following Schrage, "Zur Frontstellung," 230-31, cf. 229 n. 62. See also Heinrich Baltensweiler, *Die Ehe im Neuen Testament: Exegetische Untersuchungen über Ehe, Ehelosigkeit und Ehescheidung*, ATANT 52 (Zürich and Stuttgart: Zwingli, 1967), 159.

44. Bruns, 182, 191.

45. Bruns, 183-89, 192-93.

there is no evidence that gnostics even used the latter term. As Conzelmann remarks: "The language [in 6:12] points to a previous history in Stoicism. Only the Stoics and Cynics provide material for comparison."[46]

In the final analysis, the closest parallels to 7:4 must also be said to come from the Stoics, and indeed, from their discussions on marriage.[47] As early as the second century B.C.E., Antipater reasoned in his tractate *On Marriage* that unlike life's other friendships and affections, which resemble "juxtaposed mixings of beans," marriages were "complete fusions, as wine with water." This was because husbands and wives "not only share a partnership of property, and children . . . and the soul, but these alone also share their bodies."[48] In the first century C.E., in his lecture *Is Marriage an Impediment to the Pursuit of Philosophy?* Musonius asks, "To whom is everything thought to be common — bodies, souls, possessions — except a husband and wife?";[49] and

---

46. Conzelmann, 108. Bruns, 183, even concedes that his proposed gnostic use of ἔξεστιν may have arisen under Stoic influence. On this possibility, see Will Deming, "The Unity of 1 Corinthians 5–6," *JBL* 115 (1996): 299-303.

47. This is emphasized especially by Weiß, *Korintherbrief*, 172 n. 2.

48. Antipater (app. A), lines 24-25, οὐ γὰρ μόνον τῆς οὐσίας καὶ τῶν . . . τέκνων καὶ τῆς ψυχῆς, ἀλλὰ καὶ τῶν σωμάτων οὗτοι μόνοι κοινωνοῦσι. For non-Stoic antecedents to this idea, see Xenophon, *Oeconomicus* 10.3-5, where Ischomachus and his wife speak of themselves as sharing one another's bodies (τῶν σωμάτων κοινωνήσοντες ἀλλήλοις) and being a "partner of the body" (τοῦ σώματος . . . κοινωνός). See also Isocrates, *Nicocles* 40, which describes marriage as a "partnership of everything of life" (κοινωνία . . . παντὸς τοῦ βίου), cited by Friedrich Zucker, "Socia unanimans," *Rh. Mus.*, n.s., 92 (1944): 210-11. By contrast, see Plato, *Republic* 5.457C-466D, where the male and female guardians of a city are said to hold all things in common (κοινῇ πάντα) except their bodies. On the notion of marriage as a reciprocal relationship in the Hellenistic period, see Claude Vatin, *Recherches sur le mariage et la condition de la femme mariée à l'époque hellénistique*, Bibliothèque des Écoles Françaises d'Athènes et de Rome 216 (Paris: E. de Boccard, 1970), 33-34, 39-40, 54-56, 200-228; Emiel Eyben, "De latere Stoa over het huwelijk," *Hermeneus: Tijdschrift voor antieke Cultuur* 50 (1978): 352-53; Michel Foucault, *The Care of the Self*, History of Sexuality 3 (New York: Pantheon Books, 1986), 159-64, cf. 78-79; and Joseph Vogt, "Von der Gleichwertigkeit der Geschlechter in der bürgerlichen Gesellschaft," *Akademie der Wissenschaften und der Literatur: Abhandlungen der Geistes- und Sozialwissenschaftlichen Klasse* 2 (1960): 246-55. Cf. Paul Veyne, "La famille et l'amour sous le Haut-Empire romain," *Annales: Économies, Sociétés, Civilisations* 33 (1978): 48; and Jean-Paul Broudéhoux, *Mariage et famille chez Clément d'Alexandrie*, Théologie Historique 11 (Paris: Beauchesne et ses Fils, 1970), 17.

49. Musonius, frag. 14.94.8-9 L. (74.7-8 H.), τίσι δὲ νενόμισται κοινὰ εἶναι πάντα, καὶ σώματα καὶ ψυχαὶ καὶ χρήματα, πλὴν ἀνδρὸς καὶ γυναικός. . . . Cf. Dio Chrysostom, *Oration* 3.122: "His wife, moreover, he regards not merely as the partner (κοινωνός) of his bed and affections, but also as his helpmate in his counsel in action, and indeed in his whole life" (J. W.

in his lecture entitled *What Is the Chief Aspect of Marriage?* he states that married couples consider "everything common property and nothing one's own, not even the body itself."[50] In the following century Hierocles echoed this sentiment, saying the good husband and wife are those who "agree with one another" (συμφωνέω — cf. 7:5), having made "everything common, even as far as their bodies."[51] The popularity of this Stoic tradition in Greece, moreover, is suggested by its use in Plutarch,[52] and perhaps in an inscription from Mantinea, some forty miles southwest of Corinth.[53]

Against this comparison of 7:4 to Stoic materials, Bruns has argued that the Stoics (he cites only Musonius) insisted on the *mutual* ownership of bod-

---

Cohoon and H. Lamar Crosby, eds. and trans., *Dio Chrysostom*, 5 vols., LCL [London: William Heinemann; Cambridge: Harvard University Press, 1932-51], 1:159).

50. Musonius, frag. 13A.88.13-14 L. (67.9–68.1 H.), καὶ κοινὰ δὲ ἡγεῖσθαι πάντα καὶ μηδὲν ἴδιον, μηδ' αὐτὸ τὸ σῶμα.

51. Hierocles 54.19-22 von Arnim (Stobaeus 4.505.12-16 W.-H.), συμφωνούντων μὲν ἀλλήλοις καὶ πάντα κοινὰ πεποιημένων μέχρι καὶ τῶν σωμάτων, to which he adds, giving a new emphasis to the traditions of Antipater and Musonius, " — nay, rather, even as far as their *spirits*" (μᾶλλον δὲ καὶ αὐτῶν τῶν ψυχῶν). See also Seneca, *De beneficiis* 2.18.1-2: "Every obligation that involves two people makes an equal demand upon both. . . . it is true that a husband has certain duties, yet those of the wife are not less great. In the exchange of obligations each in turn renders to the other the service that he requires, and they desire that the same rule of action should apply to both, but this rule, as Hecaton says, is a difficult matter" (trans. John W. Basore, ed. and trans., *Seneca: Moral Essays*, LCL [London: William Heinemann; New York: Putnam, 1932-35], 3:85, 87).

52. Plutarch, *Moralia* 142F-143A *(Coniugalia praecepta)*: "As the mixings of liquids, according to what men of science say, extends throughout their entire content, so also in the case of married people there ought to be a mutual amalgamation of their bodies, property, friends, and relations" (trans. Frank Cole Babbitt, ed. and trans., *Plutarch's Moralia*, LCL (Cambridge: Harvard University Press; London: William Heinemann, 1962), 2:325. See also 138E-F, 140E-F, and *Moralia* 769F *(Amatorius)*; and cf. *Moralia* 156D *(Septem sapientium convivium)*. Regarding Stoic influence on these passages, see Helge Almquist, *Plutarch und das Neue Testament: Ein Beitrag zum Corpus Hellenisticum Novi Testamenti*, ASNU 15 (Uppsala: Appelberg, 1946), 96-97; A. A. Long, *Hellenistic Philosophy: Stoics, Epicureans, Sceptics*, 2nd ed. (Berkeley: University of California Press, 1986), 159-60; and André-Jean Voelke, *Les rapports avec autrui dans la philosophie grecque: D'Aristote à Panétius*, Bibilothèque d'histoire de la philosophie (Paris: J. Vrin, 1961), 150.

53. Wilhelm Dittenberger, *Sylloge Inscriptionum Graecarum*, 3rd ed. (Leipzig: S. Hirzel, 1917; reprint, Hildesheim: Georg Olms, 1982), 2.783.30-34. The inscription dates from the late first century B.C.E. and speaks of a wife being "commingled" (συγκερασθεῖσα) with her husband in marriage, "for lives were yoked with lives and souls with bodies" (ἐζεύγνυντο γὰρ βίοι βίοις καὶ σώμασιν ψυχαί). On Stoic usage of the term συγκεράννυμι, see Conzelmann, 214 and n. 34 (regarding 1 Cor. 12:24, "God combined the body," ὁ θεὸς συνεκέρασεν τὸ σῶμα).

ies, whereas Paul speaks of the *exchange* of authority over one's body with a spouse.[54] But this assessment is only correct as far as an isolated reading of 7:4 goes, for Bruns overlooks the emphasis on mutuality in Paul's larger argument: in 7:5 Paul speaks of abstaining from sexual intercourse only "by *mutual* consent" (ἐκ συμφώνου). Thus, if we were to carry Bruns's interpretation to its logical conclusion, 7:5 would contradict 7:4, since an "exchange" of authority would mean that a spouse could unilaterally impose continence on a marriage partner by his or her exclusive authority over the other's body. But this is not only overly casuistic; it also misreads Paul's argument. Paul, quite reasonably, imposes the requirement of mutual consent in 7:5 *on the basis of* his assertions in 7:3-4, not in contradiction to them. His demand, "Do not rob one another!" (μὴ ἀποστερεῖτε ἀλλήλους), which is the immediate justification for mutual consent in 7:5, arises directly out of his discussion of marital obligations in verses 3-4, and even reflects the language of marital obligation he introduces in verse 3.[55]

In reality, then, Paul's assertion that "the wife does not rule over her own body, but the husband does" implies no "exchange" of rights between partners. Rather, it means that the wife *alone* does not rule over her own body, but the husband does *also*, and vice versa for the husband, just as we find in Stoic documents. From a syntactical standpoint, moreover, this is not at all surprising, since Paul uses the very same manner of elliptical expression later in the chapter, in verses 32-34: "The unmarried man concerns himself with the things of the Lord . . . the married man concerns himself with the things of the world . . . and he is divided." Here again Paul seems to have set up two mu-

---

54. Bruns, 181.

55. Noted by Weiß, *Korintherbrief,* 173, and Wolbert, 81. See Exod. 21:10 LXX: "he will not deprive (ἀποστερήσει) her of her necessities, and clothing, and sexual relations." For the use of στερέομαι in marriage contracts, see Häge, 73-74, 79-80, although he notes (163-64) that the term does not occur in the common era. Regarding the possible influence of Exod. 21:10 LXX on Jewish and non-Jewish marriage contracts in Egypt, see Jacob J. Rabinowitz, *Jewish Law: Its Influence on the Development of Legal Institutions* (New York: Block, 1956), 45-47, 56-60, 65-66. Cf. Sir. 28:15; and [Aristotle] *Oeconomicus* 3.2: "Wherefore a man of sound mind ought not to forget what honours are proper to his parents or what fittingly belong to his wife and children; so that rendering to each and all their own, he may obey the law of men and of gods. For the deprivation we feel most of all is that of the special honour which is our due. . . . Now to a wife nothing is of more value, nothing more rightfully her own, than honoured and faithful partnership with her husband" (trans. Hugh Trendennick and G. Cyril Armstrong, eds. and trans., *Aristotle,* vol. 18, *Metaphysics: Books X-XIV, Oeconomica, and Magna Moralia,* LCL [Cambridge: Harvard University Press; London: Wm. Heinemann, 1935], 409).

tually exclusive categories. Yet, as several scholars have pointed out, since Paul is speaking about a Christian man in both cases, he must mean that the unmarried man concerns himself with the things of the Lord *alone,* while the married man *also* concerns himself with the things of the world. Otherwise it would be impossible to explain why the latter is "divided."[56] Thus, despite Bruns's objection, 7:4 looks a great deal like a Stoic argument that Paul has enlisted for his own purposes.

At this point let us briefly summarize our findings. The logic of 7:1-6 appears to be something like this: In 7:1b Paul quotes a Cynic view on sexual relations, "it is good for a man not to touch a woman." This represents a Corinthian position, and may come from their letter to Paul. Given the many parallels with Stoic authors in 7:1-5, it was evidently held by members of the congregation with an interest in Stoic philosophy, as Stoics sometimes held Cynic views on marriage.[57] In 7:2-6 Paul qualifies this view with Stoic assertions on the mutuality of the marriage relationship and with Judeo-Christian concerns about extramarital sexual relations. The result, in 7:5, is a modified Cynic position for married Christians that condones limited degrees of abstinence within marriage.

With this, however, our understanding of these verses is still incomplete, for there is a final aspect of 7:5 that requires our attention. In this verse Paul allows for sexual abstinence within marriage so that spouses might have leisure for prayer. This is a rather obscure notion. The rationale behind it seems to be either that sex is time-consuming or "distracting,"[58] which would be a Cynic

---

56. So Niederwimmer, 113; C. K. Barrett, *A Commentary on the First Epistle to the Corinthians,* HNTC (New York and Evanston, Ill.: Harper and Row, 1968), 179; cf. Clement of Alexandria, *Stromateis,* bk. 3, chap. 12.88.2-3 (2.236.28–237.4 Stählin); *Paedagogus,* bk. 2, chap. 10.109.4 (1.223.1-9 S.). As is often noted, Johann Albrecht Bengel, *Gnomon of the New Testament* (Philadelphia: Perkinpine and Higgins, 1864; reprint, 1888), 2:199, styled Paul's elliptical manner of expression in 7:4 an "elegant paradox."

57. On the view that the Cynic ideas here belong to Cynics, not Stoics (e.g., John T. Fitzgerald, Review of *Paul on Marriage and Celibacy,* by Will Deming, *JR 77* [1997]: 290), see Will Deming, "The Unity of 1 Corinthians 5-6," *JBL* 115 (1996): 292-93 n. 12.

58. So C. F. Georg Heinrici, *Das erste Sendschreiben des Apostel Paulus an die Korinthier* (Berlin: Wilhelm Hertz, 1880), 190-91, noting that there is no mention of ritual uncleanness here, and citing Plutarch, *Vitae 69C (Numa),* which speaks of a worshiper's need for σχολή. See also Wettstein, 2:126, and Valckenaer, 2:204-5, cited above, n. 13. For Jewish materials see Steven D. Fraade, "Ascetical Aspects of Ancient Judaism," in *Jewish Spirituality: From the Bible through the Middle Ages,* ed. Arthur Green, World Spirituality: An Encyclopedic History of the Religious Quest 13 (New York: Crossroad, 1986), 274-75; and Eliezer Diamond, *Holy Men*

view, or that it rendered one ritually impure, and hence religiously unfit for prayer.[59] It may be that these two possibilities overlap, as Niederwimmer suggests, since ritual purification itself is time-consuming.[60] In any event, the notion that sex is in tension specifically with prayer, and that these two activities must be cordoned off into distinct spaces of time, is not Stoic. Rather, our closest parallel comes from the *Testament of Naphtali*, a pseudepigraphical work dated to the period 100 B.C.E.–100 C.E. One of the purposes of this work is to instruct its readers to discern the order of God's commandments in the end time. It depicts the patriarch Naphtali telling his sons that God has made them to exist in a world of "order" (τάξις), and that they must do nothing "out of its proper time" (ἔξω καιροῦ αὐτοῦ).[61] After some ramification, this theology is summed up near the end of the testament with the following words:

> For the commandments of the Law (αἱ ἐντολαὶ τοῦ νόμου) are double, and they are fulfilled with a regular method. For there is a time for intercourse with his wife (καιρὸς γὰρ συνουσίας γυναικὸς αὐτοῦ) and a time of continence for his prayer (καιρὸς ἐγκρατείας εἰς προσευχὴν αὐτοῦ). And there are two commandments; and if they should not be in their order they produce sin. It is also thus for the other commandments. Be, therefore, wise in God,

---

and Hunger Artists: Fasting and Asceticism in Rabbinic Culture (Oxford: Oxford University, 2003), 33-54. *m. Ketubot* 5.6 speaks of "seasons [for marital duty] spoken of in the Law," with reference to Exod. 21:10 (see above, n. 55). Philo, *De Decalogo* 96-101, says the Sabbath was set aside that one might have time to philosophize and have leisure (σχολάζω) to contemplate nature, while *Jub.* 50:8 forbids sexual intercourse on the Sabbath. Clement of Alexandria, *Paedagogus*, bk. 2, chap. 10.96.2 (1.215.6-11 S.), says Christians should not use time during the day for intercourse, but for praying, reading, or doing good.

59. On ritual purity and sexual continence, see especially Richard E. Oster, Jr., "Use, Misuse and Neglect of Archaeological Evidence in Some Modern Works on 1 Corinthians (1 Cor 7,1-5; 8,10; 11,2-16; 12,14-26)," *ZNW* 83 (1992): 60-64, although he too quickly dismisses the possibility of Stoic-Cynic influence. See also Bernhard Lohse, *Askese und Mönchtum in der Antike und in der alten Kirche*, Religion und Kultur der alten Mittelmeerwelt in Parallelforschungen 1 (Munich and Vienna: R. Oldenbourg, 1969), 25-41 (with lit.); Schrage, "Zur Frontstellung," 222-23; Exod. 19:15; Lev. 15:16-18; 1 Sam. 21:4-6; Josephus, *Against Apion* 2.198, 203; and Plutarch, *Moralia* 655D (*Quaestionum convivialium*), cf. 712C.

60. Niederwimmer, 93 n. 54. In any case, there is no mention here of the idea that sex is *morally* defiling. There is also no evidence for Brown's contention that 7:5 points to "protracted bouts of abstinence, like those with which contemporary Jewish prophets prepared themselves to receive their visions" (Peter Brown, 55). The issue here is continence for prayer, not visions.

61. *T. Naph.* 2:9-10; cf. 3:1-5 and 7:1. On the idea of apocalyptic "times," see also Luke 21:24; 1 Thess. 5:1; and cf. Dan. 2:21.

and discerning, knowing the order of his commands and the ordinance of everything, so that the Lord will love you.[62]

Here we see the dichotomy between sex and prayer put forth as the paradigmatic example of how a follower of God must be careful to discern the structure of God's will in the "last times."[63] The clumsiness of the expressions "*his* wife" and "*his* prayer" in Naphtali's admonitions indicates, moreover, that it had a previous history outside of this text and is being quoted here as an established dogma.[64] The verbal similarities between *Testament of Naphtali* 8:8 and 1 Corinthians 7:5 are also noteworthy. While Paul permits continence within marriage for a "time" (πρὸς καιρόν), Naphtali knows of a "time" for continence (καιρὸς ἐγκρατείας).[65] Furthermore, just as Paul is concerned that if the Corinthians overstep this "time" they will be tempted to sin, due to their "lack of continence" (ἀκρασία), Naphtali holds that overstepping the "time of continence" will also result in sin. Finally, both the *Testament of Naphtali* and Paul speak of their teachings in the context of "commandments." The former maintains that this teaching on intercourse and prayer *is* a commandment (ἐντολή) for the last times, while Paul is explicit that his ruling in 7:5 does *not* derive from a commandment (οὐ κατ᾽ ἐπιταγήν) (cf. 7:25).

For several reasons, therefore, it would appear that 1 Corinthians 7:5 and *Testament of Naphtali* 8:7-10 draw on a common tradition. This, in turn, provides us with our first clue as to the motivation for continence among the Corinthians. Evidently, like many other Christians in the first century, the Corinthians lived in expectation of the second coming.[66] Adhering to some form of the tradition now preserved in the *Testament of Naphtali*, they held that prayer in the period before the eschaton was particularly important,[67]

---

62. *T. Naph.* 8:7-10.

63. *T. Naph.* 8:1.

64. Jürgen Becker, *Untersuchungen zur Entstehungsgeschichte der Testamente der Zwölf Patriarchen*, AGJU 8 (Leiden: Brill, 1970), 214-18, 228, has argued that the underlying sources of *T. Naph.* 2, 3, and 8 are in the style of "synagogue sermons." Given a Semitic original for this text, one could also perhaps read the disconcerting αὐτοῦ as referring to either God ("He has a time for . . .") or, as 8:7 might suggest, the Law ("it has [specifies] a time for . . ."), but then we would expect a dative rather than the genitive.

65. Cf. Paul's use of ἐγκρατεύομαι in 1 Cor. 7:9.

66. See 1 Cor. 1:7; 15:51-52; and the discussion of 7:25-31 below.

67. On the importance of prayer in apocalyptic times, see Phil. 4:5b-6, Luke 21:34-36, and

even to the extent that sexual intercourse needed to be curtailed since, for whatever reason, it inhibited prayer.

If this is correct, then Paul's argument in 7:1-6 must be understood as combining elements of Stoic philosophy with both the Judeo-Christian concern about *porneia* and apocalyptic ideas. Yet how is this possible? The link between these various spheres of thought has come about, I would suggest, through the medium of Jewish wisdom traditions, for not only is the avoidance of *porneia* an important theme in this literature, but in the Hellenistic period Jewish wisdom feeds into both popular philosophy[68] and apocalyptic texts.[69] In fact, the *Testaments of the Twelve Patriarchs,* of which the *Testament of Naphtali* is a part, may be a case in point for this type of syncretism: on the one hand, it stands somewhere between Jewish wisdom and apocalyptic traditions and takes a very pronounced position against *porneia*,[70] and on the other hand, some scholars detect the influence of Stoicism in the *Testaments*.[71]

---

1 Pet. 4:7. In Philippians and Luke prayer is contrasted with "worrying" (μεριμνάω) and with the cares or "worries" (μέριμναι) of life, which will be Paul's topic in 1 Cor. 7:32-34.

68. As seen, e.g., in Sirach, Philo, and the *Sentences of Pseudo-Phocylides.*

69. See, e.g., John J. Collins, "Cosmos and Salvation: Jewish Wisdom and Apocalyptic in the Hellenistic Age," *HR* 17 (1977): 121-42; Jonathan Z. Smith, "Wisdom and Apocalyptic," in *Map Is Not Territory: Studies in the History of Religions,* SJLA 23 (Leiden: Brill, 1979), 67-87; and Florentino García Martínez, "Wisdom and Apocalyptic in the Dead Sea Scrolls and in the Biblical Tradition," *Ephemerides Theologicae Lovanienses* 78 (2002): 536-49. The mixing of popular philosophy with wisdom and apocalyptic traditions is also attested in the synoptics; see, e.g., John S. Kloppenborg, *The Formation of Q: Trajectories in Ancient Wisdom Collections,* Studies in Antiquity and Christianity (Philadelphia: Fortress, 1987), passim; Burton L. Mack, *A Myth of Innocence: Mark and Christian Origins* (Philadelphia: Fortress, 1988), 57-62, 67-69, 73-74, 325-31; Gerd Theissen, *Sociology of Early Palestinian Christianity* (Philadelphia: Fortress, 1977), 8-16; and Theissen, *Social Setting,* 27, 39, 44-49, 50, 58. On Theissen, see Richard A. Horsley, *Sociology and the Jesus Movement* (New York: Crossroad, 1989), 46-47, 116-19.

70. See, e.g., Howard Clark Kee, "Testaments of the Twelve Patriarchs," in *The Old Testament Pseudepigrapha,* ed. James H. Charlesworth (Garden City, N.Y.: Doubleday, 1985), 1:779-80.

71. See Kee, "Testaments," 779, 782 n. 1c, 783 n. 4b; Kee, "The Ethical Dimensions of the Testaments of the XII as a Clue to Provenance," *NTS* 24 (1978): 269; and Harm W. Hollander, *Joseph as an Ethical Model in the Testaments of the Twelve Patriarchs,* SVTP 6 (Leiden: Brill, 1981), 95, 103-4 n. 56 (with literature and criticism of Kee). One possible instance of Stoic influence occurs in *T. Naph.* 2:1-10, where our author first introduces his doctrine of divine order and appropriate times. Here he employs the image of the human body, a metaphor of divine order often found in Stoic authors (see, e.g., Conzelmann, 211 and n. 8). Paul also uses this metaphor in 1 Cor. 12:12-26: compare *T. Naph.* 2:8a, "For God made all [parts of the body — see 2:8b] good,

Paul concludes his argument in 7:1-6 with a statement that may again combine wisdom and Stoic thinking. He says in verse 7: "I want all men to be as I myself also am; but each has his own *charisma* from God, one in this way, one in that way." A few scholars take the position that Paul envisions both marriage and continence as a charisma, or "gift of grace" (χάρισμα).[72] Most, however, reject this theory, arguing that Paul speaks only of continence as a gift. Niederwimmer, an advocate of the latter position, even ridicules the former position as no more than "an adventurous misunderstanding," adding, *"Marriage for Paul is not grace, rather, a sign for the dearth of grace,* namely for the dearth of the charisma of ἐγκράτεια [continence]. . . . As for the other gifts of grace, through which the married are compensated, it is self-evident that marriage (!) is not intended."[73] Yet such an extreme characterization of

---

in the correct order," with 1 Cor. 12:18, "God set the members, each one of them in the body as he wanted"; and *T. Naph.* 2:10a, "For if you should tell the eye to hear, it cannot," with 1 Cor. 12:17a, "If all the body is an eye, where is the hearing?" *T. Naph.* 8:7-10 may itself have originated as an esoteric interpretation of another wisdom tradition, namely, Eccles. 3:1-8. There we are told that "there is a proper time (καιρός/עת) for every activity under heaven." In *T. Naph.* 8:7-10 these "proper times" have been given apocalyptic significance, enabling those who are "wise in God and discerning" (8:10) to participate in God's ordering of the last times, thereby keeping themselves from sin (8:9). If Stoic-minded Corinthians had been familiar with the *Naphtali* tradition and the text from Ecclesiastes, they may have been persuaded that these traditions spoke directly to their consternations about marriage. This is because the verse immediately before Eccles. 3:1-8 promises wisdom to "the good man" (τῷ ἀνθρώπῳ τῷ ἀγαθῷ), whereas the sinner, whom *T. Naph.* 8:9 identifies as the person acting contrary to God's ordering of the times, is given "distraction," or περισπασμόν (2:26; cf. 3:10), which in the Stoic-Cynic marriage debate was the antithesis of "leisure" (σχολή). For a philosophical counterpart to this doctrine of appropriate times, see Plutarch, *Moralia* 653B-655D *(Quaestiones convivales)*, which is a treatise entitled *On the Proper Time for Sexual Intercourse* (περὶ καιροῦ συνουσίας — cf. *T. Naph.* 8:8), and the adage that Diogenes Laertius 4.42 attributes to Arcesilaus (ca. 315-240 B.C.E.): "But this very thing belongs especially to philosophy, to know the proper time of each thing" (τὸ τὸν καιρὸν ἑκάστων ἐπίστασθαι). Cf. also Clement of Alexandria, *Stromateis*, bk. 3, chap. 12.81.5 and chap. 14.94.3 (2.233.5-6; 239.16-18 S.), who refers to a proper time for begetting children (ὁ τῆς παιδοποιίας καιρός), and declares that Adam's sin was desiring the gift of marriage before the proper time.

72. E.g., David R. Cartlidge, "Competing Theologies of Asceticism in the Early Church" (Th.D. diss., Harvard University, 1969), 47; Allo, 159; and P. Tischleder, *Wesen und Stellung der Frau nach der Lehre des heiligen Paulus: Eine ethisch-exegetische Untersuchung*, NTAbh 10/3-4 (Münster: Aschendorff, 1923), 14 n. 33 (citing others).

73. Niederwimmer, 96 n. 70 (emphasis and overpunctuation Niederwimmer's); cf. Weiß, *Korintherbrief*, 176; Hans Lietzmann, *An die Korinther I·II*, rev. Werner Georg Kümmel, 5th ed., HNT 9 (Tübingen: Mohr, 1969), 30; and Conzelmann, 118. Niederwimmer is followed by Peter

7:7 finds little support in the preceding verses. If I have interpreted 7:1-6 accurately, Paul is attempting to put a damper on the inclinations of married Christians who endorse a Cynic position by arguing that only a limited degree of abstinence is possible within marriage. Since divorce for Christians is also out of the question (7:10-11), it would run counter to his purpose for Paul to conclude his discussion in verses 1-6 by implying that marriage brands one with the "stigma of the necessity of sex."[74] Unless we are to understand Paul as risking taunting his readers by announcing that some are excluded from the charisma of continence, but will be compensated with some other, unspecified gift, it makes better sense to read verse 7 as Paul's effort to reconcile these Corinthians to their fate, not to goad them regarding their presumed shortcomings.[75]

But quite aside from this, the preceding verses indicate that the contrast Paul draws in 7:7 is not one between incontinent *married* Christians, on the one side, and continent *unmarried* Christians, on the other, but between *married* Christians who are able to forgo sexual relations and those who are not. This is clearly his concern in 7:4-6, at least. Most probably, therefore, Paul's mention of the charismata is a reminder to those spouses who are advocating abstinence that all Christians, including their own husbands and wives, are not endowed with the same gifts.[76] What we see in 7:7, in other words, is both Paul's deference to the celibate tendencies of these spouses and his insistence that their demands are overbearing.

It is from this perspective, I would contend, that we should also interpret the beginning of verse 7, where Paul says, "I want all men to be as I myself also

---

Brown, 56-57, who concludes that for Paul and the Corinthians "marriage, like household slavery, was a 'calling' devoid of glamor." Brown (56-57) also refers to the gift in 7:7 as the "prophetic gift of continence" and the "apostolic gift of celibacy," which, he explains, "was too precious a thing to extend to the Church as a whole." Rather, he says, "Paul tended to solve the issue of the precise position of celibacy in the Christian church by sweeping it into the high trajectory of his own apostolic calling." This baroque elaboration on Niederwimmer derives from a very superficial reading of the text. Paul never refers to the gift in 7:7 as a "calling," nor is it possible to show that he considered it an "apostolic" or "prophetic" gift. To the contrary, we have no reason to think that the "virgins" in 7:25ff., among whom Paul promotes celibacy, are either apostolic or prophetic, and in 9:5 Paul speaks of marriage, not celibacy, as an apostolic right, noting that the "other apostles and the brothers of the Lord and Cephas" were married.

74. So Niederwimmer, 96.

75. Cf. David R. Cartlidge, "1 Corinthians 7 as a Foundation for a Christian Sex Ethic," *JR* 55 (1975): 224; Schrage, "Zur Frontstellung," 233-34.

76. This is a point that Paul makes again, more elaborately, in 1 Cor. 12.

am, *but . . ."* (θέλω δὲ πάντας . . . ἀλλὰ . . .). Since Paul lived in a celibate state himself (7:8; 9:5), these words probably function in a "diplomatic" manner, enabling Paul to identify with the Corinthians and advise them.[77] A similar manner of persuasion may be found in 1 Corinthians 14. In an attempt to quell the Corinthians' fascination for speaking in tongues (chaps. 12–14), Paul expresses both his empathy and his reservations by stating in 14:5, "I want you all to speak in tongues — *but rather* that you might prophesy" (θέλω δὲ πάντας . . . μᾶλλον δὲ . . .), and in 14:18-19, "I thank God I speak in tongues more than all of you, but. . . ."[78] And it is surely more than coincidence that the topic here, as in 7:7, is charismata.[79]

With this understanding of 7:7, let us return to our initial concern for evidence of Stoicism and Jewish wisdom here. On what basis, after all, can Paul or the Corinthians maintain that continence within marriage is a gift from God? Even though this notion is all but lacking for the first century, it does have a parallel of sorts in Wisdom of Solomon 8:20-21, where, in his zeal to possess Lady Wisdom, King Solomon fashions a plan: "As a child I was naturally clever, and was possessed of a good soul — or, rather, being good, I entered into an undefiled body. But knowing that I would not otherwise be in possession (ἔσομαι ἐγκρατής)[80] unless God should give (ἐὰν μὴ ὁ θεὸς δῷ) — and this was discretion, to know whose gift it is (τίνος ἡ χάρις) — I appealed to the Lord."[81] While modern translators are in agreement that the "posses-

---

77. So Ben Witherington III, *Women in the Earliest Churches*, SNTSMS 59 (Cambridge: Cambridge University Press, 1988), 29-30; see also Norbert Baumert, *Ehelosigkeit und Ehe im Herrn: Eine Neuinterpretation von 1 Kor 7*, FB 47 (Würzburg: Echter, 1984), 55-56.

78. On the rhetorical intent of 1 Cor. 14:5, 18-19, see Gerd Theissen, *Psychological Aspects of Pauline Theology* (Philadelphia: Fortress, 1987), 292-94; and Wayne A. Meeks, *The First Urban Christians: The Social World of the Apostle Paul* (New Haven and London: Yale University Press, 1983), 121.

79. S. Scott Bartchy, *ΜΑΛΛΟΝ ΧΡΗΣΑΙ: First-Century Slavery and the Interpretation of 1 Corinthians 7:21*, SBLDS 11 (Missoula: University of Montana Press, 1973), 149-50, also notes the similarity between 7:7a and 14:5. Niederwimmer has been persuaded completely by Paul's rhetorical strategy — see 95 ("The contrast between wish and reality determines the text. Verse 7a sounds like a deep sigh, and v. 7b like a consolation — for [Paul] himself and for the others") and 94 n. 61 ("That which Paul actually wishes is [according to v. 7] clearly celibacy").

80. The future expresses the direct discourse of the thought.

81. Cited in this connection by a number of scholars, e.g., Kümmel in Lietzmann, 176; H. Chadwick, "'All Things to All Men' (I Cor. ix.22)," *NTS* 1 (1954/55): 265 n. 3; and Weiß, *Korintherbrief*, 176 n. 1. Weiß also cites *Aristeas* 248 and 327 (177 n. 1 — the latter inverted as "237" in his text), but these refer to discretion in the behavior of children and self-control in matters of health (both times σωφροσύνη), not sexual continence. Other passages scholars sometimes

sion" of which Solomon speaks is of Lady Wisdom, and that he also desires that God give him wisdom,[82] the Greek is ambiguous. For Paul or for a Corinthian devoted to celibacy, Solomon's words could easily be construed to mean that the gift (χάρις) God gives is continence (ἐγκράτεια), which is close to what we find in 1 Corinthians 7:7b.

As for the inspiration that may have led to this particular interpretation of Wisdom 8:20-21, we may consider the following three facts. First, we have seen from 1 Corinthians 7:1-5 that a negative, "Cynic" position on sexual relations seems to have been current among the Corinthians, mediated via Stoic thought. Second, Paul's empathetic wish in 7:7a, that all could be like him, suggests that his celibate lifestyle served as a model for the Corinthians. And third, in 9:1-5, in justifying his lifestyle more generally, Paul's words closely resemble a passage from Epictetus. Paul declares, "Am I not free (οὐκ εἰμὶ ἐλεύθερος)? Am I not an apostle? Have I not seen Jesus our Lord? . . . Do I not have a right to travel with a Christian sister as a wife, as do the rest of the apostles and the brothers of the Lord and Cephas?" This we may compare with claims that Epictetus puts in the mouth of his ideal philosopher, the Cynic: "Look at me! . . . no wife, no children. . . . And what do I lack? Am I not without pain? Am I not without fear? Am I not free (οὐκ εἰμὶ ἐλεύθερος)?"[83] In light of these observations, and given the Stoic influences identified in 7:1-5, it is quite possible that the Corinthians saw in Paul (as elsewhere in their society) a Stoic model of celibacy that they sought to imitate. This, in turn, may have led them to claim a "gift" of continence on the basis of Wisdom 8:20-21, a gift which Paul, before them, may have claimed. As with the preceding six verses, therefore, 1 Corinthians 7:7 may also represent a synthesis of ideas from Stoic philosophers and Jewish sages.

---

cite include *1 Clement* 35.2 and 38.1-2, but these are dependent on Paul — see William A. Heth, "Unmarried 'For the Sake of the Kingdom' (Matthew 19:12) in the Early Church," *Grace Theological Journal* 8 (1987): 74. See also Clement of Alexandria, *Stromateis*, bk. 3, chap. 1.4.3; chap. 7.57.2 (2.197.10-11; 222.18-19 S.).

82. E.g., David Winston, *The Wisdom of Solomon: A New Translation with Introduction and Commentary*, AB 43 (Garden City, N.Y.: Doubleday, 1979), 199.

83. Epictetus, *Discourses* 3.22.47-48. On the resemblance of these two passages, see Conzelmann, 152 and n. 7, and Theissen, *Social Setting*, 39, 44.

Marriage out of Passion: 7:8-9

Our next indication of Stoic and Cynic influence in 1 Corinthians 7 comes in 7:9. In 7:8 Paul advises those who were married previously and are now single[84] to remain single. Verse 9 then adds an exception: if they cannot control themselves (ἐγκρατεύομαι), they should marry, "for it is better to marry than to burn" (κρεῖττον γάρ ἐστιν γαμῆσαι ἢ πυροῦσθαι). Although this justification for marriage is similar to what we find in 7:2, 5-6, the emphasis is not the same. There it is the prevention of a sin, *porneia*, that makes marital relations necessary. Here it is the force of one's sex drive, which Paul, along with his Stoic, Cynic, and Jewish contemporaries, seems to have considered a natural or God-given aspect of human existence.[85]

Inasmuch as this difference in emphasis is significant, we need to look beyond the Judeo-Christian concern for *porneia* if we are to locate statements that approximate the rationale of 7:9. These are found in the marriage discussions of several Stoics, including Ocellus, Musonius, and Hierocles, where nature is depicted as promoting marriage by equipping human beings with strong sexual urges.[86] An even closer parallel is provided in Epictetus's discussion of marriage for the Cynic. In the midst of offering several reasons why the Cynic cannot marry, Epictetus is interrupted by an objection: the renowned Cynic Crates married. Yes, replies Epictetus scornfully, but this was a special case. Not only was his wife Hipparchia fully his equal, being "another Crates," but this marriage was necessitated "out of passionate love" (ἐξ ἔρωτος).[87] Finally, we may point out that Paul's image in 7:9 of passionate love as something burning is also found in Jewish wisdom literature;[88] in the writings of moralists such as Seneca, Plutarch, and Philo;[89] and in an epigram in the *Greek Anthology* in

84. This is how I understand οἱ ἄγαμοι, "the unmarried" (see 7:11, 34).

85. For Paul, along with 1 Cor. 7:3-5, 7, see Rom. 1:26-27, and above, pp. 45-46. For Stoics and Jews, see next note.

86. See [Ocellus] (app. B), *De univ. nat.* 44; Musonius, frag. 14.92.9-17 L. (71.11–72.3 H.); and Hierocles 52.28–53.8 v. A. (Stobaeus 4.502.15–503.5 W.-H.). Cf. *T. Reub.* 2:2-8, which maintains that the "spirit of procreation and intercourse" was given to human beings at creation "that there be in them every work of man."

87. Epictetus, *Discourses* 3.22.76. See also 4.1.147, cited below, p. 205. A popular *Cynic* position in the time of the empire, by contrast, was that sexual desire necessitated sex, not marriage; Crates was the exception.

88. See Prov. 6:27-28; Sir. 9:8b; 23:17; *T. Jos.* 2:2.

89. Seneca, *De beneficiis* 4.14.1; *De matrimonio*, in Jerome, *Adversus Jovinianum* 1.49; Plutarch, *Moralia* 138F (*Coniugalia praecepta*), 752D, 753A, 759B-C, 765B-C (cf. 762D and 764B-D)

which Crates speaks of the difficulty of quenching the "flame" (φλόξ) of passion.[90] In Paul, moreover, it reappears in the Stoic-sounding Romans 1:27.[91]

Marriage as Slavery to an Outside Influence: 7:10-24

The Unholiness of a Non-Christian Spouse
as Grounds for Divorce (7:10-15a)

From his discussion of remarriage for formerly married Christians in 7:8-9,
Paul moves to the related topic of divorce and remarriage for Christians presently married in 7:10-11, a practice he forbids. Here he bases his position on
Jesus' prohibition of divorce, the implications of which, according to Paul,
bear on the separation of spouses as well. In 7:12-24 Paul then turns to yet another related topic, the question of divorce among Christians who have non-
Christian spouses. For some reason Jesus' words do not apply in this situation. Perhaps their validity was seen as resting on the equality of rights that
they accorded marriage partners, an equality that vanished if a non-Christian
husband or wife felt no compunction to abide by Jesus' command. In any
case, Paul is obliged to spell out his own ruling on this matter (see v. 12a). For
our purposes this is especially fortunate since the particular justifications
Paul gives allow us to postulate why the Corinthians objected to living with
non-Christian spouses. And here, again, we find Stoic and Cynic influence.

In 7:12-15a Paul considers two scenarios, both of which he presents in the
form of an "if . . . then" proposition. In verses 12-13 he states that if a non-

---

(all *Amatorius*), and in Stobaeus 4.468.21–469.3 W.-H.; Philo, *De Decalogo* 122; *De specialibus
legibus* 3.10.

90. *Greek Anthology* 9.497.

91. It also occurs in erotic and satirical authors, but since these would have scoffed at the
suggestion that the flame of sexual passion is properly extinguished in marriage, the source of
7:9b is best postulated among those writings just cited. It is also quite possible that the clause "it
is better to marry than to burn" is a maxim that Paul is quoting. This is suggested by three
things: the Attic spelling of "better" (κρεῖττον) rather than the koine spelling (κρεῖσσον) which
Paul prefers elsewhere (7:39; 11:17; Phil. 1:23); the rhetorical flourish at the end, provided by the
assonance between "to marry" and "to burn" (γαμῆσαι ἢ πυροῦσθαι), which is also indicative of
a maxim; and Tertullian's knowledge of an anecdote that parodies this clause, even though
Tertullian does not appear to be dependent on Paul when he uses it (*De exhortatione castitatis*
13.3; and *De monogamia* 17.2).

Christian spouse agrees (συνευδοκέω) to continue living with the Christian, then the Christian must not divorce him or her. A justification for this ruling follows in verse 14. In the second scenario, which comes in verse 15a, Paul considers the other possibility. He states that if the non-Christian leaves, then the Christian must simply abide by that decision. In contrast to the first, no justification follows this second ruling; rather, it concludes with the abrupt and definitive sounding "if he leaves, let him leave" (εἰ . . . χωρίζεται, χωριζέσθω). Quite reasonably, Paul felt no need to justify the actions of a non-Christian, and as the tone of his conclusion seems to indicate, he saw divorce or abandonment by a non-Christian as a fait accompli over which the Christian had no control anyway. Paul's initial justification for demanding that a Christian not divorce a non-Christian is thus contained in 7:14. Here he maintains, "For the unbelieving husband has been made holy by the wife, and the unbelieving wife has been made holy by the brother," adding further, "Otherwise (ἐπεὶ ἄρα) your children are unclean, but as it is (νῦν δέ) they are holy."

In reconstructing the issues Paul addresses in 7:12-24, it seems reasonable to assume from this verse that the Corinthians have objected to living with unbelievers based on a conviction that the latter were unclean, and that through an association as close as marriage, which, as Paul insists, must include sexual relations (7:3-5),[92] an unbeliever would render them unclean as well. In this way Paul's statement that the Christian spouse has made the non-Christian "holy" can be interpreted as a refutation of this conviction. Not only does the non-Christian not pollute the Christian, Paul says, but the reverse is true: Christians "decontaminate" a non-Christian, overcoming his or her uncleanness with their holiness.

The rest of verse 14 is Paul's substantiation of this ambitious claim. His logic, as scholars generally agree, depends on the assumption that the Corinthians considered their children to be "holy," regardless of how they viewed their spouses.[93] Why they held this position we do not know,[94] but it seems to

---

92. In contrast to the explicitness of 7:3-5, and perhaps out of deference to his audience, Paul speaks in vv. 12-13 of unbelievers agreeing to "live with" (οἰκεῖν μετά) their Christian spouses. In a section of his *Marriage Precepts* that is flavored with Stoic imagery, Plutarch makes a similar distinction between συμβιοῦν, which he considers the full union of a husband and wife, and συνοικεῖν, which he calls a lesser union (*Moralia* 142F).

93. E.g., Bachmann, 270; Lietzmann, 31; Joseph Blinzler, "Zur Auslegung von I. Kor. 7,14," in *Aus der Welt und Umwelt des Neuen Testaments: Gesammelte Aufsätze 1*, SBB (Stuttgart: Katholisches Bibelwerk, 1969), 180-82; Wolbert, 102-3.

94. Scholars generally reject the suggestion that the children's holiness stems from Jewish

make the best sense of Paul's otherwise unsupported assertion, "but as it is, they are holy." On the basis of this assumption Paul designs an argument that both establishes his own position and shows that the Corinthians' position leads to an untenable conclusion. If, he says in essence, the Corinthians are right in holding that the close associations with an unbeliever demanded by marriage render them unclean, then their children, who are the product of one of marriage's closest associations, would also be unclean.[95] But since their children are not only not unclean but instead holy, then the Corinthians' fear that the uncleanness of an unbelieving spouse is something that pollutes is unfounded — indeed, the reverse must be true: through marriage and sexual relations the holiness of the Christian spreads contagiously; the non-Christian spouse "has been made holy" by the believing wife or husband.

If this is an accurate interpretation of Paul's first argument in 7:12-24, then two aspects of 7:14 warrant our attention. First, we should note that Paul

---

proselyte baptism, our only knowledge of which comes from late rabbinic sources. See Gerhard Delling, "Nun aber sind sie heilig," in *Studien zum Neuen Testament und zum hellenistischen Judentum: Gesammelte Aufsätze 1950-1968,* ed. Ferdinand Hahn et al. (Göttingen: Vandenhoeck & Ruprecht, 1970), 264-66, and Blinzler, 166. For those supporting this interpretation see Lietzmann, 31; Herbert Braun, "Exegetische Randglossen zum 1. Korintherbrief," in *Gesammelte Studien zum Neuen Testament und seiner Umwelt,* 2nd ed. (Tübingen: Mohr, 1967), 192. Christian baptism must also be excluded as the source of their holiness, not only because it makes nonsense of Paul's argument, but also because it is irrelevant. If the children were holy by virtue of being baptized, then Paul could not prove from their holiness what he wants to prove, namely, that a Christian makes his or her unbelieving partner holy; and if the conceded point in Paul's argument was that baptism secured the holiness of the children, it is difficult to see why this whole matter surfaced in the first place, for the believing spouse was also baptized and therefore should be in no more danger of pollution than the children. On this see Blinzler, 167-69, 183; Weiß, *Korintherbrief,* 182; and Kümmel in Lietzmann, 177. If, however, it was the Corinthians' opinion that a spouse was indeed more vulnerable than the children because of the intimacy of conjugal relations, then an argument from child baptism would be even more superfluous. See next note.

95. Delling, "Nun aber sind sie heilig," 267-69; Delling, "Zur Exegese von I. Kor. 7,14," in *Studien zum Neuen Testament und zum hellenistischen Judentum,* 283; and Delling, "Lexikalisches zu τέκνον: Ein Nachtrag zur Exegese von I. Kor. 7,14," in *Studien zum Neuen Testament und zum hellenistischen Judentum,* 270-80, holds that Paul is speaking of grown children. But if Paul's point of reference was simply the children's familial association with their unbelieving parents, not their physical origin from their parents' sexual union, his argument would be extremely vulnerable. In this case the Corinthians could reply yes, but the analogy with children is inappropriate, for while a child may remain holy in his or her interaction with a non-Christian parent, this interaction is not nearly as close as that between a husband and wife (which Delling, "Nun aber sind sie heilig," 268, also admits).

designates the children of a Christian parent as "holy" (ἅγιος), and says of the unbelieving spouse that he or she "has been made holy" (ἡγίασται). By this Paul cannot mean that either the children or the spouse has been saved, for neither has acquired this holiness through faith, which is elsewhere Paul's prerequisite for salvation. Holiness has apparently been imparted to the children "genetically" at birth, while the spouse, whom Paul continues to call an "unbeliever" (v. 15a), has received it through contact with the Christian.[96] Furthermore, in verse 16 Paul speaks of the spouse's salvation as still a future possibility. This means that the concept of holiness in 7:14 must signify an acceptability or usefulness to God quite apart from salvation.[97] This is perhaps not as strange as it first appears, for in 1 Thessalonians 5:23 Paul prays that God will make the Thessalonians "thoroughly holy" (ἁγιάσαι . . . ὁλοτελεῖς). Since the Thessalonians are already Christians, this, too, must refer to something other than salvation.

The second aspect of 7:14 that warrants our attention is that Paul does not make a clear distinction in this verse between the physical and the moral spheres of human interaction. Instead of speaking of "cleanness" as the opposite of "uncleanness," or of "unholiness" as the opposite of "holiness," he mixes these categories, claiming that the children involved are not "unclean" but rather "holy." Since he also talks of holiness as something that can be transferred between spouses and from parents to children, in 7:12-24 it appears that Paul is addressing the fear of *moral* pollution via *physical* association with non-Christians. In our attempt to determine why the Corinthians have objected to living with non-Christian spouses, it will be useful to examine two other texts from the Corinthian correspondence in which the same concern appears.

The first is 1 Corinthians 5–6. From 5:9-13 we learn that Paul had already written a letter to the Corinthians on the subject of associating with non-Christians:

> I wrote to you in the letter not to mix together with sexually immoral persons — not at all meaning with the sexually immoral of this world, or with greedy persons and robbers, or idolaters. Otherwise (ἐπεὶ . . . ἄρα), you would need to go out of the world. But as it is (νῦν δέ), I wrote to you not to mix together if someone calling himself a brother should be a sexually im-

---

96. On other, less likely possibilities see Meyer, 204-5; Delling, "Nun aber sind sie heilig," 257-61.

97. The NEB translation renders this as the unbelieving spouse "belongs to God."

moral person, or a greedy person, or an idolater. . . . With such a person do not eat together. For what business is it of mine to judge outsiders?

Here we see the same fear of moral defilement through physical association that we found in 7:14, as well as the same argument *ad absurdum*. Thus 5:9 speaks of "mixing together" (συναναμίγνυσθαι) with immoral persons, while 5:11 forbids mixing and "eating together" (συνεσθίειν) with Christians who act immorally.

Several verses later, in 6:11, Paul returns to this quasi-physical language of pollution, maintaining that Christians have been "washed" of immoral behavior (ἀπολούω); and in 6:15-16 he contends, on the basis of Genesis 2:24, that Christians who "join themselves" (κολλάομαι) to prostitutes become "one flesh" with them, stating in 6:18 that this is a sin against the body.[98] These last verses also indicate that Paul's concern, as in 7:12-15a, is with associations of a sexual nature with non-Christians.[99] In fact, 6:15-18 is something of a mirror image of 7:14. In the one passage Paul rules that an illicit relationship with a non-Christian pollutes the Christian; in the other he rules that marriage with a Christian sanctifies the non-Christian. Finally, the rather surprising claim of 7:14-16, that the unbelieving spouse has been "made holy" by the Christian but not thereby saved, seems to be clarified by what Paul says in 6:1-11. In these verses he distinguishes between Christians, whom he calls the "holy ones" (ἅγιοι), and "unbelievers" (ἄπιστοι), whom he identifies as the "unjust" (ἄδικοι), by maintaining that Christians have both been made holy *and justified*. Presumably, it is this act of justification (through faith) that the unbelieving spouses in 7:12-16 lack.[100]

The second text which may add to our understanding of Paul's logic in 7:12-15a is the mysterious 2 Corinthians 6:14–7:1. While scholars still have many questions about the function of these six verses in their present context, they generally agree that they form a cohesive unit in their own right, with no obvious connection, at least, to what precedes or follows. This raises the possibility that they are either a set piece that Paul is quoting, a misplaced text, or

---

98. Meeks, *The First Urban Christians*, 153, comments that in 1 Cor. 5–6 Paul "takes as self-evident that pure/impure can be a metaphor for moral/immoral."

99. While Paul generalizes his discussion in 5:9-13 so as to include a variety of evildoers, his primary concern is with the sexually immoral (πόρνοι).

100. We should also note that in 1 Cor. 6 and elsewhere Paul specifies the agent of a Christian's holiness as Christ (1:2), or his name (6:11), or the Holy Spirit (6:11; Rom. 15:16), whereas in 1 Cor. 7:14 it is the Christian spouse.

an interpolation.[101] After an apparent break in the flow of thought at the end of 6:13, this section begins with an imperative in verse 14a, followed by a series of rhetorical questions in verses 14b-16a: "Do not be incompatibly yoked (ἑτεροζυγέω) to unbelievers (ἄπιστοι). For what communion is there with justice and lawlessness? — or what partnership (κοινωνία) with light towards darkness? What agreement (συμφώνησις) of Christ is there with Beliar? — or what share for a believer (πίστος) with an unbeliever (ἄπιστος)? What agreement does the temple of God have with idols?" Verse 16b then leads into a collection of citations from the Old Testament (16c-18), and the section is brought to a close in 7:1 with another imperative: "Let us cleanse ourselves from every defilement of flesh and spirit, making holiness perfect in fear of God."[102]

As with the problem of the passage's function, scholars have also failed to reach a consensus regarding its authorship or provenance. While some hold to a Pauline origin, others have suggested that it is non-Pauline or anti-Pauline, noting that it contains vocabulary that does not appear elsewhere in Paul's letters, and that its imagery and theology are more at home among Christians seeking to live by the Torah, or in documents from Qumran, than with Paul.[103] Yet whether it comes from Paul's hand or another's, or stems from circles associated with Qumran or those around Antioch or Corinth, we can be fairly confident, by its inclusion in 2 Corinthians, that it was an important tradition for the Corinthian church — assuming, that is, that it is not a late interpolation. If this is accurate, it is possible that the Corinthians had invoked the authority of this tradition in support of their position against marriages to unbelievers. And in fact, it is not hard to see how they might have done this.

To begin with, not only is the subject in 2 Corinthians 6:14–7:1 once again the danger of associating with unbelievers, but as in 1 Corinthians 7:12-14, the image used is defilement through physical contact with them.[104]

---

101. See the discussions in M. E. Thrall, "The Problem of II Cor. vi.14–vii. 1 in Some Recent Discussion," *NTS* 24 (1977/78): 138-48, and J. Murphy-O'Connor, "Philo and 2 Cor 6.14–7.1," *RB* 95 (1988): 62-69.

102. For a detailed analysis of the structure of this passage, see Hans Dieter Betz, "2 Cor 6:14–7:1: An Anti-Pauline Fragment?" *JBL* 92 (1973): 89-99.

103. See the discussions in Betz, "An Anti-Pauline Fragment?" 99-108; Thrall, "Problem," 133-38, 148 n. 1; Murphy-O'Connor, 56-62; and Victor Paul Furnish, *II Corinthians*, AB 32A (Garden City, N.Y.: Doubleday, 1984), 371-78, 382-83.

104. Cf. Betz's summary of the theology of this passage: "The purpose of the Christian life is to achieve the state of holiness and thus to become acceptable to God in the final judge-

2 Corinthians 6:17, for example, presents a paraphrase of Isaiah 52:11 that reads, "Come out from among them and separate yourselves . . . and do not touch (ἅπτομαι) an unclean thing"; and as we just saw, 2 Corinthians 7:1 speaks of cleansing both "body and spirit" (σαρκὸς καὶ πνεύματος) of defilement as a way of "perfecting holiness," thereby contrasting uncleanness with holiness, as does 1 Corinthians 7:14.[105] Beyond this, the opening exhortation in 2 Corinthians 6:14 against becoming "incompatibly" or "strangely" yoked (ἑτερο-ζυγέω) with non-Christians could easily have been pressed into service by the Corinthians as a prohibition of mixed marriages, especially since "yoke-partner" (σύζυγος) was a common term for wife, and marriage could be described as a process by which a man is "yoked" (ζεύγνυμι) to a woman.[106]

Finally, there are several smaller similarities between 2 Corinthians 6:14–7:1 and 1 Corinthians 7 that could indicate conceptual connections. Thus 2 Corinthians 6:14-16 derides the possibility of communion or partnership between Christians and non-Christians, as well as any "agreement," συμφώνησις, between Christ and Beliar, while 1 Corinthians 7:12-13 stipulates that marriage to an unbeliever *depends* on the unbelieving spouse's agreement to live with the Christian.[107] In 7:5, furthermore, Paul also speaks of the necessity of agreement between spouses, this time using the cognate substantive σύμφωνον. Nowhere else in Paul's correspondence do we find either talk of agreement between believers and unbelievers or words from the συμφων- stem. Again, the occurrence of "Beliar" as the name for Satan in 2 Corinthians 6:15 may clarify the background of Paul's caution in 1 Corinthians 7:5 against Satan leading Christians into sexual misconduct. The name Beliar, which is not at all common,[108] appears in both the *Code of Damascus* and the *Testament of Reuben* in descriptions

---

ment. . . . Because of this goal, any contact with people outside of the covenant must be eliminated" ("An Anti-Pauline Fragment?" 108; cf. 104).

105. Both Delling, "Nun aber sind sie heilig," 261-62, and Braun, "Exegetische Randglossen," 194, argue for the affinity of these two passages.

106. Also suggested by Jerome, *Adversus Jovinianum* 1.10; Hurd, 237; and Thrall, "Problem," 134-35, cf. 147-48. In this manner 2 Cor. 6:14ff., like 1 Cor. 6:15-18, is a mirror image of 1 Cor. 7:14, for as Thrall notes, "in I Corinthians [vii.14] the unbeliever is sanctified by a mixed marriage: in II Cor vi.14–vii.1 the Christian is polluted by it" (135). It should be further noted that Lev. 19:19, which may be the source of the word ἑτεροζυγέω in 2 Cor. 6:14, speaks of "different yokes" of cattle (ἑτερόζυγος) in the context of *mating and breeding* them.

107. 2 Cor. 6:16a prohibits an agreement (συγκατάθεσις) between the temple of God and idols. This image of the church as God's temple occurs again in 1 Cor. 3:16-17 (cf. 6:19).

108. Outside of 2 Cor. 6:14, Beliar occurs neither in the NT nor in early patristic literature.

of Satan in his role as one who provokes people to commit *porneia*.[109] Paul's warning in 7:5 may thus reflect an understanding of Satan implied in the name Beliar in 2 Corinthians 6:15.[110] That this description of Satan should appear in the *Testament of Reuben,* moreover, further enhances the attractiveness of this suggestion — for two reasons: first, because *Testament of Reuben* 4:1 speaks of God as giving Reuben's sons each a wife, for which the author uses the word "yoke-partner" (σύζυγος); and second, because *Testament of Reuben* 3:5 uses the same euphemism for sexual intercourse as 1 Corinthians 7:1, stating that the patriarch Judah never "touched" (ἅπτομαι) his wife Bilhah after her rape by Reuben. Elsewhere in Paul this word occurs only in the Isaiah paraphrase in 2 Corinthians 6:17.

Our investigation of 1 Corinthians 7:12-15a, and particularly Paul's assertion in 7:14 regarding the holiness of non-Christian spouses, has now led us to examine two other passages, 1 Corinthians 5–6 and 2 Corinthians 6:14–7:1. These passages indicate that the Corinthians held a general aversion to establishing formal relations or even associating with non-Christians, out of concern that such contact was polluting. In this context the problem Paul addresses in 1 Corinthians 7:12-24 may be understood as a particular instance of this general aversion. Hence our initial hypothesis, based on our interpretation of 7:14, appears to be confirmed, and we may conclude with a fair amount of confidence that the Corinthians objected to living with non-Christian spouses out of fear that physical association with unbelievers polluted them, thereby threatening their relationship with God.

Having thus defined the basic issues behind 7:12-15a, we may attempt to set this passage in a larger social and ideological context. To some extent the Corinthians' concerns are readily comprehensible against the backdrop of the religious syncretism that characterized much of the Greco-Roman period. It finds a broad analogy, for example, in the Hellenistic Jewish polemic against intermarriage with Gentiles,[111] or the Roman polemic against "foreign cults," which claimed that new religions destroyed marriages and households by

---

109. CD 4.15-17; *T. Reub.* 4:8, 10; 6:3; cf. *T. Sim.* 5:3.

110. According to Wolfgang Schrage, *Die konkreten Einzelgebote in der paulinischen Paränese: Ein Beitrag zur neutestamentlichen Ethik* (Gütersloh: Gütersloh, 1961), 220, 1 Cor. 7:5 is the only place in Paul "where, in a paraenetic-ethical context, Satan is expressly referred to as part of a warning." See also 1 Cor. 5:5, where Paul rules that the man guilty of the sexual offense described in 5:1 be handed over to Satan.

111. See, e.g., Gerhard Delling, "Ehehindernisse," in *RAC* 4 (1959), 681-82.

converting the wives of Roman citizens.[112] The Corinthian perspective is that of the converts, however, not the proponents of an established religion, and so the tensions evident in 7:12-15a find a more fruitful analogy among the Stoics and the Stoic writings of Philo, and in the wisdom tradition of Ben Sira, which itself bears several marks of Stoicism.[113]

In Ben Sira the "convert" is the wise man, and hence an aversion to outsiders expresses itself in the form of warnings against close association with persons not pursuing wisdom and righteousness. "Grudge every minute spent among fools, but linger among the thoughtful," says the author in 27:12 (NEB). In 9:14-16 Ben Sira advises that the righteous be one's dinner partners (cf. 1 Cor. 5:11); and in Sirach 13, in a caution against associating with rich and greedy men, we find several rhetorical questions that bear a palpable resemblance to 2 Corinthians 6:14-16:

> Will a clay pot have fellowship (κοινωνέω) with an iron kettle? (13:2)

> Will a wolf have fellowship with a lamb? — so also a sinner with a pious man. What peace does a hyena have with a dog? — and what peace does a rich man have with a poor man? (13:17-18)

Ben Sira's objection to these associations stems from his concern that the righteous wise man will be adversely influenced by the unrighteous fool. Sirach 12:13-14, for example, warns against attaching oneself to a sinner and thereby becoming involved with[114] his sins. As with the Corinthians, Ben Sira also employs the metaphor of defilement. In 13:1 he admonishes, "Whoever touches (ὁ ἁπτόμενος) pitch will be defiled, and whoever associates (ὁ κοινωνῶν) with a proud man will become like him" (RSV); and in 22:13 he advises, "Do not talk much with a foolish man, and do not visit an unintelligent man . . . and you will not be soiled when he shakes himself off."[115] In fact, ac-

---

112. See, e.g., David L. Balch, *Let Wives Be Submissive: The Domestic Code in I Peter*, SBLMS 26 (Chico, Calif.: Scholars, 1981), 65-76. Cf. the concern expressed in Wisd. of Sol. 14:22-27 that idol worship undermines marriages.

113. See Raymond Pautrel, "Ben Sira et le stoïcisme," *RSR* 51 (1963): 535-49; Martin Hengel, *Judaism and Hellenism: Studies in Their Encounter in Palestine during the Early Hellenistic Period* (Philadelphia: Fortress, 1974), 1:83-88, 147-53, 157-62.

114. Lit. "kneaded together with," συμφύρω — cf. 1 Cor. 5:6-8, where Paul uses the image of leaven and bread dough. See also Gal. 5:9 and Mark 8:15 par.

115. Cf. Wisd. of Sol. 4:10-14, and 2:16, where the ungodly say of the righteous man: "We are considered by him as something base, and he avoids our ways as unclean."

cording to Ben Sira, the very search for wisdom requires a certain purity. Recounting his own experiences in the concluding chapter of his work, he says: "I directed my soul to [Wisdom], and through purification (ἐν καθαρισμῷ) I found her."[116]

In the same way as the general concern at Corinth for associating with outsiders surfaces in Paul's discussion of marriage in 1 Corinthians 7:12-15a, Ben Sira also treats marriage as a particular instance of this broader problem. In Sirach 25:16-24 he details the disastrous consequences of a wise man having to associate with an evil wife, and in 26:7 he exclaims that an evil wife is a "rolling ox-yoke" (βοοζύγιον σαλευόμενον). The image here is of two oxen being mismatched under the same yoke, causing it to bob painfully up and down, which is reminiscent of the "incompatible yoking" of 2 Corinthians 6:14. That this image had some currency in wisdom literature as a metaphor for marriage is also indicated by Sirach 25:8, which reads "Happy is he who lives with an intelligent wife; and he who does not plow with ox and ass together."[117]

Finally, as with the Corinthians, Ben Sira sees divorce as a solution to these impossible partnerships. Thus, while Sirach 7:26 admonishes, "Do you have a wife after your own soul? — do not divorce her,"[118] 25:25-26 hands down the verdict for less fortunate marriages: "Do not give water an outlet; nor an evil wife brashness. If she does not go according to your directions, cut her off from your flesh."[119] Here a textual variant is worth our attention. In some Greek manuscripts verse 25 advises against giving an evil wife "power" (ἐξουσία) as opposed to "brashness" (παρρησία). This is similar to the advice given in Sirach 33:20: "In your lifetime do not give power over yourself (ἐξουσία ἐπὶ σέ) to son or wife, brother or friend." In 47:19, in turn, after recounting the extraordinary wisdom and success of King Solomon, Ben Sira

116. Sir. 51:20 (RSV). Cf. Wisd. of Sol. 8:20 (cited above, p. 126), where the author sees an "undefiled body," σῶμα ἀμίαντον (received at birth), as prerequisite to Solomon's search for wisdom. See also 1:3-5; 7:27.

117. Although the second clause appears only in the Hebrew and Syriac, not in the Greek, it is undoubtedly original since Ben Sira promises us ten happy thoughts (25:7), and without this clause he would have only nine. Against this interpretation, Patrick W. Skehan and Alexander A. Di Lella, *The Wisdom of Ben Sira*, AB 39 (New York: Doubleday, 1987), 340, read the second clause as a reference to a man with two contentious cowives.

118. This is the LXX; the Hebrew reads: "Do you have a wife? — do not hate her." On the Stoic-Cynic background of this verse see below, pp. 155-60 and 170.

119. The Hebrew adds here "take and divorce her." See also Prov. 18:22a (LXX), and the "one flesh" idea of Gen. 2:24.

fingers the cause of his downfall: "You laid your loins beside women and were overpowered through your body (ἐνεξουσιάσθης ἐν τῷ σώματί σου)." In all three of these passages the wording approaches the expression Paul uses in 1 Corinthians 7:4, where he asserts, evidently in response to misgivings from the Corinthians, that spouses do not have exclusive power (οὐκ ἐξουσιάζει) over their own bodies. From this the possibility emerges that the Corinthians who were married to unbelievers objected to the idea of "coming under their power" physically.[120]

As informative as these comparisons with Sirach might be, even closer parallels are to be found in Stoic authors and in the Stoic writings of Philo. Just as some Cynics nourished a strong disdain for nonphilosophers, as noted in chapter 2, there is evidence that some Stoics also shunned these "laymen," although others, like Epictetus, discouraged such an attitude.[121] But even Epictetus objected to becoming too intimate with outsiders.[122] In one lecture he speaks in terms reminiscent of Paul's assertion in 1 Corinthians 5:10 that Christians would have to "leave the world" to avoid unbelievers,[123] and elsewhere he explains that it is "for this reason that the philosophers advise us to leave even our own countries."[124] This last citation, moreover, belongs to an entire lecture on the dangers of social relations, which begins by addressing the issue of eating with outsiders[125] and describes their influence as something defiling. "We ought to enter cautiously into such social intercourse with laymen," Epictetus warns, "remembering that it is impossible for the man who brushes up against the person who is covered with soot to keep from getting some soot on himself."[126]

In Philo this philosophical apprehension toward outsiders as a source of

120. With Solomon, it should be noted, the reference is also to "outsiders," since the women who overpower him are *foreign* wives (see Sir. 47:20 and 1 Kings 11:1-8).

121. E.g., Epictetus, *Discourses* 2.12.1-4.

122. E.g., Epictetus, *Discourses* 4.2.1.

123. Epictetus, *Discourses* 1.12.18-19: "For look you, can we escape from men? And how is it possible? . . . What alternative remains, then, or what method can we find for living with them?" (trans. W. A. Oldfather, ed. and trans., *Epictetus: The Discourses as Reported by Arrian, the Manual, and Fragments,* 2 vols., LCL [Cambridge: Harvard University Press; London: William Heinemann, 1959], 1:93, 95).

124. Epictetus, *Discourses* 3.16.11, trans. Oldfather, 2:107, 109.

125. Aside from 1 Cor. 5:11, Paul addresses the question of eating with outsiders in 10:23-30.

126. Epictetus, *Discourses* 3.16.1-6, trans. Oldfather, 2:105, 107. See also *Discourses* 1.27.1-6, and Malherbe, *Paul and the Thessalonians,* 36-52, who cites texts describing the fragile condition of new converts to philosophy.

pollution is seen at the beginning of his treatise *That Every Good Man Is Free.* After introducing this most Stoic of themes with a Pythagorean maxim that the philosopher "should not walk the well-travelled ways," Philo explains that the wise have "opened up a new pathway, in which the outside world can never tread, . . . and have brought to light the ideal forms which none of the unclean may touch."[127] Later in the treatise Philo presents the Essenes, whom he describes as separating themselves from evil persons, as these would be detrimental to their souls, "like a disease brought by a pestilential atmosphere."[128]

In Philo's treatise *On the Sacrifices of Abel and Cain,* we again meet with the language of defilement and disease, although in this text Philo combines Stoic and Jewish traditions in a manner that may clarify further the background of Paul's contention that unbelievers are sanctified by a believing spouse. In considering the statement in Numbers 3:12-13 that the Levites are a "ransom" for Israel's firstborn, Philo first interprets these verses in terms of the soul's desire for freedom. But, he continues, it may be that Moses meant to illustrate another truth, "and one that we could ill spare, namely that every wise man is a ransom for the fool." This is because, as he says further on, the wise are like "physicians who fight against the infirmities of the sick."[129] Here, quite plainly, Philo has identified the Levite with the Stoic wise man in the latter's role as physician to the human soul.[130] Following this Philo gives a similar interpretation of the Levitical cities of refuge, which, according to Leviticus 25:32, are "ransomed forever." After again considering these words as a metaphor for the soul's journey toward perfection, he proposes that the Levites are good men (σπουδαῖος) who purify bad men (φαῦλος) by virtue of their holiness.[131] From these texts we can see that Philo's understanding of

127. Philo, *Quod omnis probus liber sit* 3-4, trans. F. H. Colson, ed. and trans., *Philo,* vol. 9, LCL (Cambridge: Harvard University Press; London: William Heinemann, 1929), 11, 13. This understanding of "unclean" compares well with Epictetus's statement in *Discourses* 4.11.5-8 that the philosopher must cleanse all "impurity of the soul," defining this impurity as "bad beliefs" (δόγματα πονηρά). See also *Discourses* 3.22.19, where he says the Cynic's governing principle must be "pure" (καθαρόν).

128. Philo, *Quod omnis probus liber sit* 76, trans. Colson, 55.

129. Philo, *De sacrificiis Abelis et Caini* 118-20, 121-24, trans. F. H. Colson and G. H. Whitaker, eds. and trans., *Philo,* vol. 2, LCL (London: William Heinemann; New York: Putnam, 1929), 181, 183, 185.

130. On the wise man as physician see Malherbe, *Paul and the Thessalonians,* 23 n. 71.

131. Philo, *De sacrificiis Abelis et Caini* 128. Cf. Wisd. of Sol. 6:24, "A multitude of wise men is the salvation of the world" (RSV).

the redemption of outsiders by insiders is, in part, based on Stoic social theory, even though he chooses to express this redemption largely in the language of his own Judaism. In light of this example, it is not impossible that Paul's claim in 1 Corinthians 7:14, that unclean, non-Christian spouses are "made holy" by their Christian spouses, may also rely on Stoic notions of social interaction, this time expressed in terms of Paul's Judeo-Christian faith.

Pursuing the Stoic background of 7:12-15a from still another persective, we may note that a principal source of the Stoics' attitude toward outsiders was their concept of friendship. For the Stoics friendship was a "partnership,"[132] based on the sharing of a common lifestyle. As Arius Didymus puts it, "They admit friendship among the wise alone, since only among these is there oneness of mind regarding the things pertaining to one's manner of life."[133] From Arius we also learn, however, that Stoics limited friendship to the wise because they held that friendship required trust or "faithfulness" (πίστις), which only wise men possess.[134] The dogma that trust is essential to friendship and a distinctive mark of the wise man is found in Epictetus as well. In his lecture *On Friendship*, for instance, he states that the governing principle of the bad man is "not trustworthy" (οὐκ ἔστι πιστόν),[135] and else-

---

132. κοινωνία, Arius in Stobaeus 2.74.3-5 W.-H. (*SVF* 3.27.3-4); cf. Diogenes Laertius 7.124. This passage from Arius also defines a common belief about one's manner of life as an "agreement," or συμφωνία. This is perhaps another indication of the philosophical provenance of 2 Cor. 6:14–7.1, as both terms appear in 6:14-15. See also Stobaeus 2.94.1-4; 2.106.13-15 W.-H.

133. Arius in Stobaeus 2.108.15-18 W.-H. Cf. Diogenes Laertius 7.124, who reports that Stoics held that friendship existed "only among the good, on account of their likeness." As this last reference indicates, the Stoic ideal of friendship was, to some degree, a variation on the fairly widespread notion that a friend must be a person "like oneself," or "another self." Hence, in Epictetus, when a young man asks whether the Cynic, if he falls ill, can convalesce in another's home, Epictetus understands this as a question about friendship and replies, "But where will you find me a Cynic's friend? For such a person must be another Cynic" (Epictetus, *Discourses* 3.22.62-65, trans. Oldfather, 2:153). For a discussion of this topos and Paul's use of it in Gal. 4:12, see Betz, *Galatians*, 221-23. See also David L. Balch, "1 Cor 7:32-35 and Stoic Debates about Marriage, Anxiety, and Distraction," *JBL* 102 (1983): 437, who cites Aristotle, *Ethica Nicomachea* 1170b 6-7 and *Ethica Eudemia* 1245a 30 (cf. *Ethica Nicomachea* 1170b 5-19). For Paul's use of philosophical notions of friendship in 2 Corinthians, see Peter Marshall, *Enmity in Corinth: Social Conventions in Paul's Relations with the Corinthians*, WUNT, 2nd ser., 23 (Tübingen: Mohr, 1987), 1-34, 130-258.

134. Arius in Stobaeus 2.108.18-25 W.-H.: "For true friendship, and not that which is falsely called, is impossible without trust (πίστις) and steadfastness. But among the bad, who are untrustworthy (ἄπιστοι) . . . they say there is no friendship." Cf. 2.112.9-15 W.-H (*SVF* 3.147.9-13).

135. Epictetus, *Discourses* 2.22.25

where he refers to those not living philosophical lives as "untrustworthy" (ἄπιστος).[136] On the other hand, he sees conversion to philosophy as a movement from being ἄπιστος to πιστός,[137] and several times he refers to the philosopher as πιστός, and at least once calls him ὁ πιστός.[138] These characterizations of friendship and the wise man are particularly suggestive, I would argue, since the terms πιστός and ἄπιστος also appear in 1 Corinthians 7:12-15a (as well as 1 Cor. 6:6 and 2 Cor. 6:14-15), and since both authors, like Paul, use this word group to distinguish between insiders and outsiders.[139]

One might object to this comparison, however, on grounds that Paul would have understood these terms very differently than the Stoics. That is, given his concept of salvation, Paul would have defined πιστός and ἄπιστος as "belief or trust in Christ" and "unbelief or lack of trust in Christ," rather than as "trusting/trustworthy" and "untrusting/untrustworthy." Yet this objection carries little weight when we consider that Paul uses the adjectival form πιστός to refer to faith in the divinity only *once* in his letters. This is Galatians 3:9, in a description of Abraham based on Genesis 15:6, where the reference is to faith in *God,* not Christ. Elsewhere Paul uses the term to denote the trustworthiness of God,[140] and his own or Timothy's trustworthiness as servants of God.[141] We also have slight warrant for assuming that the Corinthians themselves held this supposedly "normative" Pauline understanding of πιστός. Indeed, since Paul uses ἄπιστος only in the Corinthian correspondence,[142] it is quite possible that this pair of terms hails from Corinth and had a special significance for the church there. In light of these considerations, I suggest that the notions of "trustworthy," "trusting," and "trust in Christ or God," all of which are encompassed by the πιστός word group, were not as distinct in the minds of the Corinthians as they might have been for the Stoics or Paul. The Corinthians, in other words, may have used πιστός and ἄπιστος in both Stoic and Christian senses in distinguishing themselves from non-Christians, and 1 Corinthians 7:12-15a may be a reflection of this usage.

Finally, in considering the potential for Stoic influence on this passage,

---

136. Epictetus, *Discourses* 1.3.7; 1.29.21; 2.4.11; cf. *SVF* 2.41.16-17.

137. Epictetus, *Discourses* 4.9.17.

138. Epictetus, *Discourses* 1.4.18, 20; 2.14.13; 2.22.26-27, 29-30; 3.20.5; 4.1.133; 4.13.17-24; and 3.23.18.

139. In 1 Cor. 14:23-24 it is even coupled with ἰδιώτης.

140. 1 Cor. 1:9; 10:13; 2 Cor. 1:18; 1 Thess. 5:24; cf. 2 Thess. 3:3.

141. All in 1 Corinthians: 4:2, 17; 7:25.

142. 1 Cor. 6:6; 7:12, 13, 14, 15; 10:27; 14:22, 23, 24; 2 Cor. 4:4; 6:14, 15.

we may point out that, as with the Corinthians (and Ben Sira), the Stoics' aversion to outsiders is also seen in their understanding of marriage. An important piece of evidence in this regard comes from a non-Stoic (indeed, anti-Stoic) source. In his treatise entitled *On Common Conceptions, against the Stoics,* Plutarch complains that Stoics are inconsistent, for while they label outsiders unreliable (ἄπιστοι),[143] they nevertheless entrust (πιστεύωσιν) some with money and allow others to marry their daughters.[144] From this report we can surmise that Stoics experienced uncertainties in their relations with outsiders not unlike those which plagued the Corinthians, including uncertainties in the realm of "mixed" marriages.

From the Stoics themselves, moreover, it becomes clear why marriage with outsiders might surface as an issue, for along with their belief that a "partnership" could exist only among the wise, many of them held that marriage was life's *closest* partnership. As we noted above, Antipater, Musonius, and Hierocles all describe marriage as life's only partnership in which all things are shared, including the partners' souls and bodies; and Musonius states that no other partnership is "more necessary or affectionate."[145] Antipater, in turn, demands that there be a singleness of purpose in marriage, and insists that a man's wife be "another like himself."[146] Ocellus asserts that a man should marry a woman who is sympathetic in spirit and most like himself, or he will have division and disagreement instead of unity of purpose and agreement (συμφωνία).[147] Dio Chrysostom maintains that the welfare of the household depends on the like-mindedness of its master and mistress,[148] and Hierocles defines the beauty of a household as the "yoking" (ζεῦγος) of a man and a woman who agree (συμφωνέω) with one another.[149]

Again, as we saw above, Epictetus justifies Crates' marriage to Hipparchia on the basis that this woman was "another Crates," and even concedes that in

143. As well as "unjust" (ἄδικοι) — cf. 1 Cor. 6:1, 9.

144. Plutarch, *Moralia* 1062E-F *(De communibus notitiis adversus Stoicos),* trans. Harold Cherniss, ed. and trans., *Plutarch's Moralia,* vol. 13, pt. 2, LCL (Cambridge: Harvard University Press; London: William Heinemann, 1976), 689.

145. Musonius, frag. 14.94.2-3 L. (73.18–74.1 H.).

146. οἷον ἑαυτὸν ἕτερον, Antipater (app. A), lines 25-31 and 71-72. Cf. 66, where Antipater speaks of a married man "having become two in place of one" (δύο γεγονὼς ἀνθ' ἑνός).

147. [Ocellus] (app. B), *De univ. nat.* 48-49. Cf. 1 Cor. 7:5; 2 Cor. 6:14-15.

148. Dio Chrysostom, *Oration* 38.15, which continues, "What else is the good marriage, other than a husband's oneness of mind with his wife? And what else is the bad marriage, other than the discord of these two?"

149. Hierocles 54.19-22 v. A. (Stobaeus 4.505.12-16 W.-H.). Cf. 1 Cor. 7:5; 2 Cor. 6:14-15.

an ideal society *any* Cynic could marry, since all relationships resulting from marriage would be with other Cynics.[150] Likewise, Musonius requires that spouses be matched to one another with respect to discretion, righteousness, and virtue,[151] and then lets fly a series of rhetorical questions whose similarity to 2 Corinthians 6:14-16 rivals that of the verses we cited from Sirach 13: "For what sort of marriage without concord is good? — what sort of partnership (κοινωνία) beneficial? How could persons be like-minded with one another when they are evil? — or, how could a good person be like-minded with an evil one? No more than a straight piece of wood might fit with a twisted one, or both being twisted, fit with one another."[152]

Not surprisingly, these high expectations for marriage also raised the question among Stoics as to what happens when philosophers find themselves involved in unions that fall short of the ideal. Like the Corinthians, who looked to Paul for counsel on divorce, Musonius, too, considers this option. In a passage that describes marriage as a "yoke" (ζεῦγος), he explains that when the partnership of marriage lacks a common goal, and a spouse refuses to "pull together with his or her yoke-partner" (ὁμόζυγος), the couple often separates completely.[153] 1 Corinthians 7:12-15a suggests that the Corinthians were asking Paul if they could do just that.[154]

Thus far our investigation of 7:12-24 has shown that the dynamics as well as the rhetoric of the Corinthian situation are quite close to what we find in the Stoics and in two Jewish authors influenced by Stoicism, namely, Ben Sira and Philo. With this, however, our information on the issues behind this passage is not exhausted, for 7:14, which served as the starting point for our investigation, represents only the first justification that Paul gives for his ruling on mixed marriages. A second comes in 7:15b-24.

---

150. Epictetus, *Discourses* 3.22.68, 76; cf. *Cynic Epistle of Crates* 33.

151. Musonius, frag. 13B.90.12-13 L. (69.13-16 H.).

152. Musonius, frag. 13B.90.13-17 L. (69.16–70.3 H.). On the image of the straight and twisted sticks, see Diogenes Laertius 7.127.

153. Musonius, frag. 13A.88.15, 24-29 L. (68.2, 13-19 H.). On Musonius's use of ὁμό-ζυγος ("one of like-yoke"), cf. 2 Cor. 6:14, ἑτερο-ζυγέω ("to yoke differently"). Note also that an inscription from Mantinea which may reflect Stoic thought speaks of lives "yoked with lives and souls with bodies" (Dittenberger, 2.783.32-33, cited above, n. 53).

154. Cf. *De vita contemplativa* 2.13-18, where Philo maintains that the Therapeutae have abandoned their nonphilosophical wives and families in pursuit of the contemplative life.

Marriage to an Unbeliever as a Form of Slavery (7:15b-24)

With 7:15b Paul begins a new thought, stating that Christians have not been "enslaved" (δουλόομαι) by their marriages with unbelievers.[155] The difficulty here is in determining what exactly Paul is denying: In what way could someone be "enslaved" to his or her spouse?[156] Several scholars, emphasizing the "bondage" aspect of slavery, interpret οὐ δεδούλωται to mean "not bound like a slave," or simply "not bound."[157] Thus Roberts maintains that οὐ δεδούλωται means "not under slavery or bondage in the sense of being required to prevent separation," saying that the phrase draws on the verb "to leave" (χωρίζεσθαι) in 7:15a. Baltensweiler sees the "bond" in question as deriving from the notion in Genesis 2:24 that spouses become "one flesh," an idea, as we have seen, which surfaces in 1 Corinthians 6:15-17. And Niederwimmer, confessing that the sense of οὐ δεδούλωται is unclear, suggests three possibilities: "not bound" to the non-Christian spouse, "not bound" to the marriage agreement, and "not bound" by Jesus' prohibition of divorce, which Paul cites in 7:10-11.[158] The difficulty with all these conjectures is that in moving from "enslaved" to "slavishly bound" to simply "bound," these scholars move beyond the semantic range of δουλόω. Indeed, if Paul had meant "bound," one would expect the more natural δέδεται, as in 7:27 and 7:39.[159]

155. Paul's words in 7:15b, δεδούλωται ... ἐν τοῖς τοιούτοις, should probably be read as "enslaved ... in such matters" rather than "to such ones," since the Christian and the non-Christian are always spoken of in the singular in this passage, although either translation is possible.

156. W. M. L. DeWette, *Kurze Erklärung der Briefe an die Corinther*, ed. Hermann Messner, 3rd ed., Kurzgefasstes exegetisches Handbuch zum Neuen Testament 2/2 (Leipzig: S. Hirzel, 1855), 64, lists conjectures going back to the church fathers.

157. E.g., Lietzmann, 31; Baltensweiler, 193; Wolbert, 104; Conzelmann, 119 (cf. 123 n. 42); and the RSV. A more literal interpretation is pursued by Boaz Cohen, *Jewish and Roman Law: A Comparative Study* (New York: Jewish Theological Seminary of America, 1966), 1:394 n. 83, who suggests Paul means that "partners to such a marriage are not like slaves, whose marriage according to the Roman view, was permanent unless it was broken up by the master." But this is a very loose interpretation of Roman law, which did not even recognize marriage *(conubium)* between slaves; and it conjures up the image of both the Christian and the unbeliever as slaves under a common master, whereas Paul considers the possibility of slavery only for the Christian, giving no emphasis to the idea of a slave master.

158. R. L. Roberts, Jr., "The Meaning of *Chorizo* and *Douloo* in I Corinthians 7:10-17," *Restoration Quarterly* 80 (1965): 184; Baltensweiler, 195 n. 127; Niederwimmer, 104 n. 118.

159. So also Heinrici, *Der erste Brief*, 225, and Wolbert, 105. Even Roberts (182) feels compelled to clarify matters in this regard.

Against this, however, we should note that an older generation of scholars had argued that 7:39 actually justified the translation of οὐ δεδούλωται as "not bound," for after stating that a wife is "bound" (δέδεται) to her husband as long as her husband is alive, Paul goes on to say that when the husband dies the woman is "free" (ἐλευθέρα) to marry whom she will. Since being "bound" functions here as the opposite of being "free," these scholars surmised that "bound" and "enslaved" were practically equivalents of one another.[160] Yet the logic of this argument is not sound, for even if δέομαι (bound) and ἐλευθέρα (free) can be used as opposites, this in no way dictates that δέομαι (bound) and δουλόομαι (enslaved) are synonyms. This argument also does not give enough attention to the influence of legal terminology on the wording of 7:39, for not only is a woman's status of being "free to marry whom she chooses" a standard part of ancient divorce documents,[161] but the legalese of 7:39 is illustrated by the fuller wording of Romans 7:2-3: "the married woman is *bound by law* (δέδεται νόμῳ) to her living husband . . . but if her husband should die she is *free from the law* (ἐλευθέρα ἐστὶν ἀπὸ τοῦ νόμου)."[162] Therefore, while it is true that "bound" and "free" can function as counterparts, this pertains to legal parlance, and we have no evidence that δουλόω ever functions to describe the legal relation between spouses. Indeed, this would be especially surprising in the instance under consideration, since 7:15b has reference to both sexes — "the sister or the brother" — not simply to the wife, as in 7:39. Thus, while a wife could be legally "bound" to her husband, as opposed to being "free to marry" someone else of her own choosing, the idea that a husband could be legally "enslaved" to his wife must be ruled out as a possible interpretation of 7:15b.

The primary mistake inherent in all these attempts to explain the mean-

---

160. A. Tholuck, *Exposition, Doctrinal and Philological, of Christ's Sermon on the Mount According to the Gospel of Matthew,* 2nd ed., Biblical Cabinet 6 (Edinburgh: Thomas Clark, 1843), 1:341-42, followed by DeWette, 64; cf. Heinrich Greeven, "Ehe nach dem Neuen Testament," in *Theologie der Ehe: Veröffentlichung des Ökumenischen Arbeitskreises evangelischer und katholischer Theologen,* ed. Gerhard Krems and Reinhard Mumm (Regensburg: Friedrich Pustet; Göttingen: Vandenhoeck & Ruprecht, 1969), 76.

161. See P. W. Pestman, *Marriage and Matrimonial Property in Ancient Egypt: A Contribution to Establishing the Legal Position of Women,* Papyrologica Lugduno-Batava 9 (Leiden: Brill, 1961), 73-74, cf. 181; and Ludwig Blau, *Die jüdische Ehescheidung und der jüdische Scheidebrief* (Strassburg: Karl J. Trübner, 1912), 2:18-28, cf. 28-42, esp. 39 and nn. 3-4.

162. Several early manuscripts even read "bound *by law*" in 1 Cor. 7:39, supplying νόμῳ from Rom. 7:2-3; cf. Johannes B. Bauer, "Was las Tertullian 1 Kor 7 39?" *ZNW* 77 (1986): 284-87. On the legal background of Rom. 7:1-3, see Will Deming, "Paul, Gaius, and the 'Law of Persons': The Conceptualization of Roman Law in the Early Classical Period," *CQ* 51 (2001): 218-30.

ing of δεδούλωται is the assumption that the function of 7:15b is to explain Paul's ruling in 7:15a, "if the unbeliever leaves, let him leave." Between verses 15a and 15b, however, there is no connecting particle, and as I have suggested above, 15a seems to require no explanation. Beyond this, since the topic of slavery comes up again in 7:21-23, there is sufficient reason to believe that 15b introduces what follows rather than concludes what precedes.[163]

If we now turn from the possible legal connotations of δεδούλωται and cast an eye in the direction of the philosophers, we find that the notion of marriage as a form of slavery plays a significant role in texts connected with the Stoic-Cynic marriage debate. In his description of the Essenes in the *Hypothetica*, for example, Philo tells us that these philosophers nurture within their celibate community the "true and only real freedom." As a consequence they shun marriage, believing that when a man marries he becomes "a slave in place of a freeman."[164] Philo also recognizes that marriage is a form of slavery for the wife, although this is something he endorses. Somewhat earlier in the *Hypothetica*, in a passage indebted to the literature on household management, he maintains that in proper marriages women "serve" (δουλεύειν) their husbands.[165] Similarly Musonius, in rejecting the idea that wives who pursue philosophy will abandon their housework, praises the philosophical wife as one who does work which some consider a "slave's task" (δουλικά);[166] and in a Latin work on household management incorrectly attributed to Aristotle, the author claims that a wife will submit (*obsequor*) to her husband's wishes more conscientiously than if she had been purchased (*emptio*), adding that she has in fact been purchased inasmuch as her husband has given her a part in his life and the procreation of his children.[167] On a different note, Antipater rails against bachelors who refuse to marry because they see the entrance of a wife into their household as equivalent to a foreign garrison occupying a city. He says they hold this opinion be-

---

163. See Conzelmann, 125 n. 4; DeWette, 66.

164. ἀντ' ἐλευθέρου δοῦλος, Philo, *Hypothetica* 11.3, 17. Philo is somewhat inconsistent on his view of the Essenes' freedom, perhaps because of the influence of Jewish wisdom literature. Elsewhere he says that the Essenes' philosophy of life establishes a freedom that *cannot* be enslaved (ἡ ἀδούλωτος ἐλευθερία, *Quod omnis probus liber sit* 88), which is in line with the Stoic doctrine of philosophical freedom. It may be a similar inconsistency by the Corinthians that Paul is questioning when he introduces this Stoic doctrine of freedom in 7:17-24, contrasting it with being "slaves of [doctrines of] men" (7:23); see below.

165. Philo, *Hypothetica* 7.3 (see above, chap. 2, n. 173).

166. Musonius, frag. 3.42.8 L. (12.1-2 H.).

167. [Aristotle] *Oeconomica* 3.1.

cause they themselves are incapable of ruling (ἄρχειν), being rather "slaves of passion" (ἡδονῆς δοῦλοι) and susceptible to capture by a woman's beauty or her dowry.[168] In a similar fashion Hierocles contends that those who marry for the wrong reasons bring a "tyrant instead of a wife" into their homes.[169]

From the wider philosophical milieu of the Hellenistic period we also have several aphorisms connecting marriage with slavery. Stobaeus preserves a line from Euripides which holds that a wife's possessions "enslave the husband, and he is no longer free," and one from Anaxandrides, a poet of the Middle Comedy, to the effect that a poor man who marries becomes a slave (δοῦλος) to his wife, whether she is rich or poor.[170] Stobaeus also has three other lines from Euripides which may be relevant: "For the chaste wife is nothing but a man's slave";[171] "Yoked in wedlock, he is no longer free";[172] and "A great tyranny for a man are children and wife."[173] The popularity of these last sayings is indicated by the fact that Stobaeus records the first one twice, and it is known to Clement of Alexandria;[174] the second one Stobaeus again records twice, attributing it elsewhere to the tragedian Hippothoon;[175] and the second and third sayings also appear in the popular *Sentences* of Menander.[176] From the *Sentences,* furthermore, we have another maxim on this theme: "Having married, know that you are a slave for life."[177] That sayings of this nature may have circulated among the Corinthians or otherwise had an influence on Paul's writing of 1 Corinthians 7 is made plausible, moreover, by Paul's citation of a proverb in 15:33 which is elsewhere attributed to Menander.[178]

---

168. Antipater (app. A), lines 44-47.

169. τύραννον ἀντὶ γυναικός, Hierocles 55.11 v. A. (Stobaeus 4.506.19-20 W.-H.). See also Epictetus, *Discourses* 2.20.26-27, where it is implied that marriage is slavery.

170. Stobaeus 4.532.15 (δουλοῖ τὸν ἄνδρα, κοὐκέτ' ἔστ' ἐλεύθερος), and 4.513.7-11 W.-H. Cf. Pseudo-Phocylides, *Sentences* 200, Plutarch *Moralia* 100F. *(De virtute et vitio)*, and [Plutarch] *Moralia* 13F *(De liberis educandis)*.

171. πᾶσα γὰρ δούλη πέφυκεν ἀνδρὸς ἡ σώφρων γυνή, Stobaeus 4.494.10 W.-H., from his *Oedipus*. On this image cf. Dionysius of Halicarnassus, *Ancient Orators* 1.1.

172. ζευχθεὶς γάμοισιν οὐκέτ' ἔστ' ἐλεύθερος, Stobaeus 4.496.11 W.-H., from his *Antigone*.

173. μεγάλη τυραννὶς ἀνδρὶ τέκνα καὶ γυνη, Stobaeus 4.494.4 W.-H., from his *Oedipus*.

174. Also at Stobaeus 4.529.8-10 W.-H.; Clement of Alexandria, *Stromateis,* bk. 4, chap. 8.63.3 (2.277.10 S.).

175. Stobaeus 4.519.5-6 W.-H.

176. Menander, *Sententiae* 282, 506 Jaekel.

177. δοῦλος εἶναι διὰ βίου, Menander, *Sententiae* 529 J. Cf. Achilles Tatius 1.8.9.

178. Menander, frag. 187 Körte. On the Hellenistic background of the verses just before this one (i.e., 15:29-32), see Malherbe, *Popular Philosophers,* 78-79.

In the context of the argumentative structure of 1 Corinthians 7 and its reliance on Stoic and Cynic traditions, furthermore, there are several ways in which this philosophical characterization of marriage as slavery could have functioned. First, this characterization of marriage, which is pronounced invalid by Paul, seems to be part of a Corinthian argument. As such it could well have served to undergird the Corinthians' perspective that marriage to an outsider was an avenue by which unwanted, foreign influences imposed themselves on a believer's life. This, for example, is the image Philo has in mind in reporting that marriage ruins the idyllic community of the Essenes, and it is part and parcel of Antipater and Hierocles' description of marriage as tyranny or the hostile takeover of a city-state.[179] Second, the political metaphor for slavery used by Antipater and Hierocles reminds us that Stoics often spoke of the antithesis of slavery, personal freedom, in terms of kingship or rule. Thus, according to Diogenes Laertius, the Stoics held that "not only are the wise free, but also kings," and Philo explains that "the wise man alone is both free and rules."[180] Since the Corinthians, too, may have thought of themselves as kings in this philosophical sense,[181] their understanding of marriage to an unbeliever as a form of slavery may have intensified their negative appraisal of such unions inasmuch as these threatened their presumed royal status. That this would be a reasonable conclusion to draw within the framework of Stoic thought can be seen from Epictetus, who repeatedly maintains that marriage to a non-Cynic robs the Cynic of his kingdom.[182]

A third and final way the philosophical characterization of marriage as slavery could make sense in the context of 1 Corinthians 7 is suggested by the close connection that Stoics saw between freedom and "power" (ἐξουσία). Diogenes Laertius, for example, reports as a Stoic doctrine that freedom is the

179. In *Quod omnis probus liber sit* 45, Philo makes an explicit connection between the enslavement of a city-state by a tyrant and the slavery of an individual. We are also reminded here that 2 Cor. 6:14 speaks of being "incongruously yoked" with unbelievers, and that the image of a yoke can represent slavery as well as marriage (see, e.g., the line from Euripides just cited; see also Gal. 5:1; Acts 15:10; Sir. 28:19-20; 30:35 [Eng. 33:26/27]; 40:1).

180. Diogenes Laertius 7.122, οὐ μόνον δὲ ἐλευθέρους εἶναι τοὺς σοφούς, ἀλλὰ καὶ βασιλέας, and Philo, *De posteritate Caini* 138 (*SVF* 3.89.7-9), ὁ σοφὸς μόνος ἐλεύθερός τε καὶ ἄρχων.

181. See Paul's rebuff in 1 Cor. 4:8: "Already you are filled! Already you have become rich! Without us you have become kings (ἐβασιλεύσατε)! And would that you did reign (ἐβασιλεύσατε), so that we might rule as kings with you (συμβασιλεύσωμεν)!" On Stoic influence here see Conzelmann, 87, and *SVF* 3.158.34–159.37.

182. Epictetus, *Discourses* 3.22.72, 75, 79-81.

"power of independent action" (ἐξουσία αὐτοπραγίας),[183] and Dio Chrysostom concludes a discussion of slavery by stating, "And so, necessarily, the discerning are free, and they have the power (ἐξεῖναι αὐτοῖς) to do as they
want."[184] Philo, in turn, defines the free person as one who has power
(ἐξουσία) "to do everything and live as he wishes," saying that the one to
whom these things are "allowed" (ἔξεστιν) would be free;[185] while Epictetus
holds that wishing for something that is in someone else's power (ἐξουσία) is
to act as a slave (δουλεύειν).[186] As I proposed above on the basis of Paul's use
of the verb "to have power" (ἐξουσιάζω) in 7:4, the Corinthians he addresses
in 7:12ff. may have objected to physically coming under the power of an unbelieving spouse during sexual intercourse. If this is true, then part of their argument for viewing marriage to an unbeliever as slavery may have rested on
Stoic teachings such as these, which equated power with freedom and the loss
of power with slavery.[187]

Proceeding to the next few verses of our passage, we find still further evidence that Paul's argument here derives from a philosophical context. In 7:15c
Paul introduces the idea of the Christian "call," and asserts that Christians with
non-Christian spouses have been called by God "in peace" (ἐν εἰρήνῃ). Although

183. Diogenes Laertius 7.121. A version of this was known to Origen (SVF 3.147.7-9).

184. Dio Chrysostom, Oration 14.16 (SVF 3.87.2-3).

185. Philo, Quod omnis probus liber sit 59 (SVF 3.88.34-36). Cf. 1 Cor. 6:12 and 10:23: πάντα
(μοι) ἔξεστιν.

186. Epictetus, Discourses 4.7.10, and Encheiridion 14.2. See also Antipater (app. A), line 41,
who complains that bachelors who refuse to marry think they have been given the right
(ἐξουσία) to engage in illicit sex.

187. Paul's use of the term ἐξουσία supports this suggestion. It occurs seven times in 1 Corinthians in this sense of personal power (7:37; 8:9; 9:4, 5, 6, 12, 18), in one instance manifestly
drawing on a Stoic topos on freedom — i.e., 9:4 (on this see above, n. 83, and cf. p. 83; on 7:37 see
below, pp. 203-5). The word also occurs in 11:10 (a husband's authority as a restriction on his
wife's freedom) and 15:24 (of "cosmic powers"). In 6:12, furthermore, Paul suggests ironically
that one may be "overpowered" (ἐξουσιάζομαι) by the improper use of his or her personal
power. In his other letters (seven times altogether), the word denotes either God's power, Paul's
authority as a church administrator, or civil authority; but never personal power (2 Cor. 10:8;
13:10; Rom. 9:21; 13:1-3; cf. 2 Thess. 3:9 [freedom not to work]). In this light, it is also tempting to
consider the possibility of a connection between Paul's use of the verb "to deprive" (ἀποστερέω)
in 7:5 and the Stoic view that slavery was the "privation" (στέρησις) of independent action (Diogenes Laertius 7.122), in contrast to freedom, which was the "power" of independent action.
With his word choice in 7:4-5, Paul may be inferring that persons who are reluctant to maintain
sexual relations within marriage are actually depriving their spouses of freedom/power through
their demand for what they mistakenly (v. 4) view as their own freedom/power.

a few scholars have attempted to interpret this in the sense of God calling the Corinthians *to* peace,[188] Paul's reference is most certainly to a state of peace in which God found the Corinthians when he originally extended his call.[189] What Paul means by "peace," on the other hand, is not altogether clear, but it is likely that he is speaking of the peace between a husband and wife, for he uses this term regularly in his letters to refer to harmony between individuals.[190]

Significantly, Paul proposes this "peace" rather than "freedom" as the alternative to slavery. Since the Corinthians evidently saw their marriages to unbelievers as a form of slavery, they would naturally think of freedom, the solution to their problem, in terms of divorce or separation from their spouses. Paul's first inclination, therefore, is to promote marital peace, not emancipation. Inevitably, however, Paul must find a way to support his claim in verse 15b that the Corinthians are not enslaved. He does this in 7:17-24 with a Christian reworking of the philosophical topos that freedom and slavery have nothing to do with one's outward circumstances of life. But before Paul advances his argument in this direction, he pauses to interject another sort of challenge to the Corinthians' desire to be freed from their non-Christian spouses. In 7:16 he

188. E.g., Joachim Jeremias, "Die missionarische Aufgabe in der Mischehe (1. Kor 7,16)," in *Abba: Studien zur neutestamentlichen Theologie und Zeitgeschichte* (Göttingen: Vandenhoeck & Ruprecht, 1966), 297 n. 13, says ἐν εἰρήνῃ may be read as εἰς εἰρήνην, citing the evidence of the Greek church fathers; Cohen, 1:394 n. 83, thinks 7:15b is modeled on Judg. 21:13 ("and he called them to peace," καὶ ἐκάλεσαν αὐτοὺς εἰς εἰρήνην); and Gustav Billroth, *A Commentary on the Epistles of Paul to the Corinthians* (Edinburgh: Thomas Clark, 1837), 1:188, suggests that ἐν εἰρήνῃ = εἰρηνικῶς (peacefully).

189. See Barrett, 168-70; Neuhäusler, 45 n. 6; and Baltensweiler, 192, who sees, correctly, that 7:15b is analogous to 7:18b, ἐν ἀκροβυστίᾳ κέκληταί τις . . . ("has someone been called *in the state of uncircumcision?*").

190. 1 Cor. 14:33; 2 Cor. 13:11; Rom. 14:17-19 (which speaks of "serving," δουλεύων, Christ in peace); 1 Thess. 5:13. Elsewhere in early Christianity peace is spoken of as something belonging to a household. In Matt. 10:13//Luke 10:5-6 Jesus' disciples are described as bringing peace to households through their salutations, and Matt. 10:34-36//Luke 12:49-53 contrasts peace with the division of households. A form of this last saying is also found in *Gos. Thom.* 16 and in a third saying of Jesus on household peace at *Gos. Thom.* 48. Stoics and Cynics may also have spoken of peace in this manner. Lucian, *Demonax* 9, for example, recalls that the Cynic Demonax "was concerned both with reconciling brothers who were quarrelling, and with arbitrating peace for wives with their husbands" (καὶ γυναιξὶ πρὸς τοὺς γεγαμηκότας εἰρήνην πρυτανεύειν). This, in turn, resembles Epictetus's claim that the Cynic "oversees" humanity, determining "who is treating his wife well, who badly; who quarrels; what household is stable, what not" (*Discourses* 3.22.72); and it compares favorably to the concern for harmony between spouses that we find among the Stoics generally (see above, pp. 143-44).

follows the assertion that Christians have been "called in peace" with an explanation in the form of two rhetorical questions: "For (γάρ) what do you know (τί οἶδας), wife, if you will save (σώσεις) your husband? Or what do you know, husband, if you will save your wife?" Although the syntax of these questions is not transparent, scholars have concluded that they express either a genuine uncertainty or a mild optimism regarding the conversion of the unbelieving spouse. It is unlikely, in other words, that Paul is suggesting to his readers that they will *not* convert their spouses.[191] If this is correct, then the force of these questions is to point out to the Corinthians that far from being unholy, unclean outsiders, their non-Christian husbands and wives, with whom they were called in marital peace, are actually prime candidates for conversion.[192] Divorce, therefore, Paul is saying, must be seen as an uncalculated and overhasty course of action from this perspective as well.

The effectiveness of this supplementary argument lies, in large part, in its philosophical pedigree, for in all likelihood 7:16 has roots in a Stoic or Cynic tradition. This is suggested by two things. First, the form of this verse is the direct address of the Stoic-Cynic diatribe. From its beginning in verse 12 Paul has handled the question of mixed marriages in the third-person singular or second-person plural. In verse 16, however, we find the second-person singular, which is most satisfactorily explained as a shift to diatribe style. This conclusion is supported not only by the fact that the closest parallels to the syntax of Paul's questions, τί (γὰρ) οἶδας . . . εἰ, come from Epictetus,[193] but also by Paul's generous use of the diatribe style in the rest of 1 Corinthians 7.[194]

191. See Jeremias, "Die missionarische Aufgabe," 296-97; Sakae Kubo, "I Corinthians vii.16: Optimistic or Pessimistic?" *NTS* 24 (1977/78): 539-44, esp. 542, 544.

192. Just as Christians render their non-Christian spouses holy, Paul is saying, they may also convert them. Cf. 1 Pet. 3:1-6, where the author suggests that wives might convert their unbelieving husbands.

193. Epictetus, *Discourses* 2.20.28-31; 2.22.31 (twice); and 2.25.2 (cited in Jeremias, "Die missionarische Aufgabe," 294-96), which are of the form πόθεν οἶδας εἰ (or εἴσῃ ἄν), "whence do you know (will you know) if . . . ?" All other examples scholars have cited are of the form τίς οἶδεν εἰ, "who knows if . . ." These include: 2 Sam. 12:22; Esther 4:14; Jon. 3:9; Joel 2:14; *Joseph and Aseneth* 11.12 (cited in Jeremias, 292-94); Eccles. 2:19; 3:21 (cited in Kubo, 541-42); Tob. 13:8 (τίς γινώσκει εἰ, cited in Baumert, 85 n. 171); Achilles Tatius 7.6.2; Apuleius, *Metamorphoses* 1.15.4; 6.1.2; 6.5.4; and 10.26.2 (cited in C. Burchard, "Joseph and Aseneth," in *The Old Testament Pseudepigrapha*, 2:219 n. *i* 2).

194. Vv. 18, 21, and 27 — see below. Paul also uses diatribe style elsewhere in 1 Corinthians, e.g., at 15:35-36. On the history of research into Paul's use of the diatribe style, see Stowers, *Diatribe*, 7-78; Stowers, "The Diatribe," in *Greco-Roman Literature and the New Testament: Selected*

Our second reason for identifying the source of 7:16 as Stoic or Cynic is based on its similarity to an apocryphal saying preserved by Stobaeus, in which the issue is again one of "knowing" whether one will "save" one's spouse: "Plato, being asked, 'May I pursue philosophy if I marry?' said, 'Not knowing (οὐκ εἰδώς) that you will even save (σῴζειν) your own self, will you assist in saving (συνδιασώσεις) a wife upon your shoulders?'"[195] Although neither the date nor the provenance of this saying can be determined with certainty, its resemblance to 7:16 is, in my opinion, too striking to be dismissed as coincidence. Furthermore, while the speaker is said to be Plato, the question he is asked as well as his reply mirror the concerns of the Stoic-Cynic marriage debate. To assume that this saying had some currency in Stoic or Cynic circles in the first century, and to see it or a related saying as the inspiration for 7:16, is therefore not at all unreasonable.[196] There is, of course, an obvious difference between this saying and 7:16. In the one, "Plato" stresses the difficulty of saving a future spouse; in the other, Paul seeks to persuade the Corinthians that the salvation of their present spouses is still an open question. In light of this, it is possible that some version of the "Platonic" saying was known to the Corinthians and perhaps used by them as an argument for leaving an "unclean" spouse. Paul, by contrast, makes use of this saying by emphasizing the Corinthians' ignorance of God's ultimate intentions for their spouses. In all, Paul seems to have chosen the better argument, for while the "Platonic" saying works well as a warning against *initiating* marriage, Paul's version is a compelling argument for *staying* married, which is the issue here.

Following this supplementary argument in 7:16, Paul returns to his initial contention in 15b that Christians who are married to non-Christians are not "enslaved." He does this by using the casual transition phrase "In any event . . . ," or "Only . . ." (εἰ μή), and by elaborating on the idea of the Christian call, which he introduced in 15c.[197] In this way 7:17-24 serves as the con-

---

Forms and Genres, ed. David E. Aune, SBLSBS 21 (Atlanta: Scholars, 1988), 51-83; and Thomas Schmeller, *Paulus und die "Diatribe": Eine vergleichende Stilinterpretation,* NTAbh, n.s., 19 (Münster: Aschendorffsche Verlagsbuchhandlung, 1987).

195. [Plato] in Stobaeus 4.520.9-12 W.-H., cited in Gerhard Delling, *Paulus' Stellung zu Frau und Ehe,* BWANT, 4th ser., 5 (Stuttgart: W. Kohlhammer, 1931), 81 n. 159.

196. While Stoics and Cynics were more apt to quote a saying from Socrates and use him as their model, they also on occasion cited Plato, e.g., *Cynic Epistle of Diogenes* 44 (174.9-10 M.); Epictetus, *Discourses* 1.28.4; 2.17.6; 2.18.20; 2.22.36; 4.1.172.

197. So also Meyer, 209-10. It should be noted that 7:17b repeats the perfect κέκληκεν ("has called") of 7:15c; by contrast, vv. 20 and 24 run parallel to each other, using the aorist.

tinuation and conclusion of the argument begun in 7:15b-c.[198] It is not, as scholars often contend, a conclusion to the first half of chapter 7 or the theological centerpiece of the entire chapter.[199]

In addressing the themes of slavery and the Christian call in 7:17-24, Paul utilizes as his framework his teaching on the equality in Christ of Jews and Greeks, slaves and free, punctuating it at the beginning and end (vv. 17, 24)[200] with the admonition that Christians remain in the condition in which they were called. This teaching also appears in Galatians 3:28, where a third pair, male and female, is used.[201] But whereas in Galatians Paul focuses on the pair Jew-Greek, using the other two pairs as examples,[202] here his real subject is the pair slave-free, while the pair circumcised-uncircumcised represents the example.[203] 1 Corinthians 7:17-24 also shows itself different from Galatians 3:28 in that it emphasizes the Christian's indifference to the external conditions of life, not the oneness of those "in Christ."

The point Paul wishes to drive home in verses 17-24 is twofold: first, that no Christian can be enslaved by the circumstances of his or her life, by virtue of God's "call" to become a Christian; and second, that undue concern for changing the circumstances of one's life disregards the efficacy of God's call, and thereby represents a form of slavery in itself. In this way the pair circumcised-uncircumcised (7:18-19) functions to illustrate the general principle that outward circumstances are of no consequence to the Christian, and

198. So also Neuhäusler, 45 n. 4; Bartchy, 133; and Yarbrough, 112. Niederwimmer, 105 and n. 123, followed by William F. Orr and James Arthur Walther, *I Corinthians: A New Translation*, AB 32 (Garden City, N.Y.: Doubleday, 1976), 216, erroneously suggests that 7:17-24 is a digression on peace (v. 15c).

199. See, e.g., Weiß, *Korintherbrief*, 183; Hurd, 89, 178; and Baumert, 19, 99-160 (esp. 158). Ironically, Heinrici, *Der erste Brief*, 249, notes that several commentaries in his day saw 7:17-24 as an interpolation or a misplaced text.

200. On the meaning of 7:20, see below.

201. On the absence of this pair in 1 Cor. 7:17-24, see Betz, *Galatians*, 200 (regarding 1 Cor. 12:13).

202. Cf. Gal. 5:6 and 6:15, where only the pair circumcised-uncircumcised appears.

203. It is fairly common for Paul to join his real subject with examples in this way, thereby establishing a larger context for his argument. In 1 Cor. 12:4-6, for instance, he contrasts the variety of Christian "gifts," "services," and "workings" to the oneness of the Spirit, the Lord, and God, respectively, but from vv. 7-11 it becomes clear that his interest lies only with the *gifts* of the Spirit (see Conzelmann, 208). Likewise, in 12:8-10 he enumerates several gifts of the Spirit (cf. 12:28-30; 13:1-3), but as we soon learn from chap. 14, it is only the gifts of prophecy and speaking in tongues that really concern him. In this context, incidentally, Paul reproduces the paradigm Jew-Greek, slave-free (12:13), *both* pairs now serving as examples.

therefore a Christian should not seek to make a change in one way or the other. With the pair slave-free (7:21-22) Paul then goes a step beyond this, declaring that God's call actually *reverses* the circumstances of one's life, for the Christian slave is now the Lord's *freed*man, while those who were free before their call are now Christ's slaves. With this declaration the refrain of verses 17 and 24 that Christians should remain in the circumstances of life in which they were called now takes on new meaning. The longing to "better" one's station in life becomes, in effect, a denial of the significance of the change that God has already brought about.[204] This, in turn, makes one a "slave of men" (v. 23), by which Paul must be referring to a spiritual bondage to doctrines or ideologies "of men" (cf. 3:1-4), since the Christian slave of verses 21-22 cannot "become" (γίγνομαι) a slave of men in the physical sense, as he already is one.[205]

With regard to the issue of mixed marriages at Corinth, Paul's implied conclusion in all this is that Christians married to non-Christians are not enslaved — his initial claim in 7:15b. These Christians are in fact no more enslaved to their spouses than other Christians are slaves to earthly masters, something Paul has shown to be a matter of indifference. Any attempt by these Christians to shake off their supposed yoke of slavery by divorcing a non-Christian spouse must be viewed as a rejection of God's grace and at the same time the subjection of themselves to true slavery — that of the spirit.[206]

As it stands, with 7:17-24 Paul has fashioned a highly Stoicized version of his teaching on God's transforming grace, both in form and in content. In form these verses move with the distinctive rhythms of the Stoic-Cynic diatribe style of instruction.[207] The rhetorical pattern Paul employs here has the following elements. A statement of fact in the form of a rhetorical question[208]

204. Cf. Bartchy, 140.

205. Cf. 1 Cor. 6:20.

206. Cf. Alfred Juncker, *Die Ethik des Apostels Paulus*, vol. 2, *Die konkrete Ethik* (Halle an der Saale: Max Niemeyer, 1919), 161-62, who sees 7:17-24 as clear evidence that some Corinthians felt they had to break off marital relations in order to be holy, equal, and free.

207. Noted by several scholars, e.g., Weiß, *Korintherbrief*, 184-85; Conzelmann, 5, 126; and Bultmann, *Der Stil der paulinischen Predigt*, 69.

208. Edgar J. Goodspeed, *Problems of New Testament Translation* (Chicago: University of Chicago Press, 1945), 155-56, argues against translating the statement of fact as a rhetorical question on the basis of PTeb 421, θέλις αὐτὸ πωλῆσαι πώλησον, θέλις αὐτὸ ἀφεῖναι τῇ θυγατρί σου ἄφες, which he translates, "If you wish to sell it sell it; if you wish to give it to your daughter, give it to her." F. Blass and A. Debrunner, *A Greek Grammar of the New Testament and Other Early Christian Literature*, trans. and rev. Robert W. Funk (Chicago and London: University of Chi-

is made about someone, often in the direct address of the second-person singular. Next comes an imperative, the purpose of which is to deny the importance of this fact for future action. Lastly, an explanation that the original statement of fact is a matter of indifference is sometimes added.

In 7:17-24 this rhetorical pattern appears three times. In 7:18 we get two statements of fact and two imperatives: "Someone was called having been circumcised? — let him not remove the circumcision![209] Someone has been called in an uncircumcised state? — let him not be circumcised!" Verse 19 then gives a combined explanation: "Circumcision is nothing and uncircumcision is nothing; rather, keeping the commandments of God." In verse 21 we get the third statement of fact and the third imperative, this time followed by a qualification, the meaning of which is still disputed among scholars: "You were called as a slave? — don't let it concern you! But if indeed you can become free, rather use [it] (μᾶλλον χρῆσαι)."[210] Verse 22 then supplies an explanation: "For the slave who is called in the Lord is the Lord's freedman; likewise, the one called as a freeman is Christ's slave."[211] From verses 21-22 we see that Paul's interest in using this particular diatribe form has even prevented him from finishing the paradigm Jew-Greek, slave-free, since he cannot very well add to verse 21a, "You were called as a freeman? — don't let it

---

cago Press, 1961), 262 (§494), in turn, remark that while the statement of fact corresponds to a conditional protasis, it is unnecessary to translate it as a question. But none of these scholars takes into account the Latin and Hebrew examples from Seneca and Sirach (see below), the syntax of which calls for a question mark. Goodspeed's citation of the papyri does, however, show the kinship of the diatribe style to everyday speech patterns.

209. For the history of this intriguing medical procedure, see Emil Schürer, *The History of the Jewish People in the Age of Jesus Christ (175 B.C.–A.D. 135),* vol. 1, ed. and rev. Geza Vermes and Fergus Millar (Edinburgh: T. & T. Clark, 1973), 149 n. 28.

210. On the force of the last clause in 7:21, see Baumert, 114-56; Bartchy, *ΜΑΛΛΟΝ ΧΡΗΣΑΙ;* and Margaret E. Thrall, *Greek Particles in the New Testament: Linguistic and Exegetical Studies,* NTTS 3 (Grand Rapids: Eerdmans, 1962), 78-82. The use of a set rhetorical form in this verse opens up the possibility, of course, that the imperative here does not represent Paul's own command. In this way the qualification, which is clearly an addition to the set form, may be Paul's attempt to avoid a misunderstanding, carrying the meaning that slaves, while they should not regard their disenfranchised state as an indication of their worth before God, should also not forgo the opportunity to work toward their emancipation. See Will Deming, "A Diatribe Pattern in 1 Cor. 7:21-22: A New Perspective on Paul's Directions to Slaves," *NovT* 37 (1995): 130-37; and Deming, "Indifferent Things," in *Paul in the Greco-Roman World,* ed. J. Paul Sampley (Harrisburg, Penn.: Trinity Press International, 2003), 392-94.

211. On ὁμοίως, "likewise," in this verse as an indication of Stoic influence, see above, pp. 113-14.

concern you!" or " — don't become a slave!," for the imperative would not represent a reasonable course of action.[212] All the same, verse 22 proffers the explanation for this missing statement and imperative, just as if they were there, although the intervening remark (v. 21b) tends to obscure this inconsistency. As we shall see below, Paul retains this mention of the freeman in verse 22 in order to introduce into his discussion a Christian version of the Stoic paradox on freedom.

Parallels to this pattern of rhetoric can be found in several Hellenistic authors. The one most often cited is that by the Cynic Teles, from his treatise *On Self-Sufficiency,* and it is noteworthy that Teles employs the same elliptical expression, "use [it]," that we find in 7:21b:

> Therefore one should not try to change circumstances, but rather
> prepare oneself for them as they are, just as sailors do . . .
> And as for you, <regard> your present situation, use [it] (χρῶ).
> You have grown old? — do not seek the things of a young man!
> Again, you have become weak? — do not seek to carry and submit
> your neck to the loads of a strong man! . . .
> Again, you have become destitute? — do not seek the rich man's
> way of life . . . !
> Therefore, as I say, I do not see how circumstances themselves have
> anything troublesome, not old age or poverty or lack of citizenship.[213]

Our next examples come from an epigram attributed to Metrodorus and from its alter ego attributed to Posidippus.[214] Here we see some variation in the basic pattern inasmuch as a future and a present tense follow the statements of fact, not imperatives. "Metrodorus" writes, "You have a marriage? — your house will be the most excellent! You don't marry? — you live being even more at ease! . . . Youth is strong; grey hair, again, is pious."[215] To this

212. Noted by Meyer, 218; Weiß, *Korintherbrief,* 187; and Neuhäusler, 47; cf. Bartchy, 157.

213. Teles, frag. 2.10.65-80, trans. Edward N. O'Neil, ed. and trans., *Teles (The Cynic Teacher),* SBLTT 11/SBLGRS 3 (Missoula, Mont.: Scholars, 1977), 11, modified slightly.

214. The date and authorship of both epigrams is uncertain. See Pierre Waltz and Guy Soury, *Anthologie grecque, première partie: Anthologie Palatine* (Paris: Société d'édition "Les belles lettres," 1974), 3:183, and A. S. F. Gow and D. L. Page, eds., *The Greek Anthology: Hellenistic Epigrams,* vol. 2, *Commentary and Indexes* (Cambridge: Cambridge University Press, 1965), 502, although the suggestion of Gow and Page that these poems are post-Hellenistic does not take into account the parallels presented here.

215. *Greek Anthology* 9.360.

"Posidippus" mocks back, "You have a marriage? — you will not be without cares! You don't marry? — you live being even more alone! . . . Youth is foolish; grey hair, again, is feeble."[216]

Another sort of variation occurs in Sirach 7:22-26, which includes this diatribe form in its collection of proverbs. Instead of stressing the indifference of a certain condition through the imperative, the author uses it simply to give advice, following it with another such imperative rather than an explanation:

> You have cattle?[217] — tend them! And if they are profitable to you,
>   let them stay with you.
> You have children [i.e., sons]? — discipline them! And make them
>   obedient from their youth.
> You have daughters? — be on guard for their chastity! And do not
>   show yourself to be too lenient with them. . . .
> You have a wife? — do not despise her![218] And do not trust yourself
>   to a woman you hate.[219]

In the first century Philo, Seneca, and Plutarch also use this particular diatribe pattern. In his treatise *On Joseph*, where Philo has a tendency to present Joseph as a Stoic wise man, he describes this patriarch's rise to power in Egypt as a matter of philosophical necessity. Since life is full of disturbance and confusion (ταραχὴ καὶ ἀταξία), he explains, the statesman must come on the scene to give teachings as to the truth of things. Among these teachings are eight examples of our diatribe form:

216. Posidippus in Stobaeus 5.842.6-9 W.-H., and *Greek Anthology* 9.359. T. B. L. Webster, *Hellenistic Poetry and Art* (London: Methuen, 1964), 56 n. 3, compares Posidippus's sentiment to that found in Theophrastus, *On Marrying*. Johannes Geffcken, *Kynika und Verwandtes* (Heidelberg: Carl Winter, 1909), 10, called this epigram a "poetic diatribe"; and Wolfgang Speyer, *Naucellius und sein Kreis* (Munich: C. H. Beck, 1959), 96 n. 4, termed it "popular-philosophical discourse." On the use of diatribe in epigrams, see Geffcken, 6-13.

217. Here and in the following lines the expression used is "noun + לְךָ" (LXX, noun + σοί ἐστιν), as Hebrew has no verb "to have."

218. LXX: "You have a wife after your soul? — do not divorce her!" (γυνή σοί ἐστιν κατὰ ψυχήν . . . μὴ ἐκβάλῃς αὐτήν). On the difference between the Hebrew and the Greek, see Rudolf Smend, *Die Weisheit des Jesus Sirach* (Berlin: Georg Reimer, 1906), 70-71; Warren C. Trenchard, *Ben Sira's View of Women: A Literary Analysis*, BJS 38 (Chico, Calif.: Scholars, 1982), 28.

219. Alexander A. Di Lella, *The Hebrew Text of Sirach* (The Hague: Mouton, 1966), 58, describes the pattern here as "a vigorous and concise bit of Hebrew poetry"; Juncker, 204, compares Sir. 7:18-28 to a household code. See also Trenchard, 27-28. On Stoic influence in Sirach, see above, n. 113. Ben Sira was, of course, an eager *collector* of philosophical maxims.

This is another's? — don't desire it!

This is yours? — use [it], not misusing [it] (χρῶ μὴ παραχρώμενος)!

You have abundance? — share! For the beauty of riches is not in purses,
  but in aiding those in need.

You have little? — don't begrudge the rich! For no one would
  show compassion to a slanderous pauper.

You're famous and have received honors? — don't brag!

Your fortunes are lowly? — nonetheless, don't let your spirits fall!

All advances for you as you planned? — beware of change!

You stumble often? — hope for success! For when things turn among men,
  they tend toward their opposites.[220]

Here again, in the second line, we find the elliptical mode of expression that
occurs in 1 Corinthians 7:21b.

In his tractate *On Tranquility of the Mind,* Seneca admonishes a person to
pursue virtue, regardless of outward circumstances, giving us the following
examples:

Is he not permitted to be a soldier? — let him seek public office!

Must he live in a private station? — let him help his countrymen
  by his silent support!

Is it dangerous even to enter the forum? — in private houses, at the
  public spectacles, at feasts let him show himself a good comrade,
  a faithful friend, a temperate feaster!

Has he lost the duties of a citizen? — let him exercise those of a man!
  The very reason for our magnanimity in not shutting ourselves
  up within the walls of one city, in going forth into intercourse
  with the whole earth and in claiming the world as our country,
  was that we might have a wider field for our virtue.

Is the tribunal closed to you, and are you barred from the rostrum
  and the hustings? — look how many broad stretching countries

---

220. Philo, *De Josepho* 143-44, cited by Henry St. John Thackeray, *The Relation of St. Paul to Contemporary Jewish Thought* (London: Macmillan, 1900), 239, who also cites Philo, *Quod omnis probus liber sit* 48, where we find a ninth example of sorts, on the theme of slavery: "You're a slave? — you have no share in speech (λόγος)!" This maxim was also known to the Stoic emperor Marcus Aurelius (11.30). The use of the diatribe style in Philo's OT exegesis is noted by Paul Wendland, "Philo und die kynisch-stoische Diatribe," in *Beiträge zur Geschichte der griechischen Philosophie und Religion,* ed. Paul Wendland and Otto Kern (Berlin: Georg Reimer, 1895), 62-63, and Stowers, *Diatribe,* 69, 93.

lie open behind you, how many peoples! Never can you be blocked from any part so large that a still larger will not be left open to you.[221]

In Plutarch an instance of this diatribe configuration occurs in his work *On Borrowing*. As part of an argument against borrowing, he cites an adage showing its futility: "You have means? — don't borrow! . . . You are without means? — don't borrow!"[222] Although Plutarch is no Stoic, a Stoic origin for this saying is suggested by his explanation of it, which employs quotations from Cato and Crates as well as anecdotes about Musonius, Cleanthes, and Zeno.[223]

Finally, from the second century, Epictetus supplies us with still other examples of this rhetorical form:

Never say about anything, "I lost it," but rather, "I gave [it] back."
Your little child died? — it was given back!
Your wife died? — she was given back![224]

Remember that you must conduct yourself as in a banquet.
Has something been passed around down to you? — reach out your hand
    and politely take some!
It goes on by? — don't hold [it] back!
It hasn't come yet? — don't set your desire on [it] at a distance,
    but stay put until it is down by you!
Thus toward children, thus toward a wife, thus toward public office,
    thus toward wealth, and some day you will be worthy of the
    banquet of the gods.[225]

Just as the form of 7:17-24 borrows from Stoic-Cynic discourse, so does its content. This is seen most clearly in verses 22-23, which reflect the Stoic paradox that the wise and good man is always free although he be a slave, while the bad man is forever a slave even if he is a king.[226] The Stoics held

221. Seneca, *De tranquilitate animi* 4.3-4, trans. Basore, 2:229, punctuation modified slightly.

222. Plutarch, *Moralia* 829F (*De vitando aere alieno*), cited by Almquist, 97, who also cites *Moralia* 1103D (*Non posse suaviter*), which is a variation on this pattern.

223. Plutarch, *Moralia* 829F, 830B-D.

224. Epictetus, *Encheiridion* 11.

225. Epictetus, *Encheiridion* 15. Johannes Weiß, *Beiträge zur Paulinischen Rhetorik* (Göttingen: Vandenhoeck & Ruprecht, 1897), 23, cites Epictetus, *Discourses* 1.12.22, but the pattern is too different to be considered a parallel. The same holds for James 5:13-14.

226. Noted by several scholars, including Weiß, *Korintherbrief*, 187; Bultmann, *Der Stil der paulinischen Predigt*, 82; Betz, *Galatians*, 195; and F. Stanley Jones, *"Freiheit" in den Briefen des*

this doctrine because they believed that moral choice, not outward circumstances of life, defined freedom. To be free was to pursue virtue; to be a slave was to become entangled in human misconceptions about life, analogous to Paul's idea of becoming "slaves of men."[227] This philosophical understanding of freedom and slavery is widely attested in the Stoicism of the empire. We find it in Arius, Philo, Seneca, Dio Chrysostom, and Epictetus.[228]

One reason Paul may have considered the Stoic doctrine of freedom particularly apropos to the Corinthian situation is that it distinguished between slavery of the body and the "true" slavery of the soul.[229] Earlier in this section, with reference to 7:15b and 7:4, I suggested that the Corinthians saw their marriages to non-Christians as a form of slavery because of the control (ἐξουσία) a non-Christian spouse exercised over the Christian's body and the consequent danger of pollution via physical contact. If this is correct, Paul's insistence here on a Stoic definition of slavery and freedom has the effect of denying that such conjugal control over a Christian's body has any relevance for the issues of true (i.e., moral) slavery and freedom.

Quite justifiably, several scholars have cautioned against drawing too close an analogy between 7:22-23 and Stoic thought. The Stoics, they point out, held that freedom is achieved through the individual's own efforts to live according to nature and virtue, while for Paul freedom comes to the individual only though God's help, manifested in Christ. Thus, even though Epictetus can picture the philosopher responding to a tyrant with the words

---

Apostels Paulus: Eine historische, exegetische und religionsgeschichtliche Studie, GTA 34 (Göttingen: Vandenhoeck & Ruprecht, 1987), 27-37.

227. For discussions of the Stoic notion of freedom, see, e.g., Heinrich Greeven, *Das Hauptproblem der Sozialethik in der neueren Stoa und im Urchristentum,* NTF, 3rd ser., 4 (Gütersloh: C. Bertelsmann, 1935), 28-33, and Max Pohlenz, *Freedom in Greek Life and Thought: The History of an Ideal* (Dordrecht: D. Reidel; New York: Humanities, 1966), 113-15. See also *SVF* 3.85.21–89.24.

228. E.g., Arius in Stobaeus 2.101.14-20 W.-H.; Philo, *Quod omnis probus liber sit;* Dio Chrysostom, *Oration* 14 and 15; Epictetus, *Discourses* 4.1. For Seneca see Miriam T. Griffin, *Seneca: A Philosopher in Politics* (Oxford: Clarendon, 1976), 260. Curiously it is not found in Musonius, but this may be an indication of how incomplete our records are of his teachings.

229. Philo even lauds this as the "greatest dogma" (τὸ δογματικώτατον), declaring that the wise man is free "even if he should have a thousand masters of the body" (κἂν μυρίους τοῦ σώματος ἔχῃ δεσπότας, *De posteritate Caini* 138). See also Philo, *Quod omnis probus liber sit* 17-19; Seneca, *De beneficiis* 3.20.1-2; Dio Chrysostom, *Oration* 15.29; and Epictetus, *Discourses* 1.19.9; 3.22.38-44.

"Zeus has set me free!"[230] Epictetus has in mind Zeus as creator and sustainer of the cosmos, whose *logos* provides all persons with the means to make themselves free, not Zeus as personal redeemer. Yet this fundamental difference in theological orientation does not, as these scholars freely admit, diminish the likelihood that the Stoic paradox of freedom has left its mark on our passage.[231]

A second possibility for seeing the influence of Stoic thought on the content of 7:17-24 is Paul's statement in 7:20 that every Christian should remain "in the call (κλῆσις) to which he was called."[232] This admonition is peculiar in two ways. First, it is out of step with the rest of the section, for in verses 17, 18, 21, and 24 Paul insists that Christians should remain in the *circumstances* in which they were called, whereas here the call itself is at issue; and second, it does not, at least initially, seem to make much sense for Paul in this context to admonish Christians to remain in their Christian call, or in effect, to "remain Christians." Given these difficulties, scholars have generally opted for understanding κλῆσις as "state," "condition," or "status." This yields the translation "in the state in which he was called,"[233] and brings 7:20

---

230. Epictetus, *Discourses* 1.19.9, cited in Weiß, *Korintherbrief,* 190. Cf. Epictetus 3.24.67-68; 4.1.111-14, and Oldfather's note on this last passage (2:282 n. 1).

231. See Weiß, *Korintherbrief,* 189-90; Kümmel in Lietzmann, 177; Conzelmann, 127-28. Adolf Bonhöffer, *Epiktet und das Neue Testament,* Religionsgeschichtliche Versuche und Vorarbeiten 10 (Giessen: Alfred Töpelmann, 1911), 170-72 — followed by J. N. Sevenster, *Paul and Seneca,* NovTSup 4 (Leiden: Brill, 1961), 189-90, and Neuhäusler, 44 — maintains that Paul's demand in 7:21 that one remain a slave is un-Stoic, but this interpretation of 7:21, as we noted above, is disputed. Along these same lines, another difference between 7:22-23 and Stoic thinking on which some scholars have insisted may represent only dissimilarity rather than incompatibility. Thus Conzelmann, 128, maintains that Paul's "dialectic of freedom in servitude" in v. 22 is "alien" to Stoic thought. While this is true, a Stoic like Seneca can nonetheless give his full assent to the Epicurean saying, "If you would enjoy real freedom, you must be the slave of philosophy" *(philosophiae servias oportet),* adding that "the very service *(servire)* of philosophy is freedom *(libertas)*" (*Epistle* 8.7, trans. Richard M. Gummere, ed. and trans., *Seneca: Ad Lucilium, epistulae morales,* LCL [London: William Heinemann; New York: Putnam, 1930], 1:41). From this perspective Barrett's assessment of the matter is more exacting: "the paradoxical theme that it is in service that perfect freedom is found is for Paul focused not upon an impersonal and pantheistic *logos,* but upon the personal and historical Redeemer, Jesus Christ" (Barrett, 173). Even here, however, we should note that Paul can speak of Christians as slaves "to righteousness" (Rom. 6:18; cf. 6:17, 20, "slaves of sin").

232. Or *by which* he was called (ᾗ); see the next note.

233. In this case the relative pronoun ᾗ is seen as the equivalent of ἐν ᾗ, which, given the syntax of the sentence, poses no particular problem. See Walter Bauer, *A Greek-English Lexicon*

back into line with the other verses in this section. These meanings for the word κλῆσις are not found elsewhere in early Christian literature, however, nor are they clearly attested anywhere in ancient Greek literature.[234] Furthermore, its immediate *lexical* context in 7:17-24 seems to exclude any meaning but "[Christian] call."

In his commentary on 1 Corinthians, Weiß proposed that the difficulty with 7:20 had come about because the Christian sense of the word κλῆσις had been flavored by Stoic popular philosophy. As proof for his theory he cited Epictetus, *Discourses* 1.29.33-49 and 2.1.39.[235] In the first passage Epictetus states that the philosopher often acts "as a witness called by God" when faced with demanding situations;[236] and in the second he addresses the philosopher as one "who has trusted in him (πεποιθότως) who called you to these things," referring to the various trials a philosopher must face, such as being chained, tortured, exiled, or put to death. From these two passages Weiß concluded that Epictetus understood God's call in the sense of a philosopher receiving a "mission" *(vocatio, die Mission)* from God, and therefore it approximated the philosopher's "occupation" or "profession" *(Beruf)*.[237] Proposing, further, that the relative pronoun in 7:20 be translated in a "modal" sense,[238] Weiß maintained that Stoic influence on this verse could justify understanding it as an admonition to Christians to remain in the "form of the call" in which they were called.

All told, however, Weiß's proposal clarifies nothing, for even the meaning "occupation" and a modal interpretation of ᾗ will not allow us to translate κλῆσις as "form of call."[239] Beyond this, Epictetus's understanding of the words

---

of the New Testament and Other Early Christian Literature, rev. Frederick William Danker, 3rd English ed. (Chicago: University of Chicago Press, 2000), 727 (s.v. "ὅς, ἥ, ὅ, 1.f").

234. See, e.g., Karl Ludwig Schmidt, "καλέω," in *TDNT* 3 (1965), 491-92 n. 1; Neuhäusler, 43-44; and Walter Bauer, 549 (s.v. "κλῆσις, 2").

235. Weiß, *Korintherbrief,* 187.

236. ὡς μάρτυς ὑπὸ θεοῦ κεκλημένος, Epictetus, *Discourses* 1.29.46. At 1.29.49 Epictetus speaks of the philosopher's "call which God has called," τὴν κλῆσιν ἣν κέκληκεν — cf. 1 Cor. 7:20.

237. Weiß, *Korintherbrief,* 187.

238. Weiß, *Korintherbrief,* 187, on the basis of 7:17, "each *as* (ὡς) God has called"; but this modal reading of the pronoun is not supported by 7:24, where we find "each *in which* (ἐν ᾧ) he was called."

239. Weiß's further suggestion (*Korintherbrief,* 187) that poverty, lack of education, and low social status are themselves the κλῆσις referred to in 1 Cor. 1:26 speaks for itself. (Here Paul's statement, "consider your call," is shorthand for "consider how the event of your call took place." This shorthand does not work for 7:20, however.)

καλέω and κλῆσις is considerably more distant from Paul's than Weiß assumed. For Epictetus the philosopher is called by God *as a philosopher* to meet a particularly challenging or trying "situation" (περίστασις).[240] With Paul, by contrast, God's call *initiates* a person's conversion to Christianity; it is not an occasional commission that comes to one who is already a Christian.[241]

It is nonetheless still possible that Stoic usage lies behind the apparent difficulty in 7:20. A third passage from Epictetus, not considered by Weiß, points in this direction. This is *Enchiridion 7*, where Epictetus introduces the metaphor of a sea voyage. When a ship puts in, he explains, the passengers are allowed a brief shore leave. They may wander in search of freshwater or shellfish, but they must always be mindful of their ship. Turning about frequently, "for fear lest the captain should call (καλέω)," they must be prepared at any moment to drop what they are doing and heed his summons. Applying this metaphor to the philosophical life, Epictetus continues: "So it is also in life: If there be given you, instead of a little bulb and a small shell-fish, a little wife and child, there will be no objection to that; only, if the Captain [i.e., God] calls (καλέω), give up all these things and run to the ship, without even turning around to look back."[242]

Here we see that the philosopher's call sometimes requires him to abandon his, presumably nonphilosophical, wife and children. This raises the possibility that it is the Corinthians, rather than Paul, who had understood the notion of "call" in a Stoic sense, and that, having felt themselves thus called to respond to some unusual and trying situation, they proceeded to use a Stoic tradition like the one in *Enchiridion 7* to justify abandoning their non-Christian spouses. Although Paul does not mention any urgent situation here, a few verses later (7:26-31) we learn that the Corinthians stood face-to-face with a "present necessity" that promised "hardship in the flesh" to all who were married. Given that we have already identified apocalyptic concerns behind the celibacy in 7:5, this may have been the crisis that touched off, or at least fueled, the Corinthians' desire to be done with their non-Christian spouses.[243]

---

240. The word Epictetus uses at 1.29.33, 34.

241. See Bonhöffer, 37-39, 207-8; Juncker, 163-66; and Schmidt, 493. A possible exception may be Paul's own call to be an apostle, but this also seems to have coincided with his "conversion" (Gal. 1:15), and it has nothing to do with the sense of "call" in 1 Cor. 7:15c, 17-24.

242. Trans. Oldfather, 2:489, 491.

243. Cf. Luke 18:29, which speaks of Jesus' disciples leaving their wives for the sake of the kingdom of God (cf. Luke 14:26).

A principal advantage of this hypothesis is that it makes good sense of Paul's admonition in 7:20, that a Christian must "remain in the call in which he was called." What Paul is saying here, according to this interpretation, is that those Corinthians who are married to unbelievers must stay in their original Christian call.[244] They are not to follow an "additional" call or commission,[245] occasioned by a crisis, which, after the manner of the Stoics, would require them to leave their unbelieving spouses. This understanding of 7:20 also explains why Paul affords so much space (vv. 15c, 17-24) to the notion of God's call in discussing the meaning of God's grace for mixed marriages. In Galatians, by contrast, he uses the concept of faith to clarify the doctrine of grace. Here, however, he employs the terms καλέω and κλῆσις ten times in these few verses, as compared to twice in the rest of 1 Corinthians,[246] and sixteen more times in all his other letters.[247]

A last instance of Stoic influence on 7:17-24 is perhaps to be found in verse 19, where Paul states: "Circumcision is nothing and uncircumcision is

---

244. This also clarifies the otherwise unexpected admonition to "remain beside God" (μενέτω παρὰ θεῷ) in 7:24, which some manuscripts simply omit, and which Weiß, *Korintherbrief*, 191, labeled as "hardly to be interpreted with certainty."

245. Cf. the idea of "another gospel" in Gal. 1:6-9.

246. Namely, 1 Cor. 1:9 and 1:26. This does not count 10:27 (καλέω in the sense of being invited to dinner) or 15:9 (in the sense of being called by a title). He also uses the cognate adjective "called" (κλητός) at 1:1, 2, 24. Regarding the misunderstanding of "call" among the Corinthians, it is noteworthy that only in 1:26 and 7:20 does Paul use the term κλῆσις to speak of an individual's call (as opposed to God's calling of the individual), and only here does he speak of it with reference to the outward circumstances of the individual's life. (κλῆσις also occurs at Rom. 11:29, Phil. 3:14, and 2 Thess. 1:11.) Noteworthy, too, is the number of times words of the καλ- and κλη-group occur in 1 Cor. 1:1-9 in combination with notions that play an important part in 7:12-15a: the church at Corinth is comprised of those who are "made holy" (ἁγιάζω) and "called holy" (κλητοὶ ἅγιοι); and God is "faithful" (πιστός), through whom the Corinthians were "called" (καλέω) into partnership (κοινωνία) with Christ — all of which is in addition to Paul's use of κλητός, ἐπικαλέω, and ἐκκλησία elsewhere in these verses. This may indicate that the notion of being called was central to the Corinthian self-identity. Rom. 1:1-7 also has several words from the καλ- and κλη- group, but Romans may be styled after 1 Corinthians here, as are other parts of Romans.

247. Half of which are in Romans (cf. end of previous note): 8:30 (twice); 9:11, 24, 25 (twice), 26; 11:29. The others occur in Gal. 1:6, 15; 5:8, 13; Phil. 3:14; 1 Thess. 2:12; 4:7; 5:24 (also 2 Thess. 1:11; 2:14). This does not count Rom. 4:17 (καλέω in the sense of call into being) or 9:7 (in the sense of designate). It does, however, count Rom. 9:25 and 26, where Paul interprets Hos. 2:1, 23 to mean "call," even though the LXX meaning of καλέω is clearly "name." Paul also uses the adjective κλητός at Rom. 1:1, 6, 7; 8:28.

nothing — rather, keeping the commandments of God" (τήρησις ἐντολῶν θεοῦ). Like 7:20, the final clause in this verse appears to diverge from the overall theme of 7:17-24. Instead of encouraging Christians to remain in the condition in which they were called, it exhorts them to keep God's commandments. Consequently, just what Paul means by these "commandments" has become a matter of scholarly debate. Several scholars have seen them as the equivalent of "faith working through love," or "a new creation," on the basis of Galatians 5:6 and 6:15, where the paradigm circumcised-uncircumcised also occurs.[248] The problem with this suggestion is that it clearly derives from the context of Galatians and the issues under discussion in the Galatian churches. In 1 Corinthians 7:17-24, however, we would expect Paul to draw his conclusions about "what is important" from matters at hand in Corinth. As an alternative, Baltensweiler suggests that the "commandments of God" in verse 19b should be understood as "the will of God, which equally encompasses both Jews and pagans," taking this meaning from 7:18-19a.[249] But even this interpretation coincides more with Paul's thesis in Galatians (and Romans) than with anything in our passage.

In a very different vein, Sanders has suggested that the "commandments of God" refers to the Torah. Yet, observing further that circumcision is one of the commandments of the Law, and that the first part of verse 19 proclaims "circumcision is nothing," Sanders comes to the awkward conclusion that 7:19 is "one of the most amazing sentences that [Paul] ever wrote."[250] If anything, Sanders's analysis seems to rule out the idea that 7:19b is a reference to the Torah — a notion that is equally questionable from the perspective of Paul's denigration of "works of the law" (e.g., Gal. 2:16). Finally, Neuhäusler has proposed that the last clause in 7:19 be understood as the vestige of a pre-Pauline baptismal ceremony in which converts were exhorted to remain in their new calling by "keeping the commandments of God."[251] While this is certainly plausible, given that 7:17-24 may ultimately derive from a baptismal liturgy,[252]

---

248. So, e.g., Lietzmann, 32; Wolbert, 118; and Gottlob Schrenk, "ἐντέλλομαι, ἐντολή," in *TDNT* 2 (1964), 552, who notes gratuitously that this is "wholly in line with the meaning of the καινὴ ἐντολή [new commandment] according to the Johannine view."

249. Baltensweiler, 151.

250. E. P. Sanders, *Paul, the Law, and the Jewish People* (Philadelphia: Fortress, 1983), 103.

251. Neuhäusler, 46 and nn. 11-12.

252. Cf., e.g., 1 Cor. 12:13 and Gal. 3:27-28; and see also Matt. 28:19-20, where Jesus instructs his disciples to baptize all peoples, teaching them "to keep all that I commanded you" (τηρεῖν πάντα ὅσα ἐνετειλάμην ὑμῖν).

it cannot be the whole answer, for Paul has reworked the traditions in these verses to such a degree that we would hardly expect the intrusion of a superfluous vestige into his argument.

To my mind, the most satisfying solution to the problem of 7:19b comes from Stoic materials found in Epictetus. In his entry on ἐντολή in the *Theological Dictionary of the New Testament*, Schrenk explains that the Stoics had an aversion to this word because they associated it with a "primitive form of morality."[253] While this characterization has merit, it also requires some qualification, for in Epictetus we have five passages in which the term ἐντολαί signifies the very essence of Stoicism. Thus in book 1 of his *Discourses*, when an interlocutor asks Epictetus for moral direction (ἔντειλαί μοι), he replies, "What directions shall I give you (τί σοι ἐντείλωμαι)? Has not Zeus given you directions (ἐντέταλται)?" And in book 3, when Epictetus considers how he will justify his life before Zeus, he envisions himself demanding of the deity, "Have I in any respect transgressed Thy commands (ἐντολαί)?"[254]

In all five passages, moreover, Epictetus mentions themes integral to Paul's discussion of the Christian call in 7:17-24, including true freedom, faithfulness, the jurisdiction one has over one's own body, and the concept of power (ἐξουσία). For example, in book 4, in a passage that presents a dialogue between the philosopher and a tyrant, the latter threatens, "Am I not master of your body (σῶμα)? . . . Am I not master of exile or bonds?" To this Epictetus vaunts back, "[N]o one has authority (ἐξουσία) over me. I have been set free (ἠλευθέρωμαι) by God, I know His commands (ἐντολαί), no one has power any longer to make a slave of me. . . . I yield up to you all these things and my whole paltry body (σωμάτιον) itself, whenever you will."[255] Finally, again in book 3, Epictetus maintains that God's commandments are all-sufficient, serving as the philosopher's refuge even in the adverse circum-

---

253. Schrenk, 547.

254. Epictetus, *Discourses* 1.25.3 and 3.5.8 (trans. Oldfather, 1:157 and 2:43). The first quote continues: " — But if you keep (τηρῶν) these, are you in need of some others? — But hasn't he commanded (ἐντέταλαι) these . . . ?" (1.25.6). The other three passages are: 3.24.113-14; 4.3.9-10, 12; and 4.7.16-18. Note that at 1.25.4 and 4.3.12 Epictetus refers to Zeus's commandments as "ordinances," διατάγματα (see also 4.4.32). Likewise, in 1 Cor. 7:17 Paul uses the related verb διατάσσομαι, "I ordain." Elsewhere in Paul this verb occurs only in 1 Cor. 9:14 (regarding orders for evangelists — cf. Epictetus, *Discourses* 3.22.2-4), 11:34, and 16:1 (regarding order within the church), and once outside of 1 Corinthians, in Gal. 3:19 (of God's ordaining the Jewish Law).

255. Epictetus, *Discourses* 4.7.16-18, trans. Oldfather, 2:367; cited in Conzelmann, 128 n. 34 (on 7:23) and 110 n. 11 (on 6:12). See also Epictetus 1.25.2, 4, 5; 3.5.7; 4.3.9, 10.

stances to which he may, in the Stoic sense, be called. Thus even in the face of poverty, sickness, loss of status, or exile, Epictetus can hold his ground, asking rhetorically, "am I any longer to take thought as to where I am, or with whom, or what men say about me? Am I not wholly intent upon God, and His commands (ἐντολαί) and ordinances?"[256]

Given the similarities in theme and vocabulary between 1 Corinthians 7:17-24 and these passages from Epictetus, and given the dearth of convincing alternative hypotheses, I suggest that when Paul speaks in 7:19b of "keeping the commandments of God," he is using a Judeo-Christian expression that has Stoic implications.[257] Since for Epictetus observing what God has commanded is the equivalent of "being a philosopher," Paul would be using the expression in a general sense to mean "being a Christian." Commensurate with our understanding of 7:20, this meaning would forbid Christians from taking on any additional "calls" that might nullify their original call, since, according to Epictetus, one must hold to God's commandments even in adverse circumstances.[258]

256. Epictetus, *Discourses* 3.24.113-14, trans. Oldfather, 2:221. On the resemblance between this passage and 1 Cor. 4:9-13, see Conzelmann, 88 and n. 36.

257. Another passage that should be considered is Philo's Stoic-sounding *Legum allegoria* 1.93-95 (*SVF* 3.139.35–140.6 [partial]), where he distinguishes between three categories: injunction, prohibition, and "commandment with exhortation" (ἐντολὴ καὶ παραίνεσις). The first, he says, is designed for the person who acts correctly (κατορθόω), the second for the bad man (ὁ φαῦλος), and the third category (he mentions only "exhortation") is "for the neutral man (ὁ μέσος), he who is neither bad nor good (φαῦλος/σπουδαῖος)." This neutral man Philo depicts as an "infant" (νήπιον), saying that he is "just now learning." Elsewhere Philo elaborates on this image, saying that the souls of persons unfamiliar with either philosophical freedom or slavery are naked "like those of mere infants" (τῶν . . . νηπίων). They must, according to Philo, "be tended and nursed by instilling first, in place of milk (γάλα), the soft food of instruction given in the school subjects, later, the harder, stronger meat, which philosophy produces. Reared by these to manhood and robustness, they will reach the happy consummation which Zeno, or rather an oracle higher than Zeno, bids us seek, a life led agreeably to nature" (*Quod omnis probus liber sit* 160, trans. Colson, 101). Paul, in turn, describes the Corinthians with this image: "And I myself, brothers, was not able to speak to you as spiritual persons but as fleshly, as infants (νήπιοι) in Christ. I gave you milk (γάλα) to drink, not solid food, for you were not yet able" (1 Cor. 3:1-2; cf. 13:11). For the popularity of this image among the Stoics, see Johannes Behm, "βρῶμα, βρῶσις," in *TDNT* 1 (1964), 643 n. 7.

258. Cf. Epictetus, *Discourses* 3.24.98-99, where the philosopher is described as remaining steadfast in his station as householder. Indeed, it is possible that the Corinthians had given an apocalyptic bent not only to the Stoic concept of call, but also to their concept of commandment, in which case they may have held that a special interpretation of "the commandments"

Taking this line of interpretation one step further, I suspect that in addition to this general meaning of "keeping the commandments of God," Paul also has a more immediate point of reference in mind. The only commandment he claims to have in 7:1-24, or in the entire chapter for that matter, is Jesus' prohibition of divorce in 7:10-11. As we observed earlier, the whole discussion of mixed marriages in verses 12-24 is occasioned precisely by the recognition that this prohibition does not apply to Christians with non-Christian spouses. It is possible, then, that through his discussion of freedom and the Christian call, and through his use of the Stoic notion of commandments, Paul is inferring that Jesus' commandment indeed has a counterpart in the more encompassing "commandments" of Christian existence.[259] This, in fact, makes good sense in light of 7:17, where Paul describes how Christians married to non-Christians should live, employing the phrase "as the Lord apportioned to each one." Since "Lord" in Paul generally refers to Jesus, and since the only action of "apportioning" by Jesus in the chapter is, again, his prohibition of divorce in verses 10-11, it lies close at hand that Paul is suggesting to the Corinthians that the transforming grace of God's call governs mixed marriages in the same way that Jesus' prohibition of divorce governs Christian marriages. If this is true, 7:18-24 would then represent Paul's attempt to show the veracity of this suggestion, forming an appropriate conclusion to his treatment of mixed marriages.

Paul's Argument against Marriage by Reason of Adverse Circumstances: 7:25-28

With the phrase "Now concerning virgins" in 7:25, Paul introduces a new topic into the chapter. Until now he has addressed questions relevant to married people — whether they can separate, whether they can divorce, whether

---

was necessary in the end times, as in the *Testament of Naphtali*. See above, pp. 121-23, and cf. the notion of an interim law at Qumran — e.g., E. P. Sanders, *Paul and Palestinian Judaism: A Comparison of Patterns of Religion* (Philadelphia: Fortress, 1977), 270-71. On "keeping the commandments" in the context of wisdom and apocalyptic literature, see, e.g., Sir. 1:26 and Rev. 12:17.

259. Cf. Matt. 5:17-19, 31-32, where Jesus' interdiction of divorce is set in a discussion of "the commandments" (αἱ ἐντολαί), and 1 Cor. 14:37, where Paul speaks of a "commandment of the Lord" (κυρίου ἐντολή).

they can remarry; in 7:25ff. he will consider whether virgins should marry.[260] The first four verses of this new section contain several Stoic elements, some of which are already familiar to us from our examination of 7:1-24. In 7:26 Paul speaks of what is "good for a man" (καλὸν ἀνθρώπῳ), an expression he uses in 7:1, and for which we have analogies in Stoic authors. In contrast to 7:1, however, where Paul follows this phrase with a Cynic-like judgment on marriage, here he states explicitly that he is giving his own advice (γνώμη) as one who has been shown mercy by the Lord to be πιστός, or "trustworthy" (v. 25). As we saw from 7:12-15a, this notion of being πιστός was important to the Corinthians and appears to draw on the Stoic ideal of the trustworthy wise man. Paul will express this same thought in 7:40 in a manner more characteristically Christian when he claims support for his advice (γνώμη) from God's Spirit, verse 40 forming a ring composition, or *inclusio*, with verse 25.

The advice Paul gives in verses 25-26 is that virgins should remain unmarried in light of the "present necessity." Justification for this position is then offered in verse 27, in diatribe style: "You are bound to a wife? — don't seek release! You are released from a wife? — don't seek a wife!" The syntactical pattern of this verse is the same as in verses 18 and 21, and in the several examples we cited from Stoic and Cynic authors. Its subject matter, in turn — the indifference of both marriage and the single life — is especially close to the examples from Metrodorus, Posidippus, and Sirach 7:26 (LXX), giving the impression that Paul is dependent on a tradition here, rather than just a rhetorical style as in verses 18 and 21.[261] This impression is reinforced, moreover,

---

260. The introduction of this new topic is signaled by the parallelism between 7:1 and 7:25-26: "Now concerning what you wrote/it is good for a man/but because of . . ." vs. "Now concerning virgins/because of/it is good for a man . . ." (περὶ δὲ ὧν ἐγράψατε/καλὸν ἀνθρώπῳ/διὰ δέ vs. περὶ δὲ τῶν παρθένων/διά/καλὸν ἀνθρώπῳ). If 7:25ff. was simply a continuation of 7:1-24, we might have expected something like "To the virgins I say . . ." (τοῖς δὲ παρθένοις λέγω), after the model of 7:8, 10, 12.

261. Oddly, only the text from Posidippus has been cited as a parallel to 7:27, and only by Johannes Leipoldt, *Griechische Philosophie und frühchristliche Askese* (Berlin: Akademie, 1961), 35 n. 1. Still another version of the maxim in 7:27 is found in Clement of Alexandria, *Stromateis*, bk. 3, chap. 15.97.4 (2.241.3-4 S.), in the form of a saying of Jesus: "Again the Lord says, 'He who is married should not divorce, and he who is not married should not marry'" (ὁ γήμας μὴ ἐκβαλλέτω καὶ ὁ μὴ γαμήσας μὴ γαμείτω). Alfred Resch, *Agrapha: Aussercanonische Schriftfragmente*, TU, n.s., 15/3-4 (Leipzig: J. C. Hinrichs, 1906), 182-83 (agraphon 145), points to the similarities between this passage and 1 Cor. 7:11 and 7:32-36 (not 7:27 for some reason), and suggests that it comes from the *Gospel of the Egyptians*, an apocryphal work that Clement cites in *Stromateis*, bk. 3, chap. 15.92-93 (2.238.23-28 S.). Its more immediate context, however, is the Cynic argument against marriage in

by the realization that Paul is actually interested in only the second half of verse 27, which deals with being single and getting married. The first half deals with being married and "loosing" oneself from the relationship, which was Paul's topic in 7:1-24. To some extent, as well, verse 27a repeats the Lord's command in verses 10-11, whereas Paul has stated in verse 25 that he has no command of the Lord relevant to his present discussion.[262]

A link in verse 27 specifically with the issues of the Stoic-Cynic marriage debate can be seen in Paul's emphasis on the obligations imposed by married life. This comes through in the expressions "bound to a wife," "seek release," and "released from a wife." While being "bound" (δέομαι) to a husband, as we have seen from 7:39 and Romans 7:2, is a common manner of expressing a woman's relation to her husband, it is not the usual expression for describing a man's relation to his wife. The terms "release" (λύσις) and "released" (λύομαι), on the other hand, are rarely if ever used to describe divorce.[263] All three terms, however, function well in describing obligations between individuals as being either in force or terminated.[264] Thus here, as in 1 Corinthians 7:3-5, Paul appears to have adopted the Stoic-Cynic perspective of seeing marital *obligations* as the primary issue in considering questions of marriage.[265]

---

bk. 3, chap. 15.97.3 (2.240.27–241.2 S., cited above, p. 100 n. 241), and given Clement's inclination to link it with Jesus rather than Paul, it is possible that a version of this maxim may have had an existence in philosophical circles independent of 1 Cor. 7:27.

262. If this seeming repetition of 7:10-11 were an integral part of his argument in 7:25ff., then Paul would also be risking the implication that Jesus' prohibition of divorce was valid only in light of the "necessity" mentioned in 7:26 (noted by Doughty, "Heiligkeit und Freiheit," 204).

263. Adolf Hilgenfeld, *Die Glossolalie in der alten Kirche, in dem Zusammenhang der Geistesgaben und des Geisteslebens des alten Christenthums: Eine exegetisch-historische Untersuchung* (Leipzig: Breitkopf und Härtel, 1850), 135, notes that Eusebius, *Church History* 5.18.2, blames the Montanists for "dissolutions of marriages" (λύσεις γάμων). Otherwise, only the related verb ἀπολύω can mean "to divorce."

264. On λύσις and λύω, see Moulton and Milligan, 382, 384.

265. 1 Cor. 7:29, 32-35 also speak of marital obligations. As an alternative to this interpretation, several scholars have suggested that Paul is speaking of engagements and breaking engagements in v. 27: Johann Christian Konrad von Hofmann, *Die heilige Schrift neuen Testaments: Zusammenhängend untersucht* (Nördlingen: C. H. Beck, 1864), vol. 2.2, p. 164; Weiß, *Korintherbrief,* 194-95 (who suggests "spiritual engagement"); J. K. Elliott, "Paul's Teaching on Marriage in I Corinthians: Some Problems Considered," *NTS* 19 (1972/73): 220-23; and Baumert, 420-25. But there is no evidence that the vocabulary in 7:27 refers to engagement, about which little is known for this period in the provinces anyway; see Gordon D. Fee, *The First Epistle to the Corinthians,* NICNT (Grand Rapids: Eerdmans, 1987), 331-32. Elliott, who carries this suggestion

With verse 28a Paul completes the diatribe form begun in verse 27 in an unusual manner. As we know from our investigation of 7:18-19, 21-22, this diatribe pattern is composed of a statement and an exhortation, sometimes followed by an explanation as to why the statement is a matter of indifference, as the exhortation indeed claims. In verse 28a, however, Paul claims that the second exhortation, "don't seek a wife!" is *itself* a matter of some indifference, for if a single person marries, Paul says, he or she nonetheless does not sin. Paul then finishes out the verse by explaining to the Corinthians that those who marry will have "tribulation in the flesh," and he would spare them this by encouraging them not to marry.

Taken as a whole, what Paul has written in 7:25-28 is the Stoic argument against marriage, with an important modification. As we saw in chapter 2, Stoics who objected to marriage maintained that "circumstance" (περίστασις) often prevented one from embracing the responsibilities of married life. Cicero was familiar with this Stoic adaptation of the "Cynic" position against marriage, and we find it in Hierocles and Epictetus as well. This is also what we find here in Paul. The adverse circumstances at issue in Corinth are designated in verse 26 as "the present necessity," and Paul makes it very clear that this is the basis on which he is advising these virgins not to become "bound" by the obligations of marriage: "I think, therefore, that this is good *because of the present necessity* (διὰ τὴν ἐνεστῶσαν ἀνάγκην): 'it is good for a man' to be thus."

The most illuminating cipher for 7:25-28 is not Cicero, Hierocles, or Epictetus, however, but the writings of Cicero's contemporary Arius Didymus. In his treatment of Stoic ethical theory, Arius explains that the Stoics classified marriage as an "indifferent thing." This meant that although marriage was morally neutral, it was sometimes a practical advantage for the individual to marry, sometimes a practical disadvantage, depending on the prevailing circumstances of the individual's life. For one to marry under normal circumstances was therefore "fitting," but marrying under adverse circumstances was an error or "sin," ἁμάρτημα.[266] In 7:25-28 Paul's words reveal a

---

over into 7:29, mistakenly claims that "if [Paul] were thinking of those already married, ἔχοντες γυναῖκας ['those having wives'] would be a strange way of referring to husbands" (222). But "having a wife" is standard Greek usage for "being married" — see, e.g., 7:12-13.

266. Arius in Stobaeus 2.86.1-16 W.-H., see above, pp. 70-71. See also [Ocellus] (app. B), *De univ. nat.* 48, who says people who marry for the wrong reasons, such as wealth and social standing, "err" (ἁμαρτάνω). Cf. *T. Naph.* 8:7-10 (cited above, pp. 121-22), who maintains that things done out of their proper time (including conjugal relations) constitute sin.

knowledge of this Stoic line of reasoning point for point. His use of the diatribe pattern in verse 27 serves to define both marriage and the single life as
things of indifference; in verse 28b he points out that marriage in the present
situation is disadvantageous for the Christian, bringing "tribulation in the
flesh" to those who marry; while in verse 28a he consciously departs from
Stoic opinion, maintaining that even under these circumstances the person
who marries "did not sin" (οὐχ ἥμαρτες/ἥμαρτεν).[267] This last move would
seem to be clear evidence that Paul's Corinthian audience included some who
had so thoroughly combined their Christian faith with Stoic doctrine that
Paul was obliged to distinguish between Christian and Stoic usage regarding
such basic ideas as sin.

Paul's reason for contradicting the Stoic view of sin in verse 28a is obvious. For the Stoics the concept of sin encompassed wrong conduct in both
the moral and practical spheres of life (although the Stoics themselves would
not have drawn any absolute distinction between these spheres). Even in matters they considered morally neutral, one could commit "sin" if he or she did
not act in accord with rational thinking and utilitarian motives. For Paul,
however, "sin" has reference only to moral conduct. Something like marriage,
therefore, which both he and the Stoics considered morally neutral, cannot in
and of itself be sinful for Paul, even if it produces hardships. Interestingly
enough, almost a century and a half after Paul writes we again find evidence
that the Stoic notion of sin had influenced Christian thinking on marriage. As
part of his interpretation of the apocryphal saying of Jesus, "Eat every plant,
but do not eat the plant that has the bitterness," Clement of Alexandria writes:
"Therefore, a man ought not to think that marriage on rational principles
(κατὰ λόγον) is a sin (ἁμάρτημα), supposing that he does not look on the
bringing up of children as being bitter . . . ; but if a man regards the rearing of
children as bitter because it distracts him (μεταπερισπῶσα) from the things
of God on account of the time it takes up (διὰ τὰς χρειώδεις ἀσχολίας), he
may yet desire to marry because he does not take easily to a bachelor's life."[268]

---

267. Gnomic aorist, probably in sympathy with the gnomic character of v. 27. Note the
second-person singular of the diatribe.

268. Clement of Alexandria, *Stromateis*, bk. 3, chap. 9.67.1 (2.226.19-24 S.), trans.
Chadwick, in John Ernest Leonard Oulton and Henry Chadwick, *Alexandrian Christianity*, LCC
2 (London: SCM Press, 1954), 71. Cf. Col. 3:19. Ironically, Meyer, 191, excluded a Stoic interpretation for 1 Cor. 7 on the basis of Paul's use of "sin" here and in v. 36 (on which, see below).

Apocalyptic "Circumstances": 7:29-31

As we just saw, the argument Paul uses in 7:25-28 insists that "circumstances" of life can prevent one from marrying. For Stoics these circumstances could include such things as a person's financial misfortune, the acceptance of an important military assignment, the advancement of scholarship, or the general chaotic state of society. For Paul they are supplied by the apocalyptic situation in which he envisioned the church in Corinth. As a consequence, intertwined with and immediately following his Stoic-like argument in verses 25-28, Paul employs an appreciable amount of apocalyptic material — that is, language and themes which early Jews and Christians associated with the end of the world. In verse 26 Paul says his advice is based on the present "necessity" (ἀνάγκη), and in verse 28 he tells those who plan to marry that they will have "tribulation" (θλῖψις). Both these terms occur with some frequency in apocalyptic literature as part of a specialized vocabulary describing the distress of the last days.[269] In

---

269. E.g., Zeph. 1:15; Luke 21:23. See Wolfgang Schrage, "Die Stellung zur Welt bei Paulus, Epiktet und in der Apokalyptik: Ein Beitrag zu 1 Kor 7,29-31," ZTK 61 (1964): 131 n. 12; Heinrich Schlier, "θλίβω, θλῖψις," in TDNT 3 (1965), 144-46; and L. Legrand, "Saint Paul et célibat," in Sacerdoce et Célibat: Études historiques et théologiques, ed. Joseph Coppens, BETL 28 (Gembloux: Duculot; Louvain: Peeters, 1971), 320-21. John G. Gager, Jr., "Functional Diversity in Paul's Use of End-Time Language," JBL 89 (1970): 330-33, has argued against an apocalyptic meaning for the terms ἀνάγκη and θλῖψις in 7:26-28, noting that Paul never uses ἀνάγκη in connection with the end elsewhere, including 2 Cor. 6:4 and 1 Thess. 3:7, where it occurs together with θλῖψις (on this, see also Malherbe, Paul and the Thessalonians, 46-48). Yet with 1 Cor. 7:26-28, not only are the following vv. 29-31 apocalyptic (see below), as Gager himself recognizes (332), but Gager also overlooks the possibility that 7:26 is present apocalyptic language, for he assumes that his translation of ἐνεστῶσα ἀνάγκη as "present difficulty" (as opposed to "impending disaster," RSV) rules out an apocalyptic interpretation (on this, see below). Beyond this, Gager never provides a cogent nonapocalyptic alternative for these terms. On the one hand, he states that "Paul clearly presents [marriage] as a kind of θλῖψις" (331) — which is not supported by the text. And on the other hand, he says Paul uses ἀνάγκη in an "ambiguous manner" (meaning that it is nonetheless apocalyptic?), and compares Paul's usage to Hypothetica 11.17, where Philo gives the Essene position that a husband is either bound by the love charms of his wife or cares for his children out of the "necessity of nature" (ἀνάγκη φύσεως). From this he concludes, quite erroneously: "As in Paul, the married man or woman is lured away from his primary (religious) concern by the seductive ploys of the mate. Both Philo and Paul use the term ἀνάγκη to describe the marital situation" (331). But neither does Philo speak of both "the married man or woman," nor does Paul speak of "seductive ploys of the mate," nor can Gager show from Philo's use of ἀνάγκη how Paul uses the term to describe the marital situation, since 7:26 speaks of ἀνάγκη as a reality for both the married and the unmarried alike.

verse 29a Paul then elaborates ("I say this, brothers") with the apocalyptic theme that the "time" has been "drawn together" (καιρός/συστέλλομαι), and he concludes in verse 31b by using the apocalyptic rationale, "for the form of this world is passing away."

Between verses 29a and 31b, moreover, as part of his elaboration of the "tribulation" in verse 28, Paul introduces several lines of apocalyptic material describing how one must conduct oneself in the last days: "Henceforth, such that[270] even those having wives should be as not (ὡς μή) having, and those weeping as not weeping, and those rejoicing as not rejoicing, and those buying as not taking possession, and those using the world as not using it fully." Parallels to these verses may be found in both Jewish and Christian apocalyptic literature, and it is even possible that Paul is citing from an apocalyptic source here. The themes of buying, rejoicing, and mourning, for example, occur in Ezekiel's vision of the end time: "The time has come! Behold the day! The one buying should not rejoice; the one selling should not mourn."[271] Two passages from the Gospel of Luke, in turn, picture the eschaton as taking by surprise those who have become entrenched in the activities of buying, selling, and marrying. In Luke 14:15-24 the invited guests are shut out of the eschatological banquet because they insist on attending to their recent purchases of a field or oxen, or looking after a recently acquired wife; and in 17:26-37 Jesus tells his disciples that the Son of Man will come suddenly upon the world, destroying those who are distracted with marriages, buying, selling, eating, drinking, planting, and building. In a similar fashion, passages from the *Apocalypse of Elijah* and *Sibylline Oracles* 2 maintain that the eschaton will bring an end to buying, selling, and marrying.[272]

Along with these particular motifs, the distinctive "as not" (ὡς μή) phrases of 7:29b-31a find an analogy in two further apocalyptic texts. The first is Isaiah 24:2 (LXX), which depicts, through a series of ὡς- phrases, the radical social and economic disorientation brought on by the coming of the Lord: "And the people will be as (ὡς) the priest, and the slave as the lord, and the maid servant as the mistress. He who sells will be as he who buys, and he who lends as he who borrows, and he who owes as the one to whom he owes."[273]

270. Translating τὸ λοιπὸν ἵνα, see below.

271. Ezek. 7:12 LXX: ἥκει ὁ καιρός, ἰδοὺ ἡ ἡμέρα· ὁ κτώμενος μὴ χαιρέτω, καὶ ὁ πωλῶν μὴ θρηνείτω.

272. *Apoc. Elijah* 2:31; *Sib. Or.* 2:327-29. See also 4Q416.2.3.19-21 ("Sapiential Work A"), which states that a man must not allow marriage to distract him from the "mystery that is to be(come)."

273. Cited as a parallel by Heinrici, *Das erste Sendschreiben,* 207 n. 1.

The second text comes from 4 Ezra 15–16, a third-century Christian addition to 4 Ezra 1–14. Originally in Greek but now preserved only in Latin, this text is by far the closest parallel to 1 Corinthians 7:29b-31a:

> Hear my words, O my people; prepare for battle, and in the midst of the ca-
> lamities be like strangers on the earth. Let him that sells be like *(quasi)* one
> who will flee; let him that buys be like one who will lose; let him that does
> business be like one who will not make a profit; and let him that builds a
> house be like one who will not live in it; let him that sows be like one who
> will not reap; so also him that prunes the vines, like one who will not gather
> the grapes; them that marry, like those who will have no children; and them
> that do not marry, like those who are widowed.[274]

Because of the striking similarities between these verses from 4 Ezra 15–16 and 1 Corinthians 7:29b-31a, some scholars have questioned whether this late Christian text is not in fact dependent on the latter.[275] While this possibility must remain open, it should be noted that Schrage, who was the first to subject these texts to a detailed comparison, has offered several good reasons for assuming that both of them draw independently on a common source.[276]

Quite apart from 4 Ezra 16:40-44 and Schrage's considerations, however, other aspects of 1 Corinthians 7:29b-31a seem to indicate that Paul is not simply enlisting various apocalyptic motifs in support of his argument here, but is citing from a specific apocalyptic tradition or source. First, there is the syntax that begins verse 29b. The Greek reads τὸ λοιπὸν ἵνα, which is unusual because the conjunction ἵνα normally takes first position in its clause. While there are other instances in Paul of ἵνα standing in other than first position, none are nearly as harsh as this one. Bauer, conse-quently, included 7:29b in his discussion of this syntactical formation only with reservation,[277] and Lietzmann declared that the preceding τὸ λοιπόν "stands lost between two sentences."[278] This difficult syntax is clarified, however, if we assume that ἵνα begins a quotation. In this case it would stand first in its clause, and the words τὸ λοιπόν, "henceforth," could be un-

---

274. 4 Ezra (2 Esdras) 16:40-44 RSV (Vulgate 16:40-45).

275. For an analysis of the formal similarities between the two texts, see Schrage, "Die Stellung zur Welt," 147-49.

276. Schrage, "Die Stellung zur Welt," 139-49.

277. Walter Bauer, 477 (s.v. "ἵνα 4").

278. Lietzmann, 34.

derstood as a transitional phrase provided by Paul to introduce this quotation.[279]

A second reason for taking these verses as a quotation is that they contain several things which scholars consider untypical of Paul, and therefore not his creation. Braun, for instance, has observed that the "Stoic-like" indifference toward weeping and rejoicing expressed in 7:30 is difficult to reconcile with such passages as 1 Corinthians 16:17, Romans 12:15, or Philippians 3:18, where Paul speaks highly of and encourages such emotions.[280] Schrage has noted that in 7:29b-30a Paul writes atypically of the painful end of the old age with no mention of the glory and salvation of the new.[281] And finally, in terms of word usage, the coupling in 7:31a of the verb χράομαι (to use) with an accusative object (τὸν κόσμον, "the world") is not only singular for Paul, but very rare elsewhere in Greek literature.[282]

---

279. It is also possible that τὸ λοιπόν goes with what precedes it: "time is henceforth contracted, such that. . . ." A third possibility, less likely in my mind, is to take the entire group τὸ λοιπὸν ἵνα as the beginning of a quotation and assume that this odd syntax made better sense in the context from which Paul is citing. Scholars have also pointed out that the words in v. 29a, "I say this, brothers" (τοῦτο δέ φημι, ἀδελφοί), reappear in 15:50, where Paul may again be quoting an apocalyptic tradition. See Weiß, *Korintherbrief*, 197; Schrage, "Die Stellung zur Welt," 138-39; Siegfried Schulz, "Evangelium und Welt," in *Neues Testament und christliche Existenz: Festschrift für Herbert Braun zum 70. Geburtstag am 4. Mai 1973*, ed. Hans Dieter Betz and Luise Schottroff (Tübingen: Mohr, 1973), 486-87; and Ulrich B. Müller, *Prophetie und Predigt im Neuen Testament: Formgeschichtliche Untersuchungen zur urchristlichen Prophetie*, SNT 10 (Gütersloh: Gerd Mohn, 1975), 132-36, 158-59.

280. Herbert Braun, "Die Indifferenz gegenüber der Welt bei Paulus und bei Epiktet," in *Gesammelte Studien zum Neuen Testament und seiner Umwelt*, 166-67. Rom. 12:15, e.g., admonishes, "Rejoice with those rejoicing; weep with those weeping" (χαίρειν μετὰ χαιρόντων, κλαίειν μετὰ κλαιόντων). To the three passages cited by Braun we may add Rom. 9:1-2; 1 Cor. 13:6; 2 Cor. 2:4, 6-7; 7:7-10; and Phil. 1:18, 19; 4:4, 10.

281. Schrage, "Die Stellung zur Welt," 138-39, cf. 126-30; and Braun, "Die Indifferenz gegenüber der Welt," 162, 165. In 7:29b we also miss the man-woman/husband-wife parallelism that Paul carefully maintains in the earlier part of the chapter and continues in 7:32-34. This is true as well for 7:27, which I have also suggested is a citation. That Paul speaks only of men in 7:29b is especially noticeable since his topic, ultimately, is virgins (7:25). Some scholars have also maintained that the admonitions in 7:30-31a (concerning weeping, rejoicing, buying, and using) are not particularly relevant to Paul's discussion of the marriage of virgins. I will argue below, however, that they are. See Helmut H. Rex, "Das ethische Problem in der eschatologischen Existenz bei Paulus" (diss., University of Tübingen, 1954), 89; Schrage, "Die Stellung zur Welt," 138; Schulz, 486-87; and Vincent L. Wimbush, *Paul, the Worldly Ascetic: Response to the World and Self-Understanding according to 1 Corinthians 7* (Macon, Ga.: Mercer University Press, 1987), 28.

282. See Schulz, 486-87; Wimbush, 28 n. 22; and Blass and Debrunner, 84 (§152.4). Elsewhere Paul uses χράομαι (properly) with the dative: 1 Cor. 9:12, 15; 2 Cor. 1:17; 3:12.

Having now documented Paul's use of apocalyptic materials in verses 25-31, and possibly even an apocalyptic source in verses 29b-31a, let us consider the function of these materials in his larger discussion. In what way, in other words, do they supply the "circumstances" of the Stoic argument against marriage? Some scholars believe Paul's emphasis in these verses is on the brevity of time before Christ's imminent return. His argument in that case would be that "time is running out" for such ongoing human activities as marriage: If the world will soon end, what is the purpose of procreation? Or, as one study put it, "why undertake the responsibilities and involvements of family life if the transformation of all things is at hand?"[283] Another possibility is that Paul is discouraging marriage in anticipation of the new, heavenly existence that awaits God's chosen after the end, an existence in which they would be "as angels," no longer marrying.[284]

Yet given that 7:25-31 speaks only of the decline of the old age and not the in-breaking of the new, and points to the "necessity" and "tribulation" of that time, it does not appear that Paul's objective is to emphasize either the imminence of the end or any heavenly existence that might follow it. Rather, his focus here is on the hardships that were expected to beset the world in the period *before* the end.[285] It is these hardships, according to Paul, not the anticipation of a future millennium,[286] that require consideration as "special

283. Leander E. Keck and Victor Paul Furnish, *The Letters of Paul*, Interpreting Biblical Texts (Nashville: Abingdon, 1984), 85. See also Gager, 332; Wimbush, 32, 50, 84; and Franz Laub, *Eschatologische Verkündigung und Lebensgestaltung nach Paulus: Eine Untersuchung zum Wirken des Apostels beim Aufbau der Gemeinde in Thessalonike*, BU 10 (Regensburg: Friedrich Pustet, 1973), 174-78.

284. See L. Legrand, "The Prophetical Meaning of Celibacy — I," *Scripture* 12 (1960): 97-105, esp. 104-5, who combines these two views; and Peter Nagel, *Die Motivierung der Askese in der alten Kirche und der Ursprung des Mönchtums*, TU 95 (Berlin: Akademie, 1966), 20-34, who draws a parallel between Paul and the Montanists, among others. On the tenuous nature of such parallels see Frederick Charles Klawiter, "The New Prophecy in Early Christianity: The Origin, Nature, and Development of Montanism, A.D. 165-220" (Ph.D. diss., University of Chicago, 1975), 14-15, 17, 31-33, 96-99, 130-93; and Christine Trevett, "Apocalypse, Ignatius, Montanism: Seeking the Seeds," *VC* 43 (1989): 321-22. See also our discussion of "realized eschatology" in chap. 1.

285. Seen by several scholars: Doughty, "Heiligkeit und Freiheit," 204; Walter Schmithals, *Gnosticism in Corinth: An Investigation of the Letters to the Corinthians* (Nashville and New York: Abingdon, 1971), 235 nn. 158-59; Merklein, 248-51; Gottfried Hierzenberger, *Weltbewertung bei Paulus nach 1 Kor 7,29-31: Eine exegetisch-kerygmatische Studie*, Kommentare und Beiträge zum Alten und Neuen Testament (Düsseldorf: Patmos, 1967), 32 n. 1 (somewhat reluctantly); and Baumert, 17, 209; cf. Yarbrough, 104.

286. Nor, we might add, an eschatological reward for a life of sexual abstinence.

circumstances," since they make married life difficult by undermining the social and economic context within which marriages thrive. According to his elaboration of the expression "tribulation in the flesh," under these conditions human emotion is stifled (v. 30a), activities essential to establishing a household and providing for a family can be performed only with reservation (vv. 30b-31a), and a man must "have" his wife "as if not having" (v. 29b). This last claim is especially revealing, moreover, because it reflects the situation presupposed in 7:2-5. There husbands and wives are instructed to "have" each other (v. 2), which for Paul includes conjugal rights (vv. 3-4); but due to apocalyptic expectations, couples are nonetheless allowed to break off sexual relations to engage in prayer (v. 5). This compromise, as we have called it, between the "Cynic" position of verse 1b and the Stoic understanding of marriage in verses 3-4, is therefore also an instance of "having" a spouse "as if not having," by reason of apocalyptic circumstances.[287] In the context of Paul's attempt in 7:25ff. to dissuade virgins from marriage, this underscoring of the implications of the end time for the sexual side of marriage serves to counter the (possibly Stoic) argument of 7:9, that one should marry for the purpose of securing licit sexual gratification.

Paul's emphasis on the exigencies of the last days to the exclusion of other apocalyptic themes is also evident in the two statements that bracket the apocalyptic material in 7:29b-31a, namely, ὁ καιρὸς συνεσταλμέμος ἐστίν in 29a and παράγει γὰρ τὸ σχῆμα τοῦ κόσμου τούτου in 31b. The first is usually translated "the time is short" or "shortened,"[288] and is seen as expressing Paul's conviction that Christ's coming was imminent. This translation does not do justice to the meaning of the verb συστέλλω, however, which carries the sense of "drawing together," "gathering in," "compressing," or "contracting."[289] From these definitions it is clear that συστέλλω can describe something as "short" or "shortened" only in the sense that it is made more compact, not "*cut* short" or

---

287. There is thus no reason to hold that 7:29b contradicts or stands in tension with 7:2-5, as several scholars have suggested: Fee, 340; Elliott, 222; cf. Schrage, "Die Stellung zur Welt," 151; and Niederwimmer, 110-11.

288. By analogy with such passages as Mark 13:20: "And if the Lord had not shortened the days (ἐκολόβωσεν κύριος τὰς ἡμέρας), no flesh would be saved." On this theme in apocalyptic literature see Jörg Baumgarten, *Paulus und die Apokalyptik: Die Auslegung apokalyptischer Überlieferungen in den echten Paulusbriefen*, WMANT 44 (Neukirchen-Vluyn: Neukirchener, 1975), 222 nn. 139-40.

289. See Karl Heinrich Rengstorf, "στέλλω," in *TDNT* 7 (1971), 596-97, and Walter Bauer, 978 (s.v. "συστέλλω").

made smaller by subtraction.[290] Outside of 7:29a, moreover, it is never used with reference to time,[291] and thus it seems unlikely that Paul would resort to this particular verb if his meaning were simply that time were "short," a notion he could have expressed in several other, more common ways.

A more appropriate translation of ὁ καιρός συνεσταλμένος ἐστίν, therefore, is "the time is compressed" or "the time is contracted." Further, since the word καιρός does not denote just a period of time but a "proper" or "correct" time for something,[292] I would argue that verse 29a is best understood as "time is at a premium" or "opportunity is tight."[293] This interpretation coincides well with what follows in verses 29b-31a, where those who are married, weeping, rejoicing, or acquiring goods are told that they must live "as if not" being or doing these things. It also crosses paths with our understanding of 7:5. As our examination of this verse indicated, the language of Paul's ruling that spouses must allow for periods of sexual activity as well as prayer reflects the Corinthians' familiarity with (and deference to) an apocalyptic tradition which insisted that God had specified "proper times" (καιροί) for various activities. The idea was that the normal routine of one's life had to be changed in the last days. Since there was no longer sufficient opportunity for everything, one needed to live according to a special routine or "order" whereby certain activities alternated with one another. Thus there was a "time" for sexual intercourse and a corresponding "time" for prayer. If my understanding of συστέλλω and καιρός in verse 29 is accurate, then Paul is making reference to this apocalyptic tradition of "proper times" again here. In the words of this verse: "let those having wives be as not having them," since opportunity for such things "has been compressed."

The second statement that underscores Paul's narrow focus on the hardships of the end time is verse 31b, "for the form of this world is passing away." This apocalyptic announcement has several parallels in early Christian literature. In the synoptic Gospels, Mark 13:31 par. proclaims that "heaven and earth will pass away" (ὁ οὐρανὸς καὶ ἡ γῆ παρελεύσονται); a tradition from

290. Beyond this, the information that time was "cut short" would have been very important for a religious group expecting the eschaton (1 Cor. 1:7-8; 15:23-28, 51-58), yet it occurs nowhere else in 1 Corinthians.

291. Noted by Baumgarten, 222 n. 133, and Günter Klein, "Apokalyptische Naherwartung bei Paulus," in *Neues Testament und christliche Existenz*, 259.

292. See, e.g., Gerhard Delling, "καιρός," in *TDNT* 3 (1965), 458-62.

293. Cf. Gal. 6:10; Heb. 11:15; and Baumert, 208-11, 432-39. See also the sentiment in *Cynic Epistle of Diogenes* 44: "For there is no spare time (σχολή) — not only for the poor man to beg, according to Plato, but for the one hastening on the shortcut to well-being" (174.9-10 M.).

"Q" (Matt. 5:18//Luke 16:17) compares the passing away (παρέρχομαι) of heaven and earth to the passing away of the Law. The eucharistic blessing in *Didache* 10.6 includes the request, "let this world pass away" (παρελθέτω ὁ κόσμος οὗτος); while 1 John 2:17 declares that "the world is passing away (ὁ κόσμος παράγεται), along with its allurement," and 2 Peter 3:10 describes the coming of the Lord as a day "in which the heavens will pass away (παρελεύσονται) . . . the elements will burn and dissolve, and the earth and the works in it will be exposed." In contrast to all these parallels, however, Paul speaks in 1 Corinthians 7:31b not of this world as passing away, but the "*form* of this world." To some extent this notion may also be present in 2 Peter, since it speaks of "the earth *and the works in it*" (καὶ τὰ ἐν αὐτῇ ἔργα).[294] Yet the thing that sets Paul apart even from this passage is that he speaks *only* of the "form," or σχῆμα, of this world as passing away.

While scholars have proposed a wide range of definitions for the word σχῆμα,[295] it seems best to take its meaning from the admonitions in the preceding verses, since 7:31b provides the rationale for 7:29b-31a,[296] and since it also appears to summarize and conclude this section of Paul's argument.[297] These admonitions, as we have seen, demand a remoteness from marriage, from emotional involvement, and from the acquisition of goods and "use" of the world. From this vantage point the expression "form of this world" would describe the world's social and economic "infrastructure" — the social and economic context that makes these activities possible. Because the upheavals of the last days disrupt this infrastructure, Paul is saying, Christians living in that time must hold themselves aloof from all that depends on it, including these otherwise normal and innocuous human activities. Thus by speaking of the "form of this world" as passing away, which we should probably understand as an intentional modification of a standard apocalyptic topos, Paul once again places the emphasis on the hardships of the end time. Even though he uses the word κόσμος (cosmos, world) here, the more "cosmological" events of the eschaton — the second coming, the destruction of the earth and the creation of a new one — all recede into the background.[298]

294. 1 John 2:16, in turn, prefaces his apocalyptic announcement with a description of what is "in the world": "the lust of the flesh, and the lust of the eyes, and the pride of life"; cf. 2:15.

295. Chronicled in Hierzenberger, 61-63.

296. "*For* (γάρ) the form of this world is passing away."

297. Thus 7:32a makes a new start: "But (δέ) I want you to be without care. . . ."

298. See Jürgen Becker, "Erwägungen zur apokalyptischen Tradition in der paulinischen Theologie," *EvT* 30 (1970): 600; Baumgarten, 223-24. The "world" (κόσμος) in v. 31 is thus not

A final aspect of 7:25-31 that indicates Paul's intention of using these apocalyptic hardships as the "circumstances" of his argument against marriage is the fact that he has cast this passage in the present tense. His reference point in verse 26 is the "*present (ἐνεστῶσα) necessity*";[299] he maintains in verse 29 that the time "*is (ἐστίν) constricted*"; and he concludes this section in verse 31 with the statement that the form of this world "*is passing away*" (παράγει).[300] To be sure, this language is uncharacteristic of apocalyptic texts, which usually speak of future events. It would be wrong, however, to assume that the present tense has no place in apocalyptic thought. Not only have several scholars identified a present aspect to the apocalyptic ideas in Paul's theology,[301] but there exist other texts that speak of apocalyptic events as occurring in the present. These are 1 John 2:17 (cited above),[302] 1 Peter 4:17,[303] and 4 Ezra 4:26.[304]

---

the stage of superhuman forces and events, but the arena of mundane affairs — as in the verses immediately following (vv. 32-34).

299. Scholars generally agree that a future meaning for ἐνεστῶσα is highly unlikely. See the discussions in Allo, 178; Delling, *Paulus' Stellung*, 77; Schrage, "Die Stellung zur Welt," 131 and n. 13 (with lit.); and Baumert, 171-72. Elsewhere in his letters (Rom. 8:38; 1 Cor. 3:22; and Gal. 1:4) Paul consistently uses this verb to refer to present time; our closest parallel to 1 Cor. 7:26, namely, the variant reading at 3 Macc. 1:16, describes a prayer for help in the "present necessity": βοηθεῖν τῇ ἐνεστώσῃ ἀνάγκῃ. (Likewise, the preferred reading for 3 Macc. 1:16 is τοῖς ἐνεστῶσιν, "in the present situation.")

300. In addition, Schrage, "Die Stellung zur Welt," 148, notes that the admonitions in 7:29b-31a use the present participle whereas the parallel passage in 4 Ezra 16:40-44 is cast entirely in the future tense.

301. E.g., Weiß, *Korintherbrief*, 201; Braun, "Die Indifferenz gegenüber der Welt," 161; Schrage, "Die Stellung zur Welt," 148; and Rudolf Bultmann, "Ist die Apokalyptik die Mutter der christlichen Theologie? Eine Auseinandersetzung mit Ernst Käsemann," in *Exegetica: Aufsätze zur Erforschung des Neuen Testaments*, ed. Erich Dinkler (Tübingen: Mohr, 1967), 76-77. Cf. L. William Countryman, *Dirt, Greed, and Sex: Sexual Ethics in the New Testament and Their Implications for Today* (Philadelphia: Fortress, 1988), 212: "For Paul, the value of celibacy was directly related to the chaotic and troubling times which had *already* begun and would lead shortly to the end of this world and the inbreaking of the reign of God" (emphasis mine).

302. On the apocalyptic character of this passage, see 1 John 2:18-29 and the commentary in Raymond E. Brown, *The Epistles of John*, AB 30 (Garden City, N.Y.: Doubleday, 1982), 313-14.

303. "It is the time to begin the judgement from the house of God" ([ὁ] καιρὸς τοῦ κρίμα ἀπὸ τοῦ οἴκου τοῦ θεοῦ); cf. 4:7, "The end of all things has drawn near" (πάντων δὲ τὸ τέλος ἤγγικεν).

304. "The world rapidly hastens to pass away" (*festinans festinat saeculum pertransire*), cited by Weiß, *Korintherbrief*, 201. This text dates from circa the late first century c.e., now preserved in a Latin translation from Greek, which is probably a translation from Hebrew. See also

What Paul is suggesting by this use of the present is that the "necessity" of verse 26, which is evidently some immediate economic or political crisis so apparent to the Corinthians that it requires no further explanation, may represent but a foretaste of the apocalyptic tumult to come. He makes this connection, moreover, because the Stoic argument he is using depends on there being circumstances that presently stand in the way of marriage; speculation about future circumstances would not have met this need. By pointing out this possible link between an actual crisis at Corinth and the future hardships of the last days — a link the Corinthians themselves, in all probability, also assumed[305] — Paul can credibly argue that the current situation may not blow over, but matters could get worse: those who marry will have tribulation in the flesh, while those who have wives must "henceforth" be as not having them (vv. 28-29).[306]

That Paul or the Corinthians could so easily integrate apocalyptic and Stoic ideas might at first seem surprising. Upon closer inspection, however, it is apparent that in placing the emphasis on the tumult of the end time, Paul is tapping into a tradition of visions and expectations of ominous events that must have seemed tailor-made for the purpose. These events included war, earthquakes, and famines,[307] all of which promised to destroy the social and economic fabric of society, thereby making the responsibilities of married life difficult or impossible to fulfill. In the midst of this calamity — as the "form of this world" passed away — a man or a woman would have little opportunity to look after the needs of a spouse, raise children, or bother with establishing and managing a household.[308]

---

4 Ezra 5:55, "a creation just now growing old and passing the strength of its youth" *(iam senescentis creaturae et fortitudinem iuventutis praeterientis);* 14:10, "the times are close to growing old" *(tempora adpropinquant senescere);* and the discussion of these passages in Michael Edward Stone, *Fourth Ezra*, Hermeneia (Minneapolis: Augsburg Fortress, 1990), 93-94, 420-21.

305. See above, pp. 122-23. Note that Mark 13:8 speaks of famines, earthquakes, and war as the *beginning* of the end-time suffering.

306. On the translation of τὸ λοιπόν ("henceforth, from now on"), see Conzelmann, 130 n. 3 (lit.). The future tense of Paul's statement that those who marry "will have" (ἕξουσιν) tribulation has its immediate reference, of course, in the possibility of future marriages; it also points toward the development and duration of an apocalyptic crisis (but not its beginning).

307. E.g., Mark 13:8. See also Emil Schürer, *The History of the Jewish People in the Age of Jesus Christ (175 B.C.–A.D. 135),* vol. 2, rev. and ed. Geza Vermes, Fergus Millar, and Matthew Black (Edinburgh: T. & T. Clark, 1979), 514-15 (lit.); Strack and Billerbeck, 4.2.977-81, 986.

308. It should be noted that the "tribulation" (θλῖψις) of which Paul speaks in 7:28 is not general apocalyptic hardship, but this hardship as experienced specifically by those who marry. See

As a result, apocalyptic texts, like Paul, also warn of the disastrous effects the last days will have on marriage and take a stand against the initiation of new marriages. The prophet Joel, in preparing the Israelites for the Day of the Lord, thus commands the cessation of all weddings: "Assemble the people, sanctify the congregation (ἁγιάσατε ἐκκλησίαν) . . . let the bridegroom leave his chamber and the bride her room."[309] The book of Revelation reports that the destruction of "Babylon" will bring an end to the joyful sounds of its inhabitants, including "the voice of the bridegroom and bride";[310] and 4 Ezra 15–16, the text with so many similarities to 1 Corinthians 7:29b-31a, predicts disaster for both those planning marriage and those already married: "Virgins shall mourn because they have no bridegrooms; women shall mourn because they have no husbands. . . . Their bridegrooms shall be killed in war, and their husbands shall perish of famine."[311] In 2 Baruch the admonition against marriage is coupled with a warning against having children: "And you, bridegrooms, do not enter, and do not let the brides adorn themselves. And you, wives, do not pray to bear children, for the barren will rejoice more. And those who have no children will be glad, and those who have children will be sad."[312] The hardships of childbearing in the last days is also a motif in the synoptic tradition, coming to expression in Jesus' pronouncement of woes and blessings on people. In Mark 13:17 par. Jesus tells his disciples, "Woe to those who are pregnant and to those nursing in these days"; and in Luke 23:29 Jesus predicts that the inhabitants of Jerusalem will soon be telling their daughters, "Blessed are the

---

Johannes Weiß, *The History of Primitive Christianity*, completed following author's death by Rudolf Knopf, ed. Frederick C. Grant, vol. 2 (New York: Wilson-Erickson, 1937), 581; Niederwimmer, 107 n. 137; cf. 109; Schrage, "Die Stellung zur Welt," 131; and Wolbert, 198-99; cf. 120. Apocalyptic texts also predicted a disintegration of moral standards, which worked toward the destruction of the household. See Wilhelm Bousset, *Die Religion des Judentums im späthellenistischen Zeitalter*, ed. Hugo Gressmann, 3rd ed., HNT 21 (Tübingen: Mohr, 1926), 250-51, who cites *1 Enoch* 99:5; 100:1f.; *Jub.* 23:59; 4 Ezra 5:9; 6:24; and 2 *Bar.* 70:6. See also Mark 13:12 par. and Matt. 10:34-36. On the afamilial ethos of the eschatological "kingdom of God," see Elisabeth Schüssler Fiorenza, *In Memory of Her: A Feminist Theological Reconstruction of Christian Origins* (New York: Crossroad, 1983), 145-51, and Kevin J. Coyle, "Empire and Eschaton: The Early Church and the Question of Domestic Relationships," *Église et Théologie* 12 (1981): 35-94.

309. Joel 2:16 LXX; cf. 1:8.

310. Rev. 18:21-23 (echoing Jer. 16:1-9).

311. 4 Ezra (2 Esdras) 16:33-34 RSV; cf. Zech. 12:12-14.

312. 2 *Bar.* 10:13-14, trans. A. F. J. Klijn, "2 (Syriac Apocalypse of) Baruch," in *The Old Testament Pseudepigrapha*, 2:624; a Jewish apocalypse from the end of the first or beginning of the second century C.E.

sterile and the wombs that never conceived and breasts that never nursed," a saying also preserved in the *Gospel of Thomas* 79.[313]

From the perspective of first-century Christians living in the Greek world and familiar with both Stoic and apocalyptic thought, the integration of these two traditions in 7:25-31 is therefore perhaps not so remarkable. What gives one pause for reflection, however, is the extent to which this integration has taken place in our passage. To begin with, even the phraseology here is not clearly *either* Stoic *or* apocalyptic. As we have seen, Paul introduces the apocalyptic material in 7:29b-31a with the words τοῦτο δέ φημι, ἀδελφοί, ὁ καιρὸς συνεσταλμένος ἐστίν· τὸ λοιπόν . . . , "This I say, brothers, the time is constricted; henceforth. . . ." As Bonhöffer has pointed out, however, the expression τοῦτό φημι occurs frequently in Epictetus's *Discourses* as a means of introducing an opinion or clarification.[314] Paul's statement about the "time," on the other hand, finds its closest parallel in Dio Chrysostom's words "It is already time, henceforth . . ." (καιρὸς ἤδη τὸ λοιπόν), spoken to an angry mob intent on plundering his estate.[315] And verse 31a, "let those using the world be as not fully using [it]" (οἱ χρώμενοι τὸν κόσμον ὡς μὴ καταχρώμενοι), comes very close to the philosophical banter Philo assigns to his ideal statesman: "This is yours? — use [it], not misusing [it]!" (χρῶ μὴ παραχρώμενος).[316] In fact, Philo's words are approximately those of 7:31a set to the rhythm of the diatribe pattern we examined in connection with 7:18, 21, and 27.[317]

---

313. See also Luke 11:27-28; *Sib. Or.* 2:190-93; and cf. *Acts of Paul and Thecla* 3.5 (a beatitude formed from 1 Cor. 7:29b). Thackeray, 106, and Friedrich Guntermann, *Die Eschatologie des Hl. Paulus*, NTAbh 13/4-5 (Münster: Aschendorffsche Verlagsbuchhandlung, 1932), 89-90, also point to texts that predict complications and horrors associated with childbirth in the last times: 4 Ezra 5:8 (menstruating women giving birth to monsters); 6:21 (premature births); 1 Enoch 99:5 (sinful women practicing abortion and exposing and devouring newborns). Baumert, 192, on the other hand, claims that apocalyptic traditions about pregnancy, childbirth, and nursing are irrelevant since Paul does not mention these matters here. But the issues of pregnancy and reproduction do appear to stand behind 7:3-5, 14, and 34, and as I shall argue in the conclusion (chap. 4), Paul has good reason to avoid explicit mention of childbearing in 1 Cor. 7.

314. Bonhöffer, 199. τοῦτο φημι also occurs at 1 Cor. 15:50, and φημί by itself occurs at 10:15, 19. Outside of these four instances in 1 Corinthians, the first-person form does not appear in the NT.

315. Dio Chrysostom, *Oration* 46.13, cited by Wettstein, 2:129.

316. Philo, *De Josepho* 144, cited by Wettstein, 2:129.

317. See above, pp. 155-60, 170. As noted there, this same passage is cited by Thackeray, 239, in connection with 7:18, 21.

Aside from these examples, our nearest parallel to Paul's expression "the form of this

But the one "Stoic" or "near Stoic" feature of 7:25-31 with which scholars have been most fascinated is the expression "as not" (ὡς μή), which serves as a leitmotiv for the apocalyptic injunctions in verses 29b-31a. In the admonitions to those having wives to be "as not" having wives, to those weeping or rejoicing to be "as not" weeping or rejoicing, and to those making purchases and using the world to be "as not" owning or fully using, scholars have seen a resemblance to the Stoic ideal of mental and spiritual calmness, or ἀταραξία.[318] Weiß, for example, maintained that Stoic ἀταραξία "shines through here." Edwards writes, "If we can imagine St. Paul putting together an ethical theory after the manner of a Greek philosopher, we have the pith of it in [v. 30]"; and Legrand concurs: "the text of vv. 29-31 could have been signed by an Epictetus or a Seneca."[319] Again, Conzelmann states, "This appears at first sight to be the passage most strongly subject to Stoic influence in all of the Pauline epistles"; and Bornkamm says, "In themselves these words could be described as a classic paraphrase of the Cynic and Stoic ideal of severance from all earthly ties and detachment from all that fortune and circumstances may bring, whether good or evil."[320] Finally, Chadwick gives this assessment of the passage: "[Paul's] demand for continence is set within the

---

world" (τὸ σχῆμα τοῦ κόσμου τούτου) comes from Philostratus's *Life of Apollonius of Tyana* 8.7.7, where Apollonius asks, "And what is the form of this world?" (καὶ τί τὸ σχῆμα τοῦ κόσμου τοῦδε . . .). According to Philostratus, this is a direct quote from Apollonius's *Apologia pro vita,* which the latter had planned to give before the emperor Domitian (81-96 C.E.). Whether we may trust Philostratus on this point, however, is uncertain. Apollonius, incidentally, is said to have been a close associate of Musonius — see *Life of Apollonius* 4.46; and Lutz, 3 and n. 1. Finally, Romano Penna, "San Paolo (1 Cor 7,29b-31a) e Diogene il Cinico," *Bib* 58 (1977): 237-45, sees a parallel between 7:29b-31a and Diogenes Laertius 6.29, where Diogenes the Cynic is described as praising "those who were intending to marry and did not marry" as well as "those who were intending to raise children and did not raise children" (τοὺς μέλλοντας γαμεῖν καὶ μὴ γαμεῖν . . . καὶ τοὺς μέλλοντας παιδοτροφεῖν καὶ μὴ παιδοτροφεῖν). But this is a distant parallel and seems to me to be only a coincidence.

318. The seminal study here is Braun, "Die Indifferenz gegenüber der Welt bei Paulus und bei Epiktet"; see also the authors cited in the following notes, and Schrage, "Die Stellung zur Welt," 132-34, who surveys the literature and lists relevant passages from Epictetus.

319. Weiß, *Korintherbrief,* 199, citing from Epictetus, Teles, and Philo (198 n. 2; 200 nn. 1 and 3); Edwards, 194; Legrand, "Saint Paul et célibat," 322.

320. Conzelmann, 133; Günther Bornkamm, *Paul* (New York and Evanston, Ill.: Harper and Row, 1971), 206. Cf. Niederwimmer, 110 n. 50, who says that, separated from the framing of vv. 29a and 31b, vv. 29b-31a would be thoroughly Stoic; and Darrell J. Doughty, "The Presence and Future of Salvation in Corinth," *ZNW* 66 (1975): 72 n. 50, who speaks of "Stoic language" bracketed between apocalyptic assertions.

eschatological framework of Christian thought, fused with Stoic-Cynic ideas about the soul's detachment and ἀταραξία."321

This almost unanimous agreement among scholars seems to be warranted, moreover, by the several passages from Seneca and Epictetus (among others) that these scholars cite. Thus Seneca, in one of his *Moral Epistles*, says of possessions, "Let us use these things *(utamur illis)* . . . and let us use them sparingly *(utamur parce)*, as if *(tamquam)* they were given for safe-keeping and will be withdrawn. . . . If anyone has put his trust in goods that are most fleeting, he is soon bereft of them, and, to avoid being bereft, he suffers distress *(adfligitur)*."322 In another epistle he states that the wise man can be self-sufficient and still marry and raise children, "Yet all the good will be limited to his own being." To illustrate this he recounts the philosophical triumphs of the sage Stilbo in the wake of Megara's sacking by Demetrius I of Macedonia: "For Stilbo, after his country was captured and his children and his wife lost, as he emerged from the general desolation alone and yet happy, spoke as follows to Demetrius . . . , 'I have all my goods with me!'"323 In a similar fashion Epictetus maintains that the end of philosophy should be for each person to pass his life unto himself, "free from pain, fear, and perturbation (ἀταράχως), at the same time maintaining with his associates both the natural and the acquired relationships, those namely of son, father, brother, citizen, husband, wife. . . ."324 Elsewhere, after praising the man who does not value his person beyond its God-given worth, Epictetus advises: "Now if someone should also take this same attitude toward his property and his children and his wife, as this man takes toward his body, and under some frenzy and desperation simply be so disposed that he would in no way act so as to have these things or not have them (τὸ ἔχειν ταῦτα ἢ μὴ ἔχειν) . . . what sort of tyrant or body guards or swords of theirs would still be frightening to him?"325 A last example is Epictetus's description of Socrates as "having a wife and children, but as belonging to another."326 "Later on," he says, referring to Socrates' trial before

---

321. Chadwick, 268, cf. 267.

322. Seneca, *Epistle* 74.18, trans. Gummere, 2:125. Cf. Epictetus, *Encheiridion* 11.

323. Seneca, *Epistle* 9.17-18, trans. Gummere, 1:53. In 9.19 Seneca adds: "This saying of Stilbo makes common ground with Stoicism; the Stoic also can carry his goods unimpaired through cities that have been burned to ashes; for he is self-sufficient" (trans. Gummere, 1:55).

324. Epictetus, *Discourses* 2.14.8, trans. Oldfather, 1:309 (who inadvertently omits "husband" from his translation); cf. *Discourses* 3.24.58-60.

325. Epictetus, *Discourses* 4.7.5.

326. Epictetus, *Discourses* 4.1.159, γυναῖκα καὶ παιδία ἔχοντα, ἀλλὰ ὡς ἀλλότρια.

the Athenian people, "he didn't behave as having children or as having a wife, did he?"[327]

Despite the impressive weight of this evidence, however, many scholars, including most of those just cited, hold that 1 Corinthians 7:29b-31a ultimately cannot be understood in terms of Stoic thought.[328] Schrage, followed by Schulz, has taken this position, pointing to Paul's dependence on an apocalyptic source for these verses, which, as we have seen, is a genuine possibility. Reasoning that this dependence in itself is sufficient to exclude any Stoic influence, he concludes that any resemblance to authors such as Epictetus is purely coincidental.[329] Approaching the matter on an ideological plane, Schrage also argues that the apocalyptic motivation behind 7:29b-31a is entirely incompatible with Stoicism. The admonitions here to live "as not," according to Schrage, are inspired by Paul's belief that the end of the world was at hand: since the things of this life would shortly be no more, the Christian should avoid becoming overly involved with them. Such an expectation of the world's imminent and definitive demise, says Schrage, would be incomprehensible to an Epictetus, since Stoic eschatology saw the world as constantly in transition, subject to a steady cycle of conflagration and renewal that knew no meaningful beginning or definitive end.[330]

In reply to Schrage we may first question the exclusiveness he imputes to both apocalyptic and Stoic ideologies. On the one hand, his readiness to understand apocalyptic thought as completely separate from other modes of thought stands in need of correction.[331] As the research of others has shown,

327. Epictetus, *Discourses* 4.1.162, trans. Oldfather, 2:301, μή τι ὡς τέκνα ἔχων ἀναστρέφεται, μή τι ὡς γυναῖκα. . . . See also *Encheiridion* 11, where Epictetus says of a thing given by God: "care for it as belonging to another, as travellers care for the inn" (ὡς ἀλλοτρίου αὐτοῦ ἐπιμελοῦ, ὡς τοῦ πανδοχείου οἱ παριόντες).

328. Those who do not rule out Stoic influence include Weiß, *Korintherbrief*, 199 (who changes his position in *History of Primitive Christianity*, 583 n. 62); Braun, "Die Indifferenz gegenüber der Welt," esp. 343-44; and Chadwick, 267-68. See also Doughty, "Presence and Future," 72 n. 50; cf. Niederwimmer, 110 n. 149.

329. Schrage, "Die Stellung zur Welt," 136, 137-38; Schulz, 487 (although he discounts Schrage's argument from 4 Ezra 16:40-44).

330. Schrage, "Die Stellung zur Welt," 135-38, 153, following Braun, "Die Indifferenz gegenüber der Welt," 162, 164. Weiß, *History of Primitive Christianity*, 583 n. 62, and Deißner, 788-90, also point to the differences between Pauline and Stoic eschatology. For a general comparison of these two eschatologies, see Kee, "Pauline Eschatology," 137-40, 144-47, 151-55.

331. Cf. Conzelmann, 133 n. 26, and Balch, "Stoic Debates," 429-30: "Schrage argues in too rationalistic a manner about social influences, whether these are from Jewish apocalyptic or

apocalypticism is far from a clearly circumscribed entity, sealed off from "outside" influences.[332] Indeed, Schrage himself cautions against such absolutes in the syncretistic world of late Hellenism;[333] and his own research in other quarters has led him to the conclusion that certain topoi (in fact, *peristasis* catalogues) were actually *shared* by apocalyptic and Stoic authors.[334]

On the other hand, Schrage's observations on the apocalyptic motivation for the admonitions in 7:29b-31a — given that they are correct — hardly constitute sufficient grounds for ruling out Stoic influence on these verses. Paul was, after all, Christian, not Stoic, and the same holds true for his church at Corinth. We should expect, therefore, that any Stoic ideas in 1 Corinthians will bear a certain amount of Christian coloring. Just how much coloring is admissible before we decide that a passage is not, or is no longer, Stoic seems to me something of an open question: Do non-Stoic motivations for the Stoic ideal of mental and spiritual calmness necessarily render this ideal un-Stoic? Certainly scholars would be wary of applying this litmus test to, say, the Stoic elements in Philo.[335]

But apart from this caveat, I would maintain that Schrage has simply misread the apocalyptic motivation behind 7:29b-31a. According to him, Paul's concern here is with the imminence of the world's destruction. As I have argued above, however, Paul's immediate, if not sole, point of emphasis

---

from Stoic ethics." Ironically, Countryman, 213 n. 21, takes Balch to task for focusing too narrowly on Stoic influence and ignoring the eschatological content of Paul's argument.

332. See esp. Hans Dieter Betz, "On the Problem of the Religio-Historical Understanding of Apocalypticism," *JTC* 6 (1969): 134-56, esp. 155: "Jewish and, subsequently, Christian apocalypticism as well . . . must be seen and presented as peculiar expressions within the entire development of Hellenistic syncretism." Cf. Wayne A. Meeks, "Social Functions of Apocalyptic Language in Pauline Christianity," in *Apocalypticism in the Mediterranean World and the Near East,* ed. David Hellholm (Tübingen: Mohr, 1983), 703.

333. Schrage, "Die Stellung zur Welt," 125.

334. Wolfgang Schrage, "Leid, Kreuz und Eschaton: Die Peristasenkataloge als Merkmale paulinischer theologia crucis und Eschatologie," *EvT* 34 (1974): 143-47 (with extensive literature) shows that catalogues of trials and sufferings occur in both Stoic-Cynic diatribes and Jewish apocalyptic lists of woes; cf. 165-66, 171-72, 174. See also Conzelmann's remark on the *peristasis* catalogue in 1 Cor. 4:9-13: "The Stoic picture of the philosopher's struggle as a spectacle for the world is taken over by Paul into his world-picture . . . and reshaped in terms of his eschatology" (Conzelmann, 88).

335. See Conzelmann's remark on 1 Cor. 7:29b-31a: "Even the eschatological grounding is not in itself an objection. . . . Paul could simply have changed the world picture, and yet have taken over in his attitude toward the world the aloofness of the Stoics" (133).

in these verses pertains not to the imminence of the end, but to the social and economic upheaval that was to precede the end.[336] Insofar as my reading of this passage is correct, not only is the incongruence that Schrage sees between apocalyptic and Stoic eschatology a moot point, as it plays no part here, but further, the apocalyptic rationale for Paul's argument in 7:29b-31a finds a very close analogy in Epictetus's discourse *On Cynicism,* and, significantly, in the section of this discourse which deals with marriage. Here Epictetus explains that the Cynic will forgo marriage given the present "order of things,"[337] by which he refers not to the static transience of the world but to the dire state of society in his day, which he envisions as "arrayed for battle."[338]

Yet, these considerations aside, the main objection scholars have raised against understanding 7:29b-31a as an expression of Stoic calmness is that this ideal would contradict basic tenets of Paul's theology, and thus he could not espouse it. As Conzelmann explains, "The non-Stoic character of the relationship to the world [in 7:29b-31a] emerges only in the wider context. Paul's advice is not to withdraw into the safe and unrestricted realms of the inner life, but to maintain freedom in the midst of involvement."[339] By contrast, according to Schulz, Epictetus "demands ἀταραξία fundamentally, [and] excludes compassion and engaging oneself for the concrete needs of one's fellow human beings."[340] Likewise, Schrage points out that any notion of "nonengagement" with the world would be limited in Paul's theology by the value he places on love. For Paul compassion is something positive, whereas it

---

336. Schrage sees a sense of imminence in two places: in the word καιρός (v. 29a), which he translates "the time yet remaining before the Parousia" ("Die Stellung zur Welt," 131-32), and in the μή of the ὡς μή admonitions, which he translates "(already) no (longer)" (148). Both are blatant overinterpretations of Paul's words.

337. Epictetus, *Discourses* 3.22.69, "the order of things being such as it is" (τοιαύτης δ' οὔσης καταστάσεως); 3.22.76, "in this order of things" (ἐν ταύτῃ τῇ καταστάσει). Cf. Paul's use of σχῆμα ("form" of this world) in 7:29b.

338. Epictetus, *Discourses* 3.22.69. Cf. Yarbrough, 105: "Even Paul's eschatological argument has analogy in Epictetus's discourse on the Ideal Cynic in that the Cynic does not marry because the present order is 'like a battlefield'"; and Gager, 332: "As with Paul, the motivation for celibacy [in Epictetus] is the desire to devote oneself without distraction to a religious obligation, and justification for this is rooted in unusual, external, and presumably not permanent [?] circumstances." Note also that Plutarch claimed Cicero, early in his career, temporarily took up the contemplative life (τὸν σχολαστὴν καὶ θεωρητικὸν βίον), due to the turmoil of the political situation (*Vitae* 862A [*Cicero*]).

339. Conzelmann, 133.

340. Schulz, 487-88.

is negative for the Stoics.[341] By the same token, Schrage contends, the θλῖψις, or "pressure from outside" (as he translates it), that Paul speaks of in verse 28 would be inconceivable for Epictetus, who held that "what pressures and plagues people is not things and people, but the person himself with wrong δόγματα [beliefs]."[342]

Although the above arguments are widely accepted,[343] they are in need of qualification on two grounds: first, because they exaggerate the difference between Paul's theological principles and the Stoic ideal of ἀταραξία; and second, because they overlook the function of 7:29b-31a in Paul's discussion. While it is true that the Stoics sought to live free from inner disturbance (ταραχή) and "passion" (πάθος), this rarely led them to the conclusion that they must withdraw from the world. Indeed, as we saw in chapter 2, the central issue of the Stoic-Cynic marriage debate was whether one should engage oneself on behalf of human society. Should one establish a household? raise and educate children? participate in politics? safeguard the ancestral altar? make one's house a rampart for the city-state? — in short, should one pursue the active life over the contemplative life? These were some of the questions that occupied major Stoic teachers throughout the Hellenistic period, and mostly they elicited affirmative answers.[344]

Regarding attending to the needs of others, Antipater, Musonius, and Hierocles all agree that a man must provide for his family, sharing both his possessions and his body with his wife; and Epictetus claims that his ideal

---

341. Schrage, "Die Stellung zur Welt," 134; cf. 138; Schrage, *Die konkreten Einzelgebote*, 23 n. 42; and Schrage, "Zur Frontstellung," 223-24, 231 n. 68.

342. Schrage, "Die Stellung zur Welt," 135. These statements from Conzelmann, Schulz, and Schrage, it should be noted, are all directly dependent on Braun, "Die Indifferenz gegenüber der Welt," 166.

343. See also Kümmel in Lietzmann, 178; Hierzenberger, 43, 50; and in the older literature, Heinrici, *Das erste Sendschreiben*, 218-20; Bonhöffer, 35-36; and Allo, 180. Héring's objection to Stoic influence on 7:29b-31a on the grounds that "the Stoic forbade emotion," confuses emotion with πάθος (passion or emotional suffering detrimental to one's well-being). As we have seen, Epictetus does not forbid the emotion love (ἔρως); and Arius, on the other hand, lists "rejoicing" (χαίρειν), which Paul uses in 7:30, as a "correct" Stoic action (κατορθώματα, Stobaeus 2.96.20-21 W.-H.; cf. Diogenes Laertius 7.116; and the discussion of ἐπιθυμία on pp. 45-46 above).

344. See also the discussion of Stoic retirement into oneself in the midst of activities in André-Jean Festugière, *Personal Religion among the Greeks*, Sather Classical Lectures 26 (Berkeley: University of California Press, 1954; reprint, Westport, Conn.: Greenwood, 1984), 58-64, and the literature on *oikeiosis*, the Stoic notion of social affinity and dependency, cited in chap. 2, n. 15.

Cynic will make the entire world his family, and "in this way care for them all."[345] Some "pressure from outside" — what Hierocles called the "concerns" (μερίμναι) of day-to-day living[346] — was thus seen by these Stoics as inevitable. In fact, on these grounds Antipater encouraged taking on the additional responsibilities of married life, reasoning that a wife could keep her husband "undistracted" (ἀπερίσπαστος) from some of these concerns.[347] And while Epictetus argued that his Cynic would avoid marriage in order to remain "undistracted," it was only so the latter could take on yet greater responsibilities and concerns.[348] In either case it is difficult to overlook that Hierocles, Antipater, and Epictetus are using the same terminology to discuss this dilemma as Paul uses in 7:32-35.[349] The divide between Paul and the Stoics on the concept of ἀταραξία is therefore not nearly as great as scholars have portrayed it.

On the other hand, it would appear that it is not even necessary for us to reconcile the Stoic-like ἀταραξία of 7:29b-31a with Paul's overall theology, given the function of these verses in Paul's argument. As I suggested above, Paul is using the apocalyptic material in these verses to define the "circumstances" of his (Stoic) argument against marriage. In effect, this material constitutes the "facts" of an argument from expediency, and as such requires no theological justification. To put the matter another way, the admonitions here to live "as not" are not Paul's, but represent the authoritative voice of apocalyptic tradition describing what life in the last days in fact demands. Indeed, in light of Paul's efforts in 7:3-5 to limit sexual abstinence among spouses, it would be very odd if the admonition to have a wife "as not having" was his own. Rather, introduced with the explanatory phrase "this I say, brothers," verses 29b-31a serve as so many examples of the "tribulation" that, according to Paul, *necessarily* awaits those who marry in the "present necessity."[350]

As part of an argument against marriage based on expediency, verses

345. Epictetus, *Discourses* 3.22.81, οὕτως πάντων κήδεται; see also 3.22.72-73, 77, 83.

346. Hierocles 53.30–54.1 v. A. (Stobaeus 4.504.7-9 W.-H.)

347. Antipater (app. A), line 77.

348. Epictetus, *Discourses* 3.22.69.

349. See the next section.

350. On the various functions of apocalyptic material in ethical discourse, see Gager, "Functional Diversity in Paul's Use of End-Time Language"; Meeks, "Social Functions of Apocalyptic Language in Pauline Christianity"; Meeks, *The First Urban Christians*, 174-79; and John S. Kloppenborg, "Symbolic Eschatology and the Apocalypticism of Q," *HTR* 80 (1987): 287-306.

29b-31a thus function as a warning that marriage in the last times will *as a matter of fact* be unfulfilling. Just as some Stoics held that circumstances caused them to act uncharacteristically as Cynics, a certain amount of un-characteristic, Stoic-like detachment toward the things of married life is now required of Christians, according to Paul. Christians will act, but "as not," and husbands will have wives, but "as not," for Christian marriage in its ideal form will cease to exist, and for this reason, Paul is saying, it is "good for a man" not to get involved.

In sum, I would contend that there is no need to interpret 7:29b-31a in a manner that makes it compatible with Paul's ethic of Christian compassion, and thus no objection to our seeing these verses as an expression of Stoic calmness and detachment. This is not to deny, however, that 7:29b-31a also owes a considerable debt to its apocalyptic heritage. In the final analysis we must reckon with a high degree of integration between Stoic and apocalyptic materials here, which is one more indication that Paul's audience in Corinth stands intellectually and spiritually between Judeo-Christian and Stoic tradi-tions. It may also imply that these verses stem from some form of "Stoic-apocalyptic" thought whose source was in Corinth.

The Commitments of Married Life and Finding Time for the Lord: 7:32-35

Paul's debt in 1 Corinthians 7 to Stoic and Cynic thinking on marriage has been most apparent to scholars in 7:32-35, where he compares the allegiances of married Christians with those of unmarried Christians. The unmarried, he explains, are committed to pleasing the Lord, and consequently concern themselves with "the things of the Lord," while the married are committed to pleasing their spouses, and hence concern themselves with "the things of the world." As we noted earlier, Paul must mean that married Christians are com-mitted *both* to their spouses *and* to the Lord, since they are in fact Christians, and since this is the only way to account for his assertion in verse 34a that they are "divided."[351] From Paul's emphasis on marital obligations in verses 27 and 28b and from his mention of buying and possessing and "using the world" in verses 30-31, we may further surmise that his expression "the things of the world" has reference to the day-to-day responsibilities of a householder and

351. See above, p. 120.

his wife.[352] It is a preoccupation with these things, he contends, that divides Christians and stands in the way of their devotion to Christ "without distraction."[353]

Regarding the "unmarried woman and the virgin" in verse 34, moreover, Paul appears to have an additional message: that these women concern themselves for the things of the Lord so they might be "holy both in body and in spirit" (ἁγία καὶ τῷ σώματι καὶ τῷ πνεύματι). As our investigation of 7:3-5 and 7:12-24 indicated, part of the controversy over marriage in Corinth involved a person's control or "authority" over his or her own body. While Paul insists

---

352. Cf. Juncker, 185-86, who would include pregnancy, child rearing, and household management. Weiß, *Korintherbrief*, 201, followed by Niederwimmer, 111, posits a connection between v. 28b, Paul's desire to spare the Corinthians "tribulation in the flesh," and his statement in v. 32, "I want you to be without care."

353. See Baumert, 260-62, who correctly emphasizes that marriage brings involvement with the world, and it is this involvement, not marriage itself or the spouse, that "divides" a Christian. Thus Paul's words do not imply a direct tension between allegiance to the Lord and allegiance to one's spouse. The tension, rather, is between one's concern for "things of the world" and "things of the Lord" (cf. Weiß, *Korintherbrief*, 202). Niederwimmer's contention, on the basis of 7:29b (perhaps following Braun, "Die Indifferenz gegenüber der Welt," 160), that a wife is a "thing of this world" *(res huius mundi)*, and his assessment of 7:32-34 as meaning that the married person is "not completely a Christian" but only a "'half' Christian," is simply an attempt to sensationalize Paul (Niederwimmer, 113 and n. 164, 114; cf. 123). The same holds true for Peter Brown, 56, who says the "married lacked the supreme quality of the undivided heart," which for Paul was a "crushing disqualification." Both authors contradict what Paul himself says on grace and the circumstances of one's life in 7:17-24, as well as what he says in 7:36-40 (see below).

We should also resist the temptation to interpret the division of the married man (and presumably the married woman) in psychological terms. Marriage for Paul is not "anxiety producing," as Wimbush, 64, claims; nor is Balch, "Stoic Debates," 435, justified in making a distinction between the "distractions" spoken of by Stoics and Paul's "anxiety." As Legrand points out, commentators too often "think spontaneously of a heart divided in its affections in the modern romantic sense of the term." It is rather, he continues, that "the wife 'pleased' her husband by giving him the children he wanted . . . and by conducting the household efficiently. . . . For the husband, it was a matter of securing for his wife wealth, comfort and social consideration" (*Biblical Doctrine of Virginity*, 94, 95-96). Likewise, Moulton and Milligan, 26, say of the word ἀμέριμνος, "It will be seen that the NT meaning alone is attested from the vernacular documents. Its tone in them suggests that 'anxiety' rather exaggerates the word. So in Mt 28.14 we might paraphrase '. . . so that you need not trouble'; and in I Cor 7.32 the verb that follows clearly does not suggest *anxious* care" (emphasis Moulton and Milligan's). See also Rudolf Bultmann, "μεριμνάω," in *TDNT* 4 (1967), 591, who says μεριμνάω expresses an "intentness on something," or a "striving after something."

on the Stoic-like notion of mutual control of bodies within marriage (v. 4), some of the Corinthians seem to have objected to this because it inhibited prayer (see v. 5), or because this sort of arrangement with an unbeliever prevented them from achieving the ideals of "holiness" and freedom (see vv. 14, 15b). With this mention of holiness in verse 34, therefore, Paul is evidently bringing the issue of controlling one's body into play once again. In contrast to married women, who must share their physical existence with another, unmarried women and virgins, he argues, can be "dedicated to Christ" (so the NEB) with all their resources, both spiritual and physical.[354] That Paul says this of single women but not single men might indicate, furthermore, that the women in Corinth were concerned particularly about the burden of bearing and raising children.

Clearly, the logic of 7:32-35 runs parallel to the "Cynic" position on marriage, for as we saw in chapter 2, both Cynics and Stoics promoted a "Cynic" position against marriage, inasmuch as attending to the needs of a marriage relationship compromised their commitment to philosophy. It is not simply the logic of this passage, however, that exhibits similarities with the Stoic-Cynic marriage debate, but also Paul's choice of words. The most obvious case is ἀπερισπάστως, "without distraction," an adverb which appears at the end of 7:35. In choosing the adverbial form of this word, Paul has selected a distinctive and rare word indeed. Outside of Stoic authors and the Stoic-minded Clement of Alexandria, it occurs only five times in Greek literature before the third century — once in the historian Dioscurides, twice in Polybius, and twice in the papyri.[355] Among the Stoics it appears in Arius's account of Stoic ethics, in

---

354. So also Bachmann, 287. Neither chastity, virginity, or abstinence is the goal here; see Heinrici, *Der erste Brief,* 244; Juncker, 183-91; Tischleder, 95-97. The expression "holy in body," in turn, probably stems from the Corinthians; cf. Barrett, 181 (although I disagree with his understanding of the motivations involved): "The unmarried woman's special aim is presumably therefore to be holy not only in spirit but in body; she wishes to sanctify her body by abstinence from sexual relations. But this is not consistent with Paul's teaching in general, for he believes that all Christians, married or unmarried, must be holy in body. . . . Moreover, in the present chapter he has told married men and women that through their marriage they *sanctify* their unbelieving partners, and that the children born of these marriages are *holy.* We must conclude therefore that in *that she may be holy both in body and in spirit* we have words quoted from the Corinthian ascetical party. Paul approves the sentiment, though he would not himself confine it to the unmarried" (emphasis Barrett's). Characteristically, Niederwimmer, 115, insists that "holy in body" represents the ideal of unviolated continence, and that this is "evidently the view of the apostle."

355. Dioscurides (fourth or first century b.c.e.?), frag. 5b.60 Jacoby (in Athenaeus, *Deipnosophistai* 1.10c); Polybius 2.20.10; 4.18.6; *PTebt* 895.57 (175 b.c.e.), and *PKron* 38.17 (137

Epictetus, in Marcus Aurelius, and in Simplicius's commentary on Epictetus's *Encheiridion*.[356] In Clement's *Stromateis* it appears five times, and since three of these occurrences have no apparent connection with 1 Corinthians 7:35, Clement's propensity for this word points to his interest in Stoic philosophy rather than a reliance on Paul.[357] Also significant is the fact that the adjectival form, ἀπερίσπαστος — which, admittedly, is widely used in the Roman period — occurs in both Antipater's and Epictetus's discussions of marriage. The former claims that a man must marry in order to remain "undistracted,"[358] while the latter teaches that the Cynic must avoid marriage so as to be "undistracted," giving himself "wholly to the service of God" (ὅλον πρὸς τῇ διακονίᾳ τοῦ θεοῦ).[359] As many scholars have observed, this last phrase is materially

---

c.e.). On the papyri see Ceslas Spicq, *Notes de lexicographie néo-testamentaire*, OBO 22/1 (Fribourg: Éditions Universitaires; Göttingen: Vandenhoeck & Ruprecht, 1978), 1:123 and n. 2.

356. Epictetus, *Discourses* 1.29.58-59 (cf. Plutarch, *Moralia* 45D); Marcus Aurelius 3.6; and Simplicius, *Commentarius in Epicteti enchiridion* 104.36-37, ed. F. Dübner, *Theophrasti: characteres* (Paris: Didot, 1842), where it describes the actions of God. In Arius it is the manuscript reading at Stobaeus 2.86.16 W.-H., which Wachsmuth has emended to ἀπεριστάτως ("without special circumstances") on the strength of Diogenes Laertius 7.109. Yet on the strength of Stobaeus 2.76.9-15 W.-H., it is not clear whether this emendation is necessary or desirable. Bonhöffer, 108, 135 (perhaps too quickly), labels ἀπερισπάστως "a Hellenistic word particularly beloved of the Stoics."

357. Clement of Alexandria, *Stromateis*, bk. 3, chap. 6.53.3 (2.220.20-24 S.), where Clement denies the gnostic claim that marriage is evil, saying that some of the apostles traveled with wives, devoting themselves "undistractedly" to preaching; bk. 4, chap. 25.157.2 (2.318.5-7 S.), where he states that faith joins a Christian "inseparably" to Christ; and bk. 7, chap. 3.13.3 (3.10.23-26 S.), where, drawing on Plato, *Republic* 613B, Clement explains that the true gnostic brings himself and his followers into a "passionless" state (εἰς ἀπάθειαν) through "uninterrupted" communion with the Lord. The two instances that rely on 1 Cor. 7:35 are bk. 4, chap. 5.22.1 (2.257.31 S.), and bk. 4, chap. 23.149.2 (2.314.10 S.).

358. Antipater (app. A), line 77. Noted by Bonhöffer, 108 (cf. Balch, "Stoic Debates," 432). Cf. Clement's interpretation of 1 Cor. 7:29b, where he says that Paul intended marriage to be "free from passion" (ἀπροσπαθής) as well as "undistracted" from love for the Lord (*Stromateis*, bk. 7, chap. 11.64.2 [3.46.6-8 S.]). For other instances of Clement's use of the adjective in a philosophical context, see *Stromateis*, bk. 2, chap. 2.9.3 (2.117.19-20 S.), where, in Stoic fashion, Clement explains that knowledge relies on an "unwavering power of decision" (ἀπερίσπαστος προαίρεσις); and bk. 6, chap. 10.82.4 (2.473.7-8 S.), where he speaks of the gnostic's "continual" use of Greek philosophy.

359. Epictetus, *Discourses* 3.22.69. The adjective also occurs in Sir. 41:1 and Wisd. of Sol. 16:11, but nowhere else in the Bible. In the apostolic fathers, Ignatius's use of the adjective at *Ephesians* 20.2, in his demand that the Ephesians obey the bishop and presbytery "with an undistracted mind" (ἀπερισπάστῳ διανοίᾳ), may reflect the Stoic tradition found in Epictetus, *Discourses* 2.21.22, where Epictetus maintains that to study philosophy one must bring one's mind (διάνοια) undistracted to the class (ἀπερίσπαστον . . . εἰς τὴν σχολήν). Regarding the issue

very close to Paul's expression "undistracted devotion to the Lord" (εὐπάρεδρον τῷ κυρίῳ ἀπερισπάστως).³⁶⁰ Finally, Epictetus, Hierocles, and Clement use several other words cognate with ἀπερισπάστως when discussing marriage. Epictetus speaks of a wife and children as something by which a man might "be distracted" (περισπᾶσθαι), and calls the activities of married life "distraction" and "busyness" (περισπασμόν/ἀσχολία).³⁶¹ Similarly, Hierocles refers to the "distractions" (περισπασμοί) of a householder's life in the city-state, although he says these are abated by a wife;³⁶² and Clement describes marriage as "distracting" someone from the things of God (μεταπερισπῶσα τῶν θείων) because of the busyness (ἀσχολία) involved.³⁶³

Along with choosing what may be considered a specialized term in Stoic philosophy, however, Paul has given ἀπερισπάστως a place of particular emphasis in his argument by putting it at the very end of verse 35, far removed from any verb. The emphatic positioning of this adverb is in fact so extreme that Paul has written a sentence that is almost incomprehensible on the basis of normal Greek usage. This was apparent in the fourth century to the great translator and exegete Saint Jerome. Expressing dissatisfaction at his own Latin translation of 7:35, he exclaims, "The Latin words do not convey the meaning of the Greek. What words shall we use to render πρὸς τὸ εὔσχημον καὶ εὐπρόσεδρον [*sic*] τῷ κυρίῳ ἀπερισπάστως?"³⁶⁴ We know also that Jerome's contemporary John Chrysostom solved the problem by simply re-

---

at Corinth of physical autonomy versus the debt of conjugal relations owed to one's spouse, it is interesting to note that the adjective can also mean "without liability"; see POxy II 278.17-19 (no. 286; 82 C.E.): "[S]o that they may secure us without liability (ἀπερισπάστους) or difficulty with regard to the aforementioned debt (ὀφειλήν), and repay it (ἀποδώσειν)" — also cited above, n. 35, regarding Paul's use of τὴν ὀφειλὴν ἀποδιδότω in 1 Cor. 7:3.

360. Cf. *Sentences of Sextus* 230a: "Marriage He gives you to decline, so that you may live as a companion to God (ὡς πάρεδρος θεῷ)." This may be dependent on 1 Cor. 7:35, or both passages may be drawing on a common tradition.

361. Epictetus, *Discourses* 4.1.159; 3.22.72.

362. Hierocles 53.31–54.1 v. A. (Stobaeus 4.504.9 W.-H.), cited by Balch, "Stoic Debates," 435.

363. Clement of Alexandria, *Stromateis*, bk. 3, chap. 9.67.1 (2.226.22-23 S., cited above, p. 173). See also *De vita contemplativa* 1.1, where Philo describes the Therapeutae as "single-mindedly devoted to philosophical theory" (οἱ θεωρίαν ἀσπασάμενοι).

364. Jerome, *Adversus Jovinianum* 1.13, trans. Fremantle, in Philip Schaff and Henry Wace, eds., A Select Library of Nicene and Post-Nicene Fathers of the Christian Church, 2nd ser., vol. 6, *St. Jerome: Letters and Select Works* (New York: Christian Literature, 1893; reprint, Grand Rapids: Eerdmans, n.d.), 357. In his exegesis of 1 Cor. 7, this is the only part of the text that Jerome deems necessary to cite in Greek.

moving the offending adverb from his text; and according to Jerome, Latin translators regularly omitted the entire clause.[365]

In recent times C. K. Barrett has repeated Jerome's judgment. Giving his own paraphrase of verse 35, Barrett confesses, "close translation is scarcely possible."[366] Other commentators have elected to clarify Paul's difficult syntax by rewriting it in Greek, or by suggesting the presence of an understood verb "to be." Lietzmann, for example, proposes ἵνα καλοὶ πάρεδροι τοῦ κυρίου ἀπερισπάστως γένησθε as the equivalent of Paul's τὸ ... εὐπάρεδρον τῷ κυρίῳ ἀπερισπάστως;[367] and Billroth suggests that Paul has "added ἀπερισπάστως as if εἶναι had been employed,"[368] a notion that seems to have inspired the reading εἶναι ἀπερισπάστους in the second-century manuscript 𝔓[15].[369]

The best explanation for Paul's syntax in 7:35 is given (somewhat cryptically) by Blass and Debrunner, who propose that the adverb ἀπερισπάστως modifies the verbal aspect of εὐπάρεδρον, "devotion," a noun formed from the verb (εὐ)παρεδρεύω, "to sit beside."[370] In Latin this noun would be classified as a *gerundium*, and its modification by an adverb would be a fairly common syntax. For Greek, however, this construction is extremely rare.[371] On the basis of these observations, it appears that in selecting the rare adverb ἀπερισπάστως, and in placing it in a position of unusual emphasis, Paul has not only employed something of a Stoic watchword, but has used it in a rather dramatic way as the capstone of his discussion in 7:32-35.

Aside from ἀπερισπάστως, several other words in 7:32-35 may indicate a connection between this passage and either Stoic thought or the general philosophical milieu of the Stoic-Cynic marriage debate. One of these is the verb ἀρέσκω, "to please," which Paul uses three times in verses 32-34 in the sense of "pleasing the Lord" and "pleasing one's spouse." This word also occurs in Antipater and Epictetus, the latter claiming that a philosopher must

365. John Chrysostom, *Homily 20 on 1 Corinthians* (PG 61:159); Jerome, *Adversus Jovinianum* 1.13.

366. Barrett, 182.

367. Lietzmann, 35.

368. Billroth, 1:202.

369. Forming an *inclusio* with 7:32, ἀμερίμνους εἶναι. See also next note.

370. Blass and Debrunner, 63 (§117.1). Cf. Rückert and Wahl, who paraphrase 7:35 as τὸ ... (εὐ)παρεδρεύειν τῷ κυρίῳ ἀπερισπάστως (Rückert, 208; Christian Abraham Wahl, *Clavis Novi Testamenti Philologica*, 3rd ed. [Leipzig: Joh. Ambros. Barth, 1834], 210, s.v. "εὐπάρεδρος").

371. The one other example in the NT of which I am aware is 1 Tim. 4:3, "for reception with thanksgiving" (εἰς μετάλημψιν μετὰ εὐχαριστίας), where "with thanksgiving" modifies the verbal aspect of "reception."

be able to maintain his marital relation with spiritual composure (ἀταράχως) and at the same time "please God"; the former stating that the entire "goal and purpose" of a wife's existence is to "please her husband."[372]

In 7:35 Paul assures the Corinthians that his advice not to marry is for their "benefit," πρὸς . . . τὸ σύμφορον. Although a common term in deliberative rhetoric, σύμφορον and the cognate verb συμφέρω, "to benefit," were also popular among the Stoics.[373] Thus Ocellus speaks of the importance of forming marriages with the "benefit of the community" in mind (πρὸς τὸ συμφέρον τῷ κοινῷ).[374] Musonius describes the lawgivers' encouragement of procreation as "good and beneficial" (καλὸν καὶ συμφέρον).[375] And Hierocles champions marriage as something both "beneficial" (σύμφορον) and profitable.[376] Paul, of course, has taken the opposite, "Cynic" view, arguing that avoiding marriage is beneficial.[377]

---

372. Epictetus, *Discourses* 2.14.8, 12; Antipater (app. A), line 29. The word also has a place in Pythagorean discourse on marriage. In *Melissa to Cleareta* (late first–early second century C.E.) the author says a wife must hold it as an unwritten law to please her husband by fulfilling his wishes (3.2.19-22 Thesleff); and Stobaeus records this anecdote about Theano: "Being asked what would be fitting for a wife (τί πρέπον εἴη γυναικί), Theano said, 'Pleasing her own husband (τὸ τῷ ἰδίῳ ἀρέσκειν ἀνδρί)'" (Stobaeus 4.587.8-10 W.-H.). Beyond this, while Musonius does not use this particular word, the concept of spouses pleasing one another plays an important role in his understanding of marriage; see Musonius, frag. 3.40.25-28 and 42.5-9 L. (11.1-5 and 11.20–12.2 H.), frag. 13A.88.17-29 L. (68.6-7 H.), and frag. 14.94.2-19 (73.17–75.5 H.).

373. See Konrad Weiss, "φέρω," in *TDNT* 9 (1974), 72-73, and Margaret M. Mitchell, *Paul and the Rhetoric of Reconciliation: An Exegetical Investigation of the Language and Composition of 1 Corinthians* (Louisville: Westminster/John Knox, 1991), 33-34. Arius in Stobaeus 2.100.15-23 W.-H. says the Stoics considered συμφέρον another term for "virtue," ἀρετή. In Paul, words from the συμφερ- root occur only in the Corinthian correspondence, and mostly in 1 Corinthians (6:12; 7:35; 10:23, 33; 12:7; 2 Cor. 8:10; 12:1). On 1 Cor. 6:12, see Deming, "The Unity of 1 Corinthians 5-6," *JBL* (1996): 306. In Matt. 19:10, in light of Jesus' ruling on divorce, the disciples conclude, "it is not beneficial to marry" (οὐ συμφέρει γαμῆσαι); see our analysis of this passage, above, pp. 94-95.

374. [Ocellus] (app. B), *De univ. nat.* 48.

375. Musonius, frag. 15.96.25 L. (15A.78.4-5 H.). Theon, *Progymnasmata* 125.15 S., uses the same phrase.

376. Hierocles 53.20, 25 v. A. (Stobaeus 4.503.18, 504.1 W.-H.). Cf. 54.14 v. A. (Stobaeus 4.505.4 W.-H.), "most profitable," λυσιτελέσατος.

377. Note that Theon, *Progymnasmata* 125.15-20 S. (cited above, chap. 2, n. 107), explains that in making a case for having children one will demonstrate, among other things, that marriage is "beneficial" (συμφέρον), while in refuting this thesis one will draw on the *opposite* arguments (ἐκ τῶν ἐναντίων).

Again, in 7:32-34 Paul uses words from the μεριμνα- stem five times in an elaborate wordplay, or paronomasia, with the verb μερίζομαι, "to be divided" (v. 34a). These are the adjective ἀμέριμνος, usually translated "without care" (v. 32), and the verb μεριμνάω, "to care, be concerned about something" (vv. 32, 33, 34 [twice]). While words from this stem are common in early Christian literature, especially in the synoptic Gospels, they also occur in documents relating to the philosophical discussion of marriage. Hierocles uses the noun μέριμνα in speaking of the "cares" of the busy householder;[378] and it occurs in a popular line from one of Menander's plays, advising the character Parmenon that marriage "brings many cares to one's life" (μερίμνας τῷ βίῳ πολλὰς φέρει).[379] The adjective ἀμέριμνος, in turn, appears both in the epigram by Posidippus that we cited above,[380] and in a maxim attributed to Menander: "Do not say that a wife has a life free from care" (βίος ἀμέριμνος [ἦν γυναι]κὶ μὴ λαλῇς).[381] Especially interesting in this respect is Luke 10:38-42, which I suggested in chapter 2 also shows influence of the Stoic-Cynic marriage debate.[382] Here, in Luke's description of Martha's "concern" for the duties of a householder, we find not only the verb form μεριμνάω, together with the verb περισπάομαι, "to be distracted," which is cognate with Paul's ἀπερισπάστως, but also a description of Mary sitting at Jesus' feet, listening to his words (παρακαθεσθεῖσα πρὸς τοὺς πόδας τοῦ κυρίου ἤκουεν τὸν λόγον αὐτοῦ), in which some scholars see a dramatization of Paul's notion of "undistracted devotion to the Lord" (εὐπάρεδρον τῷ κυρίῳ ἀπερισπάστως).[383]

378. Hierocles 53.30 v. A. (Stobaeus 4.504.7 W.-H.), cited by Balch, "Stoic Debates," 431, correcting Bultmann, "μεριμνάω," 590, who states that the word "is not found in the Stoa." Plutarch's remark (Moralia 830A [De vitando aere alieno]) that freedom from care (ἡ ἀμεριμνία) is the benefit of poverty may also be inspired by its Stoic context (829F, 830B-D). See also Cynic Epistle of Anacharsis 3 (40.6 M.), which admonishes the tyrant Hipparchus to turn from his drunkenness to a life concerned with the proper things, βίος μεριμνητικός.

379. Menander, frag. 575 K. (in Stobaeus 4.517.12-14 W.-H.), cited in Wettstein, 2:129.

380. Posidippus in Greek Anthology 9.359, "You have a marriage? — you will not be without cares (οὐκ ἀμέριμνος)!" (see pp. 157-58); cited in this connection by Weiß, Korintherbrief, 201 n. 6.

381. Menander, Sententiae 14.17 J.

382. See above, pp. 95-96.

383. E.g., Weiß, Korintherbrief, 205; Robertson and Plummer, 158; Niederwimmer, 113 n. 162; and Wolbert, 200-201 n. 76. Félix Puzo, "Marta y María: Nota exegética a Lc 10,38-42 y 1 Cor 7,29-35," Estudios Eclesiásticos 34 (1960): 856, has noted, furthermore, that Jesus' statement in Luke 10:42, that Mary has chosen "the good portion (μερίς)," uses a word cognate with Paul's "to be divided" (μερίζομαι), which is integral to the paronomasia in 1 Cor. 7:34. Likewise, Jutta Brutscheck, Die Maria-Marta-Erzählung: Eine redaktionskritische Untersuchung zu Lk 10,38-42,

Finally, Paul's use of paronomasia in 7:32-34 may itself point to Stoic influence. It is well known that Stoics used etymologies or simple assonance between words (i.e., false etymologies) to uncover the religious, moral, and metaphysical truths they believed were hidden in words.[384] With regard specifically to the marriage discussions, we know that Antipater was familiar with the derivation of "bachelor" (ἤθεος) from "godlike" (ἰσόθεος),[385] while Aelius Herodianus saw a connection between "male" (ἄρσην) and the verbs "to give drink" (ἄρδω) and "to water" (ἔρδω), reasoning that the male "waters" the female and her offspring.[386] With his use of assonance in verses 32-34 Paul is employing this same method to draw a connection between the ideas of "cares" (μεριμνα-) and "being divided" (μερίζομαι). The "truth" he intends to reveal through this wordplay is that Christians with too many worldly cares are divided in their allegiance to Christ.[387]

BBB 64 (Frankfurt and Bonn: Peter Hanstein, 1986), 147, points out that Jesus reprimands Martha in Luke 10:41 not because she is concerned with worldly things, but because these concerns distract her from Jesus' teaching: she, like the married man of 1 Cor. 7:33-34, is "divided." It is also possible that Paul's use of μεριμνάω, etc., has an apocalyptic bent; see above, n. 67.

384. See Heymann Steinthal, *Geschichte der Sprachwissenschaft bei den Griechen und Römern mit besonderer Rücksicht auf die Logik*, 2nd ed. (Berlin: Ferd. Dümmler, 1890), 1:331-32, Karl Barwick, *Probleme der stoischen Sprachlehre und Rhetorik*, Abhandlungen der sächsischen Akademie der Wissenschaften zu Leipzig: Philologisch-historische Klasse 49/3 (Berlin: Akademie, 1957), 60, and G. R. Boys-Stones, *Post-Hellenistic Philosophy: A Study of Its Development from the Stoics to Origen* (Oxford: Oxford University Press, 2001), 54-56 (with lit.). On Stoic interest in etymology generally, see Cicero, *De officiis* 1.23; Barwick, 29-33, 58-69, 70-79; and Ilona Opelt, "Etymologie," in *RAC* 6 (1966), 802-4. Bultmann, *Der Stil der paulinischen Predigt*, 76, suggests that the paronomasia here has come into Paul's writing via the Stoic-Cynic diatribe.

385. Antipater (app. A), line 41. This etymology was also known to Gavius Bassus (fl. mid–first century B.C.E.), who, in addition, is said to have derived "bachelors" *(caelibes)* from "gods" *(caelites)*, noting that both groups live carefree (Quintilian 1.6.36). Richard Reitzenstein, "Etymologika," in *PW* 6.1 [half-vol. 11] (1907), 809, sees Stoic influence in this last etymology, due to its use of word compounds.

386. From his *On Marriage and Life Together*, cited in *Etymologicum Magnum*, s.v. "ἄρσην."

387. For this same theme elsewhere in early Christianity, see Mark 4:19 par.; Matt. 6:25-34; Luke 21:34-36; and Bultmann, "μεριμνάω," 590-93. In Paul the adjective ἀμέριμνος occurs only here; the verb μερίζω only in the Corinthian correspondence, two of those occurrences being here and 1 Cor. 7:17 (the others are 1 Cor. 1:13 and 2 Cor. 10:13); and the verb μεριμνάω, which appears four times here, appears elsewhere only at 1 Cor. 12:25; Phil. 2:20; 4:6. The noun μέριμνα is found in Paul only at 2 Cor. 11:28.

Good and Better, Sin and Blessedness: 7:36-40

In the last five verses of chapter 7 Paul addresses the men who are evidently the prospective husbands of "the virgins" (vv. 25ff.),[388] and he advises widows concerning remarriage. To the men Paul says in verses 36-38:

> If someone thinks he is acting unseemly (ἀσχημονεῖν) toward his virgin, if he should be over the limit (ὑπέρακμος) and it must be thus (καὶ οὕτως ὀφείλει γίνεσθαι), he should do what he wants (ὃ θέλει ποιείτω), he does not sin (οὐχ ἁμαρτάνει), they should marry. But he who stands firm in his heart, not having necessity (μὴ ἔχων ἀνάγκην), but has power (ἐξουσία) over his own will, and has decided this in his own heart, to keep his own virgin, he will do well (καλῶς ποιήσει). So both he who marries his own virgin does well (καλῶς ποιεῖ), and he who does not marry will do better (κρεῖσσον ποιήσει).

Then to the widows Paul says in verses 39-40 that a woman, in his opinion, is "more blessed" (μακαριωτέρα) if she remains a widow, although she is free to marry whom she wants, as long as the man is a Christian ("only in the Lord").

Depending on how we interpret this difficult section, we may identify several elements that indicate Stoic influence. As in 7:28, it appears that Paul again finds it necessary to distinguish between Stoic and Christian notions of sin, reassuring the men that even in adverse circumstances (v. 26) one commits no *moral* error in marrying his virgin. Further, if we understand ἀσχημονεῖν ("to act unseemly"), ὑπέρακμος ("over the limit"), and οὕτως ὀφείλει γίνεσθαι ("it must be thus") in a sexual sense, then we have the same rationale for marriage as we saw in 7:9, and for which we have a parallel in Epictetus.[389] Epictetus, as we remember, justifies Crates' marriage to Hipparchia on account of Crates' "passionate love" for her (ἐξ ἔρωτος).[390] Perhaps also relevant here is a short epigram in the *Greek Anthology* in which Crates confesses that when neither hunger nor time can quell love's "flame" (φλόξ, cf. 7:9), one's remaining remedy is the "noose" (βρόχος).[391] In verse 35

---

388. The exact relationship between these men and their virgins remains a matter of controversy among scholars; see above, chap. 1, n. 133.

389. Alternately, ὑπέρακμος could be interpreted as referring to the virgin being "over marriageable age." On the difficulties in translating this word, see Walter Bauer, 1032 (s.v. "ὑπέρακμος").

390. Epictetus, *Discourses* 3.22.76.

391. *Greek Anthology* 9.479, θεραπεία σοι τὸ λοιπὸν ἠρτήσθω βρόχος. For the noose as a restraint in a moral context, see Hierocles 52.4-8 v. A. (Stobaeus 3.733.16–734.2 W.-H.).

it is precisely this "noose" (βρόχος) that Paul denies applying to the Corinthians' necks in advising the virgins not to marry. This is the only occurrence of βρόχος in the New Testament.

Again, Paul's use of ἀσχημονεῖν, "to act unseemly," may in itself point in the direction of Stoic and Cynic philosophy, for as Bonhöffer has noted, this served as one of the Stoics' "favorite expressions."[392] This word and its cognates occur several times in the *Cynic Epistles,* Musonius, Dio Chrysostom, and Epictetus,[393] while Paul, in good Stoic fashion, speaks of male homosexuality as ἡ ἀσχημοσύνη, "shamefulness," in Romans 1:27.[394] In 1 Corinthians 7:35-36, moreover, as part of the transition from his topic in verses 32-35 to that in verses 36-38, Paul contrasts ἀσχημονεῖν with τὸ εὔσχημον, "that which is seemly." This same antithesis between what is seemly and what is unseemly or shameful is also found in the *Cynic Epistles of Crates* and in Epictetus;[395] and it recurs in 1 Corinthians 12:23-24, in a metaphor depicting the church as a human body, which, in all likelihood, Paul has taken over from Stoic philosophy.[396] As for τὸ εὔσχημον, Arius reports that the Stoics saw "seemly living" (τὸ εὐσχημόνως ζῆν) as a source of well-being,[397] and they sometimes referred to "correct actions" (τὰ κατορθώματα) as "seemly actions" (εὐσχημονήματα).[398] Finally, in Paul's stipulation that widows remarry "only in the Lord," we are reminded of the concerns he addresses in 7:12-24 regarding Christians living with non-Christian spouses, which, as we saw, have counterparts among the Stoics.[399]

Beyond these points, Paul's manner of expression throughout 7:36-40 appears to draw on language and concepts that the Stoics used to describe the wise and good man. We may illustrate this through a comparison with a passage from Philo's treatise *That Every Good Man Is Free,* where he presents three syllogistic proofs in support of this (Stoic) thesis:

392. Bonhöffer, 135; cf. 109 and n. 1.

393. E.g., Epictetus, *Discourses* 3.22.2, 8, 15, 52. In 3.22.15 (cited in this connection by Heinrici, *Das erste Sendschreiben,* 213 n. 1), Epictetus maintains that unless the Cynic puts his sexual life in order, he will disgrace himself (ἀσχημονέω) before his public.

394. Cf. Musonius, frag. 12.86.3, 8-10 L. (64.4-7 H.).

395. *Cynic Epistle of Crates* 10 (62.4-5 M.); Epictetus, *Discourses* 2.5.23; cf. 4.9.5, 8-9.

396. See Conzelmann, 211 and n. 8 (lit.).

397. Arius in Stobaeus 2.80.10-11, ἐν ᾧπέρ ἐστιν τὸ εὐδαιμόνως [sc. ζῆν].

398. Arius in Stobaeus 2.97.5-9 W.-H.

399. In line with this, Thrall, "Problem," 134-35, 147-48, suggests a correspondence between 1 Cor. 7:39 and 2 Cor. 6:14a.

He who does everything with discernment does everything well (εὖ ποιεῖ πάντα). He who does everything well, does everything correctly. He who does everything correctly also acts without sin (ἀναμαρτήτως) . . . such that he will have power to do everything and live as he wants (ὥστ᾽ ἐξουσίαν σχήσει πάντα δρᾶν καὶ ζῆν ὡς βούλεται). The one to whom these things are allowed (ἔξεστιν), he would be free. . . . Again, the man whom it is not possible to compel or impede (μήτ᾽ ἀναγκάσαι μήτε κωλῦσαι), this one would not be a slave (δοῦλος). It is not possible to compel or impede the good man. Therefore the good man is not a slave. . . . Again, if he is compelled (ἀναγκάζεται), it is clear that he does something unwillingly. But . . .[400] actions are either correct actions (κατορθώματα) from virtue, or sins (ἁμαρτήματα) from vice, or middle things and indifferents (μέσα καὶ ἀδιάφορα). Those from virtue, he is not forced but does willingly. . . . Those from vice — from these he flees, nor does he do them in his dreams. Neither [is he forced to do] indifferent things, naturally, toward which his mind is in equilibrium. . . . Wherefore it is clear that he does nothing unwillingly, nor is he compelled. But if he were a slave he would be compelled; and hence the good man will be free.[401]

From this passage we can see that just as Philo describes the wise man as doing all things well (εὖ ποιεῖ πάντα),[402] having power (ἐξουσία) to act,[403] and not being compelled (ἀναγκάζομαι)[404] in any way, not even with regard to "indifferent" things, so Paul describes the man who does not marry as doing well (καλῶς ποιέω),[405] having power (ἐξουσία) over his own will, and having no necessity (ἀνάγκη) to marry — an act, as we saw earlier, that Stoics considered to be an "indifferent."[406] Likewise, just as Philo presents his wise man as

400. The text is unclear at this point.

401. Philo, *Quod omnis probus liber sit* 59-61.

402. See also Arius in Stobaeus 2.66.14–67.2 W.-H. (*SVF* 3.148.37–149.1); *SVF* 1.53.14; and Diogenes Laertius 7.125.

403. See also Diogenes Laertius 121 (cited above, pp. 149-50), where freedom is defined by the Stoics as "power of independent action" (ἐξουσία αὐτοπραγίας).

404. See also Philo, *Quod omnis probus liber sit* 30, 61; Arius in Stobaeus 2.99.19-20 W.-H. (*SVF* 1.53.3 and 3.150.10-11); and Cicero, *De finibus* 3.26 (*SVF* 3.153.17).

405. Paul's use of καλῶς instead of εὖ is in line with the general tendency among New Testament authors to favor the former over the latter, and in this case may have been further prompted by the catchword in 7:1, 26, "it is good for a man" (καλὸν ἀνθρώπῳ). According to Arius, Stoics considered τὸ καλῶς ζῆν to be the equivalent of τὸ εὖ ζῆν (Stobaeus 2.78.1-2 W.-H.). Interestingly, Mark 7:37 says Jesus was praised as one who "has done all things well" (καλῶς πάντα πεποίηκεν).

406. The presence of both Stoic and apocalyptic (7:26) meanings of ἀνάγκη in 1 Cor. 7 is still further evidence that the Corinthians have blended these two realms of thought.

acting without sin (ἀναμαρτήτως)⁴⁰⁷ and at the same time living as he wants (ζῆν ὡς βούλεται), so Paul tells the man who marries that he should do what he wants (ὃ θέλει ποιείτω),⁴⁰⁸ he does not sin (οὐχ ἁμαρτάνει), but rather, like the man who remains single, he does well (καλῶς ποιέω).⁴⁰⁹ On the other hand, we may assume from what Paul says in verse 36 that the man who marries, unlike the man who remains single, does "have necessity." This, however, would also have been possible to reconcile with the Stoic understanding of the wise man, for, according to Epictetus, passionate love was a "special circumstance" (περίστασις) that could compel a Cynic even as great as Crates to marry.⁴¹⁰ As Epictetus explains elsewhere, "one would consider even more worthy of pardon the man who is compelled by passion (τὸν ὑπ' ἔρωτος ἀναγκαζόμενον) to do something contrary to what seems proper — seeing the better thing but being powerless to pursue it — for he is held back by something forceful, and in some sense divine."⁴¹¹

Regarding the widows in 7:39-40, Paul's statement that a woman "is free to marry whom she wants" (ἐλευθέρα ἐστὶν ᾧ θέλει γαμηθῆναι) ultimately derives, as we have seen, from the legal formulae of divorce documents.⁴¹² Even so, Paul may have selected this particular turn of phrase because, once again, it resonates with the Stoic claim that the wise man is free to do as he wants (see above). Similarly, there is a possibility that Paul's judgment of a widow who remains single as "more blessed" (μακαριωτέρα) reflects the Stoic dogma

---

407. See also Arius in Stobaeus 2.99.7-8; 2.109.7; 2.112.20 (*SVF* 1.52.29-30; 3.163.12; 3.147.16-17); Epictetus, *Discourses* 4.8.6; and Diogenes Laertius 7.122.

408. Even closer to Paul than Philo's phrase is one from Dio Chrysostom, *Oration* 14.16 (*SVF* 3.87.2-3): "it is allowed to [the discerning] to do as they want" (ἐξεῖναι αὐτοῖς ποιεῖν ὡς ἐθέλουσι).

409. Stoics also spoke of not sinning as the counterpart of doing well: Arius in Stobaeus 2.99.7-12; 2.102.20–103.1 (*SVF* 1.52.29-32; 3.149.16-22); 2.106.6-11; and *SVF* 2.41.24-25.

410. Epictetus, *Discourses* 3.22.76, just cited regarding 7:36. See also *Cynic Epistle of Crates* 35 (88.4-5, 12 M.), where Crates is depicted as advising his friend Aper not to flee necessity (ἀνάγκη), which includes living with a body (ἀνάγκη μὲν γὰρ ζῆν μετὰ σώματος).

411. Epictetus, *Discourses* 4.1.147. The divine origin of passionate love to some extent explains the contradiction between what Epictetus says concerning Crates and his statement in *Discourses* 3.13.10-11 that the teachings of the philosophers (ὁ λόγος ὁ τῶν φιλοσόφων) give one peace even from eros. Not surprisingly, there is discussion among Stoics as to whether the wise man will become a "lover" (albeit of boys). See *SVF* 3.164.1-15; 3.180.13–181.30; Epictetus, *Discourses* 2.21.7; Diogenes Laertius 7.113; and Seneca, *Epistle* 116.5; 123.15; cf. Diogenes Laertius 10.117-20 (Epicurus).

412. See above, n. 161.

that the good and wise man is "blessed" (μακάριος).[413] While this term has a solid place in early Christianity, it is also found in popular maxims about marriage. A line from Menander reads, ". . . and a thing which they call blessed, I take no wife";[414] and one from Euripides runs: "Blessed is he, whoever marries and obtains a good wife; and he who does not marry."[415]

In all, with verses 36-40 Paul appears to be ending his discussion on marriage with an effort to reconcile himself to his Stoic-minded audience. Whatever they decide on the question of marriage, Paul is suggesting, they will be acting as wise men and women, even if their decisions should contradict his own best judgment (see vv. 25-26). Yet, in giving his congregation this latitude, Paul makes his preference clear enough. Although the man who marries "does well," he says, the one who does not marry "will do *better*,"[416] and the widow who forgoes a second marriage is "*more* blessed."[417] He then underscores this position with the closing remark, " — and I, for my part, think that I have the Spirit of God."[418]

---

413. See Arius in Stobaeus 2.100.3-5 (*SVF* 1.53.9 and 3.150.16); Cicero, *De finibus* 3.31 (*SVF* 1.92.20); Philo, *De praemiis et poenis* 122 (cited above, chap. 2, n. 199); and *SVF* 3.154.3; 3.188.15; 3.190.11-20.

414. Menander, frag. 3 K. (from *Brothers*, bk. 2), χῶ μακάριόν φα<σιν>, γυναῖκ' οὐ λαμβάνω.

415. Euripides in Stobaeus 4.525.16–526.1 W.-H., μακάριος, ὅστις εὐτυχεῖ γάμον λαβὼν ἐσθλῆς γυναικός· εὐτυχεῖ δ' ὁ μὴ λαβών. See also Euripedes, *Orestes* 602-4 (Stobaeus 4.528.1-4 W.-H.). The term μακάριος is seldom in Paul. Outside of the comparative in 1 Cor. 7:40, it occurs in Rom. 4:7, 8, and 14:22, the first two instances being quotations from Ps. 32:1-2, and the third inspired by the situation in Corinth (cf. 1 Cor. 8:7-13; 10:27–11:1). There is a possibility that in 7:40 the term also has apocalyptic overtones. See Luke 23:29, "Blessed (μακάριαι) are the sterile and the wombs that never conceived and breasts that never nursed"; and the discussion of the eschatological aspects of this word in Friedrich Hauck, "μακάριος, D.1," in *TDNT* 4 (1967), 367-69.

416. Cf. Epictetus's description of the man compelled by love as one who sees "the better thing" (τὸ ἄμεινον), but is unable to do it (*Discourses* 4.1.147, just cited).

417. This use of the comparative may have been occasioned, in part, by a maxim such as the one just cited from Euripides, which pronounces both the unmarried and the married "blessed." See also *Cynic Epistle of Crates* 35 (88.4-6, 15-17 M.), where Crates says the one who recognizes necessity (ἀνάγκη) and does it is "the blessed man" (ὁ μακάριος ἀνήρ).

418. Or " — and I also think that I have the Spirit of God," which, as noted above, is a Christian counterpart to Paul's Stoic-like claim of trustworthiness in 7:25. The very popular translation of 7:40b as "and I think *that I also* have the Spirit of God" (see, e.g., Weiß, *Korintherbrief*, 210; Lietzmann, 36, 37; Barrett, 186; and the English translations JB, NEB, REB, and NRSV) is grammatically impossible: κἀγώ, which is the nominative, goes with the verb δοκῶ; it cannot be construed with ἔχειν, as if the subject of an infinitive clause. This point is also noted by Robertson and Plummer, 161, but ignored, it would seem, by everyone else, in favor of the idea that Paul is battling "pneumatics" or spiritualistic gnostics in 1 Cor. 7, a theory we dismissed in chap. 1.

4 A Nonascetic Interpretation of Paul

OUR INVESTIGATION HAS NOW come full circle. In chapter 1 we evaluated recent scholarly attempts to define the theological motivation for celibacy in 1 Corinthians 7. As we saw, the vast majority of scholars attribute to Paul and the Corinthians an ascetic way of thinking, although there is little agreement as to its nature and provenance, and the arguments leading to this conclusion do not hold up under scrutiny. In chapter 2 we examined discussions of marriage and celibacy from the Hellenistic world that reflected a debate between Stoic and Cynic moralists. Outlining the various positions of this debate, we charted the development of these discussions from pre-Hellenistic Greece to their popularization in first-century Greece and Rome, through their limited acceptance by second-century Christian authors, to their neglect by Christians in subsequent centuries. Finally, in chapter 3 we examined 1 Corinthians 7 in light of these discussions, highlighting conceptual similarities as well as parallels in argumentation and manner of expression.

In the present chapter I would like to explore the implications of these similarities and parallels for the purpose of clarifying three aspects of 1 Corinthians 7: (a) the identity of Paul's audience, (b) Paul's own understanding of marriage and celibacy, and (c) his place in the history of Christian asceticism. Briefly stated, I will argue that Paul's audience in 1 Corinthians 7 held a theological outlook that combined Stoic philosophy with apocalyptic and sapiential traditions. From this I will show that Paul's discussion in 1 Corinthians 7 is considerably more subtle than scholars have hitherto perceived, and I will pursue my contention that Paul's understanding of marriage is predicated on a positive evaluation of celibacy rather than a negative evaluation of sexuality or a theology of sexual asceticism. Finally, challenging the place customarily assigned to Paul in the history of Christian asceticism, I will argue that Paul should be placed before and outside of this history, not within it as one of its founders.

Paul's Audience in 1 Corinthians 7

We must admit from the start that we have no direct information on the recipients of 1 Corinthians 7. We have only indirect information, in the form of Paul's statements to them. If we assume, however, that Paul accurately assessed the disposition of his readership, we may be able to reach some tentative conclusions as to who these Corinthians were.

Since our investigation in chapter 3 revealed that much of 1 Corinthians 7 bears a Stoic imprint, we can reasonably assume that Paul's audience both understood and was receptive to Stoic ideas. They appear to be familiar with Stoic objections to contracting close associations with outsiders, especially through marriage (7:12-14). They seem to acknowledge Stoic notions of true slavery and true freedom, which Paul couches for them in diatribe style (7:18-19, 21-22; cf. 7:16, 27-28); and they may have been familiar with the Stoic ideal of mental and emotional detachment (7:29b-31a).

Beyond this, Paul's audience seems to have had a considerable appreciation for arguments current in the Stoic-Cynic marriage debate. The statement at the very beginning of 1 Corinthians 7, that sexual intercourse is not good for a man, finds analogies in certain Cynic authors and may have come from the Corinthians' letter to Paul mentioned in 7:1a. The Corinthians also understand the argument used by some Stoics that forbade marriage in adverse circumstances due to the claims these circumstances made on one's time (7:5, 25-35). In Stoic fashion they questioned whether marriage in these situations was a sin (7:28, 36), and they appear to accept the Stoic claims that spouses have mutual ownership of each other's bodies (7:4), and that marriage is sometimes necessitated by the circumstance of passionate love (7:9, 36).

Not only does 1 Corinthians 7 evidence a knowledge of Stoic thought by its recipients, however, it also suggests an appreciation for specialized Stoic vocabulary and phraseology. The expressions καλὸν ἀνθρώπῳ (7:1, 26), ὁμοίως δὲ καί (7:3-4), and the verb σχολάζω (7:5) all point in this direction, as do ἀμέριμνος and μεριμνάω (7:32-34), ἀρέσκω (7:33-34), σύμφορον, ἀπερισπάστως (7:35), the pair εὔσχημον/ἀσχημονέω (7:35-36), and the several expressions descriptive of the wise man in 7:36-40:

ὃ θέλει ποιείτω
οὐχ ἁμαρτάνει
μὴ ἔχων ἀνάγκην
ἐξουσίαν ἔχει
καλῶς ποιέω
ἐλευθέρα ἐστὶν ᾧ θέλει γαμηθῆναι
μακαριωτέρα

As we have seen, it is even possible that the terms πιστός, ἄπιστος (7:12-15, 25), καλέω, κλῆσις (7:15-24), and the phrases τήρησις ἐντολῶν θεοῦ (7:19), τοῦτο δέ φημι, ὁ καιρὸς συνεσταλμένος ἐστίν, τὸ λοιπόν (7:29), and χρώμενοι . . . ὡς μὴ καταχρώμενοι (7:31) also reflect a degree of Stoic flavoring in Paul's speech for the benefit of his audience.

To conclude that the Corinthians were Stoics, however, is too facile, for according to Paul they identified themselves primarily as followers of Christ. This suggests a syncretistic or popularized form of Stoicism at Corinth, something that may also be indicated by the number of similarities between Paul's statements in 1 Corinthians 7 and popular maxims from the general philosophical milieu of the Greco-Roman world — maxims attributed to Menander, Euripides, Plato, and Crates. Still another important aspect of this chapter is Paul's concern in 7:2, 5-6 for extramarital sex, or *porneia*, which he combines with the Stoic notion of marital duty (7:3-5) and follows with the idea that continence within marriage is a gift from God (7:7). This, in turn, points to a Stoicism informed by Jewish wisdom traditions similar to what we find in Sirach and Philo. Lastly, we must account for the apocalyptic elements in 1 Corinthians 7, which we find in 7:5 (combined with Stoic concerns for marital duty and Judeo-Christian concerns for *porneia*) and in 7:26-31, where Paul employs "Stoic-like" apocalyptic materials as the "circumstances" of a Stoic argument against marriage. Given that our closest parallel to 7:5 comes from the *Testament of Naphtali,* a Stoicism that draws on wisdom and apocalyptic ideas suggests itself.

In sum, Paul's language and argumentation in 1 Corinthians 7 imply that the Corinthians to whom this chapter was addressed included Christians whose faith embodied a considerable degree of integration between Stoic and Judeo-Christian belief systems. If this conclusion is correct, it holds important implications for New Testament scholarship and for classical studies. Regarding the former, our conclusions about the identity of the recipients of 1 Corinthians 7 provide new options for understanding the Corinthian correspondence as a whole. By linking one of the interest groups at Corinth to Stoic tendencies within Christianity, our work here promises to clarify other sections of 1 and 2 Corinthians from this perspective. This, in turn, has the attractive potential of dislodging time-honored theories of gnostic and enthusiastic influence at Corinth — as we have done, in part, in chapter 1 — thereby clearing the way for a new assessment of the dynamics of the Corinthian church. Beyond this, our demonstration of Paul's own facility and willingness to work with Stoic systems of thought provides us with important information on the cultural, rhetorical, and sociological aspects of his westward mission into Macedonia, Achaia, and Rome.

As for classical studies, we may now add a new source to our store of information on late Stoicism. It is, moreover, a source with several attractive characteristics. It can be dated and geographically fixed with precision to the mid–first century c.e. in Corinth. Being part of a Christian document, it provides an example of Stoic morality as adapted for use in a non-Stoic system of thought, thereby further documenting the popularization of Stoicism in the period of the empire. And it offers us direct access to an actual controversy on marriage, thus distinguishing itself from the many theoretical treatments and narrative reports that we examined in chapter 2.

Paul's Understanding of Marriage and Celibacy

Preliminary Considerations

Before we attempt to define Paul's position on marriage and celibacy, there are several matters we must address. From our identification of Paul's audience, it is evident that 1 Corinthians 7 cannot be read as a general statement on marriage and celibacy, as if it were a theological "position paper" intended for the church universal. Inasmuch as Paul has chosen to express himself in the Stoic idiom of his readers, both his logic and the details of his discussion have been shaped by the Corinthians' own moral sensibilities. For an audience in Judea, Asia Minor, or Rome, Paul might have couched his understanding of marriage and celibacy in very different terms.

We must also take into account that 1 Corinthians 7 is part of an occasional letter, written in response to a particular set of circumstances at Corinth. As we have seen, Paul's words presuppose that the Corinthians are in the grips of an economic or political crisis of potentially apocalyptic import.

Again, to a congregation not beset by these circumstances, or beset by a different set of circumstances, Paul's response may have been substantially different. We are given some indication of this in his letter to the Romans, where apocalyptic expectations play a smaller role than in 1 Corinthians.[1] Here, in contrast to 1 Corinthians 7:8-9, 39-40, Paul's brief remarks on marriage and widowhood lack any preference for the celibate life.[2] We may also point to the letter of 1 Timothy, in which the author, presumably a follower of Paul, actually advises young widows to marry, his concern being the promotion of church order rather than battening down in anticipation of the end-time tribulation.[3] To the extent, therefore, that part of what Paul says in 1 Corinthians 7 is eschatologically conditioned, it must be viewed as representing an "interim ethic."

Our investigations in the previous chapter also demonstrate that Paul is dealing with a variety of issues in 1 Corinthians 7. These include *being* married versus *becoming* celibate, *being* married to a non-Christian versus obtaining a divorce, *remaining* celibate versus *marrying* a Christian, and *marrying* a Christian versus *marrying* a non-Christian. This, in turn, should alert us to the danger of construing any one statement in Paul's discussion as constituting his position "on marriage," as if his subject throughout was the institution of marriage per se. It should also alert us to the fact that Paul's treatment of marriage in 1 Corinthians 7 is not designed to cover everything. He gives no ruling, for example, regarding remarriage for Christians whose non-Christian husbands or wives have left them, nor is it clear that his judgment limiting widows to marriage "only in the Lord" applies to all other Christians as well (see below).

The diversity of issues Paul addresses in 1 Corinthians 7 has also put limitations on his discussion in another way. Inasmuch as he argues here in favor of marriage, here against it, here in favor of celibacy, here against it, he has restricted the range of what he can say. He does not want to set the value of marriage too high and thereby discourage all forms of celibacy, nor does he wish to praise celibacy in a way that undermines the institution of marriage.

Hence Paul offers no laudation of the ends of marriage, nor does he enumerate the advantages of having a wife to watch over one's affairs. This twofold appeal also accounts for the absence of any direct mention of childbearing, a topic dear to many Stoics but anathema to those who took the Cynic

---

1. Only Rom. 13:11-14, which is parenetic and much less urgent than 1 Cor. 1:7-8; 7:26-31; 15:51-58.

2. Rom. 7:1-3.

3. 1 Tim. 5:14.

stance against marriage.[4] Even though verses 4, 14, and 34 indicate that having children was a concern for the Corinthians, Paul never addresses the matter squarely. He says only that husbands and wives must maintain sexual relations to the degree that it is demanded by either partner — a sure recipe for pregnancy in the ancient world — and that unmarried women have the good fortune of being useful to the Lord with their bodies as well as their spirits. It cannot be simply that Paul considered childbearing a moot point in view of the possible nearness of the end, or that he passes over this subject because it was a Stoic topos directed at citizens for the purpose of securing the future of their city-states, for which Paul had little interest. That would not explain why, in promoting celibacy, he forgoes the Cynic argument that raising children is one of the onerous burdens of marriage, which would have coincided nicely with apocalyptic traditions on the hardship of pregnancy and nursing in the end times. Instead, we must interpret Paul's silence on childbearing as his conscious avoidance of the subject, since its endorsement would have weakened his arguments in favor of celibacy, while a statement against it would have undercut his insistence on the necessity of conjugal relations.[5]

Given the task Paul has set for himself, it is not at all surprising that much of what he says in favor of marriage in 1 Corinthians 7 draws on the adverse consequences of prolonged celibacy. As Chadwick saw, "the chapter is wholly intelligible as a rearguard action."[6] Understandably, then, if somewhat ironi-

---

4. This absence has been noted by many scholars, e.g., Johannes Weiß, *Der erste Korintherbrief*, MeyerK 5 (Göttingen: Vandenhoeck & Ruprecht, 1925), 172; Wolfgang Schrage, *Die konkreten Einzelgebote in der paulinischen Paränese: Ein Beitrag zur neutestamentlichen Ethik* (Gütersloh: Gütersloh, 1961), 220 n. 157; and Roy Bowen Ward, "Musonius and Paul on Marriage," *NTS* 36 (1990): 286-87.

5. Cf. O. Larry Yarbrough, *Not Like the Gentiles: Marriage Rules in the Letters of Paul*, SBLDS 80 (Atlanta: Scholars, 1985), 107-8, and H. Chadwick, "'All Things to All Men' (I Cor. ix.22)," *NTS* 1 (1954/55): 268: "A remarkable feature of the chapter as a whole is the startling absence of any appeal to the doctrine of Creation. But to have made any such appeal would have put an unmistakable and decisive distance between Paul and the ascetic [*sic*] party at Corinth, and this he was manifestly anxious to avoid."

6. Chadwick, 264. Cf. William A. Heth, "Unmarried 'For the Sake of the Kingdom' (Matthew 19:12) in the Early Church," *Grace Theological Journal* 8 (1987): 69: "in all probability 1 Corinthians 7 is primarily a rehabilitation of the marital union in the eyes of the Corinthian ascetics"; and Peter Brown, *The Body and Society: Men, Women, and Sexual Renunciation in Early Christianity*, Lectures in the History of Religions, n.s., 13 (New York: Columbia University Press, 1988), 54-55: "It had not been Paul's concern to praise marriage; he strove, rather, to point out that marriage was safer than unconsidered celibacy."

cally, the delicate balance of Paul's response to the Corinthians, achieved by
so much judicious weighing of argument and counterargument, has been
taken by the church fathers and modern interpreters alike as his pronouncement of damnation on marriage through faint praise.

The foregoing considerations require us to see 1 Corinthians 7 as the
work of a practical church administrator who has entered the fray because
certain activities at Corinth threatened the stability of the church there. It is a
mistake, in other words, to interpret Paul's statements as the deliberations of
a systematic theologian formulating a general definition of Christian marriage. Although this puts limitations on our ability to gauge Paul's own understanding of marriage and celibacy, we may nonetheless draw conclusions
on some specific matters. We will begin with Paul's understanding of marriage and celibacy for married Christians and then turn to his position for
single Christians.

Marriage and Celibacy for Married Christians

Regarding marriage and celibacy for those already married, Paul assumes,
first of all, that Christians will honor all obligations of their marriage relationships to the extent that it is possible. This is true even under the potentially apocalyptic conditions presupposed in 1 Corinthians 7, whether that
means enduring physical or emotional hardship (7:28, 29-31) or being divided
in one's allegiances to the Lord (7:32-34). Sexual relations especially must
continue so as to avoid unfaithfulness by one of the spouses, even, presumably, if this results in the birth of children (7:3-7). Divorce is impossible, being
a violation of Christ's commandment (7:10-11).[7]

On the other hand, Paul recognizes that within the limits of a person's ca-
pacity certain acts of devotion to Christ, such as prayer, can take precedence
over sexual intercourse (although not marriage, 7:5). Because the individual
sexual needs of the marriage partners may differ, however, this must be done
by mutual agreement for a set period of time. Paul rejects outright the extreme position he cites in 7:1b: "it is good for a man not to touch a woman."
The ability to remain abstinent within marriage, according to Paul, is a gift

---

7. Completely unsupported by the text is Brown's contention that "fornication and its
avoidance did not preoccupy Paul greatly. He was concerned to emphasize, rather, the continu-
ing validity of all social bonds" (55, citing 1 Cor. 7:17, 21; cf. Brown, 54, 56-57).

from God. It is not something one spouse can demand of the other (7:7). Paul is a realist here, and assumes that extramarital liaisons would be the result of such an ascetic experiment (7:5). Practically speaking, however, Paul also allows for the separation of a couple in order to accommodate the unwillingness of one of the partners (he mentions only the wife) to continue the marriage. But this separation must not evolve into a divorce (7:11).

Although certain members of the Corinthian church evidently maintained that marriages between Christians and non-Christians were a special case, and therefore required separate consideration, Paul contends that the same standards apply there as well. Having an unbelieving spouse is no grounds for divorce, even in times of hardship (7:12-13). There is nothing morally "unclean" about a non-Christian husband or wife; in fact, the non-Christian's marriage to a Christian has "sanctified" the non-Christian (7:14). Neither is marriage to a non-Christian a form of slavery in any true, Christian sense (7:15, 17-24), and there is always the possibility that a Christian will convert his or her spouse (7:16). Rather than seeking a divorce, a Christian should work to preserve the couple's original marital peace (7:12-13, 15). This is a matter of keeping God's commandments (7:15) and of recognizing the grace inherent in one's Christian call (7:17-24). If the non-Christian decides to leave, however, that is his or her prerogative (7:15).

Marriage and Celibacy for Single Christians

Just as some married Corinthians seem to have argued that the threat of end-time tribulations justified divorce or the cessation of conjugal relations, Paul sees these dire circumstances as an impediment to initiating new marriages. Paul's treatment of whether single Christians should marry or remain celibate is thus based wholly on the expediency of the times — and this cannot be stressed enough. As our investigation in chapter 3 demonstrated, what Paul says in 7:27-28, in 7:29-31, in 7:32-35, and in 7:36-40 depends equally on the "necessity" (ἀνάγκη) he speaks of in 7:26. To overlook this is to overlook the underlying rationale of his argument.[8]

---

8. This has been acknowledged by a few scholars, e.g., Rudolf Schnackenburg, "Die Ehe nach dem Neuen Testament," in *Theologie der Ehe: Veröffentlichung des Ökumenischen Arbeitskreises evangelischer und katholischer Theologen*, ed. Gerhard Krems and Reinhard Mumm (Regensburg: Friedrich Pustet; Göttingen: Vandenhoeck & Ruprecht, 1969), 21, 23, 24;

To discourage his readers from *initiating* marriage in this time of crisis, Paul points out that harsh conditions foster material need — "tribulation in the flesh" — among the married (7:28). The positive aspects of married life such as sexual gratification and the ownership of goods are considerably reduced (7:29-31), while the responsibilities of marriage are made more difficult to fulfill. Those who marry will have concerns that divide their interests and draw them away from the Lord (7:32-34). Given the uncertainty of the times, Paul concludes, devotion to the Lord should take precedence over *becoming* married (7:35).

Yet Paul exercises caution in advocating this apocalyptically inspired celibacy. His words, he is careful to explain, do not represent a commandment of the Lord but the advice of a church leader who has sought guidance from the Holy Spirit (7:25, 40). If Christians feel their sexual drives demand it, they should proceed with plans to marry, even in adverse circumstances (7:36). Here again Paul shows himself to be a realist with regard to sexuality. Nowhere does he make the absolute claim that celibacy under such conditions is "best." Instead, he reasons that remaining single is "better" than subjecting oneself to almost certain hardship (7:28, 38), although marrying is "better" than being overcome with sexual desire (7:9; cf. 7:36). In Paul's opinion getting married, even in the worst of times, is a morally commendable action. Both the person who marries and the person who remains single "do well," and both are described as acting wisely (7:36-40).

Lastly, Paul leaves us with an elusive remark on Christians marrying non-Christians. For widows, he says, such a marriage is out of the question. Widows may marry "only in the Lord" (7:39). Whether this applies to other Christians, however, we cannot be sure. Passages such as 1 Corinthians 5:9-11, 7:12-14, 2 Corinthians 6:14–7:1, and similar texts from Jewish and Stoic authors allow us to speculate as to how some of the Corinthians might have answered this question, but nothing Paul himself says warrants the application of this rule beyond widows. Perhaps, given the opportunity, Paul would have extended this rule to cover other persons. It is also possible, however, that he saw widows, or even women in general, as a special case, reasoning that they

---

but it is more often denied, e.g., Kurt Niederwimmer, *Askese und Mysterium: Über Ehe, Ehescheidung und Eheverzicht in den Anfängen des christlichen Glaubens,* FRLANT 113 (Göttingen: Vandenhoeck & Ruprecht, 1975), 111-13; John G. Gager, Jr., "Functional Diversity in Paul's Use of End-Time Language," *JBL* 89 (1970): 331, 337.

were particularly susceptible to apostasy once they had been incorporated into a non-Christian household.[9]

Paul in the History of Christian Asceticism

Coming finally to Paul's place in the history of Christian asceticism, it is essential for us to be in the clear regarding two findings of this study. First, Paul's reason for both condoning and promoting celibacy at Corinth was to keep this congregation, during a period of severe tribulation, as free as possible from the distractions associated with married life in the ancient world. And second, his theological justification for this agenda depends heavily on Stoic and apocalyptic traditions of thought, neither of which denigrate human sexuality or espouse the renunciation of sexual relations as the goal of celibacy.[10] This means that sexual abstinence was not, as far as Paul was concerned, an aspiration in itself. It was only a secondary feature of celibacy, the necessary by-product of two things: a desire to live the unencumbered, single life, and the Judeo-Christian prohibition of extramarital sexual relations.[11] Indeed, Paul advises the Corinthians against the attempt to censure their (God-given) sexual drives, maintaining that if one is unsure of his or her ability to remain continent, then marriage is the better choice. Celibacy for Paul

9. See, e.g., the discussion in Margaret Y. MacDonald, "Early Christian Women Married to Unbelievers," *SR* 19 (1990): 221-34. For this reason it is also impossible to say whether the mixed marriages described in 7:12-13 were contracted (a) between two pagans, after which one of them converted to Christianity, (b) between a Christian and a pagan, or (c) between two Christians, after which one left the faith — especially since we do not know if the Corinthians had always known and followed Paul's rule.

10. On this see Wolfgang Schrage, "Die Stellung zur Welt bei Paulus, Epiktet und in der Apokalyptik: Ein Beitrag zu 1 Kor 7,29-31," *ZTK* 61 (1964): 149-50 and n. 76; Rosemary Radford Ruether, "Is Celibacy Eschatological? The Suppression of Christian Radicalism," in *Liberation Theology: Human Hope Confronts Christian History and American Power* (New York: Paulist, 1972), 51-64; cf. Peter Nagel, *Die Motivierung der Askese in der alten Kirche und der Ursprung des Mönchtums,* TU 95 (Berlin: Akademie, 1966), 20-21.

11. So also the celibacy of Jesus, John the Baptist, and the Essenes. Likewise, Epictetus's Cynic practices abstinence as the result of foreswearing marriage, at the same time professing a low opinion of other types of sexual relations — but not human sexuality per se. See *Discourses* 3.22.13, 95; cf. 4.1.143; 2.18.15-18. Epictetus's views may well reflect his teacher's strict stance against extramarital relations; see Musonius, frag. 12, *On Sexual Relations.* Cf. Elaine H. Pagels, "Paul and Women: A Response to Recent Discussion," *JAAR* 42 (1974): 542, who notes that Paul "refuses to accord religious value to celibacy," i.e., sexual asceticism — see next note.

was thus not the equivalent of sexual asceticism, a regime of self-induced privation and hardship; and although we are much less informed as to the Corinthians' theology of celibacy, it would appear that they were in basic agreement with Paul on this point.[12]

As Christianity moved into the second century, however, Christian authors began promoting a substantially different understanding of celibacy.[13] Their motivations for celibacy arose from a view of human existence which maintained that the soul was trapped within the body and thereby hindered from attaining moral perfection by the constraints of a person's physical nature. This set the aspirations of the soul in opposition to the urgings of the body, including the sexual drive. While this particular brand of body-soul dualism had been a part of Greek philosophical thinking since the time of Pythagoras,[14] it took on a new significance in the second century, as if surfacing in the world of ideas for the first time. It was propounded widely by Neoplatonists, and many leading Christians incorporated it into their theologies.

For this reason Christian discussions on marriage begin to chart a new course. For the first time a negative evaluation of human sexuality becomes an important consideration. The primary focus of these discussions is no longer the alienation of the individual from the divine will through the social and economic obligations of marriage, but alienation from God on an anthropological level. Unlike Stoics, Cynics, Paul, or the authors of apocalyptic and wisdom literature, all of whom discussed marriage in terms of conflicting allegiances within a person's "lifestyle" (βίος), this new generation of moral-

12. That such a distinction exists between celibacy and asceticism is often overlooked by scholars of early Christianity. See, e.g., David L. Balch, "Backgrounds of I Cor. vii: Sayings of the Lord in Q; Moses as an Ascetic ΘΕΙΟΣ ΑΝΗΡ in II Cor. iii," NTS 18 (1971/72): 351: "There was, at the time of the rise of Christianity, a growing concern for *sexual asceticism*. . . . Celibacy became common enough for Augustus to attempt to correct it from 18 B.C. to A.D. 9 through a series of laws" (emphasis mine). The Augustan marriage legislation, however, was directed at the refusal of Roman citizens to marry, not their foreswearing of sexual relations. By contrast, Walter Schmithals, *Gnosticism in Corinth: An Investigation of the Letters to the Corinthians* (Nashville and New York: Abingdon, 1971), 235 n. 158, writes: "Indeed, fundamentally, Paul does not think ascetically, even when, naturally, he shows no high regard of marriage. Asceticism, however, is opposition to the sexual urge itself, which Paul precisely does *not* command" (emphasis Schmithals's) — to which Niederwimmer, 84 n. 20, characteristically and quite wrongly replies, "That is a non sequitur."

13. On this development, see Elizabeth A. Clark, *Reading Renunciation: Asceticism and Scripture in Early Christianity* (Princeton: Princeton University Press, 1999), 39-42 and passim.

14. E.g., Plato, *Cratylus* 400B-C.

ists and theologians saw the problem as one of conflicting allegiances within a person's very being, between the sexual urgings of the body and the soul's yearning for God.[15]

Among many leaders of the church, human sexuality came to be seen as part of a fallen creation — a creation, as some would remark, that was brought to its knees by the carnal union of its first man and woman. The neat dichotomy that Paul could assume between conjugal relations and *porneia* still held, but the dividing line between them now moved in and out of focus. To some the activity of sexual intercourse suggested rebellion against God, surrounding the institution of marriage with inchoate misgivings and suspicions. While they continued to denounce pagan sexual practices as ungodly, unholy, impure, unrighteous, and sinful, a positive appraisal of Christian sexual practices as godly, holy, pure, righteous, and sinless came hard to these church leaders, and it chafed.[16] More radical Christians, by contrast — docetics, Marcionites, Montanists, Encratites, and various types of gnostics — denounced sexual intercourse altogether and forbade marriage.

Yet despite their suspicions about the sexual component of marriage, the orthodox were unwilling to take this final step. Unlike their heretical counterparts, who proclaimed the material world to be the handiwork of an evil or misguided Demiurge, and procreation the furtherance of his deranged will, the orthodox continued to affirm the God of the Old Testament, maker of heaven and earth, whose first decree to humanity was to "be fruitful and multiply." If the creation was in a fallen state, it remained nonetheless God's creation, and procreation continued to have a part in the divine plan.

Beginning in the second century, or shortly before, a new dynamic thus pervaded Christian thinking on marriage, pitting an aversion to sexuality, based on a material dualism, against the view that procreation was divinely sanctioned. Among the orthodox, a resolution of sorts came in the form of a graded standard of morality by which theologians declared marriage to be a legitimate, though lesser manner of life. Although marriage was perhaps nec-

---

15. Paul, of course, also knows an anthropological alienation from God (e.g., Gal. 5:16-24; Rom. 7:13-25), but this does not involve a rejection of the physical self or human sexuality, nor does it enter into his thinking on marriage; cf. Leander E. Keck and Victor Paul Furnish, *The Letters of Paul*, Interpreting Biblical Texts (Nashville: Abingdon, 1984), 85: "None of Paul's allegedly negative views of sex and marriage . . . is based on either body-soul/spirit dualism or on female inferiority."

16. See, e.g., Elizabeth A. Clark, "Antifamilial Tendencies in Ancient Christianity," *Journal of the History of Sexuality* 3 (1995): 356-80.

essary for the majority, it nevertheless involved a Christian in the question-able activity of sexual intercourse. Consistent with this, the Fathers promoted the Stoic position that intercourse should be performed only for procreation. Unlike the Stoics, however, the Fathers did not encourage physical intimacy or large families, but small families and decreased sexual activity. Celibacy, on the other hand, was promoted by the Fathers as the preferred way of life for the believer. It not only allowed one to devote oneself without distraction to the service of Christ, but it also made possible the achievement of a goal quite unknown to Paul, namely, a state of holiness won through total sexual absti-nence.[17]

Returning to the question of Paul's place in the history of Christian ascet-icism, we see that a significant gulf separates him from patristic thought. Paul's conception of marriage and celibacy was shaped by a worldview steeped in traditional Greek ideals for life in the city-state. Rather than com-manding a place at the start of the Christian ascetic tradition, Paul is one of the last participants in a marriage discussion whose antecedents reach as far back as the pre-Socratics. Fully within the parameters of that discussion, Paul assesses the value of marriage and celibacy with regard to prevailing circum-stances. For him it is not a matter of choosing a lower or higher standard of morality, but of forestalling important decisions in life on the basis of expedi-ency. For later Christians, however, the focus would shift to a dualistic under-standing of the world, cleaving the individual into body and soul, and de-manding a choice between sexuality and spirituality. This difference between Paul and the patristic authors is real and cannot be explained away either by such theories as we examined in chapter 1 or by the insistence of the Fathers themselves that their positions derive from the apostle's writings. While the Fathers often appear to speak the same language as Paul, their conceptual world is so different that even the words "sin," "holiness," "marriage," and "fornication" take on theological implications quite beyond anything Paul imagined.

---

17. See, e.g., the discussion in Rosemary Radford Ruether, "Misogynism and Virginal Fem-inism in the Fathers of the Church," in *Religion and Sexism: Images of Women in the Jewish and Christian Traditions* (New York: Simon and Schuster, 1974), 150-83. On the wholesale ascetic re-interpretation of Paul, see Clark, *Reading Renunciation,* esp. 259-329.

Antipater of Tarsus

From His *On Marriage*

The Greek text presented in this appendix is also available in *SVF* 3.254.23–257.10 and Stobaeus 4.507.6–512.7 Wachsmuth and Hense. The only other complete translation of this text is Emiel Eyben, "De latere Stoa over het huwelijk" (in Dutch), *Hermeneus: Tijdschrift voor antieke Cultuur* 50 (1978): 22-29, although Konrad Gaiser, *Für und wider die Ehe* (Munich: Heimeran, 1974), 36-39, is nearly complete. Partial translations exist in Max Pohlenz, ed. and trans., *Stoa und Stoiker,* Die Bibliothek der alten Welt: Griechische Reihe (Zürich: Artemis, 1950), 1:185-87 (sometimes lapsing into paraphrase); and Hildegard Cancik-Lindemaier, "Ehe und Liebe: Entwürfe griechischer Philosophen und römischer Dichter," in *Zum Thema Frau in Kirche und Gesellschaft,* ed. Hubert Cancik (Stuttgart: Katholisches Bibelwerk, 1972), 58-59. E. Vernon Arnold, *Roman Stoicism: Being Lectures on the History of the Stoic Philosophy with Special Reference to Its Development within the Roman Empire* (Cambridge: Cambridge University Press, 1911), 318-19, offers a running paraphrase. None of these translations makes use of Hense's edition of the text.

Ὁ εὐγενὴς καὶ εὔψυχος νέος, ἔτι δ' ἥμερος καὶ πολιτικός, θεωρῶν διότι τέλειος
οἶκος καὶ βίος οὐκ ἄλλως δύναται γενέσθαι, ἢ μετὰ γυναικὸς καὶ τέκνων·
ἀτελὴς γὰρ¹ ὥσπερ πόλις, οὐχ ἡ ἐκ γυναικῶν μόνον, ἀλλὰ καὶ ἐκ ψιλῶν
ἀνδρῶν· ὃν τρόπον τε ποίμνη ἐπιγονὴν μὴ ἔχουσα οὐ καλὴ οὐδὲ βουκόλιον
5 εὐθηνοῦν, πολὺ μᾶλλον οὐδὲ πόλις οὐδ' οἰκία· ταῦτα δὲ² δὴ κατανενοηκὼς ὁ
εὐγενὴς καὶ ὡς φύσει πολιτικὸν γενόμενον, συναύξειν τὴν πατρίδα δεῖ³ <. . .>.

Καὶ γὰρ οὐκ ἂν ἄλλως δύναιντο αἱ πόλεις σῴζεσθαι, εἰ μὴ οἱ βέλτιστοι
ταῖς φύσεσι τῶν πολιτῶν [ἢ]⁴ τῶν γενναίων παῖδες, τῶν προτέρων⁵ καθαπερεὶ
φύλλων καλοῦ δένδρου ἀπομαραινομένων καὶ ἀπορρεόντων,⁶ οὗτοι καθ'
10 ὥραν γαμοῖεν, καθαπερεί τινας γενναίους βλαστοὺς διαδόχους τῇ πατρίδι
καταλείποντες, οἳ⁷ θάλλειν αὐτὴν ἀεὶ ποιοῖεν, καὶ τὴν ἀκμὴν ἀΐδιον
φυλάττοιεν, καὶ ὅσον ἐφ' ἑαυτοῖς μηδέποτ' εὐεπίθετον τοῖς ἐχθροῖς.⁸
στοχαζόμενοι τοῦ καὶ ζῶντες καὶ μεταλλάξαντες ἀμύνειν τῇ πατρίδι καὶ
βοηθεῖν,⁹ τῶν ἀναγκαιοτάτων καὶ πρώτων καθηκόντων νομίζουσι τὸ
15 συγκραθῆναι εἰς γάμον, πᾶν μὲν τὸ τῇ φύσει ἐπιβάλλον σπεύδοντες ἐπιτελεῖν,
πολὺ δὲ μάλιστα τὸ εἰς τὴν τῆς πατρίδος σωτηρίαν καὶ αὔξησιν ἀνῆκον, καὶ ἔτι
μᾶλλον εἰς τὴν τῶν θεῶν τιμήν. εἰ γὰρ ἐκλείποι τὸ γένος, τίς τοῖς θεοῖς θύσει;
λύκοι τινὲς ἢ ταυροκτόνων γένος λεόντων.¹⁰

Συμβέβηκε δὲ καὶ τὸν μὴ πεῖραν ἐσχηκότα γαμετῆς γυναικὸς καὶ τέκνων
20 ἄγευστον εἶναι τῆς ἀληθινωτάτης καὶ γνησίου εὐνοίας. αἱ μὲν γὰρ ἄλλαι φιλίαι
ἢ φιλοστοργίαι ἐοίκασι ταῖς τῶν ὀσπρίων ἤ τινων ἄλλων παραπλησίων κατὰ

1. ἀτελὴς γὰρ: I construe ἀτελής with βίος, or οἶκος καὶ βίος as a collective. Von Arnim and
Hense add οἰκία after γὰρ.

2. ταῦτα δὲ δὴ: von Arnim and Hense (following Halm) emend this to the more common
ταῦτά τε δή.

3. δεῖ <. . .>.: This clause lacks a verb, perhaps something like ἡγεῖται, as I suggest in the
translation. Hense indicates a lacuna after δεῖ. Von Arnim inserts a raised dot here and begins a
parenthesis with the following καὶ γὰρ, which ends after βοηθεῖν in line 14, a solution I find unlikely.

4. ἢ: I delete, following von Arnim and Hense.

5. προτέρων: emended to πατέρων by von Arnim.

6. Cf. Homer, Iliad 6.145-49; and Musaeus 2 B5 Diels-Kranz.

7. οἳ: emended to καὶ by von Arnim.

8. The full stop is my punctuation; von Arnim has a raised dot; Hense has a comma.

9. The comma is my punctuation; von Arnim has a close parenthesis; Hense has a full stop
followed by τῶν <οὖν> ἀναγκαιοτάτων κτλ. (See n. 3.)

10. ταυροκτόνων . . . λεόντων: Hense ("Zu Antipatros von Tarsos," Rh. Mus., n.s., 73 [1920/
24]: 304) regards the similarity of this phrase with Sophocles, Philoctetes 400-401, as perhaps
only a coincidence; cf. Cicero, De finibus 3.66.

THE NOBLE AND COURAGEOUS youth, being, moreover, civilized and political, perceiving that household and life cannot otherwise be complete except with a wife and children — for it is incomplete as in the case of a city-state, not only one composed entirely of women, but also one composed of single men: in the same manner that a flock is not good when it has no increase, nor a herd when it does not thrive, much more so neither a city-state nor a household — and so, having observed these things, and that he is political by nature, the noble person <holds> that he must assist in increasing the fatherland.

For, surely, the city-states would not otherwise be able to prosper unless the best children, with regard to character, of the true citizens — even as the predecessors of the latter "wither and fall off," just like leaves of a good tree — unless these children would marry in due season, bequeathing, just like some true shoots, successors to the fatherland who would make it thrive eternally and protect its vigor to the extent it depended on them, never exposed to its enemies.[1] Endeavoring, both while living and having passed away, to bolster the fatherland and assist it, they consider being united in marriage among the primary and most necessary actions that are fitting, being eager to fulfill every task laid on them by nature, most especially that which furthers the safekeeping and proper growth of the fatherland, and, even more, the honor of the gods — for if the race would die out, who will sacrifice to the gods? Some wolves or a race of bull-killing lions?

Moreover, it is the case that he who has not experienced a wedded wife and children has not tasted the truest and genuine goodwill.[2] For the other friends or friendly affections of life are like the juxtaposed mixings of beans

---

1. Four generations are in view here, which is the extent of a city's life span at any given time: older citizens, leading citizens, sons, grandsons.

2. Antipater's word choice, "proper growth," "wedded wife," and "genuine/legitimate goodwill," emphasizes his view that these benefits belong exclusively to legal marriage and legitimate children. Cf. Aristotle, *Athenaion politeia* 4.2.7; Philo, *De Abrahamo* 194.

τὰς παραθέσεις μίξεσιν, αἱ δ᾽ ἀνδρὸς καὶ γυναικὸς ταῖς δι᾽ ὅλων κράσεσιν, ὡς
οἶνος ὕδατι· καὶ τοῦτο <σῶζον τὴν οἰκείαν φύσιν>¹¹ ἔτι μὲν μίσγεται δι᾽ ὅλων.
οὐ γὰρ μόνον τῆς οὐσίας καὶ τῶν φιλτάτων πᾶσιν ἀνθρώποις τέκνων καὶ τῆς
25 ψυχῆς, ἀλλὰ καὶ τῶν σωμάτων οὗτοι μόνοι κοινωνοῦσι. καὶ κατ᾽ ἄλλον δὲ
τρόπον εἰκότως μεγίστη ἐστίν. αἱ μὲν γὰρ ἄλλαι κοινωνίαι καὶ ἑτέρας τινὰς
ἀποστροφὰς ἔχουσι· ταύτας "δ᾽ ἀνάγκη πρὸς μίαν ψυχὴν βλέπειν,"¹² τὴν τοῦ
ἀνδρός. προστίθεται γὰρ σώζοντος¹³ πατρὸς καὶ μητρὸς μὴ ἀγνώμονος ἕνα
τοῦτον σκοπὸν τοῦ βίου ποιεῖσθαι καὶ τέλος, τούτῳ ἀρέσκειν, αὐτῶν <δὲ>¹⁴
30 τῶν γονέων ἑκατέρων παραχωρούντων ἑκουσίως τὰ πρῶτα τῆς εὐνοίας
ἀπονέμειν, τὴν μὲν τῷ ἀνδρί, τὸν δὲ τῇ γυναικί. οὐκ ἀπείρως <δὲ>¹⁵ τῆς πρὸς
γυναῖκα συμβιώσεως καὶ ὁ Εὐριπίδης εἰς ταῦτα ἀποβλέψας καὶ ἀποθέμενος
τὴν ἐν τῷ γράφειν μισογυνίαν ταῦτ᾽ εἴρηκεν·

γυνὴ γὰρ ἐν νόσοισι καὶ κακοῖς πόσει
35   ἥδιστόν ἐστι, δώματ᾽ ἢν οἰκῇ καλῶς,
ὀργήν τε πραΰνουσα <καὶ δυσθυμίας
ψυχὴν μεθιστᾶσ᾽·>¹⁶ ἡδὺ καὶ ἀπάται φίλων.¹⁷

τυγχάνει δὲ καὶ ἡρωϊκὸν τὸ πρᾶγμα.¹⁸

11. σῶζον . . . φύσιν: my addition, based on such texts as Alexander Aphrodesia, *De mixtione* 217.35 and 218.5-6. Hense indicates a lacuna after καὶ τοῦτο. Von Arnim emends the manuscript reading ἔτι μὲν to ἐπιμένων; Pohlenz (ed. and trans., *Stoa und Stoiker*, vol. 1, *Die Gründer, Panaitios, Poseidonios*, Die Bibliothek der alten Welt: Griechische Reihe [Zürich: Artemis, 1950], 371) suggests ὡς οἶνος ὕδατι καὶ τοῦτο <ἐκείνῳ> κτλ. My assumption is that a scribe, familiar with only the Aristotelian twofold division of mixtures, elided words that referred to the Stoic threefold division. If this is correct, Antipater's intent may have been to emphasize that the husband, like the wine, does not compromise his identity or standing in this union (see, e.g., A. A. Long and D. N. Sedley, *The Hellenistic Philosophers*, vol. 1, *Translations of the Principal Sources with Philosophical Commentary* [Cambridge: Cambridge University Press, 1987], 292-93; and see Antipater's next argument).

12. δ᾽ ἀνάγκη . . . βλέπειν: Euripides, *Medea* 247.

13. σώζοντος: my emendation of the manuscript reading σώζουσα. I take it as a genitive absolute in line with the following ἀγνώμονος and παραχωρούντων. Von Arnim suggests (προστίθεται γὰρ <οὕ>τω ἡ οὖσα πατρὸς καὶ μητρὸς μὴ ἀγνώμονος) ἕνα <τε> τοῦτον κτλ. Pohlenz (371) suggests προστίθεται γὰρ τούτῳ, <θέλημα> σώζουσα πατρὸς κτλ. Hense notes other proposals, including ἥ γε (*vel* ὡς) οὖσα (Gaisford), and σώφρονος οὖσα (Meineke).

14. δὲ: my addition.

15. δὲ: added by von Arnim and Hense (following Gesner).

16. καὶ . . . μεθιστᾶσ᾽·: restored by von Arnim and Hense (following Gesner); see next note.

17. γυνὴ . . . φίλων: a fragment of Euripides extant only here and at Stobaeus 4.496.16-20 W.-H., under the lemma Εὐριπίδου Φρίξῳ.

18. The full stop is Hense's punctuation; von Arnim has a raised dot.

or other similar things; but those of a husband and wife are like thorough blendings, as wine with water, the former <retaining its proper nature>³ while being thoroughly mixed. For not only do they hold property in common, and children (whom everyone considers extremely precious), and the soul, but these alone hold their bodies in common. And in yet another way is this partnership arguably the greatest, for while other partnerships also have some alternative diversions, these "must focus on one soul," the husband's. For while father and mother are doing well, being in sound mind, she consents to make this one man both object and goal of life, to please him. <But> when the parents of each step aside, they consent to render freely the foremost goodwill to one another: she to her husband, he to his wife.⁴ Even Euripides, having given his attention to these things, set aside the misogyny typical of his writing and, in a fashion not inexperienced in the matter of sharing life with a woman, said this:

> For a wife is most pleasant to her husband
> in sicknesses and troubles, if she manages the house well;
> both calming his anger <and setting his soul free
> from despair>. Even treachery of friends becomes something pleasant.

The thing is truly heroic.

3. The husband, like the wine, does not compromise his identity or standing in this union — see Antipater's next argument and n. 11 to the Greek text.

4. Evidently the wife is expected to devote herself entirely to her husband from the beginning of their marriage; the husband only after the death of his parents. Cf. [Aristotle] *Oeconomica* 3.2 (143.24-25): "[the husband] promising to honor his wife far above all others saving his parents" *(multo magis se post parentes uxori tradidit ad honorem).*

Νῦν δὲ ἐν ἰδίαις[19] πόλεσιν ἅμα τῇ ἄλλῃ τῇ καθεστώσῃ ἐκλύσει καὶ
40 ἀναρχίᾳ καὶ τῇ ἐπὶ τὸ καταφερὲς[20] ῥᾴθυμον ἐπικλίσει καὶ τὸ γαμεῖν τῶν
χαλεπωτάτων εἶναι δοκεῖ· τὸν δ' ἤθεον <βίον>,[21] ἐξουσίαν διδόντα πρὸς
ἀκολασίαν καὶ ποικίλων ἡδονῶν ἀπόλαυσιν ἀγεννῶν καὶ μικροχαρῶν,
ἰσόθεον νομίζουσι, τὴν δὲ τῆς[22] γυναικὸς εἴσοδον οἱονεί τινος φρουρᾶς εἰς
πόλιν εἰσαγωγήν. ἔοικε μέντοι δύσκολος ἐνίοις ὁ μετὰ γυναικὸς φαίνεσθαι
45 βίος διὰ τὸ μὴ δύνασθαι ἄρχειν ἀλλ' ἡδονῆς δούλους εἶναι, καὶ τοὺς μὲν ὑπὸ
τοῦ κάλλους τεθηρευμένους, τοὺς <δ'>[23] ὑπὸ τῆς προικός, τὰ μὲν ἀπ' αὐτῆς[24]
ἑκουσίως καταχαρίζεσθαι τῇ γυναικί. καὶ μὴ διδάσκειν περὶ οἰκονομίας
μηθὲν μηδὲ περὶ αὐξήσεως οἴκου μηδὲ τίνος ἕνεκα συνεληλύθασι, μηδὲ
περὶ θεῶν εὐσεβείας καὶ δόξης καὶ δεισιδαιμονίας ἐμποιεῖν,[25] μηδὲ τὸ τῆς
50 τρυφῆς ὀλέθριον παριστάναι μηδὲ τὸ ἀχάριστον τῶν ἡδονῶν, μηδὲ ἐθίζειν
ἀτενίζειν εἰς τὸ ἔμπροσθεν τοῦ βίου καὶ πᾶν τὸ μέλλον ὀρθῇ τῇ γνώμῃ
ἐκλογίζεσθαι, μηδὲ αὖ τυφλῶς καὶ ἀσκέπτως εὔελπιν εἶναι, μηδ' ὅτι ἐὰν ὁ
ἀνὴρ βουληθῇ, δύναται πάντως γενέσθαι ὧν ἐπιθυμεῖ· καὶ μὴ πρὸς τῷ
παρόντι μόνῳ γίγνεσθαι, ἀλλὰ καὶ αὐτὴν συνεπιβλέπειν τὸ πόθεν καὶ πῶς
55 καὶ εἰ σωτηρίως καὶ συμφερόντως εἰς τὰ ὅλα. ἐπεὶ καὶ εἴ τις ταῦτα καὶ τὰ
ἄλλα τὰ καλῶς τεθεωρημένα καὶ παραγγελλόμενα παρὰ τοῖς φιλοσόφοις
δύναιτο πράττειν, ὃ ἂν τῶν πλείστων[26] καὶ κουφότατον εἶναι βάρος γαμετὴ
γυνὴ δόξῃ.

Ὁμοιότατον[27] γάρ ἐστιν ὡς εἴ τις μίαν ἔχων χεῖρα ἑτέραν ποθὲν
60 προσλάβοι ἢ ἕνα πόδα ἔχων ἕτερον ἀλλαχόθεν ἐπικτήσαιτο.[28] ὡς γὰρ οὗτος

19. ἰδίαις: von Arnim and Hense (following Gesner) emend the manuscript reading to
ἐνίαις, unnecessarily in my view.

20. Von Arnim and Hense (following Wyttenbach) add καὶ after καταφερὲς.

21. τὸν δ' ἤθεον βίον: emended from the manuscript reading τὸν δὴ θεὸν by von Arnim and
Hense (following Meineke). Hense also lists βίον δ' ἤθεον as a possibility (following Jacobs).

22. τὴν δὲ τῆς: one manuscript reads τὴν δὲ πρὸς τῆς, which is impossible without further
emendation. See Hense, "Zu Antipatros von Tarsos," 304 n. 1.

23. δ': added by von Arnim and Hense (following Gesner).

24. ἀπ' αὐτῆς: emended by Hense (following Meineke) from the manuscript reading ὑπ'
αὐτῆς. Von Arnim suggests ἐπ' αὐτῇ . . . γυναικὶ . . . . The full stop is my punctuation; von Arnim
and Hense have no punctuation here.

25. περὶ θεῶν . . . ἐμποιεῖν: von Arnim suggests emending to περὶ θεῶν <καὶ> εὐσεβείας καὶ
δεισιδαιμονίας καλὰς δόξας ἐμποιεῖν.

26. ὃ ἂν τῶν πλείστων: von Arnim suggests ἐν ἂν τῶν ἡδίστων (cf. line 35).

27. For this argument, cf. Antiphon in Stobaeus 4.522.15–523.6 W.-H. (87 B49 [359.2-13]
Diels-Kranz).

28. ἐπικτήσαιτο: Hense's suggestion. The manuscripts read ἐκτήσατο. Von Arnim (following Wakefield) suggests κτήσαιτο.

But now in our own cities, along with the other prevailing feebleness and lawlessness and the inclination toward degrading frivolity, even marrying is reckoned to be among the most irksome things. They consider the young bachelor's <life> godlike[5] because it gives them license for licentiousness and enjoyment of various sordid and cheap pleasures, while they view the arrival of a wife as if it was the introduction of some foreign garrison into a city-state.[6] Yet it seems that living with a wife appears difficult to some men because they are unable to rule,[7] being instead slaves to pleasure. Some have been taken captive by beauty, some by the dowry, in some cases voluntarily surrendering a cut to the wife. And they are unable to teach their wives anything about household management, or the growth of a household, or for what reason they came together in the first place. Nor are they able to promote reverence and honor for the gods, or religious sensibilities; or point out the destructive nature of luxury, or how unrewarding pleasures can be. Nor are they able to accustom their wives to take stock of life's former experiences and assess all eventualities with correct judgment; and, further, not to be hopeful, blindly and without reflection; or think that what she desires can certainly come about if only her husband will consent;[8] or be engaged with the present only, but rather that she herself should consider with him the source and the means, and if something brings security and benefit to the whole. For if a man could do these and the other things that have been duly considered and recommended by the philosophers, a wife will seem to be indeed the lightest of all possible burdens.

For the closest analogy is if someone who had one hand would add another from somewhere, or, having one foot, would get an additional one from

5. Wordplay between "bachelor" and "godlike"; perhaps a reference to an early Epicurean adage. For the Latin version, see Quintilian 1.6.36.

6. On the military simile, cf. Antiphon in Stobaeus 4.521.15-16 Wachsmuth and Hense: "For marriage is a great contest for a man" (μέγας γὰρ ἀγὼν γάμος ἀνθρώπῳ); and *Sentences of Sextus* 230b: "Marry and have children, knowing each is difficult. But if, knowing that it is difficult, you would be courageous, as for battle — indeed, marry and have children" (γάμει καὶ παιδοποιοῦ χαλεπὸν εἰδὼς ἑκάτερον· εἰ δὲ καθάπερ εἰδὼς πόλεμον ὅτι χαλεπὸν ἀνδρίζοιο, καὶ γάμει καὶ παιδοποιοῦ).

7. Cf. *Sentences of Sextus* 236: "A man who divorces a wife confesses that he is not able to rule a woman" (μηδὲ γυναικὸς ἄρχειν δύνασθαι).

8. Cf. Menander, *Sentences* 143 Jaekel: "For a wife knows nothing except what she wants" (γυνὴ γὰρ οὐδὲν οἶδε πλὴν ὃ βούλεται).

πολὺ ἂν ῥᾷον καὶ βαδίσαι οὗ θέλοι κἀπελάσαι[29] καὶ προσαγάγοιτο, οὕτως ὁ
γυναῖκα εἰσαγαγόμενος ῥᾷον ἀπολήψεται τὰς κατὰ τὸν βίον σωτηρίους καὶ
συμφερούσας χρείας. ἀντὶ γοῦν δύο ὀφθαλμῶν χρῶνται τέτταρσιν καὶ ἀντὶ
δύο χειρῶν ἑτέραις τοσαύταις, αἷς καὶ ἀθρόως[30] πράττοι ἂν ῥᾷον τὸ τῶν
65 χειρῶν ἔργον. διὸ κἂν εἰ αἱ ἕτεραι κάμνοιεν, ταῖς ἑτέραις αὖ θεραπεύοιτο καὶ
τὸ σύνολον δύο γεγονὼς ἀνθ' ἑνὸς[31] μᾶλλον ἂν ἐν τῷ βίῳ κατορθοίη.

Διόπερ τὸν νομίζοντα τὴν εἴσοδον τῆς γυναικὸς καταβαρύνειν τὸν βίον
καὶ δυσκίνητον ποιεῖν ὅμοιον <οἶμαι ἂν>[32] πάσχειν, ὡς εἴ τις πλείονας πόδας
κωλύοι προσλαβεῖν, ἵν' ἐὰν πολὺ δέῃ βαδίζειν μὴ ἐφελκώμεθα πολλούς, ἢ τῷ
70 πλείονας χεῖρας κτωμένῳ μέμφοιτο· ὅταν γάρ τι δέῃ πράττειν ἐμποδίσεσθαι
ὑπὸ τοῦ πλήθους αὐτῶν. κατὰ ταὐτὰ γὰρ καὶ εἴ τις προσλάβοι οἷον ἑαυτὸν
ἕτερον (οὐθὲν γὰρ διοίσει εἴτε θῆλυ τοῦτό ἐστιν εἴτε ἄρρεν), πολὺ
ἐλαφρότερον καὶ εὐκοπώτερον πάντ' ἂν πράξειεν τὰ ἔργα. φιλαγάθῳ <δ'>[33]
ἀνδρὶ καὶ θέλοντι σχολὴν ἄγειν ἢ περὶ τοὺς λόγους ἢ τὰ πολιτικὰ ἔργα ἢ
75 ἄμφω ταῦτα, καὶ τελείως τοῦτο ἀμετάθετόν ἐστιν. ὅσῳ γὰρ μᾶλλον αὐτὸς
ἀπὸ τῆς οἰκονομίας ἀπέστραπται, τοσούτῳ μᾶλλον τὴν διαδεξομένην τὴν
<δι>οίκησιν[34] παραληπτέον καὶ περὶ τὰ ἀναγκαῖα ἑαυτὸν ἀπερίσπαστον
<ποιητέον.>[35] οὐ κακῶς καὶ ὁ κωμικὸς[36] ἐπιτέμνει <τὸ>

σχολαστής ἐστι· δεῖ δ' οἶμαι γαμεῖν
80   τὸν ἐπιμελῆ καὶ δυνατὸν οἰκονομεῖν ὄχλον πλείω,

ἐπιφωνήσας·

τὸν ἀμελῆ μᾶλλον, ἐπιθυμοῦντα δὲ
σχολῆς, ἵν' ἔχων οἰκονόμον ἀδεῶς περιπατῇ.

29. κἀπελάσαι: suggested by von Arnim and Hense; the manuscripts read καὶ γελάσαι.

30. ἀθρόως: Hense (following Elter and Meineke) suggests ἀθρόοις.

31. δύο γεγονὼς ἀνθ' ἑνὸς: cf. Plato, *Symposium* 192E, ἀντὶ δυοῖν ἕνα εἶναι.

32. οἶμαι ἂν: my addition (in view of the preceding ὅμοιον). Von Arnim adds οἶμαι; Hense adds ἂν οἶμαι.

33. δ': added by von Arnim and Hense.

34. δι-: added by von Arnim and Hense (following Gesner).

35. ποιητέον.: added by von Arnim (following Gesner's suggestion of τηρητέον); Hense indicates a lacuna.

36. ὁ κωμικὸς: Aristophanes? These two quotations are extant only here. τὸ: added by von Arnim and Hense.

some other place. For just as this person would very easily walk about and come and go where he wished, so the man who has brought home a wife will easily obtain the necessities that sustain and benefit his life. For then they make use of four eyes instead of two, and likewise four hands instead of two, which he would use collectively to make manual labor easy. Hence, even if one set would be weary, he would be served, in turn, by the other; and in general, this man would better proceed correctly in life, having become two in place of one.

Therefore, <it seems to me> that the man who thinks the entry of a wife into his house burdens life and makes it cumbersome labors under the same wrong impression as if someone would prevent us from acquiring more feet, so that if we need to walk a lot we will not be dragging many after us, or would censure the man with more hands, saying, "For when he needs to do something, he will be impeded by their number." For, according to what we have said, if someone would acquire another like himself — and it will make no difference at all whether this is a female or a male — he would do all his work much more handily and easily. Indeed, for the man who loves the good and desires leisure time to direct either to philosophical discussions or political affairs, or both these, this is a perfectly settled matter. For the more he himself has withdrawn from managing the household, the more he needs to acquire this woman who will take over the management,[9] and <make> himself undistracted by the day-to-day necessities. Not badly does the comic poet sum up <what>

> a man of leisure is: I think the man who is conscientious
> and able to manage sizable groups needs to marry;

having added,

> even more so the one who is neglectful but nevertheless desires
> leisure, so that he may go about securely, having someone
> to manage his household.

---

9. Cf. Menander, *Sentences* 155 J.: "A good wife is the rudder of a household" (γυνὴ δὲ χρηστὴ πηδάλιόν ἐστ' οἰκίας); and similarly, *Sentences* 140-41 J.

Ocellus Lucanus

On the Nature of the Universe [Spurious] 43b-51

The Greek text presented in this appendix is also available in Holger Thesleff, ed., *The Pythagorean Texts of the Hellenistic Period*, Acta Academiae Aboensis, Humaniora 30/1 (Åbo, Finland: Åbo Akademi, 1965), 135-37, and Richard Harder, *"Ocellus Lucanus": Text und Kommentar*, Neue philologische Untersuchungen, no. 1 (Berlin: Weidmann, 1926), 21-23, with commentary on 120-34. An older English translation is available in Thomas Taylor, trans., *Ocellus Lucanus, On the Nature of the Universe; Taurus, the Platonic Philosopher, On the Eternity of the World; Julius Firmicus Maternus, Of the Thema Mundi, in Which the Positions of the Stars at the Commencement of the Several Mundane Periods Is Given; Select Theorems, On the Perpetuity of Time, By Proclus* (London: Printed for the translator [by Richard Taylor], 1831), 21-25. The rendition by Kenneth Sylvan Guthrie in his *Pythagorean Library* and *Pythagoras Source-book and Library*, both published in 1920 by Platonist Press, Alpine, N.J., and now available in reprints, is simply an imprecise paraphrase of Taylor's translation.

(43b) Περὶ δὲ τῆς ἐξ ἀλλήλων ἀνθρώπων γενέσεως, ὅπως τε καὶ ἐκ τίνων ἔσται κατὰ τρόπον ἐπιτελουμένη νόμῳ τε καὶ σωφροσύνης καὶ ὁσιότητος ἐπισυνεργούσης, τάδε καλῶς ἔχειν οἴομαι. (44) πρῶτον μὲν τοῦτο ⟨δεῖ⟩[1] διαλαβεῖν, ὅτι οὐχ ἡδονῆς ἕνεκα πρόσιμεν ἀλλὰ τέκνων γενέσεως· καὶ γὰρ
5 αὐτὰς τὰς δυνάμεις καὶ τὰ ὄργανα καὶ τὰς ὀρέξεις τὰς πρὸς τὴν μῖξιν ὑπὸ τοῦ θεοῦ δεδομένας τοῖς ἀνθρώποις οὐχ ἡδονῆς ἕνεκα δεδόσθαι συμβέβηκεν ἀλλὰ τῆς εἰς τὸν ἀεὶ χρόνον διαμονῆς τοῦ γένους. ἐπειδὴ γὰρ ἀμήχανον ἦν θνητὸν φύντα θείου βίου κοινωνῆσαι, τὴν τοῦ γένους ἀθανασίαν φθειρομένοις[2] καθ᾽ ἕκαστον ἀνεπλήρωσεν ὁ θεός, ἀκατάληκτον ποιήσας καὶ συνεχῆ ταύτην τὴν
10 γένεσιν.

(45) Ἓν οὖν τοῦτο πρῶτον δεῖ θεωρεῖν ὅτι οὐχ ἡδονῆς ἕνεκα ἡ μῖξις· ἔπειτα δὲ καὶ αὐτὴν τὴν τοῦ ἀνθρώπου[3] σύνταξιν πρὸς τὸ ὅλον, ὅτι μέρος ὑπάρχων οἴκου τε καὶ πόλεως καί, τὸ μέγιστον, κόσμου συμπληροῦν ὀφείλει τὸ ἀπογινόμενον τούτων ἕκαστον, ἐὰν μέλλῃ μήτε συγγενικῆς ἑστίας
15 λειποτάκτης γίνεσθαι μήτε πολιτικῆς μήτε μὴν τῆς θείας. οἱ γὰρ καθάπαξ μὴ διὰ παιδοποιίαν συναπτόμενοι ἀδικήσουσι τὰ τιμιώτατα τῆς κοινωνίας συστήματα· εἰ δὲ καὶ γεννήσουσιν οἱ τοιοῦτοι μεθ᾽ ὕβρεως καὶ ἀκρασίας, μοχθηροὶ οἱ γενόμενοι καὶ κακοδαίμονες ἔσονται καὶ βδελυροὶ ⟨. . .⟩[4] ὑπό τε θεῶν καὶ δαιμόνων καὶ ἀνθρώπων καὶ οἴκων καὶ πόλεων.

1. δεῖ: added by Harder and Thesleff.
2. τὴν τοῦ γένους ἀθανασίαν φθειρομένοις: Thesleff's emendation for the manuscript reading τῆς τοῦ γένους ἀθανασίας φθειρομένης.
3. αὐτὴν τὴν τοῦ ἀνθρώπου: Thesleff and Harder (following Jaeger) for the manuscript reading τὴν αὐτὴν τῷ ἀνθρώπῳ. For the cause of the corruption see Harder, 127.
4. βδελυροὶ ⟨. . .⟩: a past participle seems to be required, perhaps something like νομισθέντες, as I suggest in the translation.

43b BUT CONCERNING THE GENESIS of human beings from one another, and how and by whom it will be duly accomplished, both by law and as temperance and holiness make their contribution — these things I consider to be morally beautiful. 44First, however, it is necessary to comprehend this: we have sexual intercourse not for the sake of pleasure, but the procreation of children. For, in fact, the reproductive powers themselves, and the sexual organs, and the yearnings that were given to human beings by God in order to bring on sexual intercourse happen not to have been given for the sake of pleasure,[1] but the everlasting continuation of the race. For since it was impossible that one born mortal share in divine[2] life, God supplied to each of those who perish the immortality of the race, making their genesis continuous and constant.

45So it is first necessary to observe this one thing, that sexual intercourse is not for the sake of pleasure, and, thereupon, also the very place of the human being with respect to the Whole — that, being a part of both household and city-state, and, most importantly, the *kosmos,* each part leaving these entities by death is obligated to complete the Whole,[3] if he does not wish to be a deserter either of the ancestral hearth of his household, or the altar of his city-state, or, indeed, the altar of the gods. For those who have intercourse not at all for the sake of having children do injustice to the most revered systems of partnership.[4] And if, in fact, such persons as these give birth, by means of wantonness and lack of self-control, then those born will be wretched and pitiful, and <regarded as> loathsome by gods, and divine beings, and men, and households, and city-states.[5]

---

1. Cf. Chardonas (third-second century B.C.E.), *Prooemia* 62.30-33 Thesleff: "Each man should have intercourse with a woman who is lawfully his wife, and from this woman he should have children. For no other reason should he give up sperm of his own children. He should not lawlessly waste and treat with disrespect that which is held in honor by nature and by law. For nature made sperm for the sake of having children, not wantonness."

2. I.e., immortal life.

3. Literally: ". . . each part leaving them is obligated to complete [it]."

4. I.e., marriage and the household, the city-state, and even partnership with the divine realm — see the next note as well as lines 12-15, 25-27; and Cicero, *De finibus* 3.64.

5. The enumeration here is not without rhyme or reason, as Richard Harder, *"Ocellus Lucanus": Text und Kommentar,* Neue philologische Untersuchungen, no. 1 (Berlin: Weidmann, 1926), 127, claims: failure to continue the sacrificial tradition of one's household or city-state through one's children brings censure from both divine and human realms ("in the sight of gods, and divine beings, and men"), the latter being further described in terms of its two central institutions, household and city-state.

20   (46) Ταῦτα οὖν προδιανοουμένους οὐ δεῖ ὁμοίως τοῖς ἀλόγοις ζῴοις προσέρχεσθαι τοῖς ἀφροδισίοις, ἀλλ' ὡς ἀναγκαῖον <καὶ>[5] καλὸν ἡγουμένους ὅπερ ἀναγκαῖον καὶ καλὸν εἶναι νομίζουσιν οἱ ἀγαθοὶ τῶν ἀνθρώπων, τὸ μὴ μόνον πολυανδρεῖσθαι τοὺς οἴκους καὶ τὸν πλείονα τῆς γῆς τόπον πληροῦσθαι (ἡμερώτατον γὰρ πάντων καὶ βέλτιστον ζῷον[6] ὁ ἄνθρωπος), ἀλλὰ καί, τὸ
25 μέγιστον, εὐανδρεῖσθαι. (47) διὰ γὰρ ταύτην τὴν αἰτίαν καὶ τὰς πόλεις εὐνομουμένας οἰκήσουσι καὶ τοὺς ἰδίους οἴκους κατὰ τρόπον οἰκονομήσουσι, καὶ τοὺς θεοὺς δὲ φίλους αὐτοῖς καταστήσουσι. πάρεστι δὲ θεωρεῖν ὅτι καὶ ἡ βάρβαρος καὶ ἡ Ἑλλὰς τότε μάλιστα εὐδοκιμεῖν πέφυκε[7] κατὰ τὰς πολιτείας καὶ τὰς πολιτικὰς πράξεις, ὅτε μὴ μόνον πολυπληθείᾳ ἀνθρώπων ἀλλὰ καὶ
30 ἀνδρείᾳ χορηγοῦνται.

     (48) Ὅθεν ἁμαρτάνουσι πολλοί, μὴ πρὸς τὸ μέγεθος τῆς ψυχῆς[8] μηδὲ πρὸς τὸ συμφέρον τῷ κοινῷ συνιστάντες τοὺς γάμους, ἀλλὰ πρὸς τὸν πλοῦτον ἢ τὴν ὑπεροχὴν τοῦ γένους ἀποβλέποντες. ἀντὶ μὲν γὰρ τοῦ νέαν καὶ ὡραίαν συναρμόζεσθαι συνηρμόσαντο ἂν τὴν ὑπερηλικεστέραν, ἀντὶ δὲ τοῦ συμπαθῆ
35 τὴν ψυχὴν καὶ ὁμοιοτάτην ἐπίδοξον τῷ γένει ἢ ὑπερχρήματον. (49) τοιγάρτοι ἀντὶ συμφωνίας διαφωνίαν καὶ ἀντὶ ὁμοφροσύνης διχοφροσύνην κατα-σκευάζουσι περὶ ἡγεμονίας διαμαχόμενοι πρὸς ἀλλήλους· ἡ μὲν γὰρ ὑπερέχουσα πλούτῳ καὶ γένει καὶ φίλοις ἄρχειν προαιρεῖται τοῦ ἀνδρὸς παρὰ τὸν τῆς φύσεως νόμον, ὁ δέ γε διαμαχόμενος δικαίως καὶ οὐ δεύτερος ἀλλὰ
40 πρῶτος θέλων εἶναι ἀδυνατεῖ τῆς ἡγεμονίας ἐφικέσθαι. (50) ὧν δὴ γενομένων οὐ μόνον τοὺς οἴκους κακοδαίμονας ἀλλὰ καὶ τὰς πόλεις συμβαίνει γενέσθαι. μέρη γὰρ τῶν πόλεων οἱ οἴκοι· ἐκ δὲ τῶν μερῶν ἡ τοῦ ὅλου καὶ τοῦ παντὸς σύνθεσις· εἰκὸς οὖν, ὁποῖα τὰ μέρη τυγχάνουσιν ὄντα, καὶ τὸ ὅλον καὶ τὸ πᾶν τὸ ἐκ τοιούτων συντιθέμενον τοιοῦτον εἶναι. (51) καὶ ἐν ταῖς τέχναις δὲ αἱ
45 πρῶται ἀρχαὶ[9] μεγάλα συνεργοῦσι πρὸς τὸ καλῶς ἢ τὸ κακῶς τὸ ὅλον ἔργον

5. καὶ: added by Harder and Thesleff (following Rudolph).

6. ζῷον: emended from the manuscript reading ζῴων by Harder and Thesleff (following Nogarola).

7. καταστήσουσι . . . πέφυκε: omitted by all but one manuscript.

8. μὴ πρὸς τὸ μέγεθος τῆς ψυχῆς: This is Thesleff's solution (cf. lines 34-35, τοῦ συμπαθῆ τὴν ψυχήν). The manuscripts read μὴ πρὸς τὸ μέγεθος τῆς τύχης κτλ. Harder (following Jaeger) indicates a lacuna after τὸ, and Jaeger emends the text to read μὴ πρὸς τὸ <. . . ἀλλὰ πρὸς τὸ> μέγεθος τῆς τύχης κτλ.

9. ἀρχαὶ: Harder's emendation (followed by Thesleff) for the manuscript reading οἰκοδομαί. He reasons (133-34) that a more general term is needed for the examples given (building, shipbuilding, composition), and that despite the author's intentions of treating the relationship between household and city-state as one of part to whole (μέρος/τὸ ὅλον), he actually describes it as one of beginning to end (ἀρχή/τέλος).

46Therefore, giving thought to these things beforehand, it is necessary that we do not enter upon sexual intercourse after the manner of irrational animals, but rather holding as necessary and morally beautiful that very thing which good people regard to be necessary and morally beautiful, namely, not just that households be populated, and most of the earth's surface filled[6] — for the human being is the most civilized and excellent animal of all — but, indeed, most importantly, that they abound with *good* people. 47For it is through this means they will inhabit well-governed city-states, and properly manage their own households, and establish even the gods as their friends. It is readily seen that territories both barbarian and Greek grow quite naturally to be most highly esteemed with regard to their forms of government and political practices when they are supplied not only with an abundance of people, but also with manly fortitude.

48Hence, many err by forming marriages without regard for the excellence of a person's soul or for the benefit of the community, fixing their attention on the wealth or prominence of the family. For instead of marrying a young woman in her prime, they marry[7] the one too old to have children, and instead of one sympathetic in spirit and most like them, one from a distinguished family or one who is very wealthy. 49For this very reason they bring on disagreement instead of agreement, and division instead of unity of purpose, battling with one another for control. For she, being superior in terms of wealth and family and social connections, deliberately chooses to rule her husband, contrary to the law of nature; and he, battling with justice on his side — not wanting to be second but first — is unable to attain control. 50When these things happen, not only do households turn out to be ill-fated, but city-states as well. For the households are *parts* of the city-states; and the make-up of the Whole and the Entirety derives from the parts. It is therefore reasonable that whatever sort of things the parts happen to be, the Whole and the Entirety that are composed of such parts are also like this. 51So, too, in the crafts, the first beginnings contribute greatly toward the good or the bad

---

6. For the possibility that this phrase echoes Gen. 1:28, see Harder, 128-32.
7. Gnomic aorist.

συντελεσθῆναι· οἷον ἐπὶ μὲν οἰκοδομίας θεμελίου καταβολή, ἐπὶ δὲ ναυπηγίας τρόπις, ἐπὶ δὲ συναρμογῆς καὶ μελοποιίας τάσις φωνῆς καὶ λῆψις· οὕτως οὖν καὶ ἐπὶ πολιτείας εὐνομουμένης τε καὶ κακονομουμένης οἴκων κατάστασις καὶ συναρμογὴ μέγιστα συμβάλλεται.

completion of the whole work. Just as for building it is laying down a foundation, for ship-building it is the keel, for musical composition and writing lyrical melodies it is the choice of the voice's intensity and pitch — so then also for both a well- and an ill-governed political system, the stability and internal harmony of households contributes the most.

Works Cited

Editions of Greek and Latin Texts, by Editor

Arnim, Hans von. *Hierokles ethische Elementarlehre*. Berliner Klassikertexte 4. Berlin: Weidmann, 1906.

————, ed. *Stoicorum Veterum Fragmenta*. 3 vols. Stuttgart: B. G. Teubner, 1903-5. Cited as *SVF*, by volume, page, and line.

Cohoon, J. W., and H. Lamar Crosby, eds. and trans. *Dio Chrysostom*. 5 vols. LCL. London: William Heinemann; Cambridge: Harvard University Press, 1932-51.

Crönert, Wilhelm. *Kolotes und Menedemos*. Studien zur Palaeographie und Papyruskunde 6. Leipzig: Eduard Avenarius, 1906. Pp. 53-67 contain *P. Herculaneum* 339, its columns arranged according to *P. Herc.* 155.

Diels, Herman, ed. and trans. *Die Fragmente der Vorsokratiker*. Vol. 2. Edited by Walther Kranz. 6th ed. Berlin-Charlottenburg: Weidmann, 1951.

Dittenberger, Wilhelm. *Sylloge Inscriptionum Graecarum*. Vol. 2. 3rd ed. Leipzig: S. Hirzel, 1917; reprint, Hildesheim, Zürich, and New York: Georg Olms, 1982.

Dübner, F., ed. *Theophrasti charakteres*. Paris: Didot, 1842.

Foerster, Richard, ed. *Libanii Opera*. Vol. 8. Leipzig: B. G. Teubner, 1915.

Hense, O., ed. *C. Musonii Rufi Reliquiae*. Leipzig: B. G. Teubner, 1905. Cited by page and line. Note: frags. 15A and 15B Hense are frag. 15 Lutz.

Hobein, H., ed. *Maximi Tyrii Philosophumena*. Bibliotheca Scriptorum Graecorum et Romanorum Teubneriana. Leipzig: B. G. Teubner, 1910.

Jaekel, Siegfried, ed. *Menandri Sententiae, Comparatio Menandri et Philistionis*. Academia Scientiarum Germanica Berolinensis, Bibliotheca Scriptorum Graecorum et Romanorum Teubneriana. Leipzig: B. G. Teubner, 1964.

Körte, Alfred, ed. *Menandri quae supersunt*. Vol. 2, *Reliquiae apud veteres scriptores servatae*. Bibliotheca Scriptorum Graecorum et Romanorum Teubneriana. Leipzig: B. G. Teubner, 1957.

Kroll, Wilhelm, ed. *Vettii Valentis Anthologiarum libri*. Berlin: Weidmann, 1908.

Kühn, Carl Gottlob, ed. *Claudii Galeni opera omnia*. Vol. 8. Leipzig: Carl Cnoblochi, 1824.

Long, A. A., and D. N. Sedley, ed. *The Hellenistic Philosophers.* Vol. 2, *Greek and Latin Texts with Notes and Bibliography.* Cambridge: Cambridge University Press, 1988.

Long, H. S., ed. *Diogenis Laertii Vitae Philosophorum.* Vol. 2, Scriptorum Classicorum Bibliotheca Oxoniensis. Oxford: Clarendon, 1964.

Lutz, Cora E. "Musonius Rufus 'The Roman Socrates.'" In *Yale Classical Studies* 10, edited by Alfred R. Bellinger, 3-147. New Haven: Yale University Press, 1947. Cited by fragment, page, and line.

Malherbe, Abraham J., ed. *The Cynic Epistles.* SBLSBS 12. Missoula, Mont.: Scholars, 1977.

Migne, Jacques-Paul, ed. *Patrologiae cursus completus: Series Latina.* 217 vols. Paris: Migne, 1844-55.

————. *Patrologiae cursus completus: Series Graeca.* 162 vols. Paris: Migne, 1857-66.

Oldfather, W. A., ed. and trans. *Epictetus: The Discourses as Reported by Arrian, the Manual, and Fragments.* 2 vols. LCL. Cambridge: Harvard University Press; London: William Heinemann, 1959.

O'Neil, Edward N., ed. and trans. *Teles (The Cynic Teacher).* SBLTT 11/SBLGRS 3. Missoula, Mont.: Scholars, 1977.

Pomeroy, Arthur J., ed. *Arius Didymus: Epitome of Stoic Ethics.* SBLTT 44/SBLGRS 14. Atlanta: Society of Biblical Literature, 1999.

Spengel, Leonard, ed. *Rhetores Graeci.* Vol. 2. Leipzig: B. G. Teubner, 1854. Pp. 57-130 contain Aelius Theon, *Progymnasmata.*

Stählin, Otto, ed. *Clemens Alexandrinus.* Vols. 1-4. 3rd ed. Die griechischen christlichen Schriftsteller der ersten Jahrhunderte. Berlin: Akademie, 1960-72.

Thesleff, Holger, ed. *The Pythagorean Texts of the Hellenistic Period.* Acta Academiae Aboensis, Humaniora 30/1. Åbo, Finland: Åbo Akademi, 1965.

Wachsmuth, Curtius [Kurt], and Otto Hense, eds. *Ioannis Stobaei Anthologium.* 5 vols. Berlin: Weidmann, 1884-1912; reprint, 1958. Cited by volume, page, and line.

Wehrli, Fritz, ed. *Die Schule des Aristoteles: Texte und Kommentar.* Vol. 1, *Dikaiarchos.* 2nd ed. Basel and Stuttgart: Schwabe, 1967.

Secondary Sources, Including Translations

Achelis, Hans. *Virgines Subintroductae: Ein Beitrag zum VII. Kapitel des I. Korintherbriefs.* Leipzig: J. C. Hinrichs, 1902.

————. "AGAPĒTÆ." *ERE* 1 (1926): 177-80. This is an English version of "Subintroductae," in *Realencyklopädie für protestantische Theologie und Kirche,* 3rd ed., 19 (1907): 123-27.

Adam, Alfred. "Erwägungen zur Herkunft der Didache." *ZKG* 68 (1957): 1-47.

Adkins, Arthur W. H. *Merit and Responsibility: A Study in Greek Values.* Oxford: Oxford University Press, 1960.

Allmen, Jean Jacques von. *Pauline Teaching on Marriage.* Studies in Christian Faith and Practice 6. London: Faith, 1963.

Allo, E.-B. *Première épitre aux Corinthiens.* 2nd ed. EBib. Paris: Libraire Lecoffre, 1934; reprint, 1956.

Almquist, Helge. *Plutarch und das Neue Testament: Ein Beitrag zum Corpus Hellenisticum Novi Testamenti.* ASNU 15. Uppsala: Appelberg, 1946.

Arai, Sasagu. "Die Gegner des Paulus im I. Korintherbrief und das Problem der Gnosis." *NTS* 19 (1972/73): 430-37.

Arnim, Hans von. "Ineditum Vaticanum." *Hermes* 27 (1892): 118-30.

Arnold, E. Vernon. *Roman Stoicism: Being Lectures on the History of the Stoic Philosophy with Special Reference to Its Development within the Roman Empire.* Cambridge: Cambridge University Press, 1911.

Arthur, Marylin B. "Early Greece: The Origins of the Western Attitude toward Women." In *Women in the Ancient World: The "Arethusa" Papers,* edited by John Peradotto and J. P. Sullivan, 7-58. SUNY Series in Classical Studies. Albany: SUNY Press, 1984.

Attridge, Harold W. *First-Century Cynicism in the Epistles of Heraclitus.* HTS 29. Missoula, Mont.: Scholars, 1976.

Babbitt, Frank Cole, ed. and trans. *Plutarch's Moralia.* Vol. 2. LCL. Cambridge: Harvard University Press; London: William Heinemann, 1962.

Babut, Daniel. *Plutarque et le Stoïcisme.* Paris: Presses Universitaires de France, 1969.

Bachmann, Philipp. *Der erste Brief des Paulus an die Korinther.* 4th ed. Kommentar zum Neuen Testament 7. Leipzig: A. Deichert, 1936. This is identical to the 3rd ed. of 1921 except for the additional bibliography and notes supplied by Ethelbert Stauffer, pp. 488-514.

Baer, Richard A., Jr. *Philo's Use of the Categories Male and Female.* ALGHJ 3. Leiden: Brill, 1970.

Balch, David L. "Backgrounds of I Cor. vii: Sayings of the Lord in Q; Moses as an Ascetic ΘΕΙΟΣ ANHP in II Cor. iii." *NTS* 18 (1971/72): 351-64.

―――. *Let Wives Be Submissive: The Domestic Code in I Peter.* SBLMS 26. Chico, Calif.: Scholars, 1981.

―――. "1 Cor 7:32-35 and Stoic Debates about Marriage, Anxiety, and Distraction." *JBL* 102 (1983): 429-39.

―――. "Household Codes." In *Greco-Roman Literature and the New Testament: Selected Forms and Genres,* edited by David E. Aune, 25-50. SBLSBS 21. Atlanta: Scholars, 1988.

―――. "Neopythagorean Moralists and the New Testament Household Codes." In *ANRW* 2.26.1 (1992), 380-411.

Baldry, H. C. "Zeno's Ideal State." *JHS* 79 (1959): 3-15.

Balsdon, J. P. V. D. *Life and Leisure in Ancient Rome.* New York: McGraw-Hill, 1969.

Baltensweiler, Heinrich. *Die Ehe im Neuen Testament: Exegetische Untersuchungen über Ehe, Ehelosigkeit und Ehescheidung.* ATANT 52. Zürich and Stuttgart: Zwingli, 1967.

Barns, John. "A New Gnomologium: With Some Remarks on Gnomic Anthologies." *CQ* 44 (1950): 126-37; and n.s. 1 [mistakenly 45] (1951): 1-19.

Barraclough, Ray. "Philo's Politics: Roman Rule and Hellenistic Judaism." In *ANRW* 2.21.1 (1984), 417-553.

Barrett, C. K. *A Commentary on the First Epistle to the Corinthians.* HNTC. New York and Evanston, Ill.: Harper and Row, 1968.

Bartchy, S. Scott. *ΜΑΛΛΟΝ ΧΡΗΣΑΙ: First-Century Slavery and the Interpretation of 1 Corinthians 7:21.* SBLDS 11. Missoula: University of Montana Press, 1973.

Barwick, Karl. *Probleme der stoischen Sprachlehre und Rhetorik.* Abhandlungen der sächsischen Akademie der Wissenschaften zu Leipzig: Philologisch-historische Klasse 49/3. Berlin: Akademie, 1957.

Basore, John W., ed. and trans. *Seneca: Moral Essays*. Vols. 2-3. LCL. London: William Heinemann; New York: Putnam, 1932-35.

Baudrillart, André. *Moeurs païennes, moeurs chrétiennes*. Vol. 1, *La famille dans l'antiquité païenne et aux premiers siècles du christianisme*. Paris: Librairie Bloud and Gay, 1929.

Bauer, Johannes B. "Was las Tertullian 1 Kor 7 39?" *ZNW* 77 (1986): 284-87.

Bauer, Walter. *A Greek-English Lexicon of the New Testament and Other Early Christian Literature*. Revised by Frederick William Danker. 3rd English ed. Chicago: University of Chicago Press, 2000.

Baumert, Norbert. *Ehelosigkeit und Ehe im Herrn: Eine Neuinterpretation von 1 Kor 7*. FB 47. Würzburg: Echter, 1984.

Baumgarten, Jörg. *Paulus und die Apokalyptik: Die Auslegung apokalyptischer Überlieferungen in den echten Paulusbriefen*. WMANT 44. Neukirchen-Vluyn: Neukirchener, 1975.

Becker, Jürgen. "Erwägungen zur apokalyptischen Tradition in der paulinischen Theologie." *EvT* 30 (1970): 593-609.

————. *Untersuchungen zur Entstehungsgeschichte der Testamente der Zwölf Patriarchen*. AGJU 8. Leiden: Brill, 1970.

Behm, Johannes. "βρῶμα, βρῶσις." In *TDNT* 1 (1964), 642-45.

————. "γλῶσσα, ἑτερόγλωσσος." In *TDNT* 1 (1964), 719-27.

Beker, J. Christiaan. *Paul's Apocalyptic Gospel: The Coming Triumph of God*. Philadelphia: Fortress, 1982.

Bengel, Johann Albrecht. *Gnomon of the New Testament*. Vol. 2. Philadelphia: Perkinpine and Higgins, 1864.

Berger, Klaus. "Gnosis/Gnostizismus I." In *TRE* 13 (1984), 519-35.

Betz, Hans Dieter. "On the Problem of the Religio-Historical Understanding of Apocalypticism." *JTC* 6 (1969): 134-56.

————. *Der Apostel Paulus und die sokratische Tradition: Eine exegetische Untersuchung zu seiner "Apologie" 2 Korinther 10–13*. BHT 45. Tübingen: Mohr, 1972.

————. "2 Cor 6:14–7:1: An Anti-Pauline Fragment?" *JBL* 92 (1973): 88-108.

————. *Galatians: A Commentary on Paul's Letter to the Churches in Galatia*. Hermeneia. Philadelphia: Fortress, 1979.

————. "Gottmensch II." In *RAC* 12 (1983), 234-312.

Bickel, Ernestus. *Diatribe in Senecae philosophi fragmenta*. Vol. 1, *Fragmenta de matrimonio*. Leipzig: B. G. Teubner, 1915.

Bieler, Ludwig. *ΘΕΙΟΣ ΑΝΗΡ: Das Bild des "göttlichen Menschen" in Spätantike und Frühchristentum*. Vol. 1. Vienna: Oskar Höfels, 1935.

Bien, Günther. *Die Grundlegung der politischen Philosophie bei Aristoteles*. 3rd ed. Freiburg and Munich: Karl Alber, 1985.

Billerbeck, Margarethe. *Epiktet: Vom Kynismus*. Philosophia Antiqua 34. Leiden: Brill, 1978.

————. *Der Kyniker Demetrius: Ein Beitrag zur Geschichte der frühkaiserzeitlichen Popularphilosophie*. Philosophia Antiqua 36. Leiden: Brill, 1979.

Billroth, [Johann] Gustav [Friedrich]. *A Commentary on the Epistles of Paul to the Corinthians*. Vol. 1. Edinburgh: Thomas Clark, 1837.

Blass, F., and A. Debrunner. *A Greek Grammar of the New Testament and Other Early Christian Literature*. Translated and revised by Robert W. Funk. Chicago and London: University of Chicago Press, 1961.

Blau, Ludwig. *Die jüdische Ehescheidung und der jüdische Scheidebrief.* Vol. 2. Strassburg: Karl J. Trübner, 1912.

Blinzler, Joseph. "Zur Auslegung von I. Kor. 7,14." In *Aus der Welt und Umwelt des Neuen Testaments: Gesammelte Aufsätze 1,* 158-84. SBB. Stuttgart: Katholisches Bibelwerk, 1969. Replaces the 1963 version.

Bonhöffer, Adolf. *Epictet und die Stoa: Untersuchungen zur stoischen Philosophie.* Stuttgart: Ferdinand Enke, 1890.

———. *Die Ethik des Stoikers Epictet.* Stuttgart: Ferdinand Enke, 1894; reprint, Stuttgart–Bad Connstatt: Friedrich Frommann, 1968.

———. *Epiktet und das Neue Testament.* Religionsgeschichtliche Versuche und Vorarbeiten 10. Giessen: Alfred Töpelmann, 1911.

Bornkamm, Günther. *Paul.* New York and Evanston, Ill.: Harper and Row, 1971.

Boswell, John. *The Kindness of Strangers: The Abandonment of Children in Western Europe from Late Antiquity to the Renaissance.* New York: Pantheon Books, 1988.

Bousset, Wilhelm. *Die Religion des Judentums im späthellenistischen Zeitalter.* Edited by Hugo Gressmann. 3rd ed. HNT 21. Tübingen: Mohr, 1926.

Boys-Stones, G. R. *Post-Hellenistic Philosophy: A Study of Its Development from the Stoics to Origen.* Oxford: Oxford University Press, 2001.

Braun, Herbert. "Exegetische Randglossen zum 1. Korintherbrief." In *Gesammelte Studien zum Neuen Testament und seiner Umwelt,* 178-204. 2nd ed. Tübingen: Mohr, 1967.

———. "Die Indifferenz gegenüber der Welt bei Paulus und bei Epiktet." In *Gesammelte Studien zum Neuen Testament und seiner Umwelt,* 156-67, 343-44. 2nd ed. Tübingen: Mohr, 1967.

Bréhier, Émile. *Chrysippe.* Paris: Félix Alcan, 1910.

Brennan, Tad. "Epicurus on Sex, Marriage, and Children." *CP* 91 (1996): 346-52.

Broek, R. van den. "The Present State of Gnostic Studies." *VC* 37 (1983): 41-71.

Broudéhoux, Jean-Paul. *Mariage et famille chez Clément d'Alexandrie.* Théologie Historique 11. Paris: Beauchesne et ses Fils, 1970.

Brown, Peter. "The Notion of Virginity in the Early Church." In *Christian Spirituality: Origins to the Twelfth Century,* edited by Bernard McGinn and John Meyendorff, 427-43. World Spirituality: An Encyclopedic History of the Religious Quest 16. New York: Crossroad, 1985.

———. *The Body and Society: Men, Women, and Sexual Renunciation in Early Christianity.* Lectures in the History of Religions, n.s., 13. New York: Columbia University Press, 1988.

Brown, Raymond E. *The Epistles of John.* AB 30. Garden City, N.Y.: Doubleday, 1982.

Bruce, F. F. *Paul: Apostle of the Heart Set Free.* Grand Rapids: Eerdmans, 1977.

Bruns, Bernhard. "'Die Frau hat über ihren Leib nicht die Verfügungsgewalt, sondern der Mann . . .': Zur Herkunft und Bedeutung der Formulierung in 1 Kor 7,4." *MTZ* 33 (1982): 177-94.

Brunt, P. A. *Italian Manpower: 225 B.C.–A.D. 14.* Oxford: Clarendon, 1971.

Brutscheck, Jutta. *Die Maria-Marta-Erzählung: Eine redaktionskritische Untersuchung zu Lk 10,38-42.* BBB 64. Frankfurt and Bonn: Peter Hanstein, 1986.

Bultmann, Rudolf. *Der Stil der paulinischen Predigt und die kynisch-stoische Diatribe.* FRLANT 13. Göttingen: Vandenhoeck & Ruprecht, 1910.

———. *Theology of the New Testament.* Vol. 1. New York: Charles Scribner's Sons, 1951.

————. "μεριμνάω." In *TDNT* 4 (1967), 589-93.

————. "Ist die Apokalyptik die Mutter der christlichen Theologie? Eine Auseinandersetzung mit Ernst Käsemann." In *Exegetica: Aufsätze zur Erforschung des Neuen Testaments*, edited by Erich Dinklei, /6-82. Tübingen: Mohr, 1967.

Burchard, C. "Joseph and Aseneth." In *The Old Testament Pseudepigrapha*, edited by James H. Charlesworth, 2:177-247. Garden City, N.Y.: Doubleday, 1985.

Butts, James R. "The Progymnasmata of Theon: A New Text with Translation and Commentary." Ph.D. diss., Claremont Graduate School, 1986.

Caizzi, Fernanda Decleva, ed. *Antisthenis Fragmenta*. Testi e Documenti per lo Studio dell' Antichitá 13. Milan: Istituto Editoriale Cisalpino, 1966.

Cameron, Averil. "The Exposure of Children and Greek Ethics." *Classical Review* 46 (1932): 105-14.

Cancik-Lindemaier, Hildegard. "Ehe und Liebe: Entwürfe griechischer Philosophen und römischer Dichter." In *Zum Thema Frau in Kirche und Gesellschaft*, edited by Hubert Cancik, 47-80. Stuttgart: Katholisches Bibelwerk, 1972.

Cartlidge, David R. "Competing Theologies of Asceticism in the Early Church." Th.D. diss., Harvard University, 1969.

————. "1 Corinthians 7 as a Foundation for a Christian Sex Ethic." *JR* 55 (1975): 220-34.

————. Review of *Paul, the Worldly Ascetic*, by Vincent L. Wimbush. *JBL* 108 (1989): 355-57.

Chadwick, H. "'All Things to All Men' (I Cor. ix.22)." *NTS* 1 (1954/55): 261-75.

Cherniss, Harold, ed. and trans. *Plutarch's Moralia*. Vol. 13, pt. 2. LCL. Cambridge: Harvard University Press; London: William Heinemann, 1976.

Chilton, C. W. "Did Epicurus Approve of Marriage?" *Phronesis* 5 (1960): 71-74.

Clark, Elizabeth A. "Antifamilial Tendencies in Ancient Christianity." *Journal of the History of Sexuality* 3 (1995): 356-80.

————. *Reading Renunciation: Asceticism and Scripture in Early Christianity*. Princeton: Princeton University Press, 1999.

Cohen, Boaz. *Jewish and Roman Law: A Comparative Study*. Vol. 1. New York: Jewish Theological Seminary of America, 1966.

Cohn, Hermann. "Antipater von Tarsos: Ein Beitrag zur Geschichte der Stoa." Ph.D. diss., University of Giessen, 1905.

Cohoon, J. W., and H. Lamar Crosby, eds. and trans. *Dio Chrysostom*. Vols. 1-5. LCL. London: William Heinemann; Cambridge: Harvard University Press, 1932-51.

Collins, John J. "Cosmos and Salvation: Jewish Wisdom and Apocalyptic in the Hellenistic Age." *HR* 17 (1977): 121-42.

————. "Marriage, Divorce, and Family in Second Temple Judaism." In *Families in Ancient Israel*, edited by Leo Perdue, Joseph Blenkinsopp, John J. Collins, and Carol Meyers, 104-62. Louisville: Westminster/John Knox, 1997.

Colpe, Carsten. "Vorschläge des Messina-Kongresses von 1966 zur Gnosisforschung." In *Christentum und Gnosis*, edited by Walther Eltester, 129-32. BZNW 37. Berlin: Alfred Töpelmann, 1969.

————. "Gnosis II (Gnostizismus)." In *RAC* 11 (1981), 537-659.

Colson, F. H., ed. and trans. *Philo*. Vol. 9. LCL. Cambridge: Harvard University Press; London: William Heinemann, 1929.

Colson, F. H., and G. H. Whitaker, eds. and trans. *Philo*. Vol. 2. LCL. London: William Heinemann; New York: Putnam, 1929.

Conzelmann, Hans. "Zur Analyse der Bekenntnisformel I. Kor. 15,3-5." *EvT* 25 (1965): 1-11.

——. *1 Corinthians: A Commentary on the First Epistle to the Corinthians*. Hermeneia. Philadelphia: Fortress, 1975.

Countryman, L. William. *Dirt, Greed, and Sex: Sexual Ethics in the New Testament and Their Implications for Today*. Philadelphia: Fortress, 1988.

Coyle, Kevin J. "Empire and Eschaton: The Early Church and the Question of Domestic Relationships." *Église et Théologie* 12 (1981): 35-94.

Crahay, R. "Les moralistes anciens et l'avortement." *L'Antiquité Classique* 10 (1941): 9-23.

Crouzel, Henri. "Marriage and Virginity: Has Christianity Devalued Marriage?" *The Way*, suppl. 10 (1970): 3-23. Now in: *Mariage et divorce: Célibat et caractère sacerdotaux dans l'église ancienne*, 47-65. Études d'histoire du culte et des institutions chrétiennes 2. Turin: Bottega d'Erasmo, 1982.

Csillag, Pál. *The Augustan Laws on Family Relations*. Budapest: Akadémiai Kiadó, 1976.

Dahl, Nils A. "Paul and the Church at Corinth according to 1 Corinthians 1:10–4:21." In *Christian History and Interpretation: Studies Presented to John Knox*, edited by W. R. Farmer, C. F. D. Moule, and R. R. Niebuhr, 313-35. Cambridge: Cambridge University Press, 1967.

Dassmann, Ernst, and Georg Schöllgen. "Haus II (Hausgemeinschaft)." In *RAC* 13 (1986), 801-906.

Deißner, Kurt. "Das Sendungsbewußtsein der Urchristenheit." *ZST* 7 (1929/30): 772-90.

——. *Das Idealbild des stoischen Weisen: Rede anläßlich der Reichsgründungsfeier der Universität Greifswald am 18. Januar 1930*. Greifswalder Universitätsreden 24. Greifswald: L. Bamberg, 1930.

Delatte, Armand. *Essai sur la politique pythagoricienne*. Liège and Paris, 1922; reprint, Geneva: Slatkine, 1979.

Delling, Gerhard. *Paulus' Stellung zu Frau und Ehe*. BWANT, 4th ser., 5. Stuttgart: W. Kohlhammer, 1931.

——. "Ehehindernisse." In *RAC* 4 (1959), 680-91.

——. "καιρός." In *TDNT* 3 (1965), 455-64.

——. "Nun aber sind sie heilig," "Lexikalisches zu τέκνον: Ein Nachtrag zur Exegese von I. Kor. 7,14," and "Zur Exegese von I. Kor. 7,14," all in *Studien zum Neuen Testament und zum hellenistischen Judentum: Gesammelte Aufsätze 1950-1968*, edited by Ferdinand Hahn, Traugott Holtz, and Nikolaus Walter, 257-69, 270-80, and 281-87, respectively. Göttingen: Vandenhoeck & Ruprecht, 1970.

——. "Geschlechter." In *RAC* 10 (1978), 780-803.

Deming, Will. "A Diatribe Pattern in 1 Cor. 7:21-22: A New Perspective on Paul's Directions to Slaves." *NovT* 37 (1995): 130-37.

——. "The Unity of 1 Corinthians 5–6." *JBL* 115 (1996): 291-315.

——. Review of *Asceticism*, ed. Vincent L. Wimbush and Richard Valantasis. *JR* 80 (2000): 668-69.

——. "Paul, Gaius, and the 'Law of Persons': The Conceptualization of Roman Law in the Early Classical Period." *CQ* 51 (2001): 218-30.

——. "Indifferent Things." In *Paul in the Greco-Roman World*, edited by Paul Sampley, 384-403. Harrisburg, Penn.: Trinity Press International, 2003.

Derrett, J. Duncan M. "The Disposal of Virgins." In *Studies in the New Testament,* 1:184-92. Leiden: Brill, 1977.

DeSilva, D. A. "Paul and the Stoa: A Comparision." *JETS* 38 (1994): 549-64.

Devine, Richard J. "Holy Virginity: A Study of the New Testament Teaching on Virginity and Celibacy." Ph.D. diss., University of Fribourg, 1964.

DeWette, W. M. L. *Kurze Erklärung der Briefe an die Corinther.* Edited by Hermann Messner. 3rd ed. Kurzgefasstes exegetisches Handbuch zum Neuen Testament 2/2. Leipzig: S. Hirzel, 1855.

Diamond, Eliezer. *Holy Men and Hunger Artists: Fasting and Asceticism in Rabbinic Culture.* Oxford: Oxford University Press, 2003.

Dibelius, Martin. *Der Hirt des Hermas.* HNT Ergänzungsband: Die Apostolischen Väter 4. Tübingen: Mohr, 1923.

Dibelius, Martin, and Hans Conzelmann. *The Pastoral Epistles.* Hermeneia. Philadelphia: Fortress, 1972.

Dihle, Albrecht. "Ethik." In *RAC* 6 (1966), 646-796.

Di Lella, Alexander A. *The Hebrew Text of Sirach.* The Hague: Mouton, 1966.

Dodd, C. H. *The Apostolic Preaching and Its Developments: Three Lectures.* Chicago and New York: Willett-Clark, 1937.

Donahue, John R. "Stoic Indifferents and Christian Indifference in Clement of Alexandria." *Traditio* 19 (1963): 438-46.

Doughty, Darrell J. "Heiligkeit und Freiheit: Eine exegetische Untersuchung der Anwendung des paulinischen Freiheitsgedankens in 1 Kor 7." Ph.D. diss., Göttingen University, 1965.

———. "The Presence and Future of Salvation in Corinth." *ZNW* 66 (1975): 61-90.

Dudley, Donald B. *A History of Cynicism.* London: Methuen, 1937; reprint, Hildesheim: Georg Olms, 1967.

Dungan, David L. *The Sayings of Jesus in the Churches of Paul: The Use of the Synoptic Tradition in the Regulation of Early Church Life.* Philadelphia: Fortress, 1971.

Ebeling, Gerhard. "Der Grund christlicher Theologie: Zum Aufsatz Ernst Käsemanns über 'Die Anfänge christlicher Theologie.'" *ZTK* 58 (1961): 227-44.

Edwards, Thomas Charles. *A Commentary on the First Epistle to the Corinthians.* 2nd ed. New York: A. C. Armstrong and Son, 1886.

Ehrhardt, Arnold. *Politische Metaphysik von Solon bis Augustin.* Vol. 1, *Die Gottesstadt der Griechen und Römer.* Tübingen: Mohr, 1959.

Eijk, Ton H. C. van. "Marriage and Virginity, Death and Immortality." In *Epektasis: Mélanges patristiques offerts au Cardinal Jean Daniélou,* edited by Jacques Fontaine and Charles Kannengiesser, 209-35. Paris: Beauchesne, 1972.

Elliott, J. K. "Paul's Teaching on Marriage in I Corinthians: Some Problems Considered." *NTS* 19 (1972/73): 219-25.

Elorduy, Eleuterio. *Die Sozialphilosophie der Stoa.* Philologus, suppl. 28/3. Leipzig: Dieterich, 1936.

Elze, Martin. *Tatian und seine Theologie.* Forschungen zur Kirchen- und Dogmengeschichte 9. Göttingen: Vandenhoeck & Ruprecht, 1960.

Engberg-Pedersen, Troels. *Paul and the Stoics.* Louisville: Westminster/John Knox, 2000.

Erdmann, Walter. *Die Ehe im alten Griechenland.* Münchener Beiträge zur Papyrusforschung und antiken Rechtsgeschichte 20. Munich: C. H. Beck, 1934.

Eyben, Emiel. "De latere Stoa over het huwelijk." *Hermeneus: Tijdschrift voor antieke Cultuur* 50 (1978): 15-32, 71-94, 337-59.

———. "Family Planning in Graeco-Roman Antiquity." *Ancient Society* 11/12 (1980/81): 5-82.

Fahnenbruch, Franz. "Zu 1 Kor 7,36-38." *BZ* (Freiburg i. B.) 12 (1914): 391-401.

Fee, Gordon D. "1 Corinthians 7:1 in the N.I.V." *JETS* 23 (1980): 307-14.

———. *The First Epistle to the Corinthians.* NICNT. Grand Rapids: Eerdmans, 1987.

Feldman, David Michael. *Birth Control in Jewish Law.* New York: New York University Press; London: University of London, 1968.

Ferguson, John. *Utopias of the Classical World.* London: Thomas and Hudson, 1975.

Festugière, André-Jean. *Personal Religion among the Greeks.* Sather Classical Lectures 26. Berkeley: University of California Press, 1954; reprint, Westport, Conn.: Greenwood, 1984.

Ficker, G. Review of *Virgines Subintroductae,* by Hans Achelis. *TRu* 8 (1905): 117-18.

Fiedler, Peter. "Haustafel." In *RAC* 13 (1986), 1063-73.

Field, James A., Jr. "The Purpose of the *Lex Iulia et Papia Poppaea.*" *Classical Journal* 40 (1944/45): 398-416.

Fiorenza, Elisabeth Schüssler. *In Memory of Her: A Feminist Theological Reconstruction of Christian Origins.* New York: Crossroad, 1983.

———. *Bread Not Stone: The Challenge of Feminist Biblical Interpretation.* Boston: Beacon Press, 1984.

Fischel, Henry A. "Studies in Cynicism and the Ancient Near East: The Transformation of a Chreia." In *Religions in Antiquity: Essays in Memory of Erwin Ramsdell Goodenough,* edited by Jacob Neusner, 372-411. Numen Supplements 14. Leiden: Brill, 1968.

———. *Rabbinic Literature and Greco-Roman Philosophy.* SPB 21. Leiden: Brill, 1973.

Fitzgerald, John. Review of *Paul on Marriage and Celibacy,* by Will Deming. *JR* 77 (1997): 289-90.

Ford, J. Massyngberde [also Massingberd]. "St. Paul, the Philogamist (I Cor. vii in Early Patristic Exegesis)." *NTS* 11 (1964/65): 326-48.

———. *A Trilogy on Wisdom and Celibacy.* Cardinal O'Hara Series: Studies and Research in Christian Theology at Notre Dame 4. Notre Dame, Ind., and London: University of Notre Dame Press, 1967.

Forschner, Maximilian. *Die stoische Ethik: Über den Zusammenhang von Natur-, Sprach- und Moralphilosophie im altstoischen System.* Stuttgart: Klett-Cotta, 1981.

Foucault, Michel. *The Use of Pleasure.* History of Sexuality 2. New York: Pantheon Books, 1985.

———. *The Care of the Self.* History of Sexuality 3. New York: Pantheon Books, 1986.

Fraade, Steven D. "Ascetical Aspects of Ancient Judaism." In *Jewish Spirituality: From the Bible through the Middle Ages,* edited by Arthur Green, 253-88. World Spirituality: An Encyclopedic History of the Religious Quest 13. New York: Crossroad, 1986.

Frank, Karl Suso. *Grundzüge der Geschichte des christlichen Mönchtums.* Grundzüge 25. Darmstadt: Wissenschaftliche Buchgesellschaft, 1979.

Frank, Richard I. "Augustus' Legislation on Marriage and Children." *California Studies in Classical Antiquity* 8 (1975): 41-52.

Furnish, Victor Paul. *II Corinthians.* AB 32A. Garden City, N.Y.: Doubleday, 1984.

Gager, John G., Jr. "Functional Diversity in Paul's Use of End-Time Language." *JBL* 89 (1970): 325-37.

———. *Kingdom and Community: The Social World of Early Christianity.* Englewood Cliffs, N.J.: Prentice-Hall, 1970.

Gaiser, Konrad. *Für und wider die Ehe.* Munich: Heimeran, 1974.

Geffcken, Johannes. *Kynika und Verwandtes.* Heidelberg: Carl Winter, 1909.

Geurts, Nico. *Het Huwelijk bij de Griekse en Romeinse Moralisten.* Amsterdam: H. J. Paris, 1928.

Glotz, Gustave. *The Greek City and Its Institutions.* New York: Knopf, 1951; reprint, Ann Arbor: University Microfilms, 1965.

Goessler, Lisette. "Plutarchs Gedanken über die Ehe." Ph.D. diss., University of Basel, 1962.

Goodenough, Erwin R. *The Politics of Philo Judaeus: Practice and Theory.* New Haven: Yale University Press, 1938.

Goodspeed, Edgar J. *Problems of New Testament Translation.* Chicago: University of Chicago Press, 1945.

Gottschalk, H. B. "Aristotelian Philosophy in the Roman World from the Time of Cicero to the End of the Second Century A.D." In *ANRW* 2.36.2 (1987), 1079-1174.

Goulet-Cazé, Marie-Odile. "Le cynisme à l'époque impériale." In *ANRW* 2.36.4 (1990), 2720-2833.

Gow, A. S. F., and D. L. Page, eds. *The Greek Anthology: Hellenistic Epigrams.* Vol. 2, *Commentary and Indexes.* Cambridge: Cambridge University Press, 1965.

Grafe, Eduard. "Geistliche Verlöbnisse bei Paulus." *Theologische Arbeiten aus dem rheinischen wissenschaftlichen Predigerverein,* n.s., 3 (1899): 57-69.

Grant, Robert M. *Gnosticism and Early Christianity.* 2nd ed. New York and London: Columbia University Press, 1966.

———. *Early Christianity and Society: Seven Studies.* San Francisco: Harper and Row, 1977.

———. "Early Christians and Gnostics in Graeco-Roman Society." In *The New Testament and Gnosis: Essays in Honour of Robert McL. Wilson,* edited by A. H. B. Logan and A. J. M. Wedderburn, 176-83. Edinburgh: T. & T. Clark, 1983.

Green, Henry A. *The Economic and Social Origins of Gnosticism.* SBLDS 77. Atlanta: Scholars, 1985.

Greeven, Heinrich. *Das Hauptproblem der Sozialethik in der neueren Stoa und im Urchristentum.* NTF, 3rd ser., 4. Gütersloh: C. Bertelsmann, 1935.

———. "Ehe nach dem Neuen Testament." In *Theologie der Ehe: Veröffentlichung des Ökumenischen Arbeitskreises evangelischer und katholischer Theologen,* edited by Gerhard Krems and Reinhard Mumm, 37-79. Regensburg: Friedrich Pustet; Göttingen: Vandenhoeck & Ruprecht, 1969.

Griffin, Miriam T. *Seneca: A Philosopher in Politics.* Oxford: Clarendon, 1976.

Grilli, Alberto. *Il problema della vita contemplativa nel mondo greco-romano.* Filologia e Letterature Classiche, 1st ser. Milan and Rome: Fratelli Bocca, 1953.

Grosheide, F. W. *Commentary on the First Epistle to the Corinthians.* NICNT. Grand Rapids: Eerdmans, 1955.

Grotius, Hugo. *Annotationes in Novum Testamentum.* Vol. 2. Paris: Pelé, 1646.

Gryson, Roger. *Les origines du célibat ecclésiastique: Du premier au septième siècle.* Recherches et synthèses, Histoire 2. Gembloux: J. Duculot, 1970.

Gummere, Richard M., ed. and trans. *Seneca: Ad Lucilium, epistulae morales.* 3 vols. LCL. London: William Heinemann; New York: Putnam, 1930.

Guntermann, Friedrich. *Die Eschatologie des Hl. Paulus.* NTAbh 13/4-5. Münster: Aschendorff, 1932.

Guthrie, W. K. C. *A History of Greek Philosophy.* Vol. 3, *The Fifth-Century Enlightenment.* Cambridge: Cambridge University Press, 1969.

————. *A History of Greek Philosophy.* Vol. 5, *The Later Plato and the Academy.* Cambridge: Cambridge University Press, 1978.

Güttgemanns, Erhardt. *Der leidende Apostel und sein Herr: Studien zur paulinischen Christologie.* FRLANT 90. Göttingen: Vandenhoeck & Ruprecht, 1966.

Häge, Günter. *Ehegüterrechtliche Verhältnisse in den griechischen Papyri Ägyptens bis Diokletian.* Graezistische Abhandlungen 3. Cologne and Graz: Böhlau, 1968.

Hägg, Tomas. *The Novel in Antiquity.* Berkeley: University of California Press, 1983.

Hamlyn, D. W. *A History of Western Philosophy.* Harmondsworth: Penguin Books, 1987.

Hanna, Ralph, and Traugott Lawler, eds. *Jankyn's Book of Wikked Wyves.* Vol. 1, *The Primary Texts.* Athens: University of Georgia Press, 1997.

Hansen, Günther Christian. "Molestiae nuptiarum." *Wissenschaftliche Zeitschrift der Universität Rostock: Gesellschafts- und sprachwissenschaftliche Reihe* 2, no. 12 (1963): 215-19.

Hauck, Friedrich. "μακάριος, D.1." In *TDNT* 4 (1967), 367-69.

Hauck, Friedrich, and Siegfried Schulz. "πόρνη." In *TDNT* 6 (1968), 579-95.

Heinrici, C. F. Georg. *Das erste Sendschreiben des Apostel Paulus an die Korinthier.* Berlin: Wilhelm Hertz, 1880.

————. *Der erste Brief an die Korinther.* MeyerK 5, 8th ed. Göttingen: Vandenhoeck & Ruprecht, 1896.

Helm, Rudolf. "Kynismus." In *PW* 12.1 [half-vol. 23] (1924), 3-24.

Hengel, Martin. *Judaism and Hellenism: Studies in Their Encounter in Palestine during the Early Hellenistic Period.* 2 vols. Philadelphia: Fortress, 1974.

Henrion, Lise. "La conception de la Nature et du rôle de la Femme chez les philosophes cyniques et stoïciens." Ph.D. diss., Université de Liège, 1942-43.

Hense, Otto. "Bio bei Philo." *Rh. Mus.,* n.s., 47 (1892): 219-40.

————. "Zu Antipatros von Tarsos." *Rh. Mus.,* n.s., 73 (1920/24): 290-305.

Héring, Jean. *The First Epistle of Saint Paul to the Corinthians.* London: Epworth, 1962.

Herklotz, Franz. "Zu 1 Kor 7,36ff." *BZ* (Freiburg i. B.) 14 (1916/17): 344-45.

Heth, William A. "Unmarried 'For the Sake of the Kingdom' (Matthew 19:12) in the Early Church." *Grace Theological Journal* 8 (1987): 55-88.

Hicks, R. D. *Stoic and Epicurean.* Epochs of Philosophy. New York: Charles Scribner's Sons, 1920.

————, ed. and trans. *Diogenes Laertius: Lives of Eminent Philosophers.* 2 vols. LCL. London: William Heinemann; Cambridge: Harvard University Press, 1925.

Hierzenberger, Gottfried. *Weltbewertung bei Paulus nach 1 Kor 7,29-31: Eine exegetisch-kerygmatische Studie.* Kommentare und Beiträge zum Alten und Neuen Testament. Düsseldorf: Patmos, 1967.

Hilgenfeld, Adolf. *Die Glossolalie in der alten Kirche, in dem Zusammenhang der Geistesgaben und des Geisteslebens des alten Christenthums: Eine exegetisch-historische Untersuchung.* Leipzig: Breitkopf und Härtel, 1850.

————. *Die apostolischen Väter: Untersuchungen über Inhalt und Ursprung der unter ihrem Namen erhaltenen Schriften.* Halle: C. E. M. Pfeffer, 1853.

Himes, Norman Edwin. *Medical History of Contraception.* London: Geo. Allen and Unwin; Baltimore: Williams and Wilkins, 1936; reprint, New York: Gamut, 1963.

Hock, Roland F., and Edward N. O'Neil, eds. *The Chreia in Ancient Rhetoric.* Vol. 1, *The "Progymnasmata."* SBLTT 27/SBLGRS 9. Atlanta: Scholars, 1986.

Hofmann, Johann Christian Konrad von. *Die heilige Schrift neuen Testaments: Zusammenhängend untersucht.* Vol. 2/2. Nördlingen: C. H. Beck, 1864.

Höistad, Ragnar. "Cynic Hero and Cynic King: Studies in the Cynic Conception of Man." Inaugural diss., University of Uppsala, 1948.

Holladay, Carl R. *"Theios Aner" in Hellenistic Judaism: A Critique of the Use of This Category in NT Christology.* SBLDS 40. Missoula, Mont.: Scholars, 1977.

Hollander, Harm W. *Joseph as an Ethical Model in the Testaments of the Twelve Patriarchs.* SVTP 6. Leiden: Brill, 1981.

Holloway, Paul A. *Consolation in Philippians: Philosophical Sources and Rhetorical Strategy.* SNTMS 112. Cambridge: Cambridge University Press, 2001.

Hopkins, Keith. "A Textual Emendation in a Fragment of Musonius Rufus: A Note on Contraception." *CQ,* n.s., 15 (1965): 72-74.

Hopkins, M. K. "Contraception in the Roman Empire." *Comparative Studies in Society and History* 8 (1965): 124-51.

Horsley, Richard A. "Pneumatikos vs. Psychikos: Distinctions of Spiritual Status among the Corinthians." *HTR* 69 (1976): 269-88.

————. "Wisdom of Word and Words of Wisdom in Corinth." *CBQ* 39 (1977): 224-39.

————. "'How Can Some of You Say That There Is No Resurrection of the Dead?': Spiritual Elitism in Corinth." *NovT* 20 (1978): 203-31.

————. "Spiritual Marriage with Sophia." *VC* 33 (1979): 30-54.

————. "Gnosis in Corinth: I Corinthians 8.1-6." *NTS* 27 (1980/81): 32-51.

————. *Sociology and the Jesus Movement.* New York: Crossroad, 1989.

Horst, P. W. van der. *The Sentences of Pseudo-Phocylides.* SVTP 4. Leiden: Brill, 1978.

Humbert, Michel. *Le remariage à Rome: Étude d'histoire juridique et sociale.* Università di Roma: Pubblicazioni dell' Istituto di diritto Romano e dei diritti dell' oriente mediterraneo 44. Milan: A. Giuffrè, 1972.

Hurd, John Coolidge, Jr. *The Origin of I Corinthians.* London: SPCK, 1965; reprint, Macon, Ga.: Mercer University Press, 1983.

Isaac, E. "1 (Ethiopic Apocalypse of) ENOCH." In *The Old Testament Pseudepigrapha,* edited by James H. Charlesworth, 1:5-89. Garden City, N.Y.: Doubleday, 1983.

Jeremias, Joachim. "Die missionarische Aufgabe in der Mischehe (1. Kor 7,16)." In *Abba: Studien zur neutestamentlichen Theologie und Zeitgeschichte,* 292-98. Göttingen: Vandenhoeck & Ruprecht, 1966.

————. "Zur Gedankenführung in den paulinischen Briefen." In *Abba: Studien zur neutestamentlichen Theologie und Zeitgeschichte,* 269-76. Göttingen: Vandenhoeck & Ruprecht, 1966.

Jonas, Hans. *The Gnostic Religion.* 2nd ed. Boston: Beacon Press, 1963.

————. *Gnosis und spätantiker Geist.* Vol. 1, *Die mythologische Gnosis,* 3rd ed. Göttingen: Vandenhoeck & Ruprecht, 1964.

Jones, F. Stanley. *"Freiheit" in den Briefen des Apostels Paulus: Eine historische, exegetische und religionsgeschichtliche Studie.* GTA 34. Göttingen: Vandenhoeck & Ruprecht, 1987.

Jülicher, Adolf. "Die geistlichen Ehen in der alten Kirche." *ARW* 7 (1904): 372-86.

―――. "Die Jungfrauen im ersten Korintherbrief." *Protestantische Monatshefte* 22 (1918): 97-119.

Juncker, Alfred. *Die Ethik des Apostels Paulus.* Vol. 2, *Die konkrete Ethik.* Halle an der Saale: Max Niemeyer, 1919.

Kahn, Charles H. "Arius as a Doxographer." In *On Stoic and Peripatetic Ethics: The Work of Arius Didymus,* edited by William W. Fortenbaugh, 3-13. Rutgers University Studies in Classical Humanities 1. New Brunswick, N.J.: Transaction Books, 1983.

Käsemann, Ernst. "On the Subject of Primitive Christian Apocalyptic" and "Sentences of Holy Law in the New Testament." In *New Testament Questions of Today,* 108-37 and 67-81, respectively. Philadelphia: Fortress, 1969.

Kaser, Max. *Das römische Privatrecht.* Vol. 1, *Das altrömische, das vorklassische und klassische Recht.* 2nd ed. Handbuch der Altertumswissenschaft, Rechtsgeschichte des Altertums 10.3.3.1. Munich: C. H. Beck, 1971.

Keck, Leander E., and Victor Paul Furnish. *The Letters of Paul.* Interpreting Biblical Texts. Nashville: Abingdon, 1984.

Kee, Howard Clark. "The Ethical Dimensions of the Testaments of the XII as a Clue to Provenance." *NTS* 24 (1978): 259-70.

―――. "Pauline Eschatology: Relationships with Apocalyptic and Stoic Thought." In *Glaube und Eschatologie: Festschrift für Werner Georg Kümmel zum 80. Geburtstag,* edited by Erich Gräßer and Otto Merk, 135-58. Tübingen: Mohr, 1985.

―――. "Testaments of the Twelve Patriarchs." In *The Old Testament Pseudepigrapha,* edited by James H. Charlesworth, 1:775-828. Garden City, N.Y.: Doubleday, 1985.

Kennedy, George A., trans. *Progymnasmata: Greek Textbooks of Prose Composition and Rhetoric.* Writings from the Greco-Roman World 10. Atlanta: Society of Biblical Literature, 2003.

Keyes, Clinton Walker, ed. and trans. *Cicero: De Re Publica, De Legibus.* LCL. Cambridge: Harvard University Press; London: William Heinemann, 1928.

Kidd, I. G. "Cynics." In *Encyclopedia of Philosophy,* edited by Paul Edwards, vol. 2 (1967), 284-85.

―――. "Stoic Intermediates and the End for Man." In *Problems in Stoicism,* edited by Anthony Arthur Long, 216-38. London: University of London Press, Athlone Press, 1971.

Kiefer, Otto. *Sexual Life in Ancient Rome.* London: George Routledge and Sons, 1938.

Klassen, William. "Musonius Rufus, Jesus, and Paul: Three First-Century Feminists." In *From Jesus to Paul: Studies in Honour of Francis Wright Beare,* edited by Peter Richardson and John Coolidge Hurd, 185-206. Waterloo, Ontario: Wilfrid Laurier University Press, 1984.

Klawiter, Frederick Charles. "The New Prophecy in Early Christianity: The Origin, Nature, and Development of Montanism, A.D. 165-220." Ph.D. diss., University of Chicago, 1975.

Klein, Günter. "Apokalyptische Naherwartung bei Paulus." In *Neues Testament und christliche Existenz: Festschrift für Herbert Braun zum 70. Geburtstag am 4. Mai 1973,* edited by Hans Dieter Betz and Luise Schottroff, 241-62. Tübingen: Mohr, 1973.

Kleiner, Diana E. E. "The Great Friezes of the Ara Pacis Augustae: Greek Sources, Roman Derivatives, and Augustan Social Policy." *Mélanges de l'École Française de Rome: Antiquité* 90 (1978): 753-85.

Klijn, A. F. J., trans. "2 (Syriac Apocalypse of) Baruch." In *The Old Testament Pseudepigrapha,* edited by James H. Charlesworth, 2:615-52. Garden City, N.Y.: Doubleday, 1985.

Kloppenborg, John S. *The Formation of Q: Trajectories in Ancient Wisdom Collections.* Studies in Antiquity and Christianity. Philadelphia: Fortress, 1987.

———. "Symbolic Eschatology and the Apocalypticism of Q." *HTR* 80 (1987): 287-306.

Koch, Hugo. *Virgines Christi: Die Gelübde der gottgeweihten Jungfrauen in den ersten drei Jahrhunderten,* 59-112. TU 31/2. Leipzig: J. C. Hinrichs, 1907.

Koch, Klaus. *The Rediscovery of Apocalyptic: A Polemical Work on a Neglected Area of Biblical Studies and Its Damaging Effects on Theology and Philosophy.* SBT, 2nd ser., 22. Naperville, Ill.: Alec R. Allenson, [1972].

Koester, Helmut. Review of *Weisheit und Torheit,* by Ulrich Wilckens. *Gnomon* 33 (1961): 590-95.

Kretschmar, Georg. "Ein Beitrag zur Frage nach dem Ursprung frühchristlicher Askese." *ZTK* 61 (1964): 27-67.

Kubo, Sakae. "I Corinthians vii.16: Optimistic or Pessimistic?" *NTS* 24 (1977/78): 539-44.

Kugelmann, Richard. "1 Cor 7:36-38." *CBQ* 10 (1948): 63-71.

Kümmel, Werner Georg. "Verlobung und Heirat bei Paulus (I. Cor 7 36-38)." In *Neutestamentliche Studien für Rudolf Bultmann,* edited by Walther Eltester, 275-95. BZNW 21. Berlin: Alfred Töpelmann, 1954. Now in: *Heilsgeschehen und Geschichte: Gesammelte Aufsätze 1933-1964,* edited by Erich Grässer, Otto Merk, and Adolf Fritz, 310-27. Marburger Theologische Studien 3. Marburg: N. G. Elwert, 1965.

Labriolle, Pierre de. "Le 'mariage spirituel' dans l'antiquité chrétienne." *Revue Historique* 137 (1921): 204-25.

Lacey, W. K. *The Family in Classical Greece.* Aspects of Greek and Roman Life. London: Thames and Hudson, 1968.

Ladeuze, P. Review of *Virgines Subintroductae,* by Hans Achelis. *RHE* 6 (1905): 58-62.

Lake, Kirsopp. *The Apostolic Fathers.* Vol. 2, *The Shepherd of Hermas, the Martyrdom of Polycarp, the Epistle to Diognetus.* LCL. Cambridge: Harvard University Press; London: William Heinemann, 1913.

———. *The Earlier Epistles of St. Paul: Their Motive and Origin.* 2nd ed. London: Rivingtons, 1914.

Lampe, Peter. *From Paul to Valentinus: Christians at Rome in the First Two Centuries,* translated by Michael Steinhouser and edited by Marshall D. Johnson. Minneapolis, Minn.: Fortress Press, 2003.

Lane Fox, Robin. *Pagans and Christians.* New York: Knopf, 1987.

Laub, Franz. *Eschatologische Verkündigung und Lebensgestaltung nach Paulus: Eine Untersuchung zum Wirken des Apostels beim Aufbau der Gemeinde in Thessalonike.* BU 10. Regensburg: Friedrich Pustet, 1973.

Lausberg, Marion. *Untersuchungen zu Senecas Fragmenten.* Untersuchungen zur antiken Literatur und Geschichte 7. Berlin: Walter de Gruyter, 1970.

Legrand, Lucien. "The Prophetical Meaning of Celibacy — I." *Scripture* 12 (1960): 97-105.

———. *The Biblical Doctrine of Virginity.* London: Geoffrey Chapman, 1963.

———. "Saint Paul et célibat." In *Sacerdoce et Célibat: Études historiques et théologiques,* edited by Joseph Coppens, 315-31. BETL 28. Gembloux: Duculot; Louvain: Peeters, 1971.

Legrand, Ph. E. *Daos: Tableau de la comédie grecque*. Lyon: A. Rey, 1910.

Leipoldt, Johannes. *Griechische Philosophie und frühchristliche Askese*. Berlin: Akademie, 1961.

Léon-Dufour, Xavier. "Mariage et continence selon S. Paul." In *A la rencontre de Dieu: Mémorial Albert Gelin*, edited by A. Barucq, A. George, and H. de Lubac, 319-29. Bibliothèque de la Faculté Catholique Théologie de Lyon 8. Le Puy: Xavier Mappus, 1961.

―――. "Mariage et virginité selon saint Paul." *Christus* 11 (1964): 179-94.

Lesky, E., and J. H. Waszink. "Embryologie." In *RAC* 4 (1959), 1228-44.

Lietzmann, Hans. *An die Korinther I•II*. Revised by Werner Georg Kümmel. 5th ed. HNT 9. Tübingen: Mohr, 1969.

Lohse, Bernhard. *Mönchtum und Reformation*. Göttingen: Vandenhoeck & Ruprecht, 1963.

―――. *Askese und Mönchtum in der Antike und in der alten Kirche*. Religion und Kultur der alten Mittelmeerwelt in Parallelforschungen 1. Munich and Vienna: R. Oldenbourg, 1969.

Long, A. A. *Hellenistic Philosophy: Stoics, Epicureans, Sceptics*. 2nd ed. Berkeley: University of California Press, 1986.

Long, A. A., and D. N. Sedley. *The Hellenistic Philosophers*. Vol. 1, *Translations of the Principal Sources with Philosophical Commentary*. Cambridge: Cambridge University Press, 1987.

Lovejoy, Arthur O., and George Boas. *Primitivism and Related Ideas in Antiquity*. Baltimore: Johns Hopkins University Press, 1935; reprint, New York: Octagon Books, 1973.

Lütgert, W. *Freiheitspredigt und Schwarmgeister in Korinth: Ein Beitrag zur Charakteristik der Christuspartei*. BFCT 12/3. Gütersloh: C. Bertelsmann, 1908.

Luther, Martin. *Luther's Works*. Edited by Jaroslav Pelikan and Helmut Lehmann. Vol. 28, *Commentaries on 1 Corinthians 7, 1 Corinthians 15, Lectures on 1 Timothy*, edited by Hilton C. Oswald. Saint Louis: Concordia, 1973.

Luttikhuizen, Gerard P. *The Revelation of Elchasai: Investigations into the Evidence for a Mesopotamian Jewish Apocalypse of the Second Century and Its Reception by Judeo-Christian Propagandists*. Texte und Studien zum Antiken Judentum 8. Tübingen: Mohr, 1985.

Lutz, Cora E. "Musonius Rufus 'The Roman Socrates.'" In *Yale Classical Studies* 10, edited by Alfred R. Bellinger, 3-147. New Haven: Yale University Press, 1947.

MacDonald, Margaret Y. "Early Christian Women Married to Unbelievers." *SR* 19 (1990): 221-34.

Mack, Burton L. *A Myth of Innocence: Mark and Christian Origins*. Philadelphia: Fortress, 1988.

MacMullen, Ramsay. *Enemies of the Roman Order*. Cambridge: Harvard University Press, 1966.

MacRae, George W. Review of *Gnosticism in Corinth: An Investigation of the Letters to the Corinthians*, by Walter Schmithals. *Int* 26 (1972): 489-91.

Malherbe, Abraham J. "Cynics." In *IDBsup* (1962), 201-3.

―――. "'Gentle as a Nurse': The Cynic Background to I Thess ii." *NovT* 12 (1970): 203-17.

————. "Self-Definition among Epicureans and Cynics." In *Jewish and Christian Self-Definition,* vol. 3, *Self-Definition in the Greco-Roman World,* edited by Ben F. Meyer and E. P. Sanders, 46-59. London: SCM Press, 1982.

————. *Moral Exhortation: A Greco-Roman Sourcebook.* Library of Early Christianity. Philadelphia: Westminster, 1986.

————. *Paul and the Thessalonians: The Philosophic Tradition of Pastoral Care.* Philadelphia: Fortress, 1987.

————. *Paul and the Popular Philosophers.* Minneapolis: Fortress, 1989.

————. "Determinism and Free Will in Paul: The Argument of 1 Corinthians 8 and 9." In *Paul in His Hellenistic Context,* edited by Troels Engberg-Pedersen, 231-55. Minneapolis: Fortress, 1995.

————, ed. *The Cynic Epistles.* SBLSBS 12. Missoula, Mont.: Scholars, 1977.

Marrou, H. I. *A History of Education in Antiquity.* Wisconsin Studies in Classics. Madison: University of Wisconsin Press, 1982.

Marshall, Peter. *Enmity in Corinth: Social Conventions in Paul's Relations with the Corinthians.* WUNT, 2d ser., 23. Tübingen: Mohr, 1987.

Martin, Dale B. *The Corinthian Body.* New Haven and London: Yale University Press, 1995.

————. "Paul without Passion: On Paul's Rejection of Desire in Sex and Marriage." In *Constructing Early Christian Families: Family as Social Reality and Metaphor,* edited by Halvor Moxnes, 201-15. London and New York: Routledge, 1997.

Martin, Hubert, Jr. "Amatorius (Moralia 748E-771E)." In *Plutarch's Ethical Writings and Early Christian Literature,* edited by Hans Dieter Betz, 442-537. SCHNT 4. Leiden: Brill, 1978.

Martínez, Florentino García. "Wisdom and Apocalyptic in the Dead Sea Scrolls and in the Biblical Tradition." *Ephemerides Theologicae Lovanienses* 78 (2002): 536-49.

Matura, Thaddée. "Le célibat dans le NT d'après l'exégèse recente." *NRT* 97 (1975): 481-500, 593-604.

Maurer, Christian. "Ehe und Unzucht nach 1. Korinther 6,12–7,7." *WD,* n.s., 6 (1959): 159-69.

Meeks, Wayne A. "The Image of the Androgyne: Some Uses of a Symbol in Earliest Christianity." *HR* 13 (1973/74): 165-208.

————. *The First Urban Christians: The Social World of the Apostle Paul.* New Haven and London: Yale University Press, 1983.

————. "Social Functions of Apocalyptic Language in Pauline Christianity." In *Apocalypticism in the Mediterranean World and the Near East,* edited by David Hellholm, 687-705. Tübingen: Mohr, 1983.

————. *The Moral World of the First Christians.* Library of Early Christianity. Philadelphia: Westminster, 1986.

Merklein, Helmut. "'Es ist gut für den Menschen, eine Frau nicht anzufassen': Paulus und die Sexualität nach 1 Kor 7." In *Die Frau im Urchristentum,* edited by Gerhard Dautzenberg, Helmut Merklein, and Karlheinz Müller, 225-53. QD 95. Freiburg, Basel, and Vienna: Herder, 1983. Now in: *Studien zu Jesus und Paulus,* 385-408. WUNT 43. Tübingen: Mohr 1987.

Meyer, Heinrich August Wilhelm. *Critical and Exegetical Handbook to the Epistles to the Corinthians.* Vol. 1, *First Epistle, Ch. I.–XIII.* Revised by William P. Dickson. Critical and Exegetical Commentary on the New Testament 5. Edinburgh: T. & T. Clark, 1892.

Michl, Johann. "Engel II (jüdisch)." In *RAC* 5 (1962), 60-97.

Miller, Walter, ed. and trans. *Cicero*. Vol. 21, *De Officiis*. LCL. Cambridge: Harvard University Press; London: William Heinemann, 1913.

Mitchell, Margaret M. *Paul and the Rhetoric of Reconciliation: An Exegetical Investigation of the Language and Composition of 1 Corinthians*. Louisville: Westminster/John Knox, 1991.

Mosheim, Johann Lorenz von. *Erklärung des Ersten Briefes des heiligen Apostles Pauli an die Gemeinde zu Corinthus*, edited by Christian Ernst von Windheim. 2nd ed. Flensburg: Kortem, 1762.

Moulton, James Hope, and George Milligan. *The Vocabulary of the Greek Testament: Illustrated from the Papyri and Other Non-Literary Sources*. Pts. 1-8. London: Hodder and Stoughton, 1915-29; reprint, Grand Rapids: Eerdmans, 1980.

Mulgan, R. G. *Aristotle's Political Theory: An Introduction for Students of Political Theory*. Oxford: Clarendon, 1977.

Müller, Ulrich B. *Prophetie und Predigt im Neuen Testament: Formgeschichtliche Untersuchungen zur urchristlichen Prophetie*. SNT 10. Gütersloh: Gerd Mohn, 1975.

Murphy-O'Connor, J. "Philo and 2 Cor 6:14–7:1." *RB* 95 (1988): 55-69.

Nadeau, Ray. "The Progymnasmata of Aphthonius." *Speech Monographs* 19 (1952): 264-85.

Nagel, Peter. *Die Motivierung der Askese in der alten Kirche und der Ursprung des Mönchtums*. TU 95. Berlin: Akademie, 1966.

Natali, Carlo. "*Oikonomia* in Hellenistic Political Thought." In *Justice and Generosity: Studies in Hellenistic Social and Political Philosophy*, edited by André Laks and Malcolm Schofield, 95-128. Proceedings of the Sixth Symposium Hellenisticum. Cambridge: Cambridge University Press, 1995.

Neuhäusler, E. "Ruf Gottes und Stand des Christen: Bemerkungen zu 1 Kor 7." *BZ*, n.s., 3 (1959): 43-60.

Niederwimmer, Kurt. "Zur Analyse der asketischen Motivation in 1. Kor 7." *TLZ* 99 (1974): 241-48.

———. *Askese und Mysterium: Über Ehe, Ehescheidung und Eheverzicht in den Anfängen des christlichen Glaubens*. FRLANT 113. Göttingen: Vandenhoeck & Ruprecht, 1975.

Nilsson, Martin P. *Geschichte der griechischen Religion*. Vol. 2. 2nd ed. Handbuch der Altertumswissenschaft 5/2. Munich: C. H. Beck, 1961.

Noonan, John T., Jr. *Contraception: A History of Its Treatment by the Catholic Theologians and Canonists*. Rev. ed. Cambridge: Harvard University Press, 1965.

Nussbaum, Martha C. *The Therapy of Desire: Theory and Practice in Hellenistic Ethics*. Princeton: Princeton University Press, 1994.

———. "*Erōs* and Ethical Norms: Philosophers Respond to a Cultural Dilemma." In *The Sleep of Reason: Erotic Experience and Sexual Ethics in Ancient Greece and Rome*, edited by Martha C. Nussbaum and Juha Sihvola, 76-86. Chicago: University of Chicago Press, 2002.

Oepke, Albrecht. "Irrwege in der neueren Paulusforschung." *TLZ* 77 (1952): 449-58.

———. "Ehe I." In *RAC* 4 (1959), 650-66.

Okin, Susan Moller. *Women in Western Political Thought*. Princeton: Princeton University Press, 1979.

Opelt, Ilona. "Etymologie." In *RAC* 6 (1966), 797-844.

Orr, William F., and James Arthur Walther. *I Corinthians: A New Translation*. AB 32. Garden City, N.Y.: Doubleday, 1976.

Osiek, Carolyn, and David L. Balch. *Families in the New Testament World: Households and House Churches*. Louisville: Westminster/John Knox, 1997.

Oster, Richard E., Jr. "Use, Misuse and Neglect of Archaeological Evidence in Some Modern Works on 1 Corinthians (1 Cor 7,1-5; 8,10; 11,2-16; 12,14-26)." *ZNW* 83 (1992): 52-73.

Oulton, John Ernest Leonard, and Henry Chadwick. *Alexandrian Christianity*. LCC 2. London: SCM Press, 1954.

Pagels, Elaine H. "Paul and Women: A Response to Recent Discussion." *JAAR* 42 (1974): 538-49.

Painter, John. "Paul and the Πνευματικοί at Corinth." In *Paul and Paulinism: Essays in Honour of C. K. Barrett*, edited by M. D. Hooker, 237-50. London: SPCK, 1982.

Parente, Margherita Isnardi. "Ierocle Stoico: Oikeiosis e doveri sociali." In *ANRW* 2.36.3 (1989), 2201-26.

Parker, Charles Pomeroy. "Musonius in Clement." *Harvard Studies in Classical Philology* 12 (1901): 191-200.

Pautrel, Raymond. "Ben Sira et le stoïcisme." *RSR* 51 (1963): 535-49.

Pearson, Birger Albert. *The Pneumatikos-Psychikos Terminology in 1 Corinthians: A Study in the Theology of the Corinthian Opponents of Paul and Its Relation to Gnosticism*. SBLDS 12. Missoula, Mont.: SBL, 1973.

———. "Philo, Gnosis and the New Testament." In *The New Testament and Gnosis: Essays in Honour of Robert McL. Wilson*, edited by A. H. B. Logan and A. J. M. Wedderburn, 73-89. Edinburgh: T. & T. Clark, 1983.

Pembroke, S. G. "Oikeiōsis." In *Problems in Stoicism*, edited by A. A. Long, 114-49. London: University of London, Athlone, 1971.

Penna, Romano. "San Paolo (1 Cor 7,29b-31a) e Diogene il Cinico." *Bib* 58 (1977): 237-45.

Pervo, Richard I. "Joseph and Asenath and the Greek Novel." In *SBL 1976 Seminar Papers: 112th Annual Meeting*, 171-81. SBLSPS 10. Missoula, Mont.: Scholars, 1976.

Pestman, P. W. *Marriage and Matrimonial Property in Ancient Egypt: A Contribution to Establishing the Legal Position of Women*. Papyrologica Lugduno-Batava 9. Leiden: Brill, 1961.

Petit, Madeleine, ed. *"Quod omnis probus liber sit": Introduction, texte, traduction et notes*. Les œuvres de Philon d'Alexandrie 28. Paris: Éditions du Cerf, 1974.

Philippson, Robert. "Hierokles der Stoiker." *Rh. Mus.*, n.s., 82 (1933): 97-114.

Plooij, D. "Eine enkratitische Glosse im Diatessaron." *ZNW* 22 (1923): 1-16.

Pohlenz, Max. "Philon von Alexandreia." In *Nachrichten der Akademie der Wissenschaften zu Göttingen, philologisch-historische Klasse* 4 (1942), 409-87. Now in: *Kleine Schriften*, vol. 1, edited by Heinrich Dörrie, 305-83. Hildesheim: Georg Olms, 1965.

———. "Klemens von Alexandreia und sein hellenisches Christentum." In *Nachrichten der Akademie der Wissenschaften zu Göttingen, philologisch-historische Klasse* 5.3 (1943), 103-80. Now in: *Kleine Schriften*, vol. 1, edited by Heinrich Dörrie, 481-558 (507 is out of sequence). Hildesheim: Georg Olms, 1965.

———. "Paulus und die Stoa." *ZNW* 42 (1949): 69-104. Also available as: *Paulus und die Stoa*. Darmstadt: Wissenschaftliche Buchgesellschaft, 1964; and in Karl Heinrich

Rengstorf, ed., *Das Paulusbild in der neueren deutschen Forschung*, 522-64. Wege der Forschung 24. Darmstadt: Wissenschaft, 1969.

―――. *Die Stoa: Geschichte einer geistigen Bewegung*. 2 vols. 2nd ed. Göttingen: Vandenhoeck & Ruprecht, 1959.

―――. *Freedom in Greek Life and Thought: The History of an Ideal*. Dordrecht: D. Reidel; New York: Humanities, 1966.

―――, ed. and trans. *Stoa und Stoiker*. Vol. 1, *Die Gründer, Panaitios, Poseidonios*. Die Bibliothek der alten Welt: Griechische Reihe. Zürich: Artemis, 1950.

Pomeroy, Sarah B. *Goddesses, Whores, Wives, and Slaves: Women in Classical Antiquity*. New York: Schocken Books, 1975.

Potterie, Ignace de la. "Le titre ΚΥΡΙΟΣ appliqué à Jésus dans l'Évangile de Luc." In *Mélanges bibliques: En hommage au R. P. Béda Rigaux*, edited by Albert Descamps and André de Halleux, 117-46. Gembloux: J. Duculot, 1970.

Praechter, Karl. *Hierokles der Stoiker*. Leipzig: Dieterich, 1901. Now in: *Kleine Schriften*, edited by Heinrich Dörrie, 310-474 (with original pagination in brackets). Collectanea 7. Hildesheim and New York: Georg Olms, 1973.

Preisker, Herbert. *Christentum und Ehe in den ersten drei Jahrhunderten: Eine Studie zur Kulturgeschichte der alten Welt*. Neue Studien zur Geschichte der Theologie und der Kirche 23. Berlin: Trowitzsch und Sohn, 1927; reprint, Aalen: Scientia, 1979.

―――. "Ehe und Charisma bei Paulus." *ZST* 6 (1928/29): 91-95.

Prete, Benedetto. *Matrimonio e continenza nel cristianesimo delle origini: Studio su 1 Cor. 7,1-40*. Studi Biblici 49. Brescia: Paideia, 1979.

Preysing, Konrad Graf. "Ehezweck und zweite Ehe bei Athenagoras." *TQ* 110 (1929): 85-110.

Puzo, Félix. "Marta y María: Nota exegética a Lc 10,38-42 y 1 Cor 7,29-35." *Estudios Eclesiásticos* 34 (1960): 851-57.

Quispel, G. "The Syrian Thomas and the Syrian Macarius." *VC* 18 (1964): 226-35.

Rabinowitz, Jacob J. *Jewish Law: Its Influence on the Development of Legal Institutions*. New York: Block, 1956.

Rackham, H., ed. and trans. *Cicero: De finibus bonorum et malorum*. LCL. London: William Heinemann; New York: Macmillan, 1914.

Raditsa, Leo Ferrero. "Augustus' Legislation concerning Marriage, Procreation, Love Affairs and Adultery." In *ANRW* 2.13 (1980), 278-339.

Reitzenstein, Richard. "Etymologika." In *PW* 6.1 [half-vol. 11] (1907), 808-9.

Rengstorf, Karl Heinrich. "ἀποστέλλω." In *TDNT* 1 (1964), 398-447.

―――. "στέλλω." In *TDNT* 7 (1971), 588-99.

Resch, Alfred. *Agrapha: Aussercanonische Schriftfragmente*. TU, n.s., 15/3-4. Leipzig: J. C. Hinrichs, 1906.

Rex, Helmut H. "Das ethische Problem in der eschatologischen Existenz bei Paulus." Diss., University of Tübingen, 1954. Summarized [by editorial staff] in *TLZ* 80 (1955): 240-41.

Richardson, P. "'I Say, Not the Lord': Personal Opinion, Apostolic Authority and the Development of Early Christian Halakah." *TynBul* 31 (1980): 65-86.

Riedel, Manfred. *Metaphysik und Metapolitik: Studien zu Aristoteles und zur politischen Sprache der neuzeitlichen Philosophie*. Frankfurt: Suhrkamp, 1975.

Rist, J. M. *Stoic Philosophy*. Cambridge: Cambridge University Press, 1969.

Roberts, R. L., Jr. "The Meaning of *Chorizo* and *Douloo* in I Corinthians 7:10-17." *Restoration Quarterly* 80 (1965): 179-84.

Robertson, Archibald, and Alfred Plummer. *A Critical and Exegetical Commentary on the First Epistle of St. Paul to the Corinthians.* 2nd ed. ICC. Edinburgh: T. & T. Clark, 1914.

Robinson, James M. "Kerygma and History in the New Testament." In *Trajectories through Early Christianity,* edited by James M. Robinson and Helmut Koester, 20-70. Philadelphia: Fortress, 1971.

Roetzel, Calvin. *Paul: The Man and the Myth.* Minneapolis: Fortress, 1999.

Rollins, Wayne G. "The New Testament and Apocalyptic." *NTS* 17 (1970/71): 454-76.

Rosner, Brian S. *Paul, Scripture, and Ethics: A Study of 1 Corinthians 5-7.* AGJU 22. Leiden: Brill, 1994; reprint, Grand Rapids: Baker, 1999.

Rousselle, Aline. *Porneia: On Desire and the Body in Antiquity.* New York: Basil Blackwell, 1988.

Rückert, L. J. *Der erste Brief Pauli an die Korinther.* Die Briefe Pauli an die Korinther 1. Leipzig: K. F. Köhler, 1836.

Ruether, Rosemary Radford. "Is Celibacy Eschatological? The Suppression of Christian Radicalism." In *Liberation Theology: Human Hope Confronts Christian History and American Power,* 51-64. New York: Paulist, 1972.

———. "Misogynism and Virginal Feminism in the Fathers of the Church." In *Religion and Sexism: Images of Women in the Jewish and Christian Traditions,* 150-83. New York: Simon and Schuster, 1974.

Salmon, Pierre. *Population et dépopulation dans l'Empire romain.* Collection Latomus 137. Brussels: Latomus, 1974.

Sampley, J. Paul, ed. *Paul in the Greco-Roman World: A Handbook.* Harrisburg, Penn.: Trinity Press International, 2003.

Sandbach, F. H. *Aristotle and the Stoics.* Cambridge Philological Society, suppl. 10. Cambridge: Cambridge Philological Society, 1985.

Sanders, E. P. *Paul and Palestinian Judaism: A Comparison of Patterns of Religion.* Philadelphia: Fortress, 1977.

———. *Paul, the Law, and the Jewish People.* Philadelphia: Fortress, 1983.

Schaff, Philip, and Henry Wace, eds. *A Select Library of Nicene and Post-Nicene Fathers of the Christian Church.* 2nd ser. Vol. 6, *St. Jerome: Letters and Select Works.* New York: Christian Literature, 1893; reprint, Grand Rapids: Eerdmans, n.d.

Schilling, Robert. "Vestales et vierges chrétiennes dans la Rome antique." *RevScRel* 35 (1961): 113-29.

Schlatter, Adolf von. *Paulus der Bote Jesu: Eine Deutung seiner Briefe an die Korinther.* Stuttgart: Calwer, 1934.

Schlier, Heinrich. "θλίβω, θλῖψις." In *TDNT* 3 (1965), 139-48.

Schmeller, Thomas. *Paulus und die "Diatribe": Eine vergleichende Stilinterpretation.* NTAbh, n.s., 19. Münster: Aschendorff, 1987.

Schmidt, Karl Ludwig. "καλέω." In *TDNT* 3 (1965), 487-536.

Schmiedel, Paul Wilhelm. *Die Briefe an die Thessalonicher und an die Korinther.* HKNT 2/1. Freiburg: Mohr, 1891.

Schmithals, Walter. *Gnosticism in Corinth: An Investigation of the Letters to the Corinthians.* Nashville and New York: Abingdon, 1971.

————. *Neues Testament und Gnosis.* ErFor 208. Darmstadt: Wissenschaftliche Buchgesellschaft, 1984.

Schnackenburg, Rudolf. "Die Ehe nach dem Neuen Testament." In *Theologie der Ehe: Veröffentlichung des Ökumenischen Arbeitskreises evangelischer und katholischer Theologen,* edited by Gerhard Krems and Reinhard Mumm, 9-36. Regensburg: Friedrich Pustet; Göttingen: Vandenhoeck & Ruprecht, 1969. Now in: *Schriften zum Neuen Testament: Exegese in Fortschritt und Wandel,* 414-34. Munich: Kösel, 1971.

Schniewind, Julius. "Die Leugner der Auferstehung in Korinth." In *Nachgelassene Reden und Aufsätze,* edited by Ernst Kähler, 110-39. Theologische Bibliothek Töpelmann 1. Berlin: Alfred Töpelmann, 1952.

Schottroff, Luise. *Der Glaubende und die feindliche Welt: Beobachtungen zum gnostischen Dualismus und seiner Bedeutung für Paulus und das Johannesevangelium.* WMANT 37. Neukirchen-Vluyn: Neukirchener, 1970.

Schrage, Wolfgang. *Die konkreten Einzelgebote in der paulinischen Paränese: Ein Beitrag zur neutestamentlichen Ethik.* Gütersloh: Gütersloh, 1961.

————. "Die Stellung zur Welt bei Paulus, Epiktet und in der Apokalyptik: Ein Beitrag zu 1 Kor 7,29-31." *ZTK* 61 (1964): 125-54.

————. "Leid, Kreuz und Eschaton: Die Peristasenkataloge als Merkmale paulinischer theologia crucis und Eschatologie." *EvT* 34 (1974): 141-75.

————. "Zur Ethik der neutestamentlichen Haustafeln." *NTS* 21 (1974): 1-22.

————. "Zur Frontstellung der paulinischen Ehebewertung in 1 Kor 7 1-7." *ZNW* 67 (1976): 214-34.

Schrenk, Gottlob. "ἐντέλλομαι, ἐντολή." In *TDNT* 2 (1964), 544-56.

Schulz, Siegfried. "Evangelium und Welt." In *Neues Testament und christliche Existenz: Festschrift für Herbert Braun zum 70. Geburtstag am 4. Mai 1973,* edited by Hans Dieter Betz and Luise Schottroff, 483-501. Tübingen: Mohr, 1973.

Schürer, Emil. *The History of the Jewish People in the Age of Jesus Christ (175 B.C.–A.D. 135).* Vol. 1. Revised and edited by Geza Vermes and Fergus Millar. Edinburgh: T. & T. Clark, 1973.

————. *The History of the Jewish People in the Age of Jesus Christ (175 B.C.–A.D. 135).* Vol. 2. Revised and edited by Geza Vermes, Fergus Millar, and Matthew Black. Edinburgh: T. & T. Clark, 1979.

————. *The History of the Jewish People in the Age of Jesus Christ (175 B.C.–A.D. 135).* Vol. 3, pt. 2. Revised and edited by Geza Vermes, Fergus Millar, and Martin Goodman. Edinburgh: T. & T. Clark, 1987.

Scott, I. W. "Is Philo's Moses a Divine Man?" *Studia Philonica Annual* 14 (2002): 87-111.

Seboldt, Roland H. A. "Spiritual Marriage in the Early Church: A Suggested Interpretation of 1 Cor. 7:36-38." *CTM* 30 (1959): 103-19, 176-89.

Sellin, Gerhard. "'Die Auferstehung ist schon geschehen': Zur Spiritualisierung apokalyptischer Terminologie im Neuen Testament." *NovT* 25 (1983): 220-37.

————. *Der Streit um die Auferstehung der Toten: Eine religionsgeschichtliche und exegetische Untersuchung von 1 Korinther 15.* FRLANT 138. Göttingen: Vandenhoeck & Ruprecht, 1986.

————. "Hauptprobleme des Ersten Korintherbriefes." In *ANRW* 2.25.4 (1987), 2940-3044.

Sevenster, J. N. *Paul and Seneca.* NovTSup 4. Leiden: Brill, 1961.

Shaw, Brent D. "The Divine Economy: Stoicism as Ideology." *Latomus* 44 (1985): 16-54.

Sickenberger, Joseph. "Syneisaktentum im ersten Korintherbriefe?" *BZ* 3 (1905): 44-69.

Skehan, Patrick W., and Alexander A. Di Lella. *The Wisdom of Ben Sira*. AB 39. New York: Doubleday, 1987.

Smend, Rudolf. *Die Weisheit des Jesus Sirach*. Berlin: Georg Reimer, 1906.

Smith, Jonathan Z. "Wisdom and Apocalyptic." In *Map Is Not Territory: Studies in the History of Religions*, 67-87. SJLA 23. Leiden: Brill, 1979.

Soden, Hans von. "Sakrament und Ethik bei Paulus: Zur Frage der literarischen und theologischen Einheitlichkeit von 1 Kor. 8–10." In *Urchristentum und Geschichte: Gesammelte Aufsätze und Vorträge*, vol. 1, *Grundsätzliches und Neutestamentliches*, edited by Hans von Campenhausen, 239-75. Tübingen: Mohr, 1951.

Spanneut, Michel. *Le stoïcisme des Pères de l'Eglise de Clément de Rome à Clément d'Alexandrie*. Patristica Sorbonensia 1. Paris: Éditions de Seuil, 1957.

———. *Permanence du stoïcisme: De Zéno à Malraux*. Gembloux: J. Duculot, 1973.

Speyer, Wolfgang. *Naucellius und sein Kreis*. Munich: C. H. Beck, 1959.

Spicq, Ceslas. *Notes de lexicographie néo-testamentaire*. Vols. 1-2, with supplement. OBO 22/1-3. Fribourg: Éditions Universitaires; Göttingen: Vandenhoeck & Ruprecht, 1978-82.

Spittler, R. P. "Testament of Job." In *The Old Testament Pseudepigrapha*, edited by James H. Charlesworth, 1:829-68. Garden City, N.Y.: Doubleday, 1983.

Spörlein, Bernhard. *Die Leugnung der Auferstehung: Eine historisch-kritische Untersuchung zu I Kor 15*. BU 7. Münchener Universitäts-Schriften, Katholisch-Theologische Facultät. Regensburg: Friedrich Pustet, 1971.

Städele, Alfons. *Die Briefe des Pythagoras und der Pythagoreer*. Beiträge zur klassischen Philologie 115. Meisenheim am Glan: Anton Hain, 1980.

Stauffer, Ethelbert. "γαμέω, γάμος." In *TDNT* 1 (1964), 648-57.

Steck, Rudolf. "Geistliche Ehen bei Paulus? (I. Kor. 7,36-38.)." *Schweizerische Theologische Zeitschrift* 34 (1917): 177-89.

Stegemann, Willy. "Theon, 5." In *PW*, 2nd ser., 5/2 [half-vol. 10] (1934), 2037-54.

Steinthal, Heymann. *Geschichte der Sprachwissenschaft bei den Griechen und Römern mit besonderer Rücksicht auf die Logik*. Vol. 1. 2nd ed. Berlin: Ferd. Dümmler, 1890.

Stelzenberger, Johannes. *Die Beziehungen der frühchristlichen Sittenlehre zur Ethik der Stoa*. Munich: Max Hueber, 1933.

Stone, Michael Edward. *Fourth Ezra*. Hermeneia. Minneapolis: Augsburg Fortress, 1990.

Stowers, Stanley K. *The Diatribe and Paul's Letter to the Romans*. SBLDS 57. Chico, Calif.: Scholars, 1981.

———. "The Diatribe." In *Greco-Roman Literature and the New Testament: Selected Forms and Genres*, edited by David E. Aune, 51-83. SBLSBS 21. Atlanta: Scholars, 1988.

Strack, Hermann L., and Paul Billerbeck. *Kommentar zum Neuen Testament aus Talmud und Midrash*. 4 vols. Munich: C. H. Beck, 1956.

Strugnell, John. "Flavius Josephus and the Essenes: *Antiquities* XVIII.18-22." *JBL* 77 (1958): 106-15.

Sullivan, Clayton. *Rethinking Realized Eschatology*. Macon, Ga.: Mercer University Press, 1988.

Tarn, W. W., and G. T. Griffith. *Hellenistic Civilization*. 3rd ed. London: Edward Arnold, 1959.

Taylor, Thomas, trans. *Ocellus Lucanus, On the Nature of the Universe; Taurus, the Platonic*

Philosopher, On the Eternity of the World; Julius Firmicus Maternus, Of the Thema Mundi, in Which the Positions of the Stars at the Commencement of the Several Mundane Periods Is Given; Select Theorems, On the Perpetuity of Time, By Proclus. London: [Richard Taylor], 1831.

Thackeray, Henry St. John. *The Relation of St. Paul to Contemporary Jewish Thought.* London: Macmillan, 1900.

Theissen, Gerd. *Sociology of Early Palestinian Christianity.* Philadelphia: Fortress, 1977.

———. *The Social Setting of Pauline Christianity: Essays on Corinth.* Edited and introduction by John H. Schütz. Philadelphia: Fortress, 1982.

———. *Psychological Aspects of Pauline Theology.* Philadelphia: Fortress, 1987.

Thesleff, Holger. *An Introduction to the Pythagorean Writings of the Hellenistic Period.* Acta Academiae Aboensis, Humaniora 24/3. Åbo, Finland: Åbo Akademi, 1961.

———, ed. *The Pythagorean Texts of the Hellenistic Period.* Acta Academiae Aboensis, Humaniora 30/1. Åbo, Finland: Åbo Akademi, 1965.

Thiselton, Anthony C. "Realized Eschatology at Corinth." *NTS* 24 (1977/78): 510-26.

Tholuck, A. *Exposition, Doctrinal and Philological, of Christ's Sermon on the Mount According to the Gospel of Matthew.* Vol. 1. 2nd ed. Biblical Cabinet 6. Edinburgh: Thomas Clark, 1843.

Thraede, Klaus. "Ärger mit der Freiheit." In *"Freunde in Christus werden . . . ,"* edited by Gerta Scharffenort and Klaus Thraede, 31-182. Gelnhausen: Burckhardthaus, 1977.

———. "Zum historischen Hintergrund der 'Haustafel' des NT." In *Jahrbuch für Antike und Christentum,* suppl. 8: *Pietas: Festschrift für Bernhard Kötting,* edited by Ernst Dassmann and K. Suso Frank, 359-68. Münster: Aschendorff, 1980.

Thrall, Margaret E. *Greek Particles in the New Testament: Linguistic and Exegetical Studies.* NTTS 3. Grand Rapids: Eerdmans, 1962.

———. "The Problem of II Cor. vi.14–vii.1 in Some Recent Discussion." *NTS* 24 (1977/78): 132-48.

Tischleder, P. *Wesen und Stellung der Frau nach der Lehre des heiligen Paulus: Eine ethisch-exegetische Untersuchung.* NTAbh 10/3-4. Münster: Aschendorff, 1923.

Treggiari, Susan. *Roman Marriage: "Iust Congiuges" from the Time of Cicero to the Time of Ulpian.* Oxford: Oxford University Press, 1991.

Trenchard, Warren C. *Ben Sira's View of Women: A Literary Analysis.* BJS 38. Chico, Calif.: Scholars, 1982.

Trendennick, Hugh, and G. Cyril Armstrong, eds. and trans. *Aristotle.* Vol. 18, *Metaphysics: Books X-XIV, Oeconomica, and Magna Moralia.* LCL. Cambridge: Harvard University Press; London: Wm. Heinemann, 1935.

Trevett, Christine. "Apocalypse, Ignatius, Montanism: Seeking the Seeds." *VC* 43 (1989): 313-38.

Trillitzsch, Winfried. "Hieronymus und Seneca." *Mittellateinisches Jahrbuch* 2 (1965): 42-54.

———. *Seneca im literarischen Urteil der Antike: Darstellung und Sammlung der Zeugnisse.* 2 vols. Amsterdam: Adolf M. Hakkert, 1971.

Tuckett, C. M. "1 Corinthians and Q." *JBL* 102 (1983): 607-19.

Valckenaer, Lodewijk Kasper. *Selecta e scholis Lud. Casp. Valckenarii in libros quosdam Novi Testamenti.* Edited by Everwijn Wassenbergh. Vol. 2. Amsterdam: Petri den Hengst et filii, 1817.

Vatin, Claude. *Recherches sur le mariage et la condition de la femme mariée à l'époque hellénistique.* Bibliothèque des Écoles Françaises d'Athènes et de Rome 216. Paris: E. de Boccard, 1970.

Verner, David C. *The Household of God: The Social World of the Pastoral Epistles.* SBLDS 71. Chico, Calif.: Scholars, 1983.

Veyne, Paul. "La famille et l'amour sous le Haut-Empire romain." *Annales: Économies, Sociétés, Civilisations* 33 (1978): 35-63.

———. "The Roman Empire." In *A History of Private Life,* vol. 1, *From Pagan Rome to Byzantium,* edited by Paul Veyne, 5-233. Cambridge: Harvard University Press, Belknap Press, 1987.

Viller, Marcel, and Karl Rahner. *Aszese und Mystik in der Väterzeit: Ein Abriß.* Freiburg: Herder, 1939. A free reworking of Marcel Viller, *La spiritualité des premiers siècles chrétiens* (Paris: Bloud et Gay, 1930).

Voelke, André-Jean. *Les rapports avec autrui dans la philosophie grecque: D'Aristote à Panétius.* Bibilothèque d'histoire de la philosophie. Paris: J. Vrin, 1961.

Vogt, Joseph. "Von der Gleichwertigkeit der Geschlechter in der bürgerlichen Gesellschaft." *Akademie der Wissenschaften und der Literatur: Abhandlungen der Geistes- und Sozialwissenschaftlichen Klasse* 2 (1960): 209-55.

Völker, Walther. *Der wahre Gnostiker nach Clemens Alexandrinus.* TU 57. Berlin: Akademie; Leipzig: J. C. Hinrichs, 1952.

Vööbus, Arthur. *History of Asceticism in the Syrian Orient.* Vol. 1. CSCO 184. Louvain: Secrétariat du CSCO, 1958.

Wahl, Christian Abraham. *Clavis Novi Testamenti Philologica.* 3rd ed. Leipzig: Joh. Ambros. Barth, 1834.

Waltz, Pierre, and Guy Soury. *Anthologie grecque, première partie: Anthologie Palatine.* Vol. 3. Paris: Société d'édition "Les belles lettres," 1974.

Ward, Roy Bowen. "Musonius and Paul on Marriage." *NTS* 36 (1990): 281-89.

Waszink, J. H. "Abtreibung." In *RAC* 1 (1950), 55-60.

Webster, T. B. L. *Studies in Menander.* 2nd ed. Publications of the University of Manchester 309, Classical Series 7. Manchester: Manchester University Press, 1960.

———. *Hellenistic Poetry and Art.* London: Methuen, 1964.

———. *An Introduction to Menander.* Manchester: University of Manchester Press; New York: Barnes and Noble, 1974.

Wedderburn, A. J. M. *Baptism and Resurrection: Studies in Pauline Theology against Its Graeco-Roman Background.* WUNT 44. Tübingen: Mohr, 1987.

Wehrli, Fritz, ed. *Die Schule des Aristoteles: Texte und Kommentar.* Vol. 4, *Demetrios von Phaleron.* 2nd ed. Basel and Stuttgart: Schwabe, 1968.

Weiß, Hans-Friedrich. "Paulus und die Häretiker: Zum Paulusverständnis in der Gnosis." In *Christentum und Gnosis,* edited by Walther Eltester, 116-28. BZNW 37. Berlin: Alfred Töpelmann, 1969.

Weiß, Johannes. *Beiträge zur Paulinischen Rhetorik.* Göttingen: Vandenhoeck & Ruprecht, 1897.

———. *Der erste Korintherbrief.* MeyerK 5. Göttingen: Vandenhoeck & Ruprecht, 1925.

———. *The History of Primitive Christianity.* Completed following author's death by Rudolf Knopf. Edited by Frederick C. Grant. Vol. 2. New York: Wilson-Erickson, 1937.

Weiss, Konrad. "φέρω." In *TDNT* 9 (1974), 56-87.

Weizsäcker, Carl. "Die Anfänge christlicher Sitte." *Jahrbücher für Deutsche Theologie* 21 (1876): 1-36.

———. *Das apostolische Zeitalter der christlichen Kirche.* 1st ed. Freiburg im Breisgau: Mohr, 1886.

Wendland, Paul. *Quaestiones Musonianae: De Musonio Stoico Clementis Alexandrini Aliorumque Auctore.* Berlin: Mayer und Mueller, 1886.

———. "Philo und die kynisch-stoische Diatribe." In *Beiträge zur Geschichte der griechischen Philosophie und Religion,* edited by Paul Wendland and Otto Kern, 3-75. Berlin: Georg Reimer, 1895.

———. "Die Therapeuten und die philonische Schrift vom beschaulichen Leben." In *Jahrbücher für classische Philologie,* suppl. 22 (1896), 693-771.

———. Review of *C. Musonii Rufi reliquiae,* ed. O. Hense. *Berliner philologische Wochenschrift* 26 (1906): 197-202.

Wettstein, Johann Jakob. *Novum Testamentum Graecum.* Vol. 2. Amsterdam: Dommerian, 1752; reprint, Graz, Austria: Akademische Druck- und Verlagsanstalt, 1962.

Wilhelm, Friedrich. "Zu Achilles Tatius." *Rh. Mus.,* n.s., 57 (1902): 55-75.

———. "Die Oeconomica der Neopythagoreer Bryson, Kallikratidas, Periktione, Phintys." *Rh. Mus.* 70 (1915): 161-223.

Wilkinson, L. P. *Classical Attitudes to Modern Issues: Population and Family Planning, Women's Liberation, Nudism in Deed and Word, Homosexuality.* London: William Kimber, 1978.

Wilson, Jack H. "The Corinthians Who Say There Is No Resurrection of the Dead." *ZNW* 59 (1968): 90-107.

Wilson, R. McL. "How Gnostic Were the Corinthians?" *NTS* 19 (1972/73): 65-74.

———. "Gnosis at Corinth." In *Paul and Paulinism: Essays in Honour of C. K. Barrett,* edited by M. D. Hooker, 102-44. London: SPCK, 1982.

———. "Gnosis/Gnostizismus II." In *TRE* 13 (1984), 535-50.

Wimbush, Vincent L. *Paul, the Worldly Ascetic: Response to the World and Self-Understanding according to 1 Corinthians 7.* Macon, Ga.: Mercer University Press, 1987.

Winston, David. *The Wisdom of Solomon: A New Translation with Introduction and Commentary.* AB 43. Garden City, N.Y.: Doubleday, 1979.

Witherington, Ben, III. *Women in the Earliest Churches.* SNTSMS 59. Cambridge: Cambridge University Press, 1988.

Wolbert, Werner. *Ethische Argumentation und Paränese in 1 Kor 7.* Moraltheologische Studien, systematische Abteilung 8. Düsseldorf: Patmos, 1981.

Wolff, Hans Julius. *Written and Unwritten Marriages in Hellenistic and Postclassical Roman Law.* Philological Monographs 9. Haverford, Pa.: American Philological Association, 1939.

Wood, Neal. *Cicero's Social and Political Thought.* Berkeley: University of California Press, 1988.

Yamauchi, Edwin M. *Pre-Christian Gnosticism: A Survey of the Proposed Evidences.* London: Tyndale, 1973.

Yarbrough, O. Larry. *Not Like the Gentiles: Marriage Rules in the Letters of Paul.* SBLDS 80. Atlanta: Scholars, 1985.

Zeller, Eduard. *Die Philosophie der Griechen in ihrer geschichtlichen Entwicklung.* Vols. 2-3. 5th ed. Leipzig: Fues, 1922-23.

Zucker, Friedrich. "Socia unanimans." *Rh. Mus.*, n.s., 92 (1944): 193-217.

Index of Selected Names and Subjects

Index of Selected Scripture References

Index of Selected Greek Words and Phrases

ἄγιος/ἁγιάζω, 132-36
ἀμεριμνία. *See under* μεριμν-
ἀμέριμνος. *See under* μεριμν-
ἀπερίσπαστος. *See under* περισπα-
ἀπερισπάστως. *See under* περισπα-
ἄπιστος. *See under* πιστ-
ἀποδίδωμι, 114-15
ἀποστερέω, 119, 150n.187
ἅπτομαι, 135, 136, 137
ἀρέσκω, 198, 208
ἀσχημονέω. *See under* σχημο-
ἀσχημοσύνη. *See under* σχημο-
ἀσχολέω. *See under* σχολ-
ἀσχολία. *See under* σχολ-

γαμίζω, 20, 22-23, 39n.138

ἐντολή, 121-22, 165-69, 208
ἔξεστιν, 116-17, 150, 204, 205n.408
ἐξουσία, 138-39, 149-50, 161, 167, 202-4
ἐξουσιάζω, 116-17, 139, 150, 209; cf.
ἐνεξουσιάζομαι (139)
ἐπιθυμία, 45-46
εὔσχημον. *See under* σχημο-

καλέω. *See* κλῆσις
καλόν, 77n.107, 107-11, 204n.405
καλὸν ἀνθρώπῳ, 107-12, 170, 204n.405,
208
καλῶς, 109n.10, 203-5, 209
κλῆσις/καλέω, 162-65, 209

μεριμν-
ἀμεριμνία, 200n.378
ἀμέριμνος, 5, 200-201, 208
μέριμνα, 123n.67, 192, 200-201
μεριμνάω, 95-96, 123n.67, 200-201, 208
μέριμνα. *See under* μεριμν-
μεριμνάω. *See under* μεριμν-
μεταπερισπάω. *See under* περισπα-

ὁμοίως, 114, 156n.211
ὁμοίως δὲ καί, 113-14, 208
ὀφείλει, 67
ὀφειλή, 114-15

περισπα-
ἀπερίσπαστος, 67, 83, 192, 196
ἀπερισπάστως, 5, 195-98, 208
μεταπερισπάω, 173, 197
περισπασμός, 83, 124n.71, 197
περισπάω, 95-96, 197, 200
περισπασμός. *See under* περισπα-
περισπάω. *See under* περισπα-
πιστ-
ἄπιστος, 133-34, 142-43, 209
πιστεύω, 143, 163
πίστος, 134, 141-43, 170, 209
πιστεύω. *See under* πιστ-
πίστος. *See under* πιστ-

σύμφορον, 199, 208
συμφέρει, 77n.107, 95, 199

270